Integrated Rural Development

Integrated Rural Development

The Ethiopian Experience and the Debate

John M. Cohen

The Scandinavian Institute of African Studies, Uppsala 1987

This book has been published with support from The Swedish International Development Authority (SIDA).

John M. Cohen is a tenured Fellow of the Harvard Institute for International Development and currently Senior Advisor on Rural Development in Kenya's Ministry of Planning and National Development. He has served as a Peace Corps lawyer to the Government of Ethiopia (1964-66), lecturer in Political Science at Haile Selassie I University (1971-73), and consultant to USAID and SIDA's projects in Ethiopia, most recently as a member of the joint Ethiopia-Swedish mission on villagization (1986). Prior to joining Harvard University in 1979, he was a professor in Cornell University's Rural Sociology Department.

ISBN 91-7106-267-X

Printed in Sweden by
Motala Grafiska, Motala 1987

Contents

LIST OF TABLES

LIST OF FIGURES

Abbreviations

AIDB	Agricultural Industrial Development Bank
AMC	Agricultural Marketing Corporation
ARDU	Arssi Rural Development Unit
BARDU	Bale-Arssi Rural Development Unit
CADU	Chilalo Agricultural Development Unit
DDO	District Development Office
EDDC	Ethiopian Domestic Distribution Corporation
EPID	Extension and Project Implementation Department
EthB	Ethiopian Birr (US$ 1 = EthB 2.07) called E$ prior to revolution
GPTF	Grain Purchase Task Force
MPP	Minimum Package Programme
PADEP	Peasant Agricultural Development Extension Programme
PMAC	Provincial Military Administration Committee
RDA	Rural Development Agent
RDC	Rural Development Centre
SEAD	South East Agricultural Development Zone
SIDA	Swedish International Development Authority

Foreword

The rural development project in Ethiopia called the Chilalo Agricultural Development Unit (CADU), later known by the acronyms ARDU and SEAD, is one of the oldest and best known projects supported by SIDA. Planning for the project started in the mid-1960s, Swedish support was initiated in 1967 and is still ongoing.

CADU was one of the first and also one of the best known examples of the integrated rural development approach tried in the 1960s and 1970s. From the outset it was designed to meet all or most of the needs of small farmers for raising the productivity. The project provided a wide range of different services from agricultural research to rural water supplies and from livestock breeding to rural road construction. It was designed as an autonomous entity outside of the local administration, though gradually it was incorporated into the Ministry of Agriculture.

This project offers examples of most of the possibilities, potentials, pitfalls and problems of integrated rural development projects. It has had several significant successes and some notable failures. To this day it can be cited as one of the most carefully planned rural development projects supported by SIDA. It offers a rich body of experience for the Ethiopian Government and for SIDA. From the outset its achievements have been documented in an exemplary fashion. Few projects have been so carefully monitores and evaluated.

The project has at times been highly controversial. This was the case in the early 1970s when the then Imperial Ethiopian Government was reluctant to implement a much-needed land reform and the Swedish Government was contemplating withdrawing its support. This has again been the case in recent years, at least in Sweden, due to the use of project resources to promote collectivization of agriculture.

This project therefore offers a rich field for study by scholars of social sciences and rural development. It is somewhat sad to not the comparatively few Swedish scholars have picked up this challenge, and that the project despite all is rather poorly documented in Swedish libraries.

John M. Cohen of Harvard University has by a very wide margin been the researcher who has contributed the most to documenting the experiences from the project. He wrote his Ph.D. thesis on the project in 1973and has since the been a prolific contributor of articles and monographs on rural development issues in Ethiopia and on this project in particular. This volume is, I believe, his way of concluding the debate around integrated rural development in the context of this project.

As everything he writes this book is based on exhaustive research and thoughtful analysis. It makes a most valuable contribution to the debate surrounding integrated rural development and to SIDA's records from its work in Ethiopia. It is my hope that it will also prove useful for the records of the Ethiopian Government. It is an excellent way of documenting one of SIDA's most thorough experiences from rural development.

Johan Holmberg
Assistant Director General, SIDA

Preface

Throughout the 1970s, integrated rural development was one of the most important development intervention strategies used by Third World governments and international aid agencies. Despite a promising beginning, this approach toward increasing the agricultural productivity and quality of life of rural people is being seriously questioned. Unfortunately, the emerging critique is being written by social scientists lacking detailed case studies of such projects and direct personal experience in their design or implementation. Moreover, it is being articulated with little regard for conceptual rigor by donors wishing to back away from their own initial mistakes. Finally, many of the critics appear more eager to find newer strategies likely to capture the imagination of the international aid community than to fairly test the strategy attacked.

Integrated rural development deserves a more enlightened critique based on detailed knowledge of how such projects functioned. Too many resources have been invested in this strategy to reject it on the basis of thin consulting reports and in-house donor evaluations. Too much accumulated but unreviewed project-related data has been generated to justify present tendencies of critics to reject the approach on the basis of superficial knowledge of troubled projects and deductive application of general principles from economics and public administration.

The central premise guiding this study is that under the right conditions appropriately designed integrated rural development projects can play an important role in bringing development to small-scale farmers and their regions. The task is to specify those conditions and identify design and implementation guidelines that can increase the probability of integrated rural development projects reaching their intended objectives. Such an exercise is typically carried out by academics and professionals after reviewing a large body of evidence and testing it against their own field experience. But this cannot be done when detailed case studies are lacking.

Hence, the principal objective of this book is to provide a comprehensive study of one of the most significant integrated rural development projects carried out in the Third World. The aims are to generate a reservoir of data that can enlighten the ongoing debate over integrated rural development and to offer a case study approach that will stimulate and provide a model for future studies of other important projects based on this intervention strategy.

The case study also seeks to contribute to the growing body of literature on Ethiopia, her patterns of development and the far reaching revolution she has undergone. Here the objectives are to consolidate the unpublished materials on Ethiopia's most important rural development project, to analyze the environment it operated in before and after the fall of Haile Selassie, and to elaborate the effects of the revolution and its agrarian reforms on the rural people of the Arssi Region.

Such focused objectives have importance beyond the field of Ethiopian studies. Africa is in a development crisis that is likely to last beyond the end of this century. It is a crisis resulting from low agricultural productivity and extreme poverty. Integrated rural development is a strategy with great potential for addressing these conditions. Hence, the selection of an Ethiopian case study as the basis for considering the integrated rural development debate is all the more important, for the project reviewed was carried out under many conditions similar to those found in other African nations desperate to achieve accelerated rural progress.

Research began in 1964 when as a Peace Corps lawyer I served in Addis Ababa and visited the Arssi Region, attracted by its hospitable people and mountainous beauty. It turned academic when I returned in 1971 to teach Political Science at Haile Selassie I University and write a doctoral dissertation on the processes of social change resulting from the introduction of the project that is the focus of this book. Between the end of my field work in 1973 and today I have visited the country several times, most recently in late 1986 when I gathered the final documents needed to complete this study and traveled extensively throughout the Arssi Region.

In between these years, I benefited greatly from ideas of colleagues at Cornell University and subsequently the Harvard Institute for International Development, most notably Milton J. Esman, Norman T. Uphoff, Seleshi Sisaye, John D. Montgomery, Robert E. Klitgaard, Nils-Ivar Isaksson, and Alemneh Dejene. Others who contributed to my perspectives on integrated rural development and CADU-ARDU include Uma J. Lele, David K. Leonard, Göran Bergman, and Michael Ståhl. But of all the people who influenced my analysis and made this study possible, I am most indebted to Johan Holmberg and James R. Scarritt.

Importantly, none of these persons is responsible for the errors in fact or analysis that exist in this study. Research was complicated by typographical errors, incorrect calculations and other mistakes that mar many of the government and project documents drawn upon here. It was also made difficult by inconsistent reporting of basic data on the region and the project's impact by different official project reports. In this regard, the hyperfactual character of this study can be misleading: the reader should focus on data trends rather than seek to square internal data on population, land holdings, yields, and other variables. Significantly, research was hampered by the unwillingness of the military government to allow Western academics access to rural areas for fieldwork. Hence, much of the data since 1975 has been gathered through government documents, donor reports, journalist accounts, and academic studies. Where possible, Ethiopian or Western experts with direct knowledge of the project and the revolution have been interviewed, in person or through correspondence. Finally, initial drafts of this book were submitted to such persons for criticism and corrections.

It is neither expected nor likely that those who draw on the detailed case study presented in Chapters 4-6 will reach in all cases conclusions similar to those outlined in Chapter 7. But it is hoped that this case study and the analysis surrounding it will lead to a more informed and constructive debate on the utility of integrated rural development interventions and the conditions under which they are likely to successfully promote progressive rural development for the large percentage of the world's population who live in rural areas of the Third World and seek to increase their productivity and standards of living.

J.M.C.

Nairobi, January 21, 1987

CHAPTER 1

Integrated Rural Development and the Ethiopian Case

> Best known of major rural development projects are Mexico's PIDER program, Kenya's KTDA, Ethiopia's CADU scheme, India's Panchayati Raj, and the Masagana 99 program in the Philippines.
>
> Jon R. Moris (1981)

RISE AND FALL OF INTEGRATED RURAL DEVELOPMENT

Although development historians may find deeper roots,[1] it seems most useful to place the birth of integrated rural development in the Ford Foundation's recommendations for responding to the 1966 Indian famine. Just as the first development decade was beginning, but before the acceptance of the theoretical argument that for many countries agriculture could be the engine rather than the handmaiden of economic growth, a team of Foundation specialists studying possibilities of increasing food production in India drafted a report entitled "India's Food Crisis and Steps to Meet It."[2] It argued that intensive integrated efforts were needed to stimulate India's agricultural sector and suggested a ten point program for achieving that goal: (1) adequate and accessible farm supplies; (2) adequate farm credit; (3) intensive educational programs; (4) individual farm plans; (5) stronger village institutions; (6) assured prices for agricultural products; (7) reliable marketing facilities; (8) rural public works; (9) evaluation and analysis; and (10) a coordinated approach. At the heart of the proposal lay the notion that a *package* of reinforcing activities applied to a particular area was the key to improving the productivity of small-scale farmers and promoting more effective governmental support for agricultural development.[3] Accepted by the Indian government, Ford's report became the basis of India's highly visible and widely discussed Intensive Agricultural District Program.[4]

The strategy presented by Ford's consultants largely restated what had already been tried in less self-conscious ways in other well known rural development projects.[5] But by explicitly outlining an approach different from the then dominant community development model,[6] the Foundation's report attracted widespread attention to the utility of integrating rural development activities in specific geographic areas. The step to a more specific strategy of integrated rural development came swiftly, primarily through the widely publicized Comilla Project.

In the history of international development, Comilla, or the Pakistan Academy of Rural Development, ranks as one of the most influential programs in the Third World.[7] The project was located at the district or *thana* level and centered on four major components: (1) a Thana Training and Development Center; (2) a public works program for road embankments and drainage; (3) a decentralized small-scale irrigation program; and (4) a two-tiered cooperative system. The objectives of the project were to modernize agriculture and improve the quality of rural life through formation of farmers' cooperatives and promotion of more responsive government services. A two-tiered cooperative system was formed to assist farmers through loans and the provision of agricultural inputs. At the same time the academy studied the local area, developed priorities for removing development constraints, and sought to improve the capacity of the government's development ministries and agencies to meet local needs. Integration was promoted by the Thana Training and Development Center, which housed government field agents, assigned development tasks and sought to coordinate their activities with those of local institutions and leaders. Out of the Center's efforts came the Rural Public Works Program, the Thana Irrigation Program, the Rural Education Program and the Women's Program and Family Planning. In the process of implementing these programs all kinds of local group – from Islamic religious preceptors to housewives, brickmakers, farmers and rickshaw pullers – were organized.

The image of Comilla outside East Pakistan was that of a strategy attacking agricultural production constraints through the promotion of diverse activities in one project – credit, inputs, farmer training, embankment construction, irrigation promotion, and so on. As such it helped forge the model of an integrated rural development project. Only years later was the successful image of the project questioned through evidence that richer farmers benefited more than the poor ones, that the project was too costly and management-intensive to be replicated elsewhere, and that the project had not fully succeeded in overcoming the persistent difficulties of achieving coordination among the major components of the program or in establishing it on a self-sustaining basis.[8] By then, however, the model suggested had been widely adopted in other less developed countries.

The growing influence of the new economics of growth, arguing for sustained agricultural and rural development as a key to increases in productivity and quality of life,[9] combined with the publicity given Comilla's successes to produce a rapid increase in the type of project now widely denominated as "integrated rural development." This occurred in the late 1960s, during the days of heady optimism about the promise of the green revolution. Among the best known and most significant of these first integrated rural development projects are the Puebla Project in Mexico (1967), the Chilalo Project in Ethiopia (1968), the Lilongwe Project in Malawi (1968) and the Vihiga Project in Kenya (1970).[10] There are, however, many unstudied integrated rural development projects of enormous scope and variability. The central concept underlying them will be reviewed in Chapter 2; for now it is important only to note that during the 1970s large amounts of government and donor funds were expended to promote them. For example, between 1975 and 1980 major international donors working in Latin America alone expended 20 percent of their allocations, or US$ 2 to 2.5 billion, on integrated rural development, a figure that would be greatly increased if nationally financed contributions were included.[11]

Eventually the difficulties of promoting development tarnished the image of integrated rural development. As project evaluations of these types of projects emerged, the strategy came under attack from professionals as being too costly to justify, too complex to be administered, and too politically powerless to be effectively coordinated. By the early 1980s, major multilateral and bilateral donors were deliberately backing away from using such projects as vehicles for promoting agricultural and rural development, proclaiming integrated rural development an unworkable approach for promoting rural progress. In the end, the strategy of integrated rural development suffered the same fate as community development: rejection.

To some extent the fall of integrated rural development was due to the failure of professionals, donors and governments to think carefully through the underlying strategy of the innovation.[12] More importantly, it was due to governments and donors pushing the scope and the size of these interventions beyond the knowledge base needed to guide their design and implementation and to increase the probability of their successful execution. These mistakes were compounded by the rapid proliferation of such projects, resulting in their tendency to outstrip the capacity of development ministries and donors to finance, manage, and coordinate them. As a result there have been some notable failures. These have reinforced a new donor-led trend that argues for macro policy interventions and avoidance of large, complex multisectoral projects.

The debate over the utility of the integrated rural development strategy is far from over. By the mid-1980s careful comparative studies were emerging that presented more balanced, long term perspectives on such projects. These studies found that much had been learned about how to design and implement integrated rural development projects and argued that under the right conditions the strategy had much to offer to governments and donors seeking to promote rural development.[13]

It is not easy for such arguments to emerge, for the case studies on which they are based are located within a generally negative literature. Social scientists build their reputations through critical evaluation and these highly visible interventions typically have received unfavorable treatment at their hands.[14] Often the most influential evaluations occurred when the project was still in its initial implementation phase. This fact has led proponents of integrated rural development strategies to argue that aside from consolidating the accumulated experience from a number of cases to better evaluate it, and increase the probability of designing better lesson-based guidelines for future projects, it is also essential to study the long-term impact of these projects. The anticipation is that detailed case studies with a longer time perspective will generate a set of observations justifying a return to careful use of integrated rural development as an important strategy for increasing the production of food and fiber and raising the quality of rural life.

ETHIOPIAN CASE AND THE DEBATE

The Chilalo Agricultural Development Unit (CADU) and its successor organization, the expanded Arssi Rural Development Unit (ARDU), is well suited for such a long term case study. Importantly, it provides the detailed experience needed to evaluate the often superficial critique of integrated rural development and to generate the lessons needed by professionals.

This observation is valid despite the fact that in its early years the project received critical treatment in the literature.[15] This criticism was largely due to the project's negative effects on some of its target population, effects resulting from land tenure and local government patterns characterizing its difficult task environment. However, on the administrative side, the project was well managed and its activities reasonably well coordinated. Importantly, it passed through a major revolution while influencing the directions of reforms issued by the inheritors of Haile Selassie's power. These removed the semi-feudal constraints that plagued the project's early years and overshadowed its conceptual and administrative successes. The project continued to function as planned while playing a critical role in the debate at the upper levels of the government over whether to promote the country's small-farm sector or march toward agrarian socialism. For these and other reasons, the project merits close attention by policy makers, project designers and implementation managers.

The purpose of the chapters that follow is to provide a detailed study of the project between 1967 and 1984. Towards these ends they will review CADU's initial design and objectives, summarize its pre-revolutionary successes and problems, describe its operations during the revolution, outline its present objectives, organization, and management, and identify its long term implications for both the region and the country. This will lay the needed empirical groundwork for evaluating the burgeoning secondary literature attacking integrated rural development projects. In this regard, the chapters that follow are intended to capture the essence of Samuel Paul's increasingly influential dictum: significant progress in the evaluation and adjustment of rural development strategies is more likely to occur from the study of successful projects.[16] Despite the problems and failures detailed in the case study that follows, CADU-ARDU is such a project.

Notes

1. For example the Shell Foundation's 1944 project at Borgo a Mozzano in rural Italy may be the earliest example of an integrated rural development project. See: L. E. Virone, "Borgo a Mozzano and Other Similar Projects in Rural Development Sponsored by Shell Companies," in *Change in Agriculture*, edited by A. H. Bunting (London: Duckworth, 1970), pp. 323-36.
2. Government of India, *Suggestions for a 10-Point Programme to Increase Food Production* (New Delhi: Ministry of Food, Agriculture, Community Development and Cooperation, 1959); and *Report on India's Food Crisis and Steps to Meet It* (New Delhi: Ministry of Food, Agriculture, Community Development and Cooperation, 1959).
3. As Ruttan notes: "Neither the communities themselves nor the village-level worker has access to the materials necessary for high productivity technologies, or the knowledge and authority to realize more efficient institutional performance." Vernon W. Ruttan, "Integrated Rural Development Programs: A Skeptical Perspective," *International Development Review*, XVIII, 4 (1974/75), p. 9. See: Guy Hunter, *The Administration of Agricultural Development: Lessons from India* (London: Oxford University Press, 1970); Albert Mayer, et al., *Pilot Project India* (Berkeley: University of California Press, 1959).
4. See: D. D. Brown, *Agricultural Development in Indian Districts* (Cambridge: Harvard University Press, 1971); Rakesh Mohan and Robert E. Evenson, "The Intensive Agricultural Districts Programme in India: A New Evaluation," *Journal of Development Studies*, XI, 3 (1975), pp. 135-54.
5. For example the Helmand Valley project in Afghanistan in 1946; Cornell's Vicos project begun in Peru in 1952.
6. The literature suggests that community development programs stressed a small number of services or activities, implying among other things that they were not sufficiently comprehensive to be effective. For an interesting criticism to this view see: Lane E. Holdcroft, *The Rise and Fall of Community Development in Developing Countries, 1950-65: A Critical Analysis and an Annotated Bibliography* (East Lansing: Department of Agricultural Economics, Michigan State University, Rural Development Paper No. 2, 1978).
7. The best description of the project is: Arthur F. Raper, et al., *Rural Development in Action: The Comprehensive Experiment at Comilla, East Pakistan* (Ithaca: Cornell Univ. Press, 1970); Robert D. Stevens, "Comilla Rural Development Program to 1971," in *Rural Development in Bangladesh and Pakistan*, edited by Robert D. Stevens, et al. (Honolulu: East-West Center, Univ. Press of Hawaii, 1976); Harvey M. Choldin, "An Organizational Analysis of Rural Development Projects at Comilla, East Pakistan," *Economic Development and Cultural Change*, XX (1972), pp. 671-90.
8. See for example the careful evaluation of the project by Harry W. Blair, "Rural Development, Class Structure and Bureaucracy in Bangladesh," *World Development*, VI, 1 (1978), pp. 65-82; Azizur Rahman Khan, "The Comilla Model and the Integrated Rural Development Programme of Bangladesh: An Experiment in 'Co-operative Capitalism,'" *World Development,* VII (1979), pp. 397-422; Akhter Hameed Khan, "Comilla Revisited: May-June 1977" (Paper Prepared for Department of Agricultural Economics, Michigan State University, 1977).
9. The emergent literature on agriculture led growth is summarized in Bruce F. Johnston and Peter Kilby's unimodal model: *Agriculture and Structural Transformation: Economic Strategies in Late-Developing Countries* (New York: Oxford University

Press, 1975). See also: John W. Mellor, *The New Economics of Growth: A Strategy for India and the Developing World* (Ithaca: Cornell University Press, 1976).

10. For a comparative analysis of these significant projects see: John D. Montgomery, "Decentralizing Integrated Rural Development Activities," in *Decentralization and Development: Policy Implementation in Developing Countries* , edited by G. Shabbir Cheema and Dennis A. Rondenelli (Beverly Hills: Sage Publications, 1983), pp. 234-6. Puebla is not a multi-sector project. But it is generally considered an integrated rural development approach because of the range of activities involved, the number of services provided the small farmer, and its concentration in a specific area.
11. *Ibid.*, p. 233.
12. Ruttan described integrated rural development as an "ideology in search of a methodology." "Integrated Rural Development Programs," pp. 9-16. For an analysis of this problem see: John M. Cohen, "Integrated Rural Development: Clearing Out the Underbrush," *Sociologia Ruralis*, XX, 4 (1980), pp. 195-212.
13. Consolidating reviews of lessons learned are: George Honadle and Jerry Van Sant, *Implementation and Sustainability: Lessons from Integrated Rural Development* (West Hartford: Kumarian Press, 1985); John M. Cohen, "The Administration of Integrated Rural Development Projects" (Cambridge: Harvard Institute for International Development, Development Discussion Paper No. 79, 1979).
14. For a treatment of "negative social science" see Robert Chambers, *Rural Development: Putting the Last First* (London: Longmans, 1983), pp. 28-46.
15. Most notably: John M. Cohen, "Effects of Green Revolution Strategies on Tenants and Small-Scale Landowners in the Chilalo Region of Ethiopia," *Journal of Developing Areas*, IX, 2 (1975), pp. 335-58; Michael Ståhl, *Ethiopia: Political Contradictions in Agricultural Development* (Stockholm: Libertryck, 1974).
16. Samuel Paul, *Managing Development Programs: The Lessons of Success* (Boulder: Westview Press, 1982).

CHAPTER 2

Integrated Rural Development

> The term 'IRD' no longer serves to identify a specific set of problems, nor does it suggest any distinctive strategy.
>
> Overseas Development Institute (1979)

An increasing number of articles and monographs are appearing that focus on strategies of integrated rural development. The most striking aspect of this literature is the imprecision with which the central concept is used and the insensitivity of many analysts to the diversity of conceptual meanings given to that term. Typical is G. V. Fuguitt's article where integrated rural development, one of his major concepts, is vaguely and variously described:

> Sometimes this term seems to imply an effort to help poor farmers as well as those in large scale commercial agriculture; another connotation is concern with other economic sectors along with agriculture; another is consideration of both human and natural resources; and yet another is concern with both rural and urban areas within a regional context.[1]

With no further consideration of the term, and without settling on a precise definition of this central concept in his article, he proceeds to analyze the interrelationship between integrated rural development and migration. Yet the logic of inquiry and the foundations of methodological analysis require conceptual clarity for proper analysis. Given the importance of this concept to rural development issues, it is surprising that little effort has been made to delineate its usages. On the contrary, integrated rural development has been the victim of faddish, often unthinking application or dispute, not the less heated because of the vagueness of the term. Voltaire said, "Before we debate let us define our terms." Following this dictum, this chapter attempts to set forth the emerging majority definition of the concept so it may be used consistently throughout this book.

SCOPE OF RURAL DEVELOPMENT

The key to understanding the conceptual confusion surrounding integrated rural development is to recognize the increasing number of activities which have come within the scope of rural development efforts since the 1960s.

Specifically, academics and professionals who focus their attention on the 60 percent of the world's population who live in villages have come to embrace the superficially trite but conceptually complex rule that "in rural development everything is related to everything else."

The rise of "systems analysis" perspectives during the last twenty years contributed to the tendency to view the rural development process from a broad perspective.[2] Arthur T. Mosher has been particulary influential in promoting the view of agricultural and rural development as involving the systematic interaction of numerous activities, to be carefully orchestrated if objectives for inducing growth or improving quality of life are to be reached.[3] Briefly, he begins by identifying five components essential for increased agricultural productivity: (1) markets for farm products; (2) constantly changing technology; (3) local availability of supplies and equipment; (4) improving and expanding agricultural land; and (5) national planning for agricultural development.[4] After elaborating the interdependence of these essential components, he presents a set of guidelines for reinforcing them in well-defined farming localities.[5] Here the objective is to create a range of advice for policy, program and project activities that support the emergence of a "progressive rural structure." By the end of his three volume exercise, Mosher has expanded the design and implementation of agricultural development from the inclusion of traditional activities, such as research, extension, credit, markets and roads, to the incorporation of non-agricultural but production-related activities, ranging from rural public works and local government to education, health and family planning.

Increased Emphasis on Rural Development

Mosher's pragmatic instinct to conceive of agricultural development as a complex system of diverse interrelated activities was reinforced by a dramatic change in economic development theory. Beginning in the mid-1960s two major trends evolved which shifted much of the development emphasis to the rural sector. First, widespread acceptance was given the view that for many less developed countries agriculture can be the major engine for growth.[6] Second, increased recognition was extended to arguments that small-scale farms can play a major role in agriculture-led development.[7]

Many world economic trends contributed to those shifts.[8] None was more influential than the realization that international trade patterns hampered both industry and export-led growth models, strategies that had dominated development theory since World War II. Specifically, it became clear that many industries in developing nations could not successfully compete in international trade and had only limited domestic markets because of overall poverty. Without markets, industry could not expand, and without expansion there were few urban jobs available for those forced out of the countryside by population growth and land pressure. By the late 1960s much importance was being attached to rural development efforts and the possibilities of providing not only additional food for rapidly increasing populations, but of improving the income levels of rural inhabitants, thereby helping to generate demand for industrial products.[9]

The shift toward rural-led development was accelerated by the appearance of high yielding varieties of wheat, rice and corn.[10] When matched with fertilizer, adequate rainfall or irrigation, and good farming practices, these seeds could greatly increase yields. Productivity was also improved through such land intensive strategies as multiple cropping. Finally, some progress was made in developing intermediate technologies to complement rather than displace labor, an approach suited to small farms. After initial experiences with capital intensive, labor displacing strategies in exploiting the potential of the new seed-fertilizer revolution,[11] many governments and international agencies made corrective efforts to implement laws and policies aimed at benefiting the rural population through small farm strategies. This choice was made easier by evidence that small farms could be as productive with food and non-food crops as the larger-scale commercial farms. For example, the highest yields of food grains per land unit in the world are found on small-scale holdings in Taiwan, South Korea, China and Japan.[12] Finally, increased understanding of the risks faced by small-scale farmers and the complex strategies they develop to deal with them have helped undermine the stereotype of the "fatalistic peasant" that had blocked many small farm programs or projects.[13]

AGRICULTURAL VS. RURAL DEVELOPMENT

The theoretical guidelines developed by agricultural and social scientists for making the rural sector a central focus of development efforts led to the emergence of complex, well-funded efforts in the countryside. One result of this new, broadly focused emphasis was the rise of integrated rural development projects. Another result, one that complicates the design and implementation of such projects, was the gradual blurring of the once clearly articulated distinction between agricultural and rural.

In the past, organizations and experts tended to define agricultural development as the increase in production of food and fiber, and rural development as the improvement of the quality of rural life. Despite lingering bureaucratic divisions among some major donors or development ministries in various countries,[14] rural development is increasingly considered to include both types of activities. Under this view, rural means the countryside and those villages or towns whose inhabitants are not primarily involved in the production of non-agricultural products for urban or export markets. This is because programs designed to promote one of these objectives invariably contain components that affect the other. Recognition of this expanded definition of "rural development" was clearly articulated by Albert Waterston:

> The purpose of agricultural development – to increase agricultural production – deals only with one sector, farm commodities. The purpose of rural development – to improve the standard of living of the rural population – is multi-sectoral including agriculture, industry, and social facilities.[15]

Increasing acceptance of this view during the 1970s by experts and donors reinforced the tendency to promote projects with multisectoral objectives.

ANALYZING THE UNDEFINED

By the mid-1970s the spread of projects aimed at promoting this broader notion of rural development had begun to attract considerable professional interest. This led to a wide range of articles and reports setting forth the objectives integrated rural development should seek, the strategy such interventions should follow, and the experience of particular projects to date. Characteristic of this growing literature was the tendency to prescribe what the objectives, scope, and methodology of integrated rural development should be while ignoring the conceptual roots of the approach and alternative perspectives on it. As a result, the definition of integrated rural development became increasingly generalized. A good example of this is Betru Gebregziabher's statement:

> In the final analysis, integrated rural development involves all the things that can most improve the living conditions of the rural masses.[16]

In this sense, Charles F. Sweet is correct that:

> My difficulty with the term 'integrated rural development' is that it has become a guise for almost any effort directed at a rural area.[17]

Recognizing this lack of conceptual clarity, Vernon W. Ruttan has argued that integrated rural development is an "ideology in search of a methodology or a technology."[18] Yet a close look at his article reveals that he also failed to define integrated rural development, treating the concept as synonymous with rural development broadly construed. The article considers why so many rural development projects are failures and what processes and institutions are essential to the success of future rural development programs. It does not distinguish or address the particular subset of projects that should be considered to constitute the integrated type. Ruttan shows little sensitivity to the diverse meanings that the notion of integrated rural development has taken at the hands of professionals and policy makers. In the end he attacks the emergent, overly broad concept prior carelessness has generated.

In order to avoid debating the undefined, this chapter now reviews the concept of integrated rural development in greater detail, outlining its history and describing the major types of definition that have emerged. Then it will specifically define the concept adopted for this study, so that the CADU-ARDU case can be clearly reviewed and evaluated.

EXPANSION OF INITIAL CONCEPT

Growing concern with the problems of rural poverty marked the early 1970s. Academics had produced studies critical of the first development decade's emphasis on growth rather than equity,[19] but it was the politicians who pressed for rural development strategies to address the needs of the world's poor and rural population. To a large extent this was because they were more sensitive than development analysts to events in China, Cuba, Vietnam and elsewhere where popularly supported guerrilla movements in the countryside had been critical to major political shifts in world politics. "Containing the green uprising"[20] added a counter-insurgency pressure for increased poverty-focused integrated rural development projects.

Powerful political pressures to increase rural development activities came from international organizations, foremost of which was the World Bank, as expressed in Robert S. McNamara's now famous statement:

> Without rapid progress in small-holder agriculture throughout the developing world, there is little hope either of achieving long-term stable economic growth or significantly reducing the levels of absolute poverty. The fact is that very little has been done over the past two decades specifically designed to increase the productivity of subsistence agriculture.[21]

The Bank's concern was echoed by donor legislatures which required their aid agencies to concentrate resources on the hundreds of millions of people living on the edge of survival.[22] Rural development programming received more funding. The result was a dramatic increase in rural development efforts coupled with a shift in focus to target the poorest of the rural population together with small-scale farmers. In the process, integrated rural development became one of the major approaches used by policy makers to respond to rural inequality. More such projects appeared than ever before, multiplying the diversity of designs. By 1975 Mosher could note with much support that:

> In recent years there has been a growing espousal of integrated projects and programs of rural development based largely on the argument that no one development is a

panacea; what we need are the projects and programs dealing simultaneously with a number of different aspects of rural well-being.[23]

This view also reflects the call for donor and government investment in Basic Human Needs, a strategy that argued for promoting human capital and reducing poverty as critical objectives of any rural development effort.[24] The basis of the strategy was that emphasis on increasing agricultural production alone would lead to inadequate distribution of the benefits of growth and not generate the changes essential to improving the quality of rural life. Under the influence of equity-oriented Basic Human Needs propositions, some integrated rural development projects emerged that sought to combine activities for increasing agricultural production with activities in such sectors as health, education, family planning, and water supply. With this view the innovation begun by Ford in India gave rise to a flood of quite diverse activities loosely labelled "integrated rural development."

DIVERSE VIEWS ON MEANING AND GOALS

No systematic analysis of integrated rural development project characteristics exists.[25] Yet, a review of the literature on efforts so labelled indicates they are largely focused on small-scale farmers, promoting both agricultural development – the increase in production of food and fibre – and rural development – the improvement of the quality of rural life and increase in off-farm employment opportunities. Rarely do they focus on large farm enterprises or non-farming objectives only. They tend to be either project and area specific or regional promotions. Donors appear to prefer the project approach, with a focus on specific areas. Here the most common projects appear to be those designed to link crop production with marketing, infrastructure and rural industry, or farm families with better services and income opportunities. National or regional efforts promoted as integrated rural development are typically the product of governments under the influence of multi-sector planners who emphasize the need for coordination through either multi-purpose ministries or new super-ministries forged to promote integrated national efforts. Here there is frequently an effort to promote centrally directed regional or district planning or implementation authorities.

Beyond the recognition that government efforts at integrated rural development can frequently be quite different from those promoted by donor projects, there is some agreement among analysts that these projects are: (1) identified by efforts to promote comprehensive coordination among a range of government, parastatal or private sector actors; (2) plagued by problems of integrating fragmented but complementary public and private sector resources and services; (3) guided logically by multi-sectoral planning efforts at either the national or local level; (4) designed and implemented by outside groups, such as national level development agencies or international donors, despite growing recognition that local participation and decision making is essential for success; and (5) located administratively in a particular government or bureaucratic unit, often created for the purpose.

Most would agree that such projects are of necessity diverse, there being no magic set of activities that must be present, though a widely held impression is that there are certain "natural" combinations, such as inputs, credit, marketing and roads. It is common for most discussions of the concept to list certain preconditions or essential elements, but aside from the pattern there are few commonalities among the suggestions. There has been some agreement in the literature that integrated rural development projects should emphasize the goal of simultaneity and promote popular participation. Finally, implicit in the literature, but rarely explicitly articulated, are the notions that the package of activities and services selected has a synergistic effect on the development process, that they are to bring about permanent change and not merely be relief undertakings, and that they are long term in implementation.

Beyond these common foundations, one finds the concept used in diverse ways. There seem to be four dominant approaches to defining it. The first conceives of it as a process of combining *reinforcing components or inputs* of a project that are essential for the success of the effort. The second builds its definition on the *development goals* of the project. The third defines the concept in terms of *project characteristics*. The fourth is identified with *spatial or area development*. There are some themes common to all four approaches but there are also considerable differences among them. To keep this chapter brief, only one proponent of each view will be presented.

i. Emphasis on Reinforcing Inputs

Faced with the diversity of objectives and content in projects reviewed at the 1971 FAO symposium on Agricultural Institutions for Integrated Rural Development, Mosher[26] concluded that the notion centers on the orchestration of a large number of disparate activities aimed at either increasing agricultural production or the satisfactions, economic or non-economic, of rural living. Specifically, he argues that the range and diversity of integrated rural development programs and projects result from their usually being based on only a subset of the larger system of project activities that are combined to reach a particular objective. He identifies 16 such activities: (1) markets for farm products; (2) retail outlets for farm inputs; (3) productive credit; (4) extension education; (5) local verification trials; and (6) farm-to-market roads. Non-agricultural activities include: (7) rural industries; (8) rural public works; (9) community construction projects; (10) group activities – recreational or cultural; (11) home life improvement extension services; (12) health facilities; (13) family planning programs; (14) schools; (15) local government; and (16) religious activities. Though there are undoubtedly more he sees the combinations these activities can take as falling within three types of integrated rural development projects: (1) agricultural development projects; (2) rural development projects with an agricultural component; and (3) rural development projects without an agricultural component.

Using this concept framework, Mosher can pinpoint the kinds of project activities being brought together and classify the efforts into a particular type of integrated development effort. The framework allows for the recognition of both production and quality of life objectives, providing in the process an umbrella which allows the diversity of integrated rural development programs or projects to be accommodated.

Mosher rightly recognizes that without qualification, this broad definition is virtually synonymous with rural development, leading him to amend his definition with two requisite design characteristics. Integrated rural development projects should be limited to (1) specific land areas (not nation-wide programs); and (2) to components or input activities not already present and reasonably effective in the area.

ii. Emphasis on Development Goals

The emphasis on development goals as the criteria for defining integrated rural development was promoted by experts based in the FAO. In their view the Mosher definition is too insensitive to issues of rural inequality. Representative of this group is Manfred Leupolt.[27] Building on the critique of 1960s growth models, he argues that the concept is:

> different from general agricultural and rural development because as a matter of policy, it places greater emphasis on the development and mobilization of human resource potential and on achieving a more equitable access to resources and a fairer distribution of income.[28]

What is integrated for Leupolt is not Mosher's specific project activities, but project objectives, such as access to resources, increased production, income distribution, consumption, popular participation or broad based social integration.

There are a number of development analysts who would agree with Leupolt's value laden position that integrated rural development of necessity centers on combining growth and equity objectives in a conscious social change model. For example, Herbert R. Kotter (quite incorrectly in terms of conceptual consensus) argues:

> There is common agreement that integrated rural development means rural transformation and hence the application of a programme including change not only of

methods of production and of economic institutions but of social and political infrastructure as well, and transformation of human relationships and opportunities.[29]

If this emphasis on transformation were commonly agreed upon, it would exclude many of the more well known integrated rural development projects, primarily because they lack the programmatic components necessary to promote improvements in the productivity and income of the rural poor and look the other way regarding the ultimate effects of such efforts, if successful, on political and economic institutions.[30] Many donors do this with their integrated rural development projects, leaving analysts to guess if the goal is the larger social change argued by Leupolt or the stable, prosperous, smallholding world sought by counter-insurgency oriented politicians.

Leupolt and Kotter's approach illustrates two significant points. First, most conceptual elaborations of integrated rural development, such as Mosher's, are the products of economists and pragmatic donor agency specialists. As such, they tend to be based on insights drawn from the field of agricultural economics. Aside from concerns about promoting rural stability without the drastic social restructuring that would result from land reform or rural empowerment, they are rarely linked to sociological or political theories. Second, those that do build on sociological or political theories, such as the FAO's, tend to be structural, with a bias to dependency perspectives. Even these efforts, however, are weakly linked to the theoretical frameworks they are supposedly built on.

iii. Emphasis on Project Type

Typical of approaches centered on project characteristics is the work of Uma J. Lele.[31] Her approach, based on the study of 17 projects in seven African countries, identifies five categories of rural projects: (1) commodity programs aimed at increasing production of export crops on the small-holder sector; (2) regional rural development programs focused on making an impact on a given area in a short period of time; (3) functional programs centered on removing a single critical constraint; (4) miscellaneous planned programs directed at providing services to a specific subsector or region; and (5) spontaneous efforts generated by local participation and confined to a particular area and problem. Under this typology integrated rural development projects were vaguely classified as regional rural development programs largely undertaken mainly on the initiative of donor agencies and planned and prepared by expatriates.[32]

The Lele study based on this classification was funded by the World Bank, and its position paper on rural development shaped the typology. The Bank's staff identified in 1975 three approaches to implementing rural development: (1) the minimum package approach centered on increasing agricultural output with modest but broad-based improvements; (2) the comprehensive approach divided into: (a) coordinated national programs directed at a wide population and based on detailed planning, phased multi-sectoral components and extensive changes in related structures, and (b) area development schemes focused on specific areas and tailored to local conditions; and (3) sector or special programs targeted on removing constraints or promoting services, such as rural public works, education and training, credit, electrification, health and so on.[33] The notion of integrated rural development is studiously avoided in the paper, yet most projects cited as examples of a given classification involve the integration of diverse activities that are necessary to reinforce and support a particular set of rural development objectives. As such, the World Bank approach clouds discussion of integrated rural development projects. Avoiding the term or creating synonyms for it does not solve the problem of clarifying the concept so that the strategy can be properly evaluated and debated.

iv. Emphasis on Spacial Planning

A confusing aspect of the literature is found in the tendency of area planners focused on urban-rural linkages to call their spatial planning exercises "integrated rural development planning." This perspective finds its modern roots in the work of E. A. J. Johnson, who sees the relationship between urban centers and the countryside, and the emergence of spatial patterns in convenient central places, as the key to economic development.[34] Proponents of this perspective tend to use the notion of a development center as the foundation of their "integrated rural development plans."[35] John Friedman's work comes the closest to relating area development to integrated rural development. He defines his "spatial framework" as based on the concept of a "rural service center" and targeted on five objectives: (1) a comprehensive strategy designed to achieve greater productivity, income, and employment in agriculture as well as a steady improvement in the social conditions of rural people; (2) a planning process that effectively links local projects for rural development to a long-term national strategy for balanced urban and regional development; (3) a program designed to benefit primarily the small, low income farmer as well as populations living in agriculturally-based service towns; (4) a method of operation that seeks actively to involve local people in the planning and implementation of programs that benefit primarily themselves; and (5) a process that will provide for the coordinated delivery of mutually supportive services for rural development.[36]

While there is obviously much in common between this view and the three previously described, there are also important differences. Unfortunately, these are not consciously spelled out in relation to the larger literature. Careless use of this perspective by planners compounds the conceptual problems surrounding integrated rural development. Not surprisingly, this literature, like the project-related views criticised by Ruttan, has also been charged with a failure to get beyond ideology to methodology.[37]

SEMANTICS AND ANALYSIS

The diversity of definitions reviewed and the problems of clarity that mark them hamper debate over the strategy. This problem is highlighted in the summary of five regional consultations involving 80 experts on integrated rural development. After extensive discussions at Colombo, Jakarta, Nairobi, Bogota and Lome in 1975 and 1976, it was concluded:

> The review of various concepts of rural development – with or without the prefix "integrated" – does not leave us with the comfortable feeling that a consensus on the concept is about to emerge.[38]

Typical of discussion about the concept, the report noted that the Bogota session stressed the importance of integrated rural development without recording what was meant by it, the Lome participants took no position on its meaning, and the other three sessions discussed the term only in the most general manner.[39]

Clearly, many experts and academics debating integrated rural development have failed to live by one of the central canons of inquiry: conceptual clarity. It might be argued, however, that the large percentage of the world's population who live in villages have little concern whether strategies that seek to reach them are called "integrated rural development." Conceptual debates among social scientists and professionals are far removed from the task of feeding people and improving the quality of their lives. It also might be argued no one has the legitimacy to issue one definition by edict, that efforts to do so are doomed to be inconsequential academic exercises. Both arguments miss the point, since concepts are obviously essential to effective policy making, coherent project design and implementation, meaningful evaluation, and useful comparative analyses of project experiences.

The lack of conceptual definition discussed here results in part from the origins of integrated rural development as an operational rather than theoretical term. It appeared at the same time new approaches to economic development were just beginning to emerge and shape projects seeking to address rural poverty. Rapid application gave rise over a decade to a variety of working definitions. While this diversity proved useful to different national or international agencies, foundations, government institutions and the professionals who work in them, it should hardly be continued now that development specialists are in the field designing and implementing complex integrated rural development strategies and academics are busy analyzing and discussing in greater detail various dimensions of these strategies in their literature.

Surely the problem noted here, that frequently we are talking past each other about different notions of integrated rural development, is a storm warning about deeper problems. At the heart of these is the sometimes careless jargon of some international development experts, so well summarized by V. T. Vittachi as "a language designed to cloud the mind and blur every meaning."[40] A clear example of such problems is seen in observations by others that the lack of conceptual rigour in defining "integrated" or "coordination" is a handy means to avoid responsibility, to conceal ignorance or vague understanding.[41]

CONCEPTUAL FRAMEWORK FOR ANALYSIS

The need for conceptual clarity and rigor in analyzing integrated rural development projects in general and CADU-ARDU in particular is exhibited in the conclusions of a leading Ethiopian economist who with no reference to the history and literature reviewed here concludes that CADU-ARDU is *not* an integrated rural development project:

> The evidence available does not seem to indicate a clearly established method of "integrated rural development" has been evolved for Arsi. The CADU/ARDU projects have certainly affected the lives of thousands of peasants in Arsi, but not necessarily because of the achievement in evolving the 'right' type of integrated development strategy.[42]

To the contrary, it is a central position of this book that CADU-ARDU is a classic example of integrated rural development that offers substantial insight into strategy, design and implementation debates surrounding such projects. So it is essential to conclude this chapter by specifying the conceptual definition of integrated rural development used here.

Having reviewed the range of definitions, this study agrees with Ruttan's recent reconsideration of the concept that the most useful and widely agreed upon definition is that set forth by Mosher.[43] His approach has the attraction of avoiding arguments that integrated rural development projects must contain specific components, facilitating the comparison of different projects for analytical purposes,and outlining a technically appropriate way to describe the strategy. Importantly, it lends itself to direct programmatic application unencumbered by ideology or disciplinary wars. From a more operational perspective, Mosher's framework allows project components and activities to be tailored to local conditions and needs rather than rigidly imposed on the basis of a preconceived set of interventions. In particular, it allows designers to be sensitive to the potential for agricultural growth and the degree of community development possible under existing cultural, political, and economic conditions.

Mosher gradually evolved his framework in a series of papers.[44] As noted earlier, the result is a broad definition that links major components of agricultural development to a non-inclusive list of important types of activities carried out in projects aimed at increasing the production of food and fiber and improving the quality of rural life. These two lists are reflected in Columns A and B of the diagram presented in Figure 1.

It is important to note that the six "agricultural project activities" presented in the box in Column B are merely illustrative of the activities that might be undertaken in a project focused on "rural agricultural support." Any one of the major components of agricultural development, or a combination of them, can be drawn upon, determining thereby the more specific activities the integrated rural development project is likely to undertake. For example, CADU-ARDU carried out activities related to several of these major components of overall agricultural development. It is also important to note that Mosher's definition accepts the broader notion of "rural development" described earlier: namely, the promotion of increased production of food and fiber while improving the quality of life on farms and in the small towns that serve them.

Based on Columns A and B, three types of integrated rural development projects are possible, their classification dependent on their mix of agricultural and non-agricultural activities and services. These are summarized in Column C of the diagram. Importantly, the resulting schema is broad enough to cover the wide range of activities, services, funding sources, executing agencies, and administrative strategies that have been combined over the past two decades to produce the diverse projects labeled the integrated rural development type.

At the heart of the framework is the notion of "bringing activities and services together and administering them." Here, "integrated" is a term of administration, the planned supply of simultaneous activities and services that enables a rural development program to become operational.[45] Explicit in this term is the requirement that the administration be located in a single executing agency that has control over the activities and services being integrated. In this regard, the established definition of the term "project" is adopted, namely "an action oriented enterprise that mobilizes resources aimed at achieving specific objectives in a particular geographic area with a time bounded period."[46] In this sense the term, as Albert O. Hirschman argues, "connotes purposefulness, some minimum size, a specific location, the introduction of something qualitatively new, and the expectation that a sequence of further development moves will be set in motion."[47] From this perspective, an integrated rural development project has specific goals but is not an end in itself. Rather it is a concrete enterprise designed to achieve

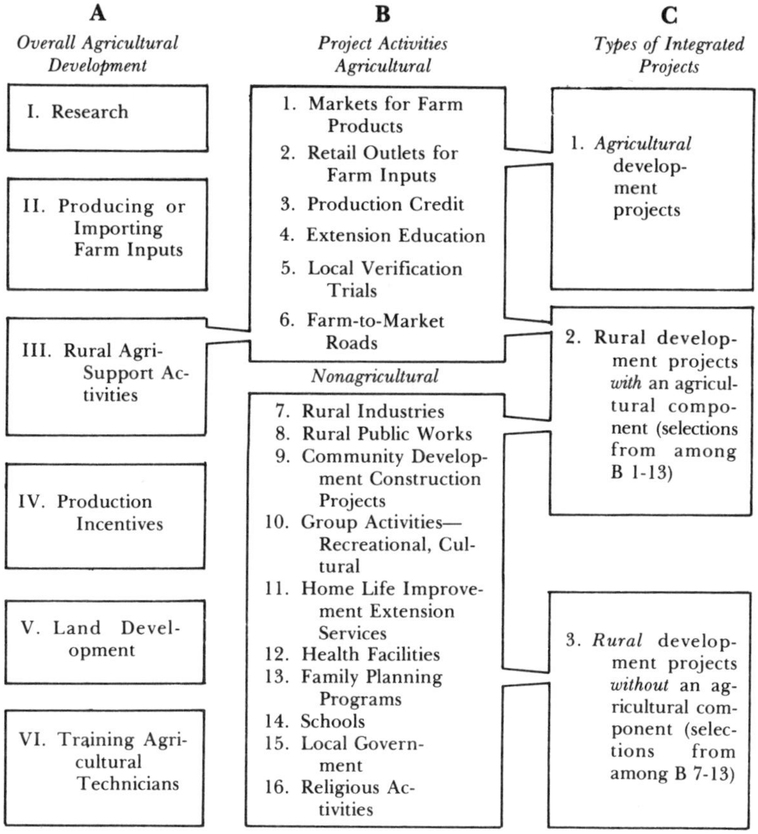

Figure 1: *Components, Activities and Types of Integrated Rural Development Projects*

Source: Mosher, *Thinking About Rural Development,* p.54.

larger development goals. Finally, the terms "activities" and "services" are used under this framework in a broad sense so that they include obvious services such as extension agent visits, the management of institutional credit or the provision of literacy teachers in elementary schools, and actions not usually defined as services, such as the construction of physical infrastructure or the training of local government officials in decentralized planning techniques. Hence, "administration of integrated activities and services" as used here means the planning, combining, and coordinating of financial, technical, material or manpower resources and their application to rural development efforts.

Within this tolerance for diverse types of project centered provision of activities and services are the specific requirements that the project be: (1) limited to a specific area or region of a country; (2) time bound in terms of meeting established objectives; (3) charged with carrying out two or more reinforcing activities or services not already present or effectively provided; and (4) implemented by an executing agency responsible for promoting the integration necessary to successfully provide those activities and services.[48]

It is also the case that most integrated rural development projects fitting the definition presented here have their conceptual origins in international aid agencies and are largely funded by foreign contributions. For the most part this is a function of their relative size, complexity and cost. But it also results from the fact that they have proven to be good vehicles for moving aid money, perhaps the primary criteria donors use for measuring success. But since such projects can be carried out solely by governments, this pattern is extended from the terms comprising the definition used here.

Based on the definition of terms and statements of requirements underlying Mosher's conceptual framework, it is submitted that the CADU project is of the second type: an integrated rural development project combining both agricultural and non-agricultural activities and services. This is significant, for these types of projects are typically the most complex to implement and the most likely to fail. As such it provides an ideal case study for evaluating the potential for integrated rural development projects to be successfully implemented in the difficult task environments of the Third World.

Notes

1. G. V. Fugitt, "Population Movements and Integrated Rural Development," *Sociologia Ruralis*, XIX, (2/3), p. 102.
2. Thomas G. Armor, George Honadle, Craig Olson and Peter Weisel, "Organizing and Supporting Integrated Rural Development Projects: A Twofold Approach to Administering Development," *Journal of Administration Overseas*, XVIII, 4 (1979), p. 276.
3. This has been achieved largely through the publication of three sequential, broadly distributed books: A. T. Mosher, *Getting Agriculture Moving* (New York: Agricultural Development Council, 1966); *Creating a Progressive Rural Structure: To Serve a Modern Agriculture* (New York: Agricultural Development Council, 1969); and his *To Create a Modern Agriculture* (New York: Agricultural Development Council, 1971).
4. Mosher, *Getting Agriculture Moving*, pp. 63-180.
5. Mosher, *Creating a Progressive Rural Structure, passim.*
6. For a summary of this shift see Michael P. Todaro, *Economic Development in the Third World: An Introduction to Problems and Policies in a Global Perspective* (London and New York: Longman, 1977), pp. 204-33.
7. For a summary of the literature on small farm strategies see: Robert D. Stevens, "Transformation of Traditional Agriculture: Theory and Empirical Findings," in *Tradition and Dynamics of Small-Farm Agriculture: Economic Studies in Asia, Africa and Latin America* (Ames: Iowa State University Press, 1977), pp. 3-24, 237-55.
8. Among those which might be discussed are increased maldistribution of income, increased population growth and unemployment, higher food prices and increased food grain scarcities, improved seed-fertilizer strategies, widespread unrest among the world's poor, increased donor concern with equity and economic justice, and better under-standing of the economies of less developed countries.
9. The theoretical underpinnings of this food grain linkage approach centered on agriculture as an engine for change is found in: Bruce F. Johnston and John W. Mellor, "The Role of Agriculture in Economic Development," *American Economic Review*, LI (1961), pp. 565-93; John W. Mellor, *The Economics of Agricultural Development* (Ithaca: Cornell University Press, 1966). The specific arguments are well presented in: John W. Mellor and Uma J. Lele, "Growth Linkages of the New Food Grain Technologies," *Indian Journal of Agricultural Economics*, XXVIII (1973), pp. 35-55 and their "Jobs, Poverty and the 'Green Revolution,'" *International Affairs* (1972), pp. 20-32. A recent consolidation of such models is: Bruce F. Johnston and Peter Kilby, *Agriculture and Structural Transformation: Economic Strategies in Late-Developing Countries* (New York: Oxford University Press, 1975).
10. A good summary of the emergence of the green revolution and the initial optimism surrounding it is: Lester R. Brown, *Seeds of Change: The Green Revolution and Development in the 1970s* (New York: Praeger Publishers, 1970).
11. The critique of the green revolution and its effect on inequality is well illustrated by: Keith Griffin, *The Political Economy of Agrarian Change: An Essay on the Green Revolution* (Cambridge: Harvard University Press, 1974); Harry M. Cleaver, Jr., "The Contradictions of the Green Revolution," *American Economic Review*, LXII, 2 (1972), pp. 177-86.
12. See for example: Wyn F. Owen, "The Significance of Small Farms in Developing Countries," in *Small Farm Agricultural Development Problems* , edited by Huntly H. Biggs and Ronald L. Tinnermeier (Fort Collins: Colorado State University, 1974), pp. 31-6.

13. Illustrative of the new tendency to see peasants as "economic men" is: Davydd J. Greenwood, *The Political Economy of Peasant Family Farming: Some Anthropological Perspectives on Rationality and Adaptation* (Ithaca: Cornell University, Center for International Studies, Occasional Paper No. 2, 1973); A. V. Chayanov, "Peasant Farm Organization," in A. V. Chayanov, *The Theory of Peasant Economy* (Homewood: Richard D. Irwin, Inc., 1966); William Foote Whyte, *Organizing for Agricultural Development* (New Brunswick, N. J.: Transaction Books, 1975).
14. The earlier division is still reflected in USAID's distinction between agricultural and rural development offices – as well as health, education and population offices – in both Washington and the overseas missions. The U.S. Department of Agriculture and legislation such as the Rural Development Act of 1972 still maintain this distinction.
15. Office of Development Information and Utilization, "Development Information on Integrated Rural Development" (Draft Document, Development Support Bureau, Agency for International Development, Washington, D.C., October 1978), p. 79.
16. Betru Gebregziabher, *Integrated Rural Development in Rural Ethiopia: An Evaluative Study of the Chilalo Agricultural Development Unit* (Bloomington: International Development Research Center, PASITAM, University of Indiana, 1975), p. 3.
17. Charles F. Sweet, "Perspectives on the Process Approach to Rural Development" (Washington, D.C.: Development Alternatives, Inc., Occasional Paper No. 4, 1978), p.8.
18. Vernon W. Ruttan, "Integrated Rural Development Programs: A Skeptical Perspective," *International Development Review*, XVIII, 4 (1974/75), pp. 9-16.
19. Typical are: Dudley Seers, "The Meaning of Development," *International Development Review,* XI, 4 (1969), pp. 2-6; Mahbub ul Haq, "Employment in the 1970s: A New Perspective," *International Development Review*, XIII, 4 (1971), pp. 8-12. The literature on the effects of growth without equity on the rural poor majority are summarized in: Charles Elliott, *Patterns of Poverty in the Third World: A Study of Social and Economic Stratification* (New York: Praeger, 1975).
20. The concern with the revolutionary potential of peasants and the threat to Western interests and political stability is well exhibited in the influential chapter "Containing the Green Uprising" in Samuel P. Huntington, *Political Order in Changing Societies* (New Haven: Yale University Press, 1968), pp. 433-61. The image of the well-off post industrial countries threatened by a worldwide majority of poor and oppressed peoples is perhaps best expressed by: Robert L. Heilbroner, *An Inquiry into the Human Prospect* (New York: W. W. Norton & Co., 1974).
21. Robert S. McNamara, "Address to the Board of Governors, Nairobi, Kenya, September 1972" (Washington, D.C.: World Bank, 1973), p. 14.
22. Best known of these is the so called "Congressional Mandate" by which the U.S. Congress in its 1973 Foreign Assistance Act made clear the need to end the trickle down approach to development and concentrate on the lower 40 percent of the population of the less developed countries. See: *Implementation of "New Directions" in Development Assistance* (Report Prepared by AID for Committee on International Relations on Implementation of the Foreign Assistance Act of 1973, 94th Congress, 1st Session, July 22, 1975).
23. Arthur T. Mosher, *Thinking About Development* (New York: Agricultural Development Council, 1976).
24. See for example: World Bank, *Poverty and Basic Needs* (Washington, D.C.: World Bank, 1980); Paul Streeten, "The Distinctive Features of a Basic Needs Approach to Development," *International Development Review*, XIX, 3 (1977), pp. 8-16.
25. A brief effort was made by ODI. It identified types but made no effort to evaluate them. Rather it concluded that integrated rural development is used in so diverse a way

as to be a slogan. Overseas Development Institute, "Integrated Rural Development" (London: ODI Briefing Paper No. 4, 1979), pp. 1-4. Still ODI's effort was more rigorous and less biased than the chaotic effort of Rainer Wulf, "On the Concept of Integrated Rural Development," *Economics*, XVII (1978), pp. 63-80.

26. A. T. Mosher, "Projects of Integrated Rural Development" (Reprint Paper, Agricultural Development Council, Inc., December 1972).
27. Manfred Leupolt, "Integrated Rural Development: Key Elements of an Integrated Rural Development Strategy," *Sociologia Ruralis*, XVIII, 1/2 (1977), pp. 7-28.
28. *Ibid.*, p. 13.
29. H. R. Kotter, "Some Observations on the Basic Principles and General Strategy Underlying Integrated Rural Development," *Monthly Bulletin of Agricultural Economics and Statistics*, XXIII, 4 (1974), p. 2, citing in part P. Coombs, et al., "New Paths to Learning," *ICED* (1973), p. 22.
30. This is certainly in the World Bank's approach: Montague Yudelman, "Integrated Rural Development Projects: the Bank's Experience," *Finance and Development*, XIV, 1 (1977), pp. 15-18.
31. Uma Lele, *The Design of Rural Development: Lessons from Africa* (Baltimore: The Johns Hopkins University Press, 1975).
32. *Ibid.*, p. 14. Examples of projects classified as integrated rural development by Lele are: the Chilalo Agricultural Development Unit (CADU) in Ethiopia; the Lilongwe Land Development Program (LLDP) in Malawi; the Zones d'Action Prioritaires Integrées (ZAPI) and the Societé de Développement du Nkam (SODENKAM) settlement scheme, both in Cameroon. Projects can also be undertaken by governments, such as the Special Rural Development Program in Kenya.
33. World Bank, *Rural Development: Sector Policy Paper* (Washington, D.C.: World Bank, 1975), pp. 40-57.
34. E. A. J. Johnson, *The Organization of Space in Developing Countries* (Cambridge: Harvard University Press, 1970).
35. Typical of this literature is: Dennis A. Rondinelli and Kenneth K. Ruddle, "Urban Functions," in their *Rural Development: An Analysis of Integrated Spacial Development Policy* (Washington, D.C.: Office of Urban Development, Agency for International Development, 1976); D. G. R. Belshaw, "Rural Development Planning: Concepts and Techniques," *Journal of Agricultural Economics*, XXVIII, 3 (1977), pp. 279-91; Ian Livingstone, "On the Concept of 'Integrated Rural Development' in Less Developed Countries," *Journal of Agricultural Economics*, XXX, 1 (1979), pp. 49-53.
36. John Friedmann, "A Spatial Framework for Rural Development: Problems of Organization and Implementation," *Economie Appliquée*, XXVIII, 2-3 (1975), pp. 519-20.
37. See: Livingstone's critique of Belshaw, "On the Concept," p. 53.
38. FAO, *Report on the FAO/SIDA/DSE Inter-Regional Symposium on Integrated Rural Development* (Rome: Food and Agriculture Organization of the United Nations, 1978), p. 14. The FAO's confusion is not helped by the articles of its staff officer M. A. Zaman. See his: "Some Experiences in the Implementation of Integrated Rural Development (IRD) Programmes," *Agricultural Administration*, IV (1977), pp. 307-16; and his "Integrated Rural Development: FAO/SIDA Expert Consultation on Policies and Institutions," *Agricultural Administration*, V (1978), pp. 239-73.
39. *Ibid.*, pp. 14-18.
40. V. T. Vitachi, "Words We Can Do Without," *Newsweek*, March 24, 1980, p. 4.
41. See: Robert Chambers, *Managing Rural Development* (Uppsala: Scandinavian Institute of African Studies, 1974), pp. 24-5; Armor, et al., "Organizing and Supporting," p. 277.

42. Fassil G. Kiros, "Learning From ARDU: Toward a Regional System of Rural Development in Ethiopia" (Paper Presented to the Seminar on Regional Planning and Development in Ethiopia, Ambo, April 1983), p. 14.
43. Ruttan, "A Historical Perspective," p. 394.
44. The evolving framework is described in several widely available articles. See footnotes 3 and 23; and his "Custom-Made Systems," *Ceres*, V, 4 (1972), pp. 33-7.
45. J.J. Ahmad, "Administration of Integrated Rural Development Programmes," *International Labour Review*, CXI, 2 (1975), p. 141.
46. Dennis A. Rondinelli, "Planning and Implementing Development Projects: An Introduction," and Wayne Weiss, Albert Waterston and John Wilson, "The Design of Agricultural and Rural Development Projects," in *Planning Development Projects*, edited by Dennis A. Rondinelli (Strausburg: Dowden, 1977), pp. 1-25, 95-139.
47. Albert O. Hirschman, *Development Projects Observed* (Washington, D.C.: Brookings Institute, 1967), p. 1.
48. Administration can be achieved through either coordination or control. The unit which administers the project can have varying mixes of coordination or control over the full range of activities and services it seeks to orchestrate--or "bring together and run." It might be a division of a ministry, the field office of a ministry, a local government body, an agency of the government, a parastatal organization, a quasi-public body, a private voluntary association, or local community development association, for example. But it is singular.

CHAPTER 3

Rural Development in Ethiopia and Chilalo

> ...agriculture should be in the forefront of the development process. One hears so much of the fertility of Ethiopia's soil, the excellence of her climate and the abundance of her resources that one is tempted to believe she can be the bread basket of the Middle East. But people do not live on potential alone. It demands realization.
>
> Aseffa Bequele and Eshetu Chole (1969)

Ethiopia is the oldest independent African nation and one of the continent's most underdeveloped countries.[1] It also is one of the largest and most populous countries in Africa, covering an area of 1,221,900 square kilometers and containing a population of 23 million in 1965 and 42 million two decades later. Development specialists visiting Ethiopia in the 1960s described it as having the potential to be the bread basket of the Horn of Africa and the Middle East. The country's natural endowment of adequate land mass, generally fertile soils, sufficient rainfall, variety of climates and elevations, and large, hard working peasantry supported this observation.[2] Yet Ethiopia's agricultural sector was unable to fulfill this promise. By the mid-1960s it was increasingly clear that Ethiopia's stagnant economy resulted from the neglect of the great majority of the country's population who were subsistence farmers.[3] Arguing that overall economic and social development of the country had to rest on increased small-holder productivity and the penetration of markets into rural areas, Swedish experts designed a major rural development project aimed at demonstrating how to achieve these objectives. The subsistence economy the Swedes hoped to alter with this project and the region where it was to be located are the subjects of this chapter.

AGRICULTURE AND ECONOMY IN THE 1960S

In the mid-1960s the Ethiopian economy was dominated by an agricultural sector which, with the exception of limited commercial farming carried out in the lowlands on large-scale irrigated lands or in a few highland areas, was characterized by subsistence holdings, rain-fed production, limited capital investment, and low agricultural yields. Since no census had been completed it was impossible to know exactly how many Ethiopians were peasants. However, it was generally estimated that 8 percent of the population lived in urban areas, with 85 percent of the 21.1 million rural population living in households engaged in peasant agriculture.[4] Most of these households farmed two hectares and used three for pasture, since five hectares was generally thought to be the optimum holding for a household using traditional tools in dry-farming regions. In 1965 their agrarian production, as a percentage of Gross Domestic Product, was one of the highest in the world, ranging between 55 and 60 percent. Moreover, the non-monetary agricultural sector probably accounted for three-quarters of the total agricultural contribution. Of the 25 percent of agricultural output marketed, coffee, sugar and cotton accounted for about 35 percent, cereals, pulses, and oilseeds 30 percent, and livestock 20 percent.[5]

Although productive area was relatively high, the amount of land devoted to crop production was low. Over half the nation's land area of some 122 million hectares was used as permanent pasture, much of which could be placed under plow or tractor. Forests occupied only slightly less than the area devoted to cropland.[6]

In the 1960s, Ethiopia also had one of the largest livestock populations in Africa. Farmers and pastoralists used a great deal of potentially cultivable land to support some 55 million domestic animals yet gained little economic benefit from them. Widespread disease and a fragmented marketing system prevented the livestock sector from making a major contribution to local and national economic growth. Most animals were kept for subsistence uses. Not more than 25 percent of the cattle pulled plows, the rest being held as savings for major purchases or for consumption. Daily meat supply in rural areas came from sheep, goats, and poultry. Horses, mules, and donkeys were used for transport.

Agriculture's monetary sector accounted for more than 90 percent of total foreign exports, with coffee comprising 60 percent of that figure. Hides and skins constituted an additional export commodity, but Ethiopia had not promoted their export despite profitable overseas markets. Oilseeds and pulses comprised the rest of the country's exports, but the government made little effort to swing farming from cereal production to these attractive cash crops, in spite of the fact that Ethiopia was mineral poor and had to earn foreign exchange in order to generate capital to finance its modernization. Finally, the marketing potential for Ethiopia's agrarian output was favorable because of rising world-wide and domestic demand due to increasing urbanization.

Despite this base and its potential, the annual agricultural growth rate averaged just above two percent per year, probably less than the overall population growth during the same period.[7] As a result of this slow growth in agricultural productivity and steady increase in population, Ethiopia had one of the lowest per capita income levels in the world. In the mid-1950s Ethiopian Gross National Product per capita ranked ahead of only Burma and Nepal, with a value of US$ 54 per person; throughout the 1960s Ethiopia scarcely improved this relative position.[8]

Agricultural Policy Under Haile Selassie

Between 1957 and 1974 the government attempted to address the country's slow economic growth through a series of national development plans. For more than a decade these plans gave insufficient emphasis to agriculture in general and the large peasant sector in particular.[9] Their overall approach was based on development theories of the 1950s, when economic growth was held to be linked primarily to capital accumulation for investment in industry and the creation of large-scale commercial farms to feed a growing urban labor force and generate export earnings. Hence, the first two plans emphasized investments in infrastructure, manufacturing and technology, and plantation agriculture. But gradually over this long period the importance of the small-farm sector to national economic growth was recognized and a strategy proposed in the third and fourth plans to raise its productivity. However, because of land tenure and other structural constraints only limited progress was made in transforming peasant agriculture prior to the revolution.

The First Five Year Plan (1957-62) gave priority to infrastructure development.[10] It stressed investments in transportation, communication, electric power, manufacturing, and housing. The plan's agricultural strategy aimed at building an infrastructure base that would stimulate increased marketing of export crops. Specifically it concentrated on surveying the irrigation potential of Ethiopia's major rivers, developing a sugar factory, improving farm labor productivity on commercial farms, and stimulating an export oriented livestock industry. The overall achievement of the first plan was low and its impact on agricultural production minimal.

The Second Five Year Plan (1963-68) emphasized investment in manufacturing, mining, and electricity.[11] Its planned investments in the agricultural sector were aimed at generating foreign exchange through increased exports and raising local food production so that imports could be reduced. The plan proposed a range of investments to promote agricultural production. These included improving the collection and analysis of agricultural data, building research stations, increasing field trials, strengthening the extension system, expanding veterinary services and establishing college level training programs to provide specialists to support such expanded services. The plan's proposed investments in the agricultural sector were largely intended to promote commercial farming, but the document did call for progressive tenancy and landownership reforms. In this way serious constraints hampering small-holder production were at least acknowledged.

But during the plan period the government made little progress in promoting the strengthening and expansion of agricultural services. Even less progress occurred in addressing more political objectives set forth in the plan, such as carrying out cadastral surveys, drafting land tenure legislation, reforming agricultural taxation, improving the administration of agriculture, and establishing the Ministry of Agriculture as the general agency responsible for the agrarian sector. In part this resulted from low expenditure rates, the agricultural sector receiving only about 6 percent of total investment under the plan. The document did facilitate, however, the establishment of the Ministry of Land Reform and Administration in 1966 and a planning ministry that was to be more open to the potential of small-holder agriculture to promote economic growth.

The Third Five Year Plan (1968-73) sought to deal more directly with the constraints to agricultural growth identified in the second plan.[12] But the draftsmen of the plan continued to view large commercial farms as the key to agricultural progress. The annual agricultural growth rate of 3.1 percent set by the plan was to be achieved by government policies aimed at stimulating increased mechanization of farms, establishment of raw material processing industries, and expansion of agricultural exports.

Tractors and plant protection chemicals were exempt from import duties. Fuel tax exemptions stimulated mechanization, and large agrarian investments above US$ 200,000 were given three to five years income tax relief. Relatively cheap credit was made available through the establishment of agricultural development banks. A number of agricultural entrepreneurs in many areas of the country took advantage of these policies. In general, the largest of their farms and plantations were run by foreign concessions and commercially experienced businessmen. Some Ethiopians followed their example, although on a smaller scale. But while incentives were given, commercial agriculture was underfunded, for it received only 10 percent of the investment expenditures under the plan, the other 90 percent going to communication infrastructure, mining schemes, power plant construction, and industry promotion. Even if commercial agriculture had been adequately funded it is doubtful this would have led to adequate growth because of the shortage of skilled managers and the sector's low absorptive capacity relative to capital. As for the peasant sector, the plan earmarked only one percent of total expenditures.

The Third Plan's strategy for promoting peasant agriculture was labelled a "package approach." It sought to concentrate financial and manpower resources on the development of a few promising highland areas. Essentially an integrated rural development strategy, the package approach argued for combined investments in agricultural research and extension with initiatives to improve the distribution of seeds and fertilizer, provide credit, develop market facilities, diffuse better implements, expand storage facilities, promote rural health, and raise functional literacy. As conceived, the package approach was to concentrate such investments in a few programs that were well financed and coordinated. The main premise behind the approach was that the constraints hampering small farm productivity were too complex and interrelated to be solved any other way. In essence the plan chose to avoid distributing limited resources to small-holders throughout the country and to concentrate resources in a few areas where they could have maximum impact.

This small-holder strategy was attractive to the government for political reasons. It allowed the regime to begin the process of bringing the peasant sector into a modernizing economy while limiting destabilizing effects to specific regions until reforms could be implemented that protected landed interests. The package program approach also had financial advantages. The changed development theory and donor policies described in Chapter 2 were leading to an emphasis on small-farm agriculture and Ethiopia's package approach provided a funding mechanism for channeling increased foreign aid to the peasant sector. As a result of the incorporation of these projects into the Third Plan, agriculture's share of external aid increased from 7 percent in 1970 to 25 percent two years later.[13]

This change in funding patterns came largely because donors had pressured the government to provide an opportunity to fund small-holder projects and succeeded in getting it written into the plan. In fact, when the Third Plan was published, a Swedish funded package approach to small-holder development was already being implemented in Arussi Province. This integrated rural development project, the Chilalo Agricultural Development Unit (CADU), is the focus of this book. It was followed shortly by the donor funded large-scale package projects,[14] and a nation-wide minimum package program begun during the third plan period.[15] Still, little progress was made by 1973 in either substantially increasing agricultural productivity in the peasant sector or in removing constraints recognized at the end of the second plan as hampering development interventions targeted on Ethiopia's small-holder sector.

Progress was made in building the institutional capacity to support a modernizing small-holder sector. Just prior to the first plan there was a weak Ministry of Agriculture unable to provide core services in an integrated way; for example, research stations lacked seed multiplication capacity and fertilizers were promoted without the availability of credit inducements. The ministry also lacked Ethiopians trained to carry out the agricultural research, extension, and other activities called for by the government. Generally there were few outlets for agricultural inputs, no organized credit channels, a limited road network, and a poorly organized market for farm products. By the late 1960s, however, the Ministry of Agriculture was firmly established as an organization, an achievement notwithstanding its limited administrative capacity, insufficient trained specialists, and inadequate budgetary support.[16] In addition, the country's research institutions were improving, agricultural training institutions were turning out college graduates, a growing network of roads and markets was emerging, irrigation schemes were expanding and the large and minimum package schemes were introducing higher yielding seeds, fertilizer and credit into a number of small-holder areas. Beyond this, the central government had increased the availability of education and health facilities in provincial towns, although evidence suggests that such facilities benefited primarily the provincial elite, not the rural peasantry.

From the late 1960s to the revolution, the government and aid agencies debated how the potential of the peasant sector could be promoted. This debate was informed by CADU's experience. Indeed, the project's quick success in increasing the productivity of small-holders, described in Chapters 4 and 5, reinforced donor pressure on the government to view agriculture in general and small-holder productivity in particular as the country's major engine of growth.

The strategy that emerged was set forth in the initial drafts of the Fourth Five Year Plan.[17] The revolution prevented the publication of this plan. Yet it is important to review because it was strongly influenced by the CADU project and envisioned promoting an increase in agricultural output by 3.1 percent over the plan period through investments in large-scale and minimum package projects.[18]

World Bank analysis provided the conceptual basis for the plan.[19] It centered on two assumptions: (1) that an adequate agricultural resource base and favorable product market outlook existed; and (2) that given the rapidly growing population and heavy dependence on agriculture as a source of exports and employment, the agricultural sector had to receive far more emphasis than in the past. The strategy specifically pinpointed the need to remove the following major constraints: insufficient government finance, lack of trained technical and administrative manpower, inaccessibility of much of the subsistence farming areas, shortage of technical and economic data, and lack of proven agricultural techniques. Because of the constraints the Bank argued for concentration of efforts on areas of high potential, to avoid spreading limited resources too thin, and to allow expansion into adjacent areas as projects succeeded in their areas of focus. The strategy was already in effect in the on-going large-scale package programs and the nationwide minimum package program.

The strategy within the areas of concentration was to be built on cereals and pulses. In order to increase farm output and activate the economy, the Bank advocated expansion of roads, establishment of grassroots cooperatives, provision of credit at low interest rates, introduction of improved seeds and fertilizers, improvement of marketing facilities, networks of exchange, statistics and long range planning, training of agricultural manpower, and development and dissemination of agrotechnology through expanded research and extension efforts.

To the Bank's credit it recognized that these approaches would not succeed without greater public investment in the peasant sector, strong commitment by the government to improve provincial administration and the performance of development ministries in the field, and the promulgation of basic land tenure reforms. Bank experts laid out a set of interim changes in the land tenure system which they felt were a necessary prelude to full reform and considered essential to stimulate small-holder agriculture. But these recommendations were noted only in passing, for those who drafted the strategy realized the social upheaval such reforms were likely to bring. Some senior Ethiopian planning and development professionals were also aware of the need for such changes.[20] But they were constrained from effectively promoting them by powerful political forces operating to protect the landed interests and social power of those who ruled Ethiopia.

Explanations of Agricultural Stagnation

Until the late 1960s the conclusion of many analysts was that the weight of tradition and strong cultural patterns held back economic development.[21] They argued that the country's conservative religious institutions, historical isolation, and feudal structures had created an inward looking peasantry not open to agricultural innovation and development. This cultural explanation was broadened by historical studies of the rise of the state,[22] which sharpened awareness of the relationship between land and power. These supported a series of political economy studies focused on the effects of autocracy and patron-client relations on government policy, the rise of the centralized bureaucracy and suppression of powerful regional lords, the emergence of central elites oriented toward development, and the landbased interests of powerful imperial supporters in the nobility, civil service and military.[23] The rise of structural theories that rejected cultural and psycho-behavioral explanations of underdevelopment,[24] the shift in Western economic development models from industrial to agricultural-led growth strategies, and the realization that the peasant was neither lazy nor fatalistic, generated detailed consideration of the development potential of Ethiopia's dominant rural sector. The increased availability of land tenure data in the mid-1960s[25] and the opening of rural areas to research by anthropologists and rural sociologists led to a rapid increase in the understanding of Ethiopia's unfulfilled agrarian potential.

By the early 1970s the explanation of Ethiopia's underdevelopment came to center on the relationship between peasant agriculture and the economy, the historical attitude of the government toward agrarian production, the general patterns of land holdings, the failure of the land reform movement, and the constraints such patterns collectively imposed on efforts to stimulate agricultural productivity.[26] The emergence of land based explanations of

Ethiopia's underdevelopment and agricultural stagnation were consolidated by the political economy concept of "Ethiopian feudalism."[27] Proponents of this view argued that Ethiopian development was constrained by a land based economy that supported the power and wealth of the emperor and ruling elites through the absorption of peasant output by means of tribute, taxation and rent.[28]

Leftist critics of Haile Selassie's regime tended to use the notion of feudal based land tenure as the only explanation of Ethiopia's underdevelopment.[29] However, most development experts and academics who used the term fully realized that the situation was different from that which had prevailed in medieval Europe, obscured to some extent the colonial pattern of Amhara domination in Southern provinces,[30] and was only one of several important factors causing agrarian stagnation and amplifying the constraints generated by the relationship between land tenure, wealth, and power.[31] They also were well aware that new social classes and a modern economy were emerging independent of the traditional sector.[32] But they were of the opinion that policies supportive of the emerging modern sector would not be effective without the transformation of the moribund rural economy and that any efforts to promote increased productivity, higher incomes, and expanded job opportunities would be unsuccessful without land tenure reform and a shift in government policy on the small farm sector. Most importantly, they believed that such changes would be difficult to achieve because the imperial government, and the central and provincial elites that supported it, understood that progressive agrarian reform would undermine the system of rural exploitation that ensured their control of the economy and polity.

In short, proponents of the feudalism explanation argued that Ethiopia was a blocked society. The stagnant rural sector kept the overall economy from moving forward and the constellation of interests that bound landed and urban elites together precluded the possibility of implementing the kinds of land, governmental, and societal-wide reforms that had roused such countries as Taiwan and South Korea. The emperor and his policy makers were locked into gradual reform at best, hesitant and piecemeal steps that had not been taken by the time the revolution began. That this political economy explanation of Ethiopia's agrarian stagnation was valid will be demonstrated in Chapters 4 and 5. There it will be used to analyze constraints that prevented the CADU project from reaching its full potential.

PROFILE OF THE CHILALO REGION IN 1965

The increasing emphasis on small-holder production that occurred during the last decade of Haile Selassie's rule and the social, economic, and political constraints that hampered its effective implementation are clearly reflected in the history of the CADU project. Before turning to that history it is essential to survey the physical and social patterns that marked the Chilalo region just before the CADU project began.

i. Geography and Administrative Units

The principal geological feature that differentiates Chilalo from the rest of Ethiopia is the Rift Valley.[33] This enormous geological scar on the face of Africa crosses Ethiopia diagonally from the southwest to the northeast, creating in the process the western plateau, the land of historical Abyssinia, and the eastern plateau, the locus of the Arussi highlands and Chilalo.

Most of Chilalo's land mass is highland plateau, with only small regions in the north and west at the lower elevations of the Rift Valley. Chilalo comprises 10,100 square kilometers or 1,010,000 hectares (25,000 *gashas* in Ethiopian land measurement units).[34] The administrative boundaries of Chilalo follow the physical characteristics of the surrounding region, for it is a geographical unit clearly demarcated by the lakes of the middle Rift Valley to the west, the Awash River to the north, the Wabi Shebelli River in the south, and the spine of the Chilalo massif which runs the length of the eastern border of the region.[35]

As an administrative unit, Chilalo is one of three sub-provinces, or *awrajas*, in Arussi Province. It is internally divided into 10 districts or *woredas*. Their boundaries also largely follow the physical topography of the region.

ii. Ecological Environment and Climate

The Ministry of Agriculture divided the *awraja* into its own development zones, which provide a useful set of geographical areas for defining and organizing the area's internal geography, as well as ecological environments, agricultural resources and population, and settlement patterns.[36] These zones, as well as administrative boundaries are set forth in Figure 2. A brief description of them suggests the ecological diversity of Chilalo.

Zone D is a lowland area of the Rift Valley. Its features also characterize the extreme western part of Zone B. The region averages 1,500 to 1,800 meters in elevation and is marked by cinder cones. In the northern part near Dodota there are gently sloping, monotonously flat plains. To the south toward Iteya the escarpment separating the Rift Valley from the higher Chilalo plateau is more rugged, being characterized by terraces, stepped faults, and ridges. Zone A is plateau region, marked by a gradual upward slope from the edge of the escarpment to the higher mountains. Since this is the main cultivated region of the *awraja*, it is important to note that the rolling plateau plains of Zone A have relatively rich dark gray prairie and

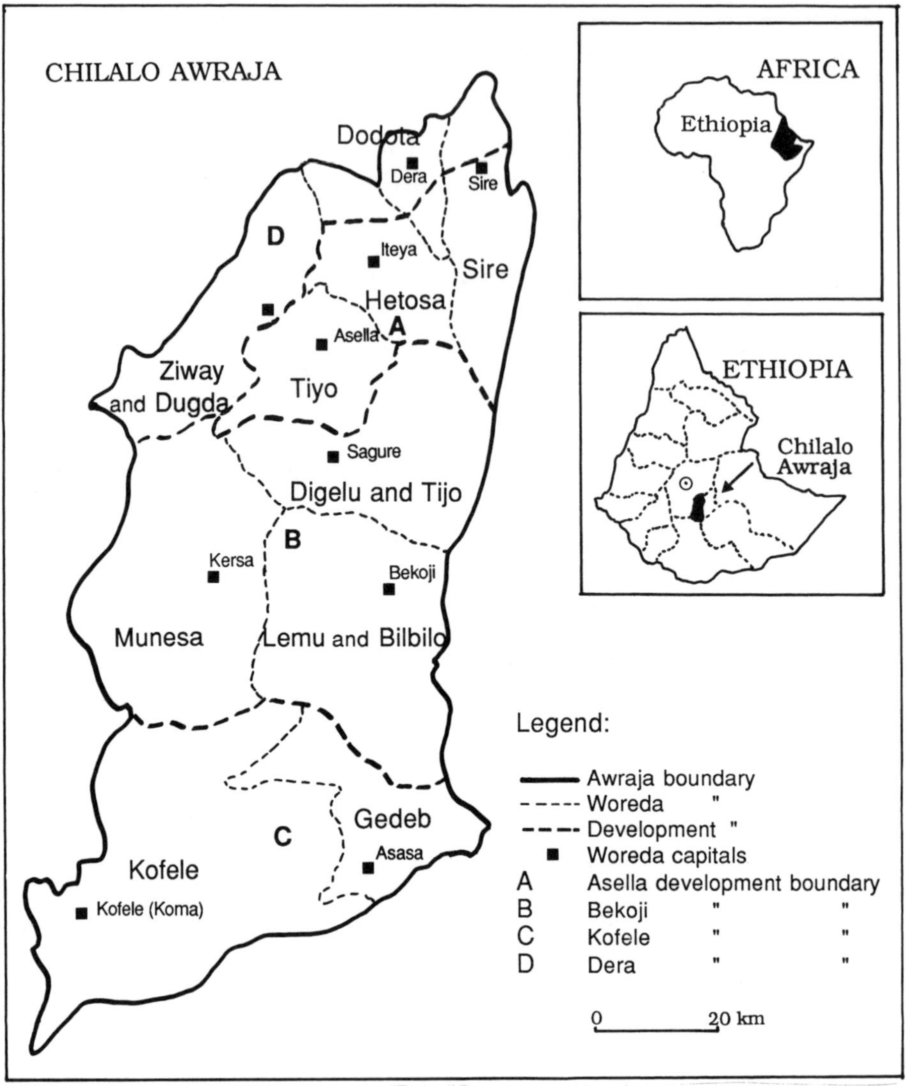

Figure 2: *Map of Administrative and Development Divisions of Chilalo Awraja*

reddish brown clay soils. The *awraja* and provincial capital, Asella, is located in this zone at a point where the plateau is the narrowest.

From Asella to Sagure the plateau gradually descends until it widens into an undulating area well suited for grazing and agricultural production. The main part of Zone B between Bekoji and Asasa consists of a region of dome shaped hills. To the west of them are wide plains. Foothills and the slopes of mountains mark the boundaries of both zones B and C and are gentle in slope. Zone C, in the extreme south, is divided into the sandy, semi-arid plains of Gedeb in the east and the rolling, evergreen regions of Kofele in the west.

The year is divided into the major rainy season, occurring during the months of July, August, and September, the minor rainy season covering the months of March and April, and the dry season that ranges over the rest of the year.[37] Despite these seasonal divisions, Chilalo's highlands receive some rainfall in every month, a fact which contributes greatly to the agricultural advantages of the area.[38] Temperatures are highly variable depending on altitude and climatic season, but in general they are conducive to the growing of a wide variety of crops on a year-round basis.[39]

Chilalo has a complex hydrological drainage system. The streams of the middle region drain into the lakes of the west, while those of the north are tributaries of the Awash River basin and those of the south flow into the Wabi Shebelli River. Many streams are seasonal, leading to a pronounced water shortage in Chilalo during the dry season. The water of all rivers and streams is used primarily for human and livestock consumption.

In the dry season most rural inhabitants were located more than five kilometers from the nearest source of available water. This required women to use much labor time carrying it to farming households. Furthermore, the need to drive cattle to distant dry season water sources every other day lowered both milk production and quality of meat. This of course had an important impact on agricultural production both in terms of rural health, available agricultural labor hours, and livestock exploitation. Some *awraja* towns in 1960 had severe water shortages, whereas others did not. But it was clear then that the development of an adequate infrastructure for inducing rural change necessitated, among numerous other requirements, that towns be provided with adequate and safe water facilities.

In the mid-1960s irrigation was limited to a few farms north of Asella and at the edge of the escarpment in the northern area of the *awraja*.[40] The only commercial uses of water power in the area were the hydroelectric station near Dodota on the Awash River, which produces electricity for some of the small towns in the north, and a few water driven grain mills.

iii. History of the Region

Prior to the end of the nineteenth century, Chilalo was occupied by pastoral Arssi-Oromo people who had seized it from earlier groups. As a culture they exhibited many of the social and political characteristics of other Oromo peoples.[41] The most important of these centered on leadership and clan land rights. Leadership of each clan was based on genealogical descent and the basis of social and political control was that of the *gada* system, a complex form of organization providing rules and regulations of social interaction as well as establishing rule making, rule application and rule adjudication of powers of various degrees in the different levels of the culturally controlled *gada* life cycles.[42] Finally, the land was owned by the clans and distributed and withdrawn by clan leadership. But while there was little stratification conflict caused by maldistribution of land, there was continuing conflict between clan leadership over the extent and powers of land custodianship.

From the early 19th century to the 1880s, intermittent fighting occurred on the borders of Arssiland, largely between Shoan troops and Arssi pastoralists.[43] Then in the mid-1880s Emperor Yohannes IV began more serious campaigns with the aid of Shoan troops. Menelik carried out these campaigns, first as a regional lord and subsequently as emperor. Despite the greater superiority of Menelik's troops and arms, it took until the end of the century for the Arssi to be fully subdued.

Since Menelik's principal objective was permanent occupation of the conquered territories, he tended to give his enemies an opportunity to yield without resistance. When an area so yielded he often granted it a measure of local autonomy and fair treatment by his soldiers and administrators. But when opposed, he directed a ruthless policy of conquest which crushed the resisting area. The result of fierce Arssi resistance was borne by their descendents.

Menelik settled a large army in the area. Since the population was not dense, this placed a heavy burden on the Arssi, most of whom were turned into tenants in support of the military forces.[44] The need to support troops in the area, its distance from the imperial capital, and the cultural differences between administrators and the southern peoples led to the establishment of a system of land tenure prevalent in the region in 1965.

In Chilalo, Menelik's representatives refused to recognize the validity of Arssi clan ownership and confiscated all of the land.[45] Of the land seized, part of it – sometimes one-third and other times one-fourth – was granted to local people, usually clan leaders or other local opportunists seeking benefit for themselves, their families, and their followers by collaborating with the Amhara. These individuals gained the title of *balabat* and became responsible to the crown and the provincial administrators as local agents for conveying the writ of the government to rural areas.[46]

The remainder was either kept by the crown, distributed as government land to soldiers and administrators, or granted to the church, imperial favorites, and northern farmers moving southward to colonize.[47] Governing forces received the land and its revenue as their maintenance salary, for rather than being paid by Menelik's government, they were required to derive their income from the districts they administered. Most Arssi became tenants under these administrators and were required not only to deliver the bulk of their crop to those who held the land but to give them personal service.

As the fertility of the Chilalo region became known, increasing numbers of Amhara and Shoa-Oromo settlers arrived from the north. The central government stimulated this migration both by granting land to new settlers and by allowing sale of government land by soldiers and administrators.[48] In addition, a number of large grants were made to nonresident nobles, military officers, and civil servants who lived in or near the imperial court. Many of these recipients held more land than they could farm and rented out their holdings to landless Arssi-Oromo or Shoa-Oromo, migrating from the north. During this colonization process, the Amharas imposed a variation of their own feudal pattern of social organization, and integrated the region into the empire with the establishment of a local government system which emphasized tax extraction and the maintenance of order.[49]

Between 1890 and 1930 the area remained sparsely settled. Farming was confined generally to areas surrounding Asela and Iteya. Continuous, although unorganized, fighting between the Arssi and immigrants into the area made colonization in southern Chilalo dangerous. The immigration of Shoa-Oromo in the early 1900s was largely responsible for generating such conflicts. Resistance was, however, unsuccessful and pastoral Arssi were forced to retreat to lowland areas where the Amharas and Shoa-Oromo had no intention of settling.

Although Italy occupied the area early in World War II, their presence brought little change to the rural populace, despite Italian promises to improve Arssi life and break the domination northern Christians held over them.[50] The Italians built an all-weather road from the rail town of Nazareth southward to Asella and a dry-weather road with bridges from Asella to Bekoji.[51] This construction had significant impact on the area, assuring more rapid and reliable contact with the administrators and markets of Addis Ababa. The other main Italian contribution to the Chilalo area was the development of a seed improvement and multiplication center at Simba, which was later renamed Kilumsa and taken over by the Ministry of Agriculture and CADU. Migration into Chilalo occurred throughout the Italian occupation, largely because of the absence of patriot resistance. Arriving northerners continued to bring more modern cultivation methods and crops to Chilalo and land pressure slowly forced the remaining Arssi pastoralists to become agriculturalists, in most cases as tenants of the Amhara and Shoa-Oromo. Government land grants in the area accelerated after the emperor, with British help, reconquered Arssiland. In the early years after the restoration, substantial areas of land in the Chilalo region were distributed to officers and veterans of the armies who had fought in the 1936 war or as guerrilla patriots during the occupation. Land was distributed to these men on the basis of rank and length of service, and these grantees were usually of Amhara and Shoa-Oromo ethnicity.

These migrations increased the number of officials, merchants, and petty traders in the region. A whole chain of administrative and commercial towns grew up along the Italian built road, and Amharas, Tigres, Gurages and Yemenis established themselves as townsmen, living on the economic growth that final pacification and increased settlement had brought. By the mid-1960s most of the population farmed. Only in the southern parts of the Chilalo was there sufficient uncultivated land to provide a last refuge for the Arssi who remained pastoralists.

During the first half of the twentieth century, Asella was at most a minor market center, but the Italian occupation and road had dramatically changed Arussiland, and Asella became the provincial as well as the *awraja* capital. A whole new administrative organization was created by a set of deconcentrated interlocking authority centers extending downward from the provincial governor to the *awraja* governor, the *woreda* governor, the *balabat* and finally the *chika shum*.[52] As a result of these changes, the system developed a more refined extractive capacity. New administrators used their powers to gain lands and settle tenants on them, to squeeze bribes out of local peoples and to collect taxes for the central government.

iv. Population Characteristics and Settlement Patterns

Baseline data, particularly for population, land holdings, and farm size are inconsistant and difficult to square. Table 1 suggests that in 1969, Chilalo had a population of 398,592 people in 92,997 households,[53] and that some 627,000 hectares of private, church and government land were registered.[54]

By rough estimate, 45 percent of the overall population were under 15 years of age and perhaps no more than 15 percent over 55. Probably more than 90 percent of the population were illiterate, with some 10 to 20 percent of the 7-12 age group children attending secondary schools. However, it was estimated that about every third or fourth family had one member possessing the functional literacy necessary to take care of most financial or social needs.[55]

Accurate data on ethnic and religious patterns is lacking, for the government discouraged such inquiry. Knowledgeable observers estimate the Oromo made up two-thirds of the rural population, with Amhara and Tigre migrants comprising the remaining one-third and dominating the towns.[56] The same uncertainty characterizes religious patterns. But it appears the population was roughly divided on a one-third Muslim, two-thirds Christian basis, with perhaps as much as 10 percent of Chilalo's inhabitants still pagan in practice.[57]

More than 90 percent of the *awraja's* population were thought to be engaged in agriculture. A 1966 survey in the area estimated that of this

Table 1: *1969 Population of Chilalo Awraja by Woreda*

Woreda	Population	Households	Hectares
Sire	47,206	10,110	61,040
Dodota	25,970	5,598	38,160
Hetosa	45,709	7,742	53,440
Tiyo	29,612	5,070	76,200
Dighelu & Tijo	40,779	11,571	44,960
Zeway & Dugda	38,763	4,600	49,040
Munessa	32,007	10,392	71,080
Limu & Bilbilo	47,678	12,106	78,360
Gedeb	63,328	19,492	85,360
Kofele	27,540	6,316	69,960
Total	398,592	92,997	627,600

Source: CADU, Planning and Evaluation Section, *General Agricultural Survey 1970* (Asella: Chilalo Agricultural Development Unit, Publication No. 71, 1971), p. 60.

percentage, 82 percent were settled agriculturalists, 17 percent semi-nomadic pastoralists, and one percent settled herdsmen.[58] The urban population at this time was estimated in one study at 23,960, engaged primarily in administrative, commercial, and farming activities.[59] Since the bulk of the population farmed, the more densely settled areas were confined to the central upland and highland plateau regions.[60] Most of the settled herdsmen lived in Kofele *Woreda*. The remaining semi-nomadic pastoralists inhabited the Rift Valley lowlands and the open grasslands of the southern part of the *awraja*.[61] The average population density for the whole *awraja* was estimated at approximately 35 persons per square kilometer.[62]

Rural settlements ranged from individual and isolated *ensete* (false banana)[63] farms in the south to cereal producing farmhouse clusters in the north. Settlement was scattered and the predominant pattern was one of individual homesteads and clusters of family compounds. Although some hamlets existed, they were exceptions to general settlement patterns.

v. Agrarian Patterns and Resources

The most developed agricultural areas of Chilalo were in the north, mainly between Iteya and Asella. Some agricultural experts estimated the total amount of land in the *awraja* under cultivation in 1965 was approximately 150,000 hectares, with more pasture land being placed under plow and tractor every year. Perhaps 500,000 hectares of additional fertile or semi-fertile farmland were thought to remain unexploited. In the north traditional and modernized techniques were used to produce wheat while in regions south of Asella the peasants were engaged mainly in the production of barley. In the far south, on the Gedeb-Asasa Plain, there was some farming of flax and in the evergreen parts of Kofele there were ensete plantations. The lowlands in the Rift Valley region were used for cattle herding and the production of maize on a harsh and often shifting basis.[64]

Nearly all the rural people of Chilalo kept domesticated animals for household food and traction. Few actively raised animals for market.[65] Between crop production and animal husbandry, it was estimated that 60 to 70 percent of the *awraja's* land was used for agrarian and livestock production.[66]

The characteristics of land occupation and tenure will be discussed in greater detail in Chapters 4 and 5. Here it is important to note only that existing studies showed that although some 50 percent of the farmers were tenants, they plowed only 20 percent of the cultivated land.[67] The majority of peasants were said to have holdings smaller than 10 hectares. For the *awraja* in general, average cultivated area was estimated at 4.7 hectares, with landowners averaging 5.6 hectares and tenants 3.2.[68]

Most small-holders grew crops on a subsistence basis with traditional, inefficient methods.[69] But there were a small but growing number of farmers using tractors. In 1971 150 farmers had mechanized some 30,000 hectares of land.[70] Their farms were confined mostly to the northern *woredas* and they produced wheat for sale in the urban areas of Nazareth and Addis Ababa.

Just to the northeast of the *awraja*, in the Awash Valley, was the Wonji sugar plantation, one of the main farming concessions in the empire. At Wonji modern farming methods and irrigation practices were used to produce cane sugar for domestic and foreign sales through Dutch capital and management. Inside the *awraja*, concession farming was developing in Zeway & Dugda *Woreda*. Contract farms were also increasing. Under this system urban bureaucrats or investors whose principal occupation was not farming rented large blocks of land for long term periods and fixed rent schedules from local landowners, and had foreigners or Ethiopian graduates of the nation's few agricultural schools manage their investment holdings. The owners of large commercial farms exhibited strong entrepreneurial instincts and a notable eagerness to adopt technical innovations such as improved seeds, fertilizers, mechanization, and modern farm management techniques. These commercial farmers also improved their profit margin by adopting more modern storage and marketing approaches that enabled them to take advantage of shifting wheat prices throughout the year. The largest of these farmers owned their own lorries and transported their crops directly to grain buyers and higher prices in Addis Ababa.

The Chilalo region suffered extensive deforestation after the Italian occupation because of fuel and construction needs of northern immigrant settlers and urban demand for charcoal production.[71] Although there were forest reserves in the Kofele and Munessa regions, the only significant remaining forest in the *awraja* was Munessa, covering an area of perhaps

15,000 hectares near Kersa. Fortunately eucalyptus had been introduced into Chilalo around the turn of the century, providing a more stable supply of firewood and construction material.[72] Although the introduction of eucalyptus helped control deforestation, the damage was already done, for soil erosion had been accelerated by the absence of the area's once extensive tree cover.[73]

There were several areas in the *awraja* where reliable grasslands predominated. This was true of the large plain between Sagure and Bekoji and the regions of Kofele, Gedeb, and Asasa to the south. These areas were well suited for grazing, and livestock production was a principal activity among the inhabitants.

iv. Town Environment

The percentage of the Chilalo population living in urban settlements was low in comparison to other regions of Ethiopia, ranging between five and six percent of the total population.[74] *Woreda* capital towns are found in Figure 2.

Asella was the only large town in 1965. It served as the administrative center of both the province and the *awraja* as well as the area's principal commercial and marketing center.[75] The population of the remaining *awraja* towns was small, the largest having the following population counts: Bekoji 1,899; Dera 1,848; Huruta 4,501; Kofele 3,359 and Sire 3,185.[76]

The urban environment of Chilalo can be described by three town profiles. First, Asella was a town dominated by northerners and Christians, nearly half of whom were native born. It had several main streets and a large number of secondary ones. A bustling commercial center, it contained a wide range of commercial establishments, from hotels and general stores to photography shops and pharmacies. Its main market was open all week, although its busiest day was Saturday. Large grain wholesalers, transporters, craftsmen, and government employees supported the commercial sector. Inhabitants' houses were interspersed with commercial establishments and government offices throughout the town. There was a large secondary school, primary schools and a hospital. Increased economic activity had led to the installation of an electrical generator and some improvement in the town's water supply. But in 1965 Asella had no sewerage system and was a sorry sight after the provincial governor ordered all trees cut to make the town look modern.

The second town, Bekoji, was far more rural than Asella. As the administrative capital of Limu & Bilbilo *Woreda*, it contained the district governor's offices, the *woreda* treasury and court and some local security facilities. There was fairly rapid transport between Bekoji and Asella via the all-weather road and there were also telecommunications links between the two towns. Bekoji had its major market day on Saturday and a minor one on

Tuesday. Trade centered on buying of crops by middlemen, trading of livestock, seed sales and private barter and exchange of foodstuffs. There were small retail outlets and market vendors who provided for household needs. Most commercial buildings were occupied by drinking establishments, and the sale of alcoholic beverages was an important factor in the local economy. There was one 600-student government school of eight grades, a priest school and a small private primary school. Sanitary conditions were poor but Bekoji did have a sealed spring and piped-in water system as well as a badly run government health station and private pharmacy. The town had no electricity. The population was half Amhara and overwhelmingly Christian. Immigrants from Shoa and Harar Provinces accounted for most inhabitants, many of whom were born in the town.

Ketar-Genet, the third town, was an exclusively commercial and marketing town of approximately 900 people. Located in the southwestern part of Tiyo *Woreda* and connected to the *awraja* capital only by dry weather tracks, the town's periodic markets took place on Tuesday and Friday. They drew heavily from the farmers of the Ketar River basin area around the escarpment edge. Perhaps 2,000 to 3,000 people came on market days. The only public facility in the town was a small government administered primary school. Water supplies came from the Ketar River, about one kilometer away, and there was no electricity, clinic or pharmacy.

vii. Basic Human Services

Malaria, tuberculosis, smallpox, and leprosy were the most visible diseases in Chilalo. But water borne illnesses were the main cause of disability and early death, the high rate of mortality among children being due largely to gastrointestinal infections. Schistosomiasis was frequent around the lowland lakes, and relapsing fever, infective and parasitic diseases, and respiratory tract problems further lowered the productivity of the region's peasantry.

There were major health centers in Asella and Sagure, government health stations in some minor towns and a scattering of mission clinics. Asella had a 52-bed hospital staffed by several doctors. The mission clinics were generally well equipped and run by qualified people. But the health stations were poorly supplied and did not provide a high standard of medical service.[77] Unsafe water supplies and a lack of public awareness of rudimentary health practices called for preventive measures, but the government failed to provide them.

A number of private rural pharmacies dispensed prescriptions and gave injections on the basis of the owner's diagnosis. Traditional healers also prescribed herb medicines, treated fractures and dislocations, and performed circumcisions. In practice, the rural pharmacies provided curative medicines while the governmental and mission clinics concentrated on curative care, with particular emphasis on leprosy, tuberculosis and trachoma.

Historically, those who received education in Chilalo did so in religious schools.[78] Few who entered these priest or Koranic schools gained literacy or knowledge beyond religious tenets. It was not until the 1950s that the government's schools began to appear in the region. By the mid-1960s the *awraja* had 27 primary schools with 9,850 students, 8 junior secondary schools with 900 students and one senior secondary school with 500 students.[79] Primary schools were located in all 10 *woredas*. Only Zeway & Dugda, Gedeb, Tiyo, and Munessa *woredas* had junior secondary schools, and Asella was the site of the only senior secondary school.

Attrition between the first and fourth grades was substantial.[80] Competitive national examinations at sixth and eighth grade reduced the number reaching senior secondary school. Non-Amhara children constituted a high percentage of those who dropped out.

Although some rural parents sent their brightest child, most sent the youngest or weakest since they needed the others for agricultural work. Primary education had little meaning for rural children or the lives they would lead. When it came to higher education it was essential for the student to move to larger towns. This gave an immediate advantage to urban children and those of wealthy parents, for it was usually only landowners and rich peasants who could afford to support a child in a distant town while he got an education. Urban children found more meaning in the curriculum and their absence from home was seldom as noticed as in the case of a rural child. Thus it was the rural child who left school, and since most of the Arssi Oromo and Muslims were rural people, it was the Christian Amhara and Shoa Oromo who dominated the junior and senior secondary school.[81] But few of those students who reached the Chilalo senior secondary level passed the exam leading to the national university.[82]

Only a few girls were sent to primary school and the percentage of female attendance dropped off even more sharply after sixth grade.[83] There were substantially fewer girls in rural schools than in larger *awraja* towns,[84] because of early female marriage and traditional attitudes rejecting the need for female education. The motivation of the province's teachers was reduced by low status and income. Their ability to teach was hampered by an inadequate supply of textbooks and materials, administrative inefficiency in the Ministry of Education, lack of established curriculum and the absence of opportunities for self improvement. As a result, the schools of Chilalo tended to attract people who could not find alternative employment, who were not committed to their profession.

viii. Markets, Transport and Infrastructure

There were 53 market towns in Chilalo in 1965, 31 of which had markets one day per week and 22 one major and one minor market day each week.[85]

The major markets were spread fairly uniformly across the *awraja*, there being at least one in each *woreda.*

Nearly every homestead in Chilalo was within walking distance of a market. Although walking time was often as much as six hours, few would miss the market for social as well as economic reasons. In both large and small towns, the market was the linchpin of the overall trading system, and hundreds to thousands of people might attend any given market.

These markets were characterized by poor sanitary conditions, inadequate product protection, and substantial waste. There was a pressing need in 1965 for market platforms, rain shelters, storage facilities, fencing for livestock, and enforcement of health rules.

Most markets were poorly connected to the principal *awraja* trading centers,[86] permitting middlemen with transport to prosper and forcing most rural producers to accept uncompetitive prices. All-weather roads were primarily confined to the route from Dodota to Bekoji in the north and one that passed through Kofele in the south. Northern and southern parts of the *awraja* were not connected by all-weather roads, so that it was frequently necessary to drive north from Asella to Mojo, then south to Shashemene in order to get to Kofele, Munessa and Gedeb Woredas. By the late 1960s there were only 90 kilometers of all-weather road and 150 kilometers of dry-weather road in Chilalo. These were fed by a network of rough dirt roads and trails.[87]

Adequate bus service ran between Addis Ababa and Asella, as well as between all of the towns located along the Dodota-Bekoji road and through the south via Kofele. However, the motor service to smaller marketing towns was confined to lorries and public passenger Land Rovers and operated on an irregular basis decided by the area's rainfall. Otherwise, horses, mules, donkeys and manpower were used to transport agricultural produce to and from markets.

Telecommunications links existed between Addis Ababa and Dire, Sire, Iteya, Asella, Sagure and Bekoji, with indirect links between Asella and Kofele via Shashamene. There were also various radio telephone links operative between Asella and other *awraja* capitals in the province. Asella had a post office. A field agent of the Ministry of Information distributed the country's English and Amharic newspapers within a day of their publication. Because of the altitude of Asella and the intervening Rift Valley lowlands, it is possible to receive radio and television programs broadcast by the government in Addis Ababa.[88]

Finally, the Ethiopian Electric Light and Power Authority maintained a generator station in Asella. The only other towns with electricity were Dera and Melkassa, which draw on a small hydroelectric plant located on the Awash River. In 1960 there were plans to electrify Bekoji from this plant, providing electricity to all the towns along the power line, including Asella. Doubting that such a project would be undertaken, some of the larger towns debated authorizing private revenue generating schemes. For most Chilalo inhabitants, however, after-dark lighting facilities would come from kerosene and petromax oil lamps for the rest of the century.[89]

ix. Rural Social Life

As with most of Ethiopia, the Chilalo region was socially stratified. This was the result of the region's history and the way northern conquerors had formed land tenure systems and local government institutions, promoted provincial elite domination, and organized rural and town markets. Chilalo's land tenure, local government, and rural market systems are outlined in detail in Chapters 4 and 5. Here it is necessary to conclude with only a brief overview of traditional organizations and provincial elite patterns.

Although a number of community organizations were found in Chilalo, none were undertaking the kind of developmental activities that caught the attention of sociologists elsewhere in Ethiopia.[90] Four types of voluntary associations existed: religious, mutual aid, savings, and labor or services.[91] The principal thread running through all these was that of self-interest. The main force behind religious associations was the psychological desire to ensure that one's funeral was well-attended and honorable. Savings associations were merely a way to build funds and their meetings rarely took on any social connotations. Labor or service organizations provided group membership activities toward focused activities such as plowing, planting, weeding, harvesting, and house construction; however, they were driven by individuals seeking to augment labor rather to promote mutual aid. Indeed, savings group members at times backed out of agreements once they had won their lot, labor pool members often found excuses to avoid providing reciprocal work after they had benefitted, and hosts receiving group labor were known to serve inferior meals after the work was completed. Based on an awareness of these behavior patterns, the designers of CADU did not envision these groups being mobilized for community development interests.

Trade associations and cooperatives were beginning to appear in Ethiopia in the mid-1960s but none operated in Chilalo *Awraja* when the CADU project began.[92] However, development associations were emerging at that time. These were formed by landowners, local government officials, and grass roots leaders for self-help purposes, often to open up roads for the economic advance of a particular area. Self-help activities were promoted because local officials and elites were unable to obtain government development expenditures. Total contributions in 1965 probably ran E$ 100,000 for all Chilalo, not including labor. Raising such money and obtaining labor placed an additional burden on rural people who had heavy tax and rental obligations and often did not benefit from the project.[93] Government pressure was sometimes needed to ensure contributions of money and labor.

Resistance was compounded by the fact that some projects were never built, their funds disappearing when a local official was transferred to another post. It was clear that these corrupt practices undermined the attempt to stimulate community self-help efforts.[94]

The provincial elites of Chilalo included: (1) landowners, mechanized farmers, grain merchants, and businessmen who dominated the economy; (2) *woreda* and *awraja* officials, municipality officers, members of parliament, and field agents of the central government ministries who set and implemented political goals; (3) elders, judges, advocates, police officers and leaders of voluntary associations who maintained societal order and integration; and (4) priests, sheikhs, members of leading families, and religious and secular school teachers who represented and socialized the main values of the community.[95] Most of these men were Amharas and townsmen. They owned land and actively tried to acquire more. As a group they were overwhelmingly Christian. Most importantly, they used their positions to protect their vested interests in the land tenure system, the political arena, and the economic markets of Chilalo.

Forged by processes of historical conquest, land distribution and government control, these individuals were the social guardians and political entrepreneurs of the Chilalo region and on the whole they controlled the community and guided its response to agricultural and rural policies, programs, and projects considered or imposed by Haile Selassie's government. As big men of the little community, they had the power to hamper the project the Swedes were about to begin and it was their vested interests, and those of thousands like them throughout the empire, that led to the blocked society described in the first part of this chapter.

Notes

1. The continuous historical traditions of Abyssinia, the role of feudalism in the social system, the patrimonial aspects of the polity, the lack of colonial experience, and a number of other major factors make Ethiopia very different from many of the countries found in most broad studies of rural development, such as Tanzania, India, or Chile. For an introduction to Ethiopian history and society, see: Harold D. Nelson and Irving Kaplan, *Ethiopia: A Country Study* (Washington, D.C.: U.S. Government Printing Office, 1981); Donald N. Levine, *Greater Ethiopia: The Evolution of a Multiethnic Society* (Chicago: University of Chicago Press, 1974).
2. Data on geology, soils, climate, and ecological zones are presented in: Mesfin Wolde Mariam, *An Atlas of Ethiopia* (Asmara: Il Poligrafico, Priv. Ltd. Co., 1970).
3. The analysis that follows is largely based on: H. Huffnagel, *Agriculture in Ethiopia* (Rome: Food and Agriculture Organization of the United Nations, 1961); International Bank for Reconstruction and Development, *The Economy of Ethiopia*, 5 vols., (Washington, D.C.: International Development Association, African Department, Report No. AF 60a, 1967); Assefa Bequele and Eshetu Chole, *A Profile of the Ethiopian Economy* (Addis Ababa: Oxford University Press, 1969); International Bank for Reconstruction and Development, *Agricultural Sector Survey, Ethiopia*, 3 vols. (Washington, D.C.: Agricultural Projects Department, Report No. PA-143a, 1973).
4. Mesfin Wolde Mariam, "The Population of Ethiopia: A Review," *Ethiopian Geographical Journal*, V, 2 (1967), pp. 15-18. Initial surveys were not published until 1971: Ethiopia, Central Statistical Office, *Population of Ethiopia: Results from the National Sample Survey 1st Round, 1964-67* (Addis Ababa: Central Statistical Office, Statistical Bulletin 6, 1971).
5. Of total GDP in 1969, agriculture accounted for 56 percent, of which 14 percent was monetary and 42 percent non-monetary. IBRD, *Agricultural Sector Survey*, p. I, 3. Crops comprised 71 percent of agricultural output in that year and livestock 29 percent. Cereals made up nearly half of the crop output. *Ibid.*, p. I, 4.
6. It was estimated that 9.7 million hectares or 7.9 percent of total land area was used for crops in the mid-1960s; 1.7 million hectares (1.4 percent) was fallow, 66.8 million hectares (54.7 percent) grassland, 0.7 million hectares (0.6 percent) coffeeland, 8.8 million hectares (7.2 percent) forest, and the rest swamp, desert or waste land. USAID/ Ethiopia Mission, "Ethiopia Fact Sheet" (Unpublished Mimeograph, n.d.), p. 1.
7. The World Bank, *Accelerated Development in Sub-Saharian Africa: An Agenda for Action* (Washington, D.C.: The World Bank, 1981), p. 144, 176.
8. See comparative figures for Africa, Middle East and South Asia 1961-65 and 1971 in: World Bank, *Annual Report 1974* (Washington, D.C.: World Bank, 1974), pp. 76-7.
9. It is estimated that during the decade of the 1960s the gross fixed monetary investment in agriculture averaged about 6 percent of total investment. For a review of this period see: Eileen Stommes and Seleshi Sisaye, "The Administration of Agricultural Development Programmes: A Look at the Ethiopian Approach," *Agricultural Administration*, VI, 3 (1979), pp. 221-39; VI, 4 (1979), pp. 253-67; VII, 1 (1980), pp. 1-23.
10. Ethiopia, *First Five Year Development Plan* (Addis Ababa: Imperial Ethiopian Government, n.d.).
11. Ethiopia, *Second Five Year Development Plan* (Addis Ababa: Berhanena Selam Printing Press, 1962).
12. Ethiopia, *Third Five Year Development Plan 1968-1973* (Addis Ababa: Berhanena Selam Printing Press, 1968), p. 189.

13. Sileshi Sisaye, "Foreign Aid and Rural Development in Ethiopia: A Study of the Role of International Donor Organizations in Agricultural Development Programmes," *International Studies*, XX, 314 (1981), p. 569.
14. These included the Wolamo Agricultural Development Project in Sidamo (World Bank), the Ada District Development Project (USAID) and the Humera Agricultural Development Program (World Bank). See: Tesfai Tecle, *The Evolution of Alternative Rural Development Strategies in Ethiopia: Implications for Employment and Income Distribution* (East Lansing: Michigan State University, African Rural Employment Paper No. 12, 1975).
15. On the first two phases of the Minimum Package Program see: Stommes and Seleshi Sisaye, "Administration of Agricultural Development," *passim*.
16. The Ministry of Agriculture and the provincial ministerial system is described in: John M. Cohen and Peter H. Koehn, *Ethiopian Provincial and Municipal Government: Imperial Patterns and Postrevolutionary Changes* (East Lansing: Michigan State University, Ethiopian Monograph No. 9, 1980), especially pp. 226-31.
17. Their position was summed up in three widely circulated papers: Imperial Ethiopian Government, *A Statement of Development Strategy and Policies Presented to the First Meeting of the Consultative Group for Ethiopia* (Addis Ababa: April 1971); Imperial Ethiopian Government, *A General Framework for the Fourth Five-Year Development Plan (1974/75-1978/79)* (Addis Ababa: Prepared for the Second Meeting of the Consultative Group for Ethiopia, June 1973); James T. Goering, "Some Thoughts on the Future Strategies for Agricultural Development" (Paper Presented to Seminar on Development Administration, Institute of Public Administration, Addis Ababa, 1971).
18. Planning Commission Office, "Final Report of the Programme Sub-Committee, Programmes and Strategies for Integrated Rural Development" (Working Group No. 11, Report for Fourth Five Year Plan, Addis Ababa, June 19, 1973). "Study Reveals Sketch of 4th Five Year Plan," *Ethiopian Herald*, September 1, 1974, p. 1.
19. The strategy is described in full in: IBRD, *Agricultural Sector Survey*, I, pp. 14-51.
20. For example, the Minister of Land Reform and Administration: John M. Cohen, "Foreign Involvement in the Formulation of Ethiopia's Land Tenure Policies," *Northeast African Studies*, VII, 2 (1985), pp. 29-31.
21. Such themes are to be found in: E. W. Luther, *Ethiopia Today* (Stanford: Stanford University Press, 1958); David Korten, *Planned Change in a Traditional Society: Psychological Problems of Modernization in Ethiopia* (New York: Praeger, 1972). The most sophisticated analysis of these factors is set forth in: Donald N. Levine, *Wax and Gold: Tradition and Innovation in Ethiopian Culture* (Chicago: University of Chicago Press, 1965).
22. This is the general thrust of such studies as: Margery Perham, *The Government of Ethiopia*, 2nd ed. (Evanston: Northwestern University Press, 1969); Richard D. Greenfield, *Ethiopia, A New Political History* (London: Pall Mall Press, 1965); Robert L. Hess, *Ethiopia: The Modernization of Autocracy* (Ithaca: Cornell University Press, 1970).
23. These variables are explored in such studies as: Christopher Clapham, *Haile-Selassie's Government* (New York: Frederick A. Praeger, 1969); Peter Schwab, *Decision-Making in Ethiopia: A Study of the Political Process* (Rutherford: Fairleigh Dickinson University Press, 1972).
24. On this shift in theoretical perspectives see: A. Eugine Havens, "Methodological Issues on the Study of Development," *Sociologia Ruralis*, XII, 314 (1972), pp. 252-72. One interesting critique of the behavioral model of the 1960s is: Siegfried Pausewang, *Methods and Concepts of Social Research in a Rural Developing Society:*

A Critical Appraisal Based on Experience in Ethiopia (München: Weltforum Verlag, 1973).

25. A series of provincial studies became available on land tenure patterns in most provinces. Ethiopia, Ministry of Land Reform and Administration, *Reports on Land Tenure Survey of Arussi, Bale, Begemdir-Simien, Eritrea, Gemu Gofa, Illubabor, Kefa, Shoa, Sidamo, Tigre, Welo and Wallega* (Addis Ababa: Department of Land Tenure, 1967-1970). Data was also contained in: Central Statistical Office, *National Survey Sample of Arussi, Begemdir, Gemu Gofa, Gojjam, Hararge, Illubabor, Kefa, Shoa, Sidamo, Tigre, Wallega and Welo* (Addis Ababa: Central Statistical Office, 1963-67). In addition, some specific studies appeared, such as: Mahtama S. W. Maskal, "Land Tenure and Taxation from Ancient to Modern Times," *Ethiopia Observer*, I, 9 (1957), pp. 283-301; Gebre-Weld-Ingida Worq, "Ethiopia's Traditional System of Land Tenure and Taxation," *Ethiopia Observer*, V, 4 (1962), pp. 302-39.
26. Examples of studies on these factors include: H. C. Dunning, "Land Reform in Ethiopia: A Case Study in Non-Development," *U.C.L.A. Law Review*, XVIII, 2 (1970), pp. 271-307; Doreen Warriner, "A Report on Land Reform in Ethiopia" (Paper Prepared for the United Nations Economic Commission for Africa, Addis Ababa, 1970); Siegfried Pausewang, "The History of Land Tenure and Social Personality Development in Ethiopia," *Rural Africana*, XI (1970), pp. 82-9.
27. The literature surrounding this concept is set forth in: John M. Cohen, "Ethiopia: A Survey on the Existence of a Feudal Peasantry," *Journal of Modern African Studies*, XII, 4 (1974), pp. 665-72. Two studies attempt to illustrate the existence of feudalism as the concept is used by social theorists: Fredrick C. Gamst, "Peasantries and Elites Without Urbanism: The Civilization of Ethiopia," *Comparative Studies in Society and History*, XII, 44 (1970), pp. 373-92; Allan Hoben, *Land Tenure Among the Amhara of Ethiopia* (Chicago: University of Chicago Press, 1973). A critique of the notion as applied to Ethiopia is found in: Gene Ellis, "The Feudal Paradigm as a Hindrance to Understanding Ethiopia," *Journal of Modern African Studies*, XIV, 2 (1976), pp. 275-95. For a reply to Ellis see: Legesse Lemma, "Review: The Feudal Paradigm...," *Ethiopianist Notes*, II, 1 (1978), pp. 71-3.
28. The arguments underlying this view are summarized in: John Markakis, *Ethiopia: Anatomy of a Traditional Polity* (London: Oxford University Press, 1974); John M. Cohen and Dov Weintraub, *Land and Peasants in Imperial Ethiopia: The Social Background to a Revolution* (Assen: Van Gorcum & Co., 1975); Michael Ståhl, *Ethiopia: Political Contradictions in Agricultural Development* (Stockholm: Liber Tryck, 1974).
29. Most of their critiques were published abroad or circulated as underground tracts. They were available in Ethiopian intellectual and student circles. Examples include: Haile Menkerios, "The Present Systems of Land Tenure in Ethiopia: An Introduction," *Challenge: Journal of the Ethiopian Students of North America*, X, 2 (1970), pp. 4-24; Dessalegn Rahmato, "Conditions of the Ethiopian Peasantry," *Challenge*, X, 2 (1970), pp. 25-49; Eshetu Chole, "The Mode of Production in Ethiopia and the Realities Thereof," *Challenge*, XXII, 1 (1971), pp. 3-22.
30. See the comments of: P.T.W. Baxter, "Ethiopia's Unacknowledged Problem: The Oromo," *African Affairs*, LXXVII, 308 (1978), p. 286.
31. Among the most important of these were seen to be: (1) the rapid increase in the rate of population growth; (2) the historical isolation of Ethiopia and its rural sector from international markets, finance capital, and technology; (3) the lack of an adequate road system and the resulting high cost of transporting agrarian output to markets; (4) the failure of the central government to commit itself to creating conditions that promote economic growth and rural development; (5) the specific failure to build a research and

extension system that reached a large percentage of the Ethiopian peasantry; (6) the inability of local government institutions to generate change because of the power of provincial elites, supported by elites at the national center, to maintain the status quo; and (7) the negative effect of all these factors on those development oriented ministries and field agents attempting too bring about rural change.

32. Donald N. Levine, "Class Consciousness and Class Solidarity in the New Ethiopian Elites," in Peter Lloyd, ed., *Elites of Tropical Africa* (Oxford: Oxford University Press, 1966), pp. 312-27. The rise of such elites generally is described by Marina Ottaway, "Social Classes and Corporate Interests in the Ethiopian Revolution," *Journal of Modern African Studies*, XIV, 3 (1976), pp. 469-86.
33. F. Dixey, *The East African Rift System* (London: Her Majesty's Stationery Office, 1956); John Walter Gregory, "The Abyssinian Section of the Rift Valley Between Lake Rudolph and the Red Sea," in *The Rift Valleys and Geology of East Africa* (London: Seeley, Service, 1921).
34. 1 hectare = 2.471 acres. There are 40 ha. in 1 official *gasha* and 1 *gasha* (or 40 ha.) = 98.84 acres. Because of historical reasons and/or inaccurate measurement, the size of any given *gasha* in the *awraja* is likely to vary.
35. A full geographical description of Chilalo *Awraja* is found in: Yelma Kabada, "Chilalo Awraja," *Ethiopian Geographical Journal*, V, 1 (1967), pp. 25-36.
36. The description of these zones is largely drawn from CADU, *Tentative CADU Program 1970/75*, (Asella: CADU, 1970), pp. 26-9, which in turn is largely derived from Yelma Kabada, "Chilalo Awraja," pp. 25-6.
37. The physical timing of these seasons is highly variable both throughout the country and within a given climatic region. Huffnagel, *Agriculture in Ethiopia*, pp. 57-73. Kabbada Tateto, "Rainfall in Ethiopia," *Ethiopian Geographical Journal* , II, 2 (1964), pp. 28-36.
38. Throughout the year the plateau rainfall averages between 750 and 1,500 mm. per year and the precipitation in the Rift Valley averages 500 mm. per year. Bengt Nekby, *CADU: An Ethiopian Experiment in Developing Peasant Farming* (Stockholm: Prisma Publishers, 1971), p. 18. 250 mm. can fall per month in the rainy season and it is common for 20 mm. to 40 mm. to fall on most regions in the dry season. For an extensive set of precipitation records in the *awraja* see: CADU, Planning and Evaluation Section, CADU, *Statistical Digest* (Addis Ababa: Chilalo Agricultural Development Unit, Publication No. 15, 1969).
39. Maximum and minimum temperatures remain fairly uniform throughout the year, ranging from 20 to 28 decrees centigrade at the high end of the scale and 10 to 15 degrees at the low end. Frost occurs at the higher elevations between November and January, and temperatures can range as much as 20 degrees centigrade between day and night in certain seasons. CADU, *Statistical Digest*, May 21, 1970 Supplement, pp. 1-13.
40. Some farmers used irrigation water from the Ketar and Gonde Rivers in the north, in Zeway and Dugda *Woreda*, and in the area immediately south of Melkassa. These farmers primarly produced vegetables and fruits. Although some pump irrigation was appearing on some northern plateau farms, there was generally little available water for irrigation in the north. There are possibilities for irrigation in Lukuche Plain near Sagure and in the basin of the Asasa River on the Gedeb-Asasa Plain. Carl-Gösta Wenner, *Water Resources and Supplies Within CADU's First Project Area* (Asella: Chilalo Agricultural Development Unit, Publication No. 53, 1970), p. 99; Yelma Kabada, "Chilalo Awraja," pp. 26-7.
41. On the Oromo see: Eike Haberland, *Galla Sud-Äthiopiens* (Stuttgart: Kohlhammer for Frobenius Institute, 1963); Karl Eric Knutsson, *Authority and Change: A Study of the*

Kalu Institution Among the Macha Galla of Ethiopia (Göteborg: Ethnografiska Muséet, 1967); Lewis, *A Galla Monarchy*; and Herbert Samuel Lewis, "Wealth, Influence and Prestige Among the Shoa Galla," in *Social Stratification in Africa*, edited by Arthur Tuden and Leonard Plotnicov (New York: The Free Press, 1970).

42. The social organization of the Arssi Oromo is very complex as well as highly variable. For a description of leadership and organization in the Chilalo area see: Arne Lexander, *Land Ownership, Tenancy and Social Organization in the Wajji Area* (Addis Ababa, Chilalo Agricultural Development Unit, Publication No. 50, 1970), pp. 70-4. See also: Asmarom Legesse, *Gada: Three Approaches to the Study of African Society* (New York: Free Press, 1972).
43. The historical background of Abyssinian conquest of Arssi-Oromoland is described in Harold G. Marcus, "Imperialism and Expansion in Ethiopia from 1865-1900," in *Colonialism in Africa*, edited by Lewis H. Gann and Peter Duighan (Cambridge: Cambridge University Press, 1969), pp. 420-61; H. G. Marcus, "Motives, Methods and Some Results of Territorial Expansion in Ethiopia During the Reign of Menelik II," in *Proceedings of the Third International Conference of Ethiopian Studies* (Addis Ababa: Haile Selassie I University, Institute of Ethiopian Studies, 1969); and Arne Lexander, *The Changing Rural Society in Arussiland* (Addis Ababa: Chilalo Agricultural Development Unit, Publication No. 7, 1968), pp. 10-18.
44. Richard K. Pankhurst, *State and Land in Ethiopia* (Addis Ababa: Oxford University Press, 1966), p. 139.
45. Haberland, *Galla Sud-Äthiopiens*, pp. 18, 26, 360, 375, 420.
46. The institution of *balabat* is delineated in Lexander, *Land Ownership in Wajji*, pp. 75-8. The confiscation of clan land led to the decline of the *gada* and the rise of the *balabat* whose authority was confirmed independently of the clan. This led to the fragmentation of Arssi social organization and the rise of former clan leaders to positions as patrons in a feudalized local gentry: Knutsson, *Authority and Change*, p. 184; Lexander, *Arussiland*, p. 12.
47. These grants led to the creation of the complex patterns which mark land tenure in the area. For an introduction to these tenures in Arussi Province, see: Pankhurst, *State and Land in Ethiopia*, pp. 137-9.
48. Pankhurst writes that a captain of 50 men would be granted five *gashas* of which three could be sold. A chief of 100 men received 10 *gashas* of which several could be sold and a chief of 300 men could receive 20 *gashas* of which 13 could be sold. This varied from area to area. For example, near Asella, an ordinary soldier, depending on his years of service, could hold four or five *gashas*. Pankhurst, *State and Land*, p. 136.
49. The acquisition of the land, its conversion into government land tenure, the mechanics of its distribution, and a description of the recipients of land grants are set forth in John M. Cohen, "Ethiopia After Haile Selassie: The Government Land Factor," *African Affairs*, LXXII, 289 (1973), pp. 365-82. The land tenure system, economic organization, hierarchical political system and culture of provincial Ethiopia is generally described in Cohen and Weintraub, *Land and Peasants in Imperial Ethiopia*. The characteristics of these specific patterns in the Chilalo region are described in Lexander, *Land Ownership in Wajji*.
50. The Italians had hoped to carve out an Oromo state as a balance against Amhara power, by building anti-Amharaism out of the depressed economic conditions of the Oromo peasant. The matter had been studied before the occupation but never successfully implemented during the limited colonial period. Czeslaw Jesman, *The Ethiopian Paradox* (London: Oxford University Press, 1963), p. 58.
51. Lexander, *Arussiland*, p. 17.

52. These officials are described generally in: Cohen and Koehn, *Ethiopian Provincial and Municipal Government*, pp. 19-37; for Chilalo in particular see: Lexander, *Land Ownership in Wajji*, pp. 18-20, 75-86.
53. These CADU figures were gathered in a 1969 survey by the provincial governor and confirmed by CADU's investigations. They differed from official figures set forth in: Central Statistical Office, *Report on a Survey of Arussi Province* (Addis Ababa: Central Statistical Office, 1966), pp. 4, 13. The governor or *enderassie* of Arussi Province had a penchant for data collection and had produced a body of data which was uncommon for most provinces. The demographic data were collected by grassroots officials under administrative supervision of the *woreda* governors and the explicitly stated instructions of the *enderassie*. Because these officials received little compensation, did not appreciate the importance of such data, were limited in literate abilities, rarely travelled extensively in their areas, did not necessarily know their boundaries, and were not educated in registration work, this demographic information was unreliable.
54. The number of hectares registered represented only inhabited areas and does not include barren land, higher elevations and swamps. Not all land inhabited was farmed or used as pasture. Hence, farm size calculations based on the figures in Table 1 are misleading. See Chapter 5.
55. Based on general tables in: Central Statistical Office, *Report on a Survey of Arussi*.
56. A sample of 53 produced an estimate of 37.7 Amhara, 54.7 Oromo, 1.9 Sidama, 5.7 Wollamo for all of Arussi Province. Central Statistical Office, *Draft Report on Rural House Hold Expenditure and Consumption* (Addis Ababa: Central Statistical Office, 1971), p. 17.
57. Data drawn from Dighelu and Tijo *Woreda*, situated halfway between what is generally called the Christian-Amharaized north and the Muslim south, supported this position. The *enderassie* survey of 1966 produced a population of 37,476 of which 60% were Christian and 40% Muslim. A sample in southern Tiyo *Woreda*, more in the Christian area, indicated 48.5% Christian, 33.1% Muslim and 18.4% unknown of a total sample of 100 tenants and landowners. Lexander, *Land Ownership in Wajji*, p. 18. Finally, the CSO study found 71.7% of a 53 sample in Arussi Province to be Christian and 28.3% Muslim. Central Statistical Office, *Report on Rural House Hold*, p. 18.
58. Central Statistical Office, *Report on a Survey of Arussi*, p. 21.
59. *Ibid.*
60. Most of these settled agriculturalists were concentrated in the central part of the *awraja*, roughly between the marketing towns of Dera and Bekoji, where fertile clay soils, heavy and consistent rainfall, altitudinal and ecological conditions and the *awraja's* major all-weather road contributed to the heavy population density of the 100 km. long agricultural corridor. It was estimated in 1967 that 40% of the *awraja* inhabitants were confined to this area. Yelma Kabada, "Chilalo Awraja," p. 29.
61. The sandy and stony soil of the Gedeb-Asasa Plain, the water and heat problems of the Rift Valley, and the forested parts of the Kofele and Munessa regions all contributed to the low population density and the absence of extensive agricultural activity there.
62. This figure was obviously highly variable. For example, Dodota *Woreda* – one of the smallest in size – had the highest density at 91 persons per sq. km., and Munessa – one of the largest – has the lowest density at 21 persons. Yelma Kabada, "Chilalo Awraja," pp. 29-30.
63. *Ensete* or plantain production was found primarily in the southern *woredas* of Kofele and Gedeb, but the production of *ensete* was spreading rapidly and small clusters or single plants could be found in many parts of Chilalo. *Ensete* is a false banana tree whose root has a heavy food yield allowing *ensete* areas to support high densities of

population. The basic cultural complex comes from Gurage or Sidama peoples in the region. See: S. Stanley, "Enset in the Ethiopian Economy," *Ethiopian Geographic Journal*, IV (1966), pp. 30-7; Taye Bezuneh and Asrat Felequa, "The Production and Utilization of the Genus Enset in Ethiopia," *Economic Botany*, XX, 1 (1966), pp. 6. 70.

64. Of course a broader range of crops was grown in each area. In 1970 in the north wheat constituted 49% of the crop land cultivated, barley 26%, and beans, peas, maize, teff and other crops the remaining 25%; in the south barley, at 59%, took up the most cultivated land, followed by 18% wheat, 15% flax, and 8% beans and peas. These figures varied each year depending on marketing incentives. CADU, Planning and Evaluation Section, *General Agricultural Survey 1970* (Asella: Chilalo Agricultural Development Unit, Publication No. 71), pp. 61-3.
65. The average farmer in the northern area was thought to have 8 to 9 livestock units and the southern farmer 12 to 13 units. *Ibid.*
66. CADU, *General Agricultural Survey 1970*, pp. 61-3.
67. Surveys estimated that in the north 53% of the farmers were landowners, 29% tenants and 17% tenants on relatives' land. In the south 40% were landowners, 39% tenants and 32% tenants on relatives' land. These are 1970 figures. Because of ongoing mechanization in the north and resulting eviction of tenants, it can be estimated that in the mid-1960s the tenancy figure in the north was well over 50%. CADU, *General Agricultural Survey 1970*, pp. 6-7.
68. *Ibid.*, pp. 8-10.
69. For descriptions of agricultural patterns of production by peasants and small-scale landowners, as well as the role of agricultural activities in their daily social life, see: Lars Leander, *A Case Study of Peasant Farming in Dighelu and Yelma Areas, Chilalo Awraja, Ethiopia* (Addis Ababa: Chilalo Agricultural Development Unit, Publication No. 22, 1969); Nekby, *CADU*, p. 37; Lexander, *Arussiland*, pp. 55-7.
70. Arussi Provincial Office of Ministry of Agriculture, Archives, Register of Tractor and Land Size for Fuel Tax Waiver File. CADU studies estimate that approximately 70% of the total area mechanized had been converted from peasant farming patterns since 1967: CADU, Planning and Evaluation Section, *Preliminary Investigation on Mechanized Farming and Its Effects* (Asella: Chilalo Agricultural Development Unit, 1971), p. 8.
71. For example, the once extensive acacia forests in the northern Dodota Plain had been almost completely destroyed in order to produce charcoal. Yelma Kabada, "Chilalo Awraja," pp. 27-8.
72. In Chilalo, as elsewhere in Ethiopia, the introduction of eucalyptus at the end of the 19th century dramatically changed Ethiopian foresty problems by providing a rapid growing tree which regenerated from its harvested stump without any reforestation practices. See generally: R. K. Pankhurst, "The Origins of Eucalyptus," *Addis Reporter*, I, 23 (1969), pp. 14-17.
73. The erosion patterns indicate how recently settled and exploited the land in the *awraja* was. Erosion was not yet severe and occurred mainly near recently made roads and on grasslands and wooded areas converted to cultivated land. Gunnar Poulsen, *Some Reflections on Water Erosion in Chilalo Awraja* (Addis Ababa: Chilalo Agricultural Development Unit, Publication No. 2, 1967). Kebede Tato, *A Preliminary Survey of Soil Erosion in the Chilalo Awraja* (Addis Ababa: Chilalo Agricultural Development Unit, Special Study No. 1, 1970).
74. Central Statistical Office, *Survey of Major Towns in Ethiopia* (Addis Ababa: Central Statistical Office, 1968), pp. vii, 1, 7-10.

75. In 1937 the population of Asella was approximately 500: Jean Comhaire, "Urban Growth in Relation to Ethiopian Development," *Cultures et Développement*, I, 1 (1968), p. 26. Asella was undergoing a population boom in the late 1960s due to increased economic activity in the *awraja*, for in 1966 the population was determined to be 13,886: Central Statistical Office, *Survey of Major Towns in Ethiopia* , p. 1. In 1965, Asella had one of the smallest populations among the Ethiopian provincial capitals, with only Lekempt and Gobe being smaller. *Ibid*., pp. vii, 7-10.

76. *Ibid*. These figures can be taken as only rough indicators and may be 10% or more higher.

77. Stig Lundin, *Survey of Health Facilities of Arussi: 1969-70* (Asella: Chilalo Agricultural Development Unit, Publication No. 57, 1970).

78. See: Haile Gabriel Dagne, "Non Government Schools in Ethiopia," in M. Bender, et al., editors, *Language in Ethiopia* (London: Oxford University Press, 1976), pp. 339-70.

79. Ministry of Education, *School Census for Ethiopia 1967-68*, Part II (Addis Ababa: Office of Planning and Statistics, 1968), pp. 19, 60-2. 80. Gunilla Bjerén, *Makelle (Ethiopia) Elementary School Drop-Out 1967* (Uppsala: The Scandinavian Institute of African Studies, Research Report No. 5, 1969).

81. The lack of educational opportunities for Oromo children and the implications of this problem are set forth in: Mordechai Abir, "Education and National Unity in Ethiopia," *African Affairs*, LXIX, 274 (1970), pp. 44-59.

82. Haile Wolde Mikael, "The Problems of Admission to the University Through School Leaving Certificate Examination" (Unpublished Paper, 1968), p. 3.

83. In a 1971 study of Asella schools, 44% of primary school children, 25% of junior secondary school children, and 12% of senior secondary school were girls. Of the total 5,922 children in all three tiers, 3,616 in primary school, 757 in junior secondary and 1,549 in senior secondary, 1,973 or 33% were girls. Bergman, *Decision Making*, p. 17.

84. For example, while 44% of primary school pupils in Asella were girls, only 10% of the Munessa primary school, 2% of the Ogelcho primary school, 13% of the Gedeb-Asasa primary school, and 20% of the Kersa primary school were girls. Ministry of Education, *School Census 1967/68*, pp. 60-62.

85. Lars Leander, *Feasibility Study on Local Roads and Market Places in Chilalo Awraja* (Addis Ababa: Chilalo Agricultural Development Unit, Publication No. 33, 1969), p. 58.

86. This problem was uniform throughout the entire country. There were not more than 7,000 km. of all-weather roads and 45,000 km. of dry weather roads in Ethiopia, with the bulk of these being located in the favored provinces of Shoa, Wollo and Eritrea. It was variously estimated that the great majority of Ethiopian people lived more than half a day by mule from a dry weather road, that only eight percent of the land area was within half a day by mule from a dry weather road, and that more than half the country was more than 30 km. from roads of any kind. Assefa Bequele and Eshetu Chole, *A Profile of the Ethiopian Economy*, pp. 34, 91-4. See: Chester C. Burdick, "Highways in Ethiopia," *Ethiopia Observer*, I, 12 (1958), pp. 401-4. Harjinder Singh, "Transport in Ethiopia's Economic Development," *Africa Quarterly*, VI (July-Sept. 1966), pp. 155-9.

87. On the road system see: CADU, *Tentative CADU Program 1970/75* , p. 46. Leander, *Feasibility Study*, pp. 5-9. Another study placed 147 km. of all-weather road and 400 km. of dry weather road. Yelma Kabada, "Chilalo Awraja," p. 34.

88. Not more than three percent of the estimated 500,000 radio sets in Ethiopia in the mid-1960s were in Arussi Province. Sidney W. Head, "The Beginnings of Broadcast

Audience Research in Ethiopia," *Journal of Ethiopian Studies*, VI, 2 (1968), pp. 77-92; Phillips Company, "Possible Future Sales Potential" (Market Research Report, Addis Ababa, 1967).

89. See generally: CADU, Planning and Evaluation Unit, *Feasibility Study on the Electrification of Sagure Town* (Addis Ababa: Chilalo Agricultural Development Unit, Publication No. 19, 1968).

90. For example, the Alem Gena-Wollamo road construction organization. Beginning on the basis of Gurage associations, it built a road of 250 km., ran 30 buses on it, administered capital of over E$ 1 million, and had over 100 employees. The Gurage people raised money for the road construction and donated it to the government to provide more public services in their areas. It should be clearly noted that the Gurage for both ecological and cultural reasons had a greater predisposition toward community activity than did other major rural ethnic groupings in Ethiopia: Fecadu Gadamu, "The Social and Cultural Foundation of Gurage Association," in *Proceedings of the Third International Conference of Ethiopian Studies*, Institute of Ethiopian Studies, Haile Selassie I University, 1970), pp. 203-13.

91. The only source of data for Chilalo Awraja is in the Wajji area: Lexander, *Arussiland*, pp. 68-72. More generally see: Richard Pankhurst and Endreas Eshete, "Self-Help in Ethiopia," pp. 354-64; Asfaw Damte, "Ekub," *University College of Addis Ababa Ethnological Society Bulletin*, 8 (1958), pp. 63-76; Temesgien Gobena, "Gege, Dabo and Other Communal Labors Mainly Among the Oromo of Western Sawa and Wallaga," *University College of Addis Ababa Ethnological Society Bulletin*, 7 (1957), pp. 65-76; Million Tesfaye, "Mutual Aid Associations Among the Kotta Galla of Harar", *University College of Addis Ababa Ethnological Society Bulletin*, II, 1 (1961), pp. 71-80; Andargatchew Tesfaye, "The Funeral Customs of the Kottu of Harar," *University College of Addis Ababa Ethnological Society Bulletin* , 7 (1957), pp. 77-80.

92. The best example of a trade association was that organized in Sidamo by coffee growers to avoid marketing middlemen exploitation. Beginning in 1962 this group developed a store, bought a mill and truck, and paid dividends to its members. See: Hammer, "Voluntary Association," pp. 73-91. The cooperative movement had just begun in Ethiopia, regulated (1966 and 1968 legislation) by the Ministry of Community Development and Social Affairs.

93. See the case study of the Bekoji Water System Project in: John M. Cohen, "Rural Change in Ethiopia: A Study of Land, Elites, Power and Values in Chilalo Awraja" (Unpublished Ph.D. diss., University of Colorado, 1973), pp. 459-64.

94. At the 1971 meeting of governors general and *enderassies*, this problem was discussed. It was suggested that funds be properly recorded and supervised. The Ministry of Interior and Ministry of National Community and Social Affairs drafted regulations which were submitted to the Council of Ministers in 1970/71. The Council decided registration and supervision of funds should be handled by Interior and supervision of collection by Community Development. This arrangement was unworkable because of the extractive instincts of many local officials and the low administrative capacity of Community Development. Ministry of Interior, "Minutes of 1971 Meeting," Archives, 1971 Governors General/Enderassy Meeting File.

95. The background values and interest of these Chilalo elites is described in: John M. Cohen, "Ethiopian Provincial Elites and the Process of Change," *Journal of Ethiopian Studies*, IX, 2 (1973), pp. 83-111.

CHAPTER 4

Strategy, Organization and Activities of CADU: 1967-73

> CADU was one of the earliest experiments in integrated rural development. Its designers sought to group physically several ministerial functions in one administrative unit in order to better serve... small farmers... it was hoped, this development administration could both (1) foster a balanced development where social goals were not sacrificed to economic advance and (2) assist the farmers in accelerating development through substantial rises in farm income.
>
> CADU Evaluation Team (1981)

In late 1964, the Swedish Government commissioned a far ranging review of strategies, programs, and projects appropriate for promoting agriculture based rural development in low income countries.[1] Its June 1965 report recommended that Sweden concentrate assistance programs in a few carefully selected countries and promote area-specific small-holder projects similar to those developed by the Comilla project in Bangladesh and the Integrated Agricultural District Program in India. Guided by this report, several aid recipient country requests for agricultural assistance were reviewed, including one from the Ethiopian government dated November 1965. Subsequently, Ethiopia was selected as a probable place for substantial Swedish aid, a decision based on long historical links,[2] the willingness of the Ethiopian government to experiment with small-farm strategies, and the suitability of highland Ethiopia to the transfer of Swedish experience with wheat and livestock production.[3]

In March 1966 the newly formed Swedish International Development Authority (SIDA) and the Ethiopian government signed an agreement authorizing the donor to investigate the possibilities for a large regional agricultural development project, select an area for focus, and prepare a project paper for joint consideration. Shortly thereafter a 10 person design team was mobilized and in the field, all members of which were Swedes, Ethiopians merely providing information and setting up government contacts.[4]

After studying five farming areas recommended by the government, the Chilalo region was selected. Official reasons for the choice were: (1) natural conditions suitable for intensive farming; (2) availability of transport and marketing facilities; (3) favorable land tenure conditions compared with those prevailing elsewhere in the empire; (4) desire for progress on the part of the area inhabitants; and (5) possibility for expanding the initial project into a larger area of Arussi Province.[5] Initially, little attention was given the larger policy environment and need for its reform, because the team had "neither instructions nor competence to judge the political situation in Ethiopia (for) the Swedish Parliament had already confirmed the choice of Ethiopia as one of the main receivers of Swedish assistance."[6]

The design team recommended a "package approach" strategy. This was defined as an intervention that integrates: (1) green revolution inputs; (2) adequate farm credits; (3) individual farm plans; (4) intensive extension education programs; (5) improvement in grassroots institutions; (6) assured prices for agricultural products; (7) reliable marketing facilities; (8) rural public works; and, most importantly, (9) coordination of all elements under a single authority.[7] This brief description clearly falls within the dominant definition of "integrated rural development" presented in Chapter 2: a project limited to a specific area, providing inputs and services not already present or reasonably effective in that area, and the administrative integration of those mutually reinforcing components essential to the project's success.

In October the SIDA design team submitted its draft proposal to both governments. A committee of Ethiopian technicians quickly reviewed it and recommended its acceptance to a ministerial committee. Five months elapsed before approval was granted. In part the delay was due to the need for senior officers to study and accept the new integrated rural development concept underlying the proposed project. More significantly, these officials were concerned with the political difficulties likely to arise from the introduction in a limited area of concentrated resources aimed at economic and social change for small-holders. Delays on the Swedish side occurred as a result of the high costs of the project, current limitations on SIDA's budget, and technical concern that the proposed project design had never been tested in Ethiopia. Underlying these concerns was a deeper one focused on rural inequality in the proposed project area, most notably high tenancy rates.

Both sides overcame their concerns, the Ethiopian government concluding it could confine the project's impact to economic growth compatible with the existing system, and SIDA believing that conditions in the Chilalo region minimized land tenure problems and accepting the Ethiopian government's assurances that a land reform bill would be submitted to Parliament during the project's first few years. There is no evidence on record that either side was concerned about the capacity of Ethiopia's ministerial and local government systems to provide the coordination and resources needed to make this large, complex project work.

So eager were the Swedes to experiment with integrated rural development in Ethiopia that they ignored one of the central principles of foreign aid enunciated by the Swedish Parliament in 1962 and 1968. It required SIDA to direct development assistance toward increasing "political democracy and social equality," and to avoid contributing to the "conservation of an anti-progressive social structure."[8] This disregard of this principle came back to haunt the designers as the project's initial phase unfolded.

Between the February 1967 Ethiopian approval and the signing of an initial 34 month project agreement on September 8, 1967, SIDA kept a small start-up staff of experts at work in the field undertaking initial technical and social science based studies. By June 1968 this group produced a flexible plan of action sensitive to the limited data available on the task environment and lack of experience with integrated rural development projects in Ethiopia. Their plan outlined a work program and detailed staffing requirements, job descriptions, building priorities, equipment needs, and budget requirements. When the project agreement was signed, members of this interim group became staff officers of CADU.

After its initial years of operation the agreement was first extended to December 1970 and subsequently to a five year second phase, running to July 1975. Additional agreements have carried the project and its Swedish support up to 1987, albeit in a different task environment and with revised objectives, activities, and areas other than those described in this chapter. Between 1967 and the beginning of the 1974 revolution, CADU spent E$ 37 million.[9]

Administrative Setting

From 1967 to 1971, CADU operated as an autonomous agency of the Ministry of Agriculture supervised by an interministerial committee chaired by the Minister of Agriculture and charged with overseeing the performance of the project and coordinating its activities with other ministries of the Ethiopian government.[10] Aside from the set of integrated services and activities comprising the project's own responsibilities, the initial *Plan of Operation* specified a number of additional supporting services and activities outside the project's administrative control. The committee was charged to organize and facilitate them. These included: (1) construction of major roads by the Imperial Highway Authority; (2) increased primary school enrollment by the Ministry of Education and Fine Arts; (3) improvement of health conditions by the Ministry of Public Health; (4) priority implementation of proposed tenancy reforms, cadastral surveys, and title registration by the Ministry of Land Reform and Administration; (5) improved local government administration by the Ministry of Interior; (6) provision of capital for the project's marketing activities by the Development Bank (later the Agro-Industrial Development Bank); (7) completion of surveys and expansion of electrical services by the Ethiopian Electric Light and Power Authority; (8) expansion of communications networks by the Imperial Board of Telecommunications;

and (9) protection of the area's river basin water for development purposes by the Ministry of Water Resources. In addition, it was clear that the project would need to work effectively with the Grain Board and Grain Corporation, the Ministry of Commerce and Industry, the Ministry of Community Development and Social Affairs, the Ministry of Information, the Ministry of Public Works, and the Planning Commission.[11]

Obtaining the support of these ministries and agencies was difficult. Ministry of Agriculture officials and staff tended to see CADU as outside their jurisdiction, the Ethiopian bureaucracy was inexperienced in inter-ministry coordination and distrustful of the project's special semi-independent status, and the field staff of development ministries often were hostile to the project's activities.[12] Yet reasonable cooperation was obtained by CADU's managers because they identified powerful supporters at the senior level of the Ministry of Agriculture and used them to facilitate government-wide coordination during the project's first two years.

By late 1970 other integrated rural development projects were being designed and implemented, requiring the government to rationalize jurisdictional responsibility over them. Towards this end, SIDA funding helped establish an Extension and Project Implementation Department (EPID) in the Ministry of Agriculture. EPID was to supervise integrated rural development projects, promote liaison between those projects and other development ministries, and manage the newly established Minimum Package Programs throughout Ethiopia.[13] While technically CADU's Executive Director reported to the head of EPID, in practice he dealt directly with a powerful Vice Minister who between 1971 and 1974 proved very effective in promoting the project's interests.

Both before and after 1971, the head of SIDA's Development Assistance Office in Addis Ababa appointed jointly with the government CADU's Executive Director and evaluation teams, received and reviewed all staff reports, managed the recruitment of expatriate employees, and carried out most overseas project purchases. Such activities kept SIDA fully informed about the project and provided access to influence CADU staff or government officials on changing project organization, strategies and activities, or national policies affecting the project's task environment.

OBJECTIVES OF THE PROJECT

The initial objectives of CADU were: (1) to bring about economic and social development; (2) to give the population an increased awareness of and responsibility for development processes; (3) to verify methods of agricultural development; and (4) to train staff not only for CADU but for similar projects elsewhere.[14] Targeted on small-scale landowners and tenants, the project aimed at raising their production levels and standards of living.

The basic premise in this early stage was that economic change would be given priority and social change would be expected to follow from success in raising agricultural productivity.[15] More specifically, CADU's strategy was to establish markets where fair prices prevailed and use extension agents and model farmers to stimulate the target population to use improved seeds and fertilizers. To facilitate this process the project made available low interest credit, undertook agricultural research, developed rural water systems, improved feeder roads, provided livestock services, and engaged in a broad range of community education and development activities.

After the signing of a second phase agreement in 1971, the initial objectives of the project were restated and expanded to reflect project experience and constraints: (1) to achieve economic and social development throughout the project area; (2) to conduct project activities in a manner that ensures the participation of the project area population in and their assuming of increasing responsibility for those activities; (3) to avoid adverse employment effects (tenant evictions) and to observe opportunities to create additional employment; (4) to direct project activities toward farmers in low income brackets; (5) to increase the financial resources of the region by raising the incomes and improving the tax paying capacity of the project area population; (6) to promote the application of CADU experience in agricultural development activities elsewhere in Ethiopia; and (7) to develop suitable methods for bringing about agricultural development in Ethiopia in an integrated manner.[16]

CADU's objectives were never made more specific. Nor were priorities explicitly set among them. However, technical and economic activities could and were deduced from them. These were translated into activity targets identified by CADU's various divisions, departments, and sections in their published annual reports. Social development objectives were never well articulated or translated into clearly justified activity targets, a fact due as much to the state of project design knowledge in the late 1960's as the fact that the senior CADU staff was dominated by agricultural scientists and economists. No sociologist, political scientist, or anthropologist served in senior positions during the 1967-73 period. This lack of specificity was to make evaluation of the project difficult and lead the project staff to underemphasize social development during the initial years of project activity.[17]

Organization and Activities of the Project

In keeping with its experimental approach, the organizational format of the project was altered several times during the 1967-73 period. Figure 3 presents the organization of the project during its critical initial years of operation.[18] Under this scheme, all divisions, sections, and units operated

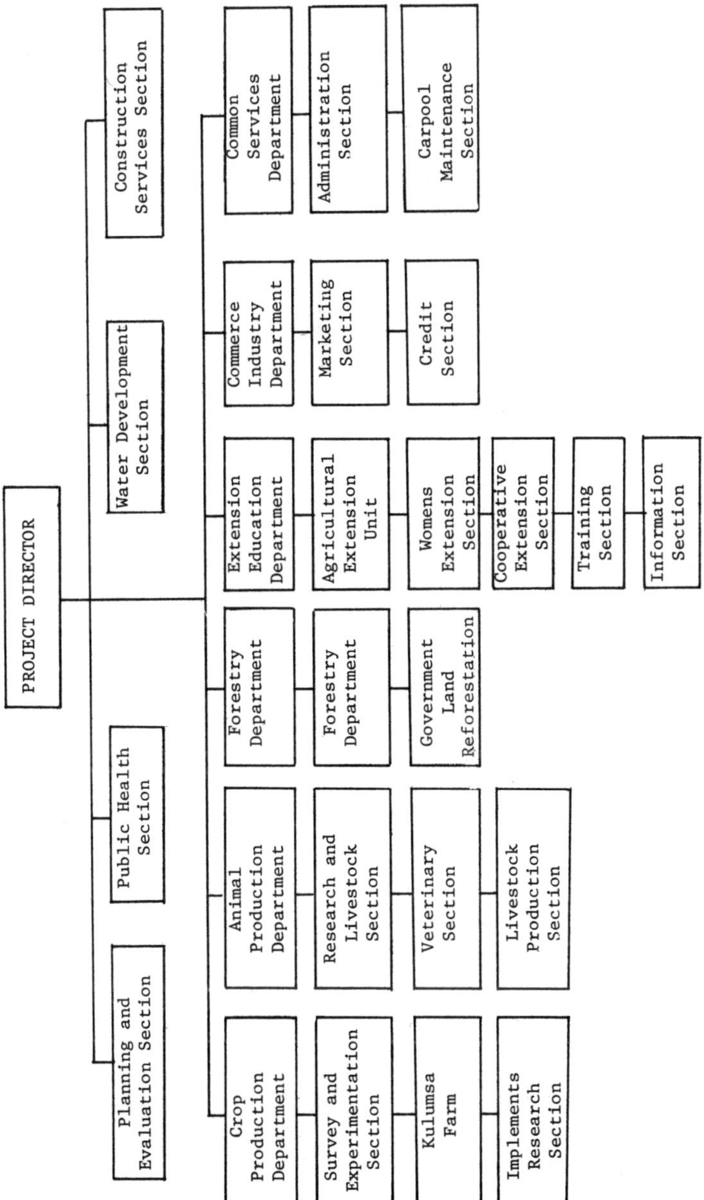

Figure 3: *CADU Organizational Format up to July 1971*

under the direction of an Executive Director appointed by SIDA in consulta-tion with the Ministry of Agriculture. Together with assistant executive directors he was responsible for preparing work plans and budgets, super-vising work schedules, hiring and dismissing personnel in accordance with regulations, promoting coordination with central and local authorities, acquiring working capital for the marketing and credit activities of the project, and submitting progress reports and an annual report.

The Planning and Evaluation Section was charged with maintaining a continual evaluation of the entire organization, ensuring efficiency in its various units, recommending ways to improve the attainment of project goals, identifying and conducting feasibility studies on potential projects and activities, and elaborating a development methodology informed by the project's experience.

The Crop Production Department had three subdivisions. The Survey and Experimentation Section directed its activities toward finding new crops and plant varieties, determining the optimal growing techniques for different crops and varieties, establishing methods for pasture improvement, controlling seed production with respect to trueness to variety, cleanliness, and germination, improving knowledge of soil conditions and determining possibilities for drainage and erosion control, establishing suitable methods of seed control, and developing an extension staff trained in new techniques. Its project farms produced improved seed varieties for sale at profit levels that covered costs of production. The goals of the Implements Research Section were to develop tools for soil preparation, crop handling, and transport, to increase knowledge of conditions under which more mechanized operations could be profitably employed, to train extension staff in the use of new equipment, and to train artisans in production and maintenance.

There were three sections in the Animal Production Department. The Research and Livestock Section was to establish optimal breeding and management methods for dairy cattle, sheep, and poultry, and to train extension staff in new methods. The Veterinary Section's aims were to increase knowledge of prevailing livestock diseases, to promote disease prevention services, to maintain the health of cross-bred cattle through vaccinations, to produce semen from cross-bred bulls, to create a cadre of inseminators and vaccinators, to train extension staff in veterinary fundamentals, and to ensure milk hygiene. Finally, the production and sale of grade cattle for the improvement of milk production was the task of the Gobe Livestock Production Section.

The Forestry Department through its various sections aimed at establishing nursery techniques and methods of planting and management of plantations, finding suitable tree species for the various ecological zones, increasing planting of trees, especially for fuel and construction purposes and for soil erosion control, producing seedlings, establishing timber plantations, and reforesting government land in Munessa Forest and at Asasa.

The Agricultural Extension Unit, Women's Extension Unit, Cooperative Extension Unit, Training Unit, and Information Unit were the components of the Extension and Education Department. The Agricultural Extension Unit tried to promote the adoption of new products, methods, and inputs for agricultural development through demonstrations, advice, and assistance regarding credit applications, to improve knowledge of agricultural conditions through an annual analysis of demonstration results, and to prepare for the extension of the project's geographic coverage. The Women's Extension Unit was occupied with increasing the general concept of development among women in the project area, training them in home economics, and establishing women's groups. The goal of the Cooperative Extension Unit was to create a basis for the establishment of cooperative societies that would involve themselves in the marketing of produce and the procurement of supplies and credit. The Training Unit took as its major tasks the selection of community groups to be given special training in rural development activities, the training of specialized project staff such as marketing foremen and extension workers, the inservice training of CADU staff, the offering of courses for agricultural staff from other projects, and the practical training of selected students from agricultural colleges and institutions. The aim of the Information Unit was to increase knowledge of development programs and project objectives and achievements, to create special campaigns to promote various project activities, to disseminate in cooperation with the government information about legislation pertinent to project goals, to promote self-help schemes, particularly in regard to water and educational projects, and to advance adult literacy.

The Commerce and Industry Department concentrated on the establishment of economic incentives by ensuring marketing outlets and fair prices, including premiums for improved quality, the provision of seed, fertilizer and other inputs recommended by the Extension and Education Department, provision of assistance in the acquisition of such inputs through credit extension, promotion of capital accumulation for development through savings schemes, offering assistance toward the creation and management of cooperative societies, and covering its own operating costs. Finally, the Water Development Section sought to organize self-help schemes for building water supply systems, to create water supply facilities in accordance with a master plan, and to increase existing knowledge of hydrological conditions in the region.

The project's format changed in mid-1971 when the initial interministerial coordinating committee was abolished and the project placed under the Ministry of Agriculture's new unit, EPID. The new format, presented in Figure 4, remained largely unchanged up to the revolution.[19] As noted earlier, the Executive Director of CADU reported in principle to the head of EPID while carrying out the same functions assigned to him when the project began. Under the revised system, the Executive Director, assisted by

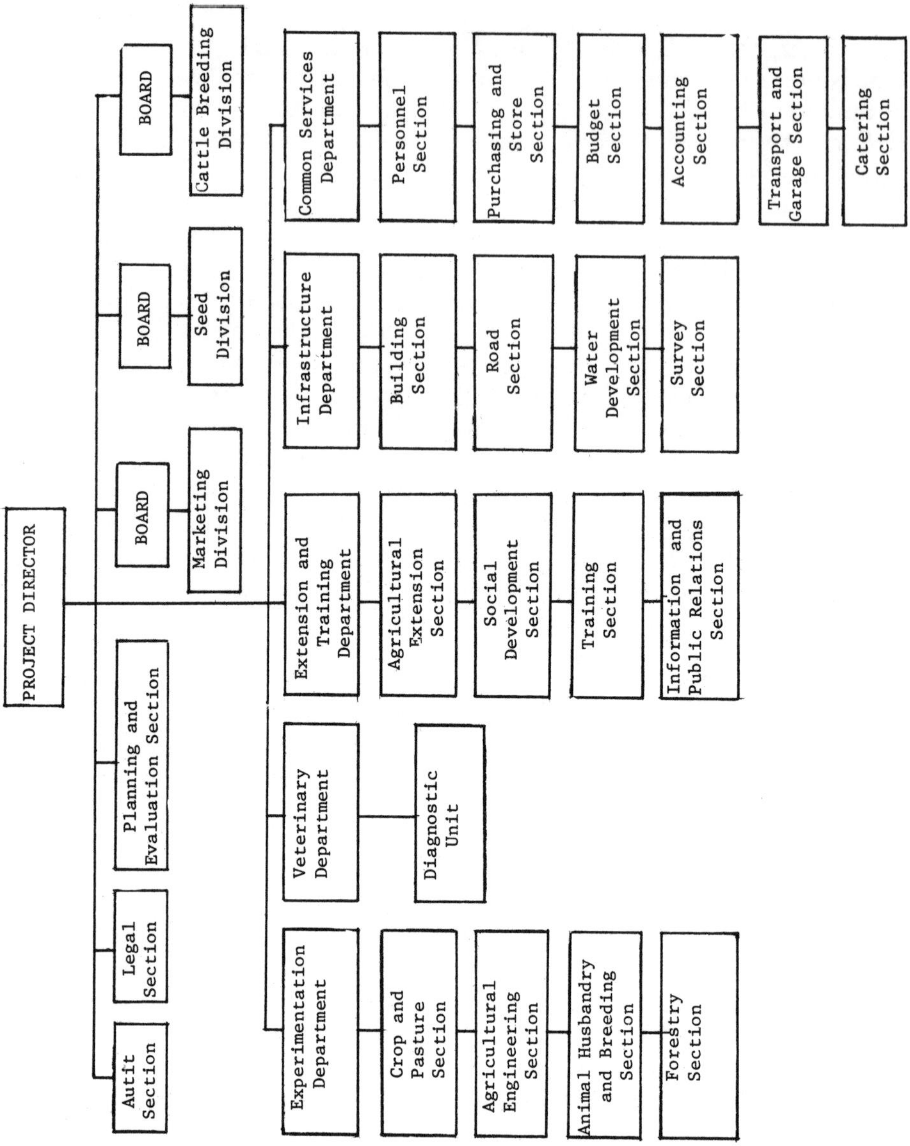

Figure 4: *CADU Organizational Format Between July l971 and l974*

the Planning and Evaluation Unit, now supervised four major departments and three autonomous divisions.[20]

CADU used its incorporation into EPID to revise its organizational structure to increase the project's efficiency and take on new functions identified by the first few years of project experience. First, the former Crop Production, Animal Production and Forestry Departments were, with the exception of the Seed Production, Cross-Bred Dairy Cattle Breeding and Veterinary Sections, consolidated into one new department labeled the Experimentation Department. Added to its functions was an additional task of identifying, testing, and improving, through nurseries, improved tree species suitable for fuel, construction, and soil erosion control. Secondly, the veterinary section was separated from livestock research and production and raised to a separate division in recognition of its expanding responsibilities. Third, the former Extension and Education Department was streamlined, renamed, and given the additional responsibility of increasing public knowledge of the objectives and philosophy of CADU, development problems of the region, CADU and government development campaigns, and changes in government legislation and policies related to rural development.[21] Fourth, the Common Services Division was expanded to reflect the growing complexity and size of the project. Fifth, the Public Health Section's activities were handed over to the Ministry of Public Health. Finally, the Water Development and Construction Services Section were rationalized and consolidated into the Infrastructure Department, in part to take advantage of the economies of scale gained from placing construction engineers, equipment, and supplies in one unit.

Aside from these six major changes, the 1971 reform established three autonomous divisions governed by boards. The purpose of this change was to ensure financial cost coverage to pave the way for their gradual takeover by the cooperative societies the project proposed promoting as of 1972. The former Kulumsa Farm Section turned into a board-governed Seed Division, the goals of which were to produce clean seed of improved varieties on two farms at a level of efficiency needed to cover costs and make a 10 percent profit on capital after depreciation and interest. The former Animal Production Department's responsibilities for producing and selling grade dairy cattle for improved milk yields were transferred to a semi-autonomous Cattle Breeding Division. A third semi-autonomous board-governed Marketing Division was created to replace the former Commerce and Industry Department. Its objectives were to: (1) establish economic incentives by ensuring market outlets at fair prices, including premiums for improved quality; (2) provide inputs recommended by the extension service; (3) assist in the acquisition of such inputs through the provision of credit; (4) promote capital accumulation through savings schemes; and (5) assist in the creation and management of cooperative societies.

Carrying out all these activities required a large staff. By 1973 CADU employed approximately 100 senior level personnel, 900 middle and lower level contract employees, and 1000 temporary daily laborers. Upper levels of staff management were filled by either Swedes or Ethiopians who were not permanent residents of the region. Nor were Ethiopians employed in middle level positions recruited from Chilalo. This latter point is significant given the patterns of Amhara colonization and the differences between Amhara and Oromo interests reviewed in Chapter 3.

From the beginning the project aimed at replacing Swedish staff with qualified Ethiopians. There were clear financial reasons for doing so, as some 25 percent of project funds went to expatriates who made up only four percent of project staff but took up 65 percent of payroll expenditures.[22] However, institution building reasons were more important. The director noted in 1972 that the potential for the project to be replicated in other regions would be enhanced if reductions in high expatriate salary and benefit costs could be coupled with increased capacity of Ethiopians to carry out senior level administrative and technical functions.

Ethiopianization at senior levels occurred quickly. In 1968, most departments and sections were headed by Swedes. At that time Swedish expatriates held about 40 top positions. Gradually Ethiopians were made unit heads and Swedes appointed as their deputies. By 1974 there were only five Swedes in senior positions, although more than a dozen still worked for CADU in technical positions. The initial project director was Bengt Nekby, a Swedish development expert. At the end of the first contract agreement, he was replaced by an Ethiopian who had served as assistant executive director for two years. This man, Paulos Abraham, was viewed by his staff as "a man with a dominant personality, organizational capability, deep commitment to innovation, and ability to persuade key staff members to identify their own interests with the welfare of the project."[24] After 1972 there were two assistant executive directors, one an Ethiopian, the other a Swede. For middle positions CADU recruited nationwide for talented Ethiopians and ran training programs for its own field staff at facilities on the project's compound.

Swedish commitment and Ethiopian leadership built a competent project staff. Their working relations with Swedish counterparts reinforced managerial and operational skills, and senior Swedish and Ethiopian leadership generated high motivation and commitment to project objectives. This was reinforced by a management style promoting staff participation in operational management, achieved through the use of a permanent Policy Advisory Committee composed of department and division heads, and the use of interdepartmental committees and task forces,[25] remarkable access of senior officers to middle and lower level staff, and an emphasis on team work. Clearly, rapid promotion of nationals, open channels of communication, and broadened staff participation were important to project success.

Salaries and benefits offered to senior and middle level Ethiopian staff were above the governmental scale. However, by the early 1970s CADU was experiencing difficulties recruiting qualified personnel for key positions because of the appearance of additional large-scale and national rural development programs. These forced CADU to compete with the World Bank or USAID for Ethiopian personnel. CADU was in part disadvantaged in this competition because it did not have an overseas training component,[26] suggesting the importance of a large project having a fellowship program that seeks to attract local professionals. Lower level salaries and benefits were equitable and the entire personnel system well run.

STRATEGY, ACTIVITIES AND RESULTS

Despite all the activities spelled out in CADU's annual reports and summarized by its organization charts, the project's principal programs centered on agricultural extension, input distribution, and output marketing. Operations on these programs began in the northern *woredas* of Chilalo *Awraja* in 1968. By 1971 these and other activities had expanded CADU's presence into all of Chilalo's ten *woredas*. These were organized into four project-defined development zones (see Figure 2), each with an administrative center overseeing implementation and coordination of project activities.[27] Just before the revolution began to unfold, most farming areas of Chilalo were covered. At that time they were served by 414 model farmers in 31 extension areas and 33 trade centers.

i. Marketing Strategy

The key to this rapid expansion of project activities was CADU's initial emphasis on promoting attractive market opportunities for the area's small-scale producers.[28] In part, that this strategy was selected by default, for the project began after the 1967 planting season. Still, the project initially focused on marketing because existing patterns of land tenure and exploitation required new economic opportunities as a prerequisite to gaining the peasantry's attention. The project offered peasants the chance to sell their agricultural products at fair and stable prices. The object of this strategy was to influence market prices upward through CADU-induced competition, in anticipation that higher prices would stimulate the target population to adopt the improved inputs, credit, and husbandry advice the project was soon to offer. In the meantime it was assumed that the government would deliver basic tenant protection that would add to the incentives generated by higher prices.

Trading centers purchasing milk and wheat were opened in the project's early months of operation. At this time Chilalo's markets were controlled by

Table 2: *Milk Purchases by CADU Collection Stations 1967-71*

Year	Number of stations	Litres collected
1967-68	1	4,000
1968-69	5	136,000
1969-70	6	318,000
1970-71	8	159,000
1971-72	8	147,133
1972-73	9	109,908

Source: CADU Annual Reports 1967-68 to 1972-73
Note: CADU documents are inconsistent in regard to litres collected.

petty traders, middlemen, and grain merchants who bought at low prices and frequently used scales off by as much as 15 percent.[29] Milk and wheat were chosen because the area was well suited to their production and larger urban markets were favorable for such products. Purchase prices for both milk and wheat were maintained above the local market prices, which was not difficult to do given the profit margins established by the area's traders and middlemen. To obtain the economies of scale resulting from increased purchases, CADU bought grain and milk from all farmers.

Prior to the arrival of CADU, there were few opportunities to market milk, despite the economic potential of cattle raising in the area. But by 1971 eight milk collection stations were operating on the Asella to Bekoji road. Milk was collected once a day, tested, and processed with CADU dairy equipment in Asella. The collection stations paid farmers fair prices on delivery and aimed at a wholesale markup of 35 percent after processing.

Milk purchases rose steadily during the first two years, reaching a peak of 318,000 collected litres in 1969-70. After that they declined, a trend documented in Table 2. CADU analysts attributed this to poor conditions of forage, high butter prices in the private sector, and, most importantly, farmer recognition that wheat farming was more profitable than dairying, diverting more of their land and labor to its production.

Initially CADU planned to sell milk in the larger markets of Nazareth and Addis Ababa. But in mid-1971 most of the milk being collected was sold to CADU employees and Asella townsmen. Efforts to begin sales to Addis Ababa's major dairy had been hampered by difficulties in obtaining the daily 1,400 liters needed to cover the costs of collection and transport. This problem continued through 1973, leading the Livestock Production Section to propose installing a milk cooling station in Asella so that milk did not have to be shipped on a daily basis. CADU's inability to raise milk production led staff to study pasture conditions, introduce supplementary feeding during the dry season, and cross-breed local stock with imported animals to increase dairy sales. Cross-bred animals raised by CADU's animal hus-

Table 3: *Crop Purchases by CADU 1967/68-1971/72*

Year	Wheat	Crop in quintals Barley	Flax
1967-68	480	-	-
1968-69	2,300	-	710
1969-70	6,314	-	798
1970-71	23,980	520	6,100
1971-72	93,887	12,149	3,327

Source: CADU Annual Reports 1967-68 to 1972-73

bandry unit sold for more than E$ 500, so CADU had to maintain its milk marketing activities through subsidization. Anticipating milk sales to increase as cross-heifers came into production, CADU viewed milk marketing losses in 1973-74 as an acceptable cost of development.

CADU's crop market interventions initially were confined to wheat. This benefitted the project, for between 1967 and 1971 prices for that crop steadily increased.[30] Within two years the project's centers were buying barley and flax as well.[31] CADU sought to cover its marketing costs by sales, an objective reached in all but the initial period and the 1971-72 fiscal year. The rapid expansion of such crop purchases is documented in Table 3.

During the 1967-73 period CADU followed three different wheat marketing strategies.[32] From 1967 to 1972 it paid prices two to seven percent higher than those prevailing in local markets, stored grain until prices had risen, and then resold it at a price 15 to 20 percent higher than that paid local farmers.[33] The objectives of this strategy were to increase farmer's incentives to adopt CADU inputs, to create market competition, and to promote seasonal price stabilization. However, CADU suffered losses pursuing these objectives. When these reached an estimated E$ 68,000 during the 1970-71 season, CADU adopted a second strategy based on offering farmers a guaranteed price set by forecasts of average prices for the year.[34] This approach led to even higher losses when unanticipated imports by the Ethiopian Grain Corporation in 1971-72 and generally high production in the country dropped wheat prices below CADU's guaranteed level. To maintain farmer confidence, CADU purchased at the set rate and held large carry-over stocks at the end of the fiscal year. Finally, in 1972-73, project officials implemented a third strategy based on shared marketing risks. Under this system farmers received 90 percent of the at-harvest market value of the crop as a first payment, with a second payment promised if CADU's gains later in the year exceeded storage and marketing costs. These terms were unacceptable to farmers and many refused to deliver their grains to CADU. In order to avoid losing the gains made since 1967 toward increasing competitiveness and prices in local markets, CADU was forced to return to its earlier strategy of purchasing grain at E$ 4.00 below the on-going Addis Ababa price and bearing the risk that market prices might fall prior to sale or that storage and sale costs might be greater than the purchase-sale margin.

Given the total budget of CADU, losses in wheat marketing did not seriously threaten the financial viability of the project.[35] What was important about these marketing problems was the way local elites tried to use them to undermine the credibility of CADU. This is best illustrated by the 1971-72 price fall, in part because it serves as a preview of the kinds of issues addressed in Chapter 5. Briefly, merchants and traders threatened by CADU marketing strategies spread rumors that project officials were depressing the market to make profits, that CADU was now revealing itself as an agency aimed at exploiting Chilalo's people. These rumors hurt CADU activities for at least a year, notwithstanding the effects of economic rationale just described.

These wheat marketing problems suggest that fair prices and adequate stabilization are necessary to induce small-scale farmers to adopt productivity increasing innovations, that even large integrated rural development projects control too small a share of the market to pursue a strategy based on influencing market prices upward, and that it is difficult to modify a marketing strategy once introduced and accepted by project farmers. The appropriate approach is probably to induce the government to pursue supportative price policies and the project to promote more effective private market systems through investments in infrastructure for transport, storage, and improved market information.[36] However, given the patterns of the political economy of Ethiopia and the Chilalo region described in Chapter 5, it is not at all clear that such an alternative approach would have been any more successful than the one CADU followed.

ii. Extension Program

CADU's extension program began in 1968, its building blocks being project extension agents, model farmers, and demonstration plots. By 1973 the project area was divided into 31 extension areas organized into the project's four development zones. These were defined by natural and man-made physical features, as well as established local and grassroots administrative boundaries. Most extension areas served 1,500 to 2,000 farm households.

Extension activities in an area began with the selection of a model farmer.[37] Farmers living within designated 800-hectare areas were called together by project staff and asked to form a committee to nominate from among themselves five candidates, one of whom was then selected by CADU to be a model farmer. Those recommended were supposed to be full time farmers, residents of their community for at least three years, holders of farms typical for the area, and persons of good moral character known to be receptive to new ideas. The extensive patron-client system that prevailed in Chilalo should have resulted in many of the candidates being recommended by the local gentry, unchallenged by tenants or poorer landowners. But no systematic study was done of these farmers, so that it was not possible to know the percentage who were tenants or the amount of land they farmed.[38] Most were probably medium size landowners. Still, the majority proved to be good choices who shared their newly acquired knowledge with all farmers in their areas. Where possible the agent tried to keep the nominating committee functioning to facilitate his other activities. This was particularly the case after 1971 when the project sought to establish Model Farmer Area Development Committees and Extension Area Development Committees. These are described in Chapter 5. Here it need only be noted that their purpose was to facilitate contact by CADU with non-adopters through the model farmer.

Model farmers were instructed by extension agents on the use of project recommended inputs.[39] This exercise was facilitated using part of a model farmer's land as a demonstration plot where the agent could hold the field days needed to carry CADU's message to 100 or so farmers who typically lived in the model farm areas.[40] In addition, extension agents established and managed other demonstration plots located near major roads, churches, and market centers. Field days were held on these plots as well. The object of these demonstrations was to induce small-scale farmers and tenants to adopt CADU innovations.[41]

This strategy, supported by good wheat and milk prices, led to the rapid expansion of the extension program and helped agents reach an increasing number of farmers. The goal of CADU prior to 1974 was to have 40 extension agents overseeing 15 to 20 model farmers each, with every model farmer reaching 100 farm families with information on and demonstration of seeds, fertilizer, tools, implements, animal production, and forestry.[42] However, when the revolution began, CADU's extension program had established only 31 areas with 414 model farmers.[43] Of these, some 370 model farmer committees were functioning and most extension areas had a higher level Extension Area Development Committee. Perhaps 1,600 Chilalo farmers belonged to such committees. Hence, the distribution of model farmers and committees, even though below target levels, was sufficient to allow nearly all Chilalo farmers easy access to the extension information provided by the project.

The model farmer approach proved reasonably successful. Senior staff estimated the project's messages were reaching three-quarters of the project area's farmers, all but the most remote landowners and tenants at least observing or hearing the project's messages. CADU concluded such model farmers were "eminently suitable information-disseminators... a relatively cheap method for reaching the 'grass root levels'."[44] A 1974 study suggested that their success getting other farmers to adopt CADU inputs was strongly influenced by their being respected farmers.[45] Adoption was also stimulated by the fact that the project's inputs did not demand major changes in husbandry practices and generated immediate yield increases. The model farmer approach should, therefore, not be given unqualified credit for the project's rapid expansion of activities. In this regard, by 1974 some extension agents argued CADU should work with clusters of 20 to 30 innovative farmers rather than a single model farmer, forming "progressive farmers clubs" that could influence the area.

Typical of most projects of the late 1960s, CADU gave haphazard attention to the role of women in development and homemaking.[46] Without the benefit of focused research, or the existence of a clear strategy for approaching or benefitting women, a home economics program was begun in 1968. It viewed women's activities as being more social than productive and focused its energies on home economics. To a large extent this was because the economic role of women on the farm was unappreciated by the project's designers and senior officers. Initially, the extension unit sought to place two home economics agents in each of the project's extension areas and charged them with forming groups of 15-20 farm housewives who could participate in weekly demonstrations in child care, food preparation, poultry raising, housing, gardening, personal hygiene, latrine and garbage pit construction, marketing, and literacy. Typically they used model farmer's wives as points of contact. Scattered households tested the agents' stamina, and local languages or dialects their ability to communicate effectively. These activities were not linked to CADU's other extension efforts focused on male farmers, nor were programs pursued that promoted horticulture, improved weeding practices, or taught marketing, all of which could have reinforced CADU's production objectives.

Between 1968 and 1971 the women's extension unit used locally identified organizers. They were given short courses and asked to conduct classes for the newly formed women's groups.[47] After 1971, CADU-trained home economics agents attempted to make this program more professional and development oriented. They began to promote income generating activities and alert extension agents to the importance of women in farm household decision making and field operations. By 1974 CADU had 32 women's extension agents who were reported as reaching 34,920 women with home economic lessons in 1973-74, a number considerably below the 83,436 said to have been reached two years earlier.[48] Since these lessons were held in groups of 15 to 20 farm wives several times per year, the actual number of meetings held in 1973-74 was about 2,900. Perhaps an additional 2,500 individual household visits also took place in that year.

There is little recorded information on the formation, procedural rules, or internal elections of women's groups, though it is thought that they deteriorated into social gatherings and were plagued by infighting and dominated by wives of bigger farmers.[49] And it is thought that peasant women were not very effective teachers in their own houses or those of other women in the neighborhood. Little data was collected to give evidence that lessons on sanitation or nutrition were adopted, much less diffused to others. It is known that Chilalo women's major interests were in literacy, an interest shared by the agents themselves. To meet this demand, some planned programs had to be dropped. This lack of knowledge on the needs of women and the effectiveness of initial efforts held back expansion of women-focused activities, project directors deciding not to invest further resources until the program received a comprehensive evaluation. Little progress was made in doing this prior to 1974.

A voluntary youth extension program began in 1973. It sought to involve rural youth between 10 and 25 years of age in recreational and learning groups. The aim was to develop notions of self-education, team work, and cooperation. Groups were formed and urged to choose leaders. Local communities were asked to elect parents and teachers as volunteer counselors. They received some training in special orientation workshops and were helped by extension workers. A major activity of these groups was to be involved in community development efforts. Again little is recorded about them other than the fact that 2,000 youth were said to have been participating by 1974.[50]

Given the limited number of senior managerial staff, the national shortages of extension agents, and the increasing number of complex demonstration, farm planning, credit appreciation, and trade center management activities staff were asked to perform (described shortly), it seems clear that the project expanded its extension areas too rapidly. To a large extent this resulted from internal project drive to have a major rural development success and local political pressure from areas neighboring on established extension areas to get CADU to create one covering their area.

Project designers recognized in 1967 that there was a serious shortage of trained personnel to run an expanding project. So in 1968 a training center with modest classroom and dormitory facilities was established at CADU headquarters. Regarded as a complement to existing government facilities, the Asella center focused on producing field agents who had ten years of schooling, knowledge of Chilalo's principal local language, Oromo, and some rural background. By the end of 1973 its short and long term courses had graduated more than 400 Ethiopians trained to serve as market foremen or their assistants, extension and assistant extension agents, home economics agents, cooperative agents, and model farmers. Sixty percent of those trained worked for CADU, the rest serving EPID in other areas of the country.[51]

Prior to 1972, extension agents were trained in two 7 month phases. The first emphasized basic theoretical training and the second practical husbandry. The latter phase aimed at promoting student devotion to agriculture, appreciation of hard work, and self-confidence. After 1972 this course was redesigned into three phases: 6 months of theory, 10 months of practical work, and four months for theoretical follow up training.[52] Marketing agents were given 22 months, some of it at a government community development training center in another province. Their courses also had theoretical and practical components, with special emphasis on cooperative principles and practices, book-keeping, and accounting. Shorter inservice training courses were given to extension and marketing agents, project orientation sessions were run for new CADU staff, and special training programs developed for livestock agents, youth extension volunteers, forestry demonstrators, and selected cooperative members.

While the staff of CADU's school was not large and there was a general shortage of books, teaching facilities and residential dormitories, the program showed substantial promise as a vehicle for raising staff performance, reducing thereby the project's dependence on the government's own training schools and programs. If there were any shortcomings they were inadequate attention to socializing students in CADU's basic philosophy and stimulating greater commitment to reaching the poorest segments of the rural community.

iii. Research Activities

Research in support of these extension efforts was carried out by CADU's Crop Production and Animal Production Departments, units consolidated as sections into an Experimention Division in 1971. Initial surveys were carried out on rainfall, natural vegetation, soil, farming practices, and weeds, pests, and diseases.[53] Based on this preliminary data, CADU staff identified four agro-ecological zones to guide scientific planning, research, and recommendations.[54] Information on precipitation levels, soil water holding capacity, and frost occurrences were essential to carry out research, but the most striking finding came from studies of present farming practices. These noted that most crop species were of local origin and that yields were held back by mixing of varieties in individual fields, low seed quality, insufficient soil and seedbed preparation, and unsatisfactory weeding during the growing period.

Guided by these findings and the fact that improved seeds and fertilizer were rarely used in Chilalo, the Crop Production Department centered its initial activities on variety and fertilizer trials for grain and forage crops. Here it gave particular attention to wheat because it was the region's principal crop.

Experiments on 21 different cereals were carried out at CADU's Kulumsa farm. Legumes and oilseed crops were also studied. Early in the project adaptive research based on wheat material obtained from the experimentation station at Debra Zeit and agricultural research programs in Kenya and Mexico yielded promising results. Soon the project was ready to issue a higher yielding wheat variety backed by a package of fertilizer and husbandry recommendation. The achievement was due to CADU's in-project adaptive research capacity, and no doubt the motivation team membership gave CADU crop production specialists.

While CADU-released varieties needed constant monitoring and occasional replacement, they led to substantial yield increases for wheat. Project recommendations for fertilizer and improved husbandry practices contributed to yield increases for other Chilalo crops as well. Such impact is suggested by tables in Chapter 5. According to CADU specialists, good husbandry practices matched with CADU's improved wheat and fertilizer packages had the potential to raise yields on farms with good soil and adequate rainfall by 60 percent or more. Because of this, the area under wheat in Chilalo dramatically increased from 27,000 hectares in 1968 to an estimated 150,000 hectares in 1973,[55] demonstrating in the process the importance of establishing small, effective research units in integrated rural development projects.

CADU's crop production specialists also sought to identify, adapt, and formulate recommendations for alternative cash crops, such as maize, rape seed, teff, sunflower, feed barley, malting barley, and haricot beans. If any important research areas were neglected, they were probably those related to maintenance of soil fertility through the use of farm manure and crop rotation and the promotion of crop protection through weed control methods.[56]

In the opinion of experts evaluating the project in early 1974, CADU's adaptive research had the potential to benefit farmers in the surrounding highland areas of Shoa and Bale Provinces.[57] This is important, for prior to CADU's arrival, there was only one functioning experimental station in central Ethiopia, and it was in Debra Zeit on the other side of the Rift Valley. Hence, in-project research targeted on immediate adaptive results yielded benefits beyond project boundaries.

Early in the project CADU began growing high quality improved seed varieties on its own farms. Because of demand it also contracted for seed from capable local growers. Besides growing seed CADU cleaned and tested it in order to maintain quality control and ultimately the confidence of the farmer. Its operations peaked in the early 1970s when its two farms at Kulumsa and Asasa produced more than 22,000 quintals of improved wheat seed on 798 hectares of land.[58] In addition, CADU farms produced barley, maize, rape, sunflower, linseed, and teff seeds. Run with substantial profits in some years, the Seed Division set an example of how efficiently and effectively to manage one of the critical components of an agriculture production oriented integrated rural development project.[59]

Together with the Cattle Breeding Division, the Animal Husbandry and Breeding Section made substantial progress in upgrading local dairy cattle by cross-breeding selected local heifers with European stock through artificial insemination.[60] The focus was on milk production, because the domestic market for high quality beef was viewed as limited. Research was carried out on feeding, milking, fencing, cattle shed building, concentrate mixtures, and simple systems for improving hygienic milking practices. Based on findings from these activities, CADU's livestock specialists began producing cross-bred animals capable of increasing yield per lactation from 300 liters to 1000 liters, when proper husbandry practices were followed. Researchers demonstrated that the management of such exotic cross-breds was not beyond the ability of local farmers. For example, after the import of 40 Friesian heifers in 1969, 15 were sold on credit to model farmers living along the Asella-Sagure road. The farmers received training in the management of dairy animals and were visited every fortnight by extension agents. Lessons from this exercise were used to improve the overall program. Most importantly, the success of this exercise and experiments with other animals led CADU to step up its efforts to cross-breed local and exotic animals, to demonstrate them to local farmers attracted by the new milk marketing opportunities, and either to sell these animals to local farmers or make artificial insemination (AI) services available to them.

Original production of cross-bred cattle took place on 250 hectares outside Asella, then moved to a 2,800 hectare farm in Gobe. To establish the farm, CADU's Road Section had to construct an 18 kilometer all-weather road to Kofele and the project had to resettle some 250-300 tenants on a farm near Asasa, where they took up 1900 of 2500 hectares. Some tenants were to return to Gobe during the revolution and substantially set back cross-breeding programs, a problem described in subsequent chapters.

Production of animals increased steadily, numbering nearly 2,500 by 1972.[61] In that year a bull station was established with a semen laboratory and a liquid nitrogen plant, part of an effort to ensure semen supply and lower AI costs. During 1972 the Cattle Breeding Division artificially inseminated 2,626 cows in its herd, yielding 866 crosses of which 509 were the desired type. Unlike the Seed Division, this unit had difficulty meeting the goal of economic self-sufficiency set by the 1971 project reforms. Just before the revolution it appeared to be near the breakeven point of producing 600 high quality cross-bred dairy cows per year for local sale. Aside from cattle, the Division's chief success was in the improvement of local sheep bred through the use of imported rams.

Some critics believe the project's livestock research over emphasized the dairy program.[62] They argue the unit overlooked substantial opportunities for promoting integrated crop-livestock production strategies, such as zero-grazing, and did not test their assumptions about the potential for beef production in the region and meat marketing outside it.

Artificial insemination, disease control, and milk quality testing were the responsibility of the Veterinary Department. By 1973 it operated a bull station that collected and stored doses of semen.[63] A 17 stop AI run was established on the Gonde to Bekoji road, with pre-established time table and inexpensive service charges. Efforts were made to expand services beyond this road.[64] However, the number of peasant farmers using it, some 350 in 1973, was lower than expected, suggesting that either inadequate demonstration had been done or farmers believed the risks too high. Local cattle owners did demand veterinary services, the Department giving more than 170,000 vaccinations for rinderpest and CBPP, anthrax, blackleg, FMD, and brucellosis in 1971-72.[65]

Milk hygiene tests during the same period showed that substantial improvements were needed in milking sanitation and collection center quality control if the project was to reach its target of effectively entering the Addis Ababa market. Towards better understanding of animal diseases and milk hygiene, a laboratory with equipment for parasitological, bacteriological, and pathological work was established in late 1972. Among the early activities, however, were the carrying out of surveys on animal health and the training of staff.

During the early years of CADU, the project's research on pasture and fodder crops sought to lay a foundation for intensive livestock production in Chilalo. Indeed, CADU's efforts here were among the most significant in the country. Pasture experimentation was carried out on grasslands south of Asella and trials took place with fodder beets and pea-oat forage crops. Experimentation also occurred with regard to stocking rate strategies, periodic grazing, and paddock fencing. New varieties of pasture grasses and fodder crops were also tested, while indigenous grasses and legumes were studied for their potential.[66] Trials quickly established that substantial increases of 4,000 to 6,000 kilograms per hectare of dry matter were possible when phosphorus and nitrogen fertilizers were applied and fencing strategies followed. While such increases tripled the carrying capacity of experimentation station pastures, few farm level trials were held and little information on pasture improvement was disseminated by extension agents. So, while farm land expansion and CADU livestock programs increased overgrazing, the project neglected to promote its findings on pasture improvement.

On the whole, CADU resisted the temptation to introduce wholly foreign implements and techniques. The one exception occurred early on when CADU provided tractor services to farmers in the area. This was stopped in 1970 when it became clear that it led to tenant evictions. From then on CADU emphasized intermediate technology. Toward this end, the Implements Research Section focused on designing farm tools and developing the capacity of local craftsmen to manufacture and maintain them. Research activities centered on: (1) soil preparation – improving the local plow, developing a harrow, producing simple bags for seed and fertilizer broadcasting, and designing a new hand hoe; (2) harvest, threshing, cleaning, and storage – developing a better sickle, introducing a new scythe, demonstrating better grain storage systems, and producing a small mobile threshing machine; and (3) transport – the improvement of current animal transport by introducing wheelbarrows and ox-drawn carts to support the increased marketing of crops CADU's seed-fertilizer packages generated.

Prototypes of plows, harrows, carts, stationary threshers, and seed cleaners were eventually produced and tested,[67] perhaps to the neglect of the potential in traditional implements.[68] While local production of these implements promised to create jobs, sales lagged, only the ox-drawn harrow and cart innovations having some success.[69] Reflecting on this in 1974, the acting head of the unit surmised such low acceptance was due to lack of adaptation to the area's different soil and terrain zones and failure to consider farmer preferences and constraints, an example of which was the ox-drawn plow that was rejected by farmers as too heavy to shoulder carry to the field or be pulled by oxen.[70] The failure of the ox-drawn cart to sell well was probably due to cost, for aside from being quite heavy it appeared well adapted to lowland or flat terrain and attractive to farmers. The most promising innovations as of 1973 were a newly developed portable thresher suitable to smallholder needs and a harrow that seemed attractive to farmers.

iv. Credit and Input Provision

It was clear from the very beginning that the demonstration of seeds and fertilizer and the creation of fair markets would achieve little success if tenants and small-scale land-owners could not afford them. The provision of credit, therefore, began prior to the sowing of the 1968 crop.

A project-based credit program was essential because there were no public or private institutional sources of small farm credit in Arussi.Tenant farmers were considered poor credit risks because of the lack of secure title to guarantee loans. So Chilalo's small-holders and tenants were forced to obtain credit from local merchants and money lenders at high interest rates.[71]

CADU changed this pattern by providing input purchase loans at the lowest possible cost, generally estimated as being approximately 12 percent per annum in the early 1970s. Because of poor cost records, the amount of subsidy underlying this rate is difficult to determine. But one study estimated that an interest rate of 25 percent was needed for CADU to break even.[72]

In 1968-69 there were nine trade centers and seven extension areas. Together they serviced 868 farmers who had decided to take advantage of new varieties of seed and/or fertilizer. By 1972-73 there were 33 trade centers and 31 extension areas providing credit to 13,302 farmers, a slight decline from the 14,146 borrowers of 1970-71. During this same period the amount of credit increased from E$ 15,700 to E$ 1,703,491, a trend demonstrated by Table 4.[73]

The extension of credit was done through the trade centers under the supervision of extension agents and trade center foremen. Credit came in the form of seeds and fertilizer rather than cash. The farmer and extension agent prepared a loan application supported by a simple farm plan accepting the new inputs and related agricultural techniques. If the application was approved, the farmer obtained from the trade center the requested supplies against a certain percentage of cash payment determined by the size of the applicant's farm and the input.[74] Unfortunately, this created hardships because the down payment came when poor farmers were most short of cash. A nine-month loan agreement terminating after harvest covered the remainder of the cost of inputs.[75] The loan agreement had to be backed by a guarantor and, if the credit taker was a tenant, a written lease. The purpose of this latter requirement was to strengthen the position of tenants, not to ensure credit repayment. While the effects of these additional constraints were not measured, some project officers felt they hampered peasant access to credit.

Table 4 documents the rise in participation of Chilalo farmers between 1967 and 1971. It was driven by an effectively run project, rising wheat prices, and a seed-fertilizer package offering good probabilities of increased yields on individual farmers' fields. Clearly the project succeeded in increasing peasant access to credit at fair prices. It also pioneered a credit management system that worked better than any other effort in Ethiopia and most schemes elsewhere in the developing world. Yet, managing such credit flows was not easy for CADU's overburdened staff, and efforts to computerize the system in the early 1970s did not succeed. By 1973 it was estimated that the extension agents were spending up to 50 percent of their time facilitating the provision and collection of credit. Not only did this limit time for carrying production increasing messages to farmers, but it affected the important bond of trust that must exist between agent and farmer. Hence, in 1973 the project was reviewing ways to transfer this function to the marketing and cooperative units.[76]

The administrative costs of managing the program were not really known, much less added into the interest charged farmers. Reflecting on the complexity of delivering this credit in a manpower short task environment and the amount of subsidy built into the credit provided, several experts argued that the experience suggested the CADU credit system would be too costly to extend to the rest of the country.[77] (But it eventually was, through a scaled-down, largely successful version adopted by EPID.) They recommended that since the package was successful farmers should begin paying cash for inputs after the second year and that savings groups be stimulated to mobilize capital as part of the project's cooperative development pro-

Table 4: *Amount of Credit and Number of Loans Extended by CADU 1967/68-1972/73*

Year	Number of Loans	Total Amount Credit Extended (E$)	Average Credit per Farmer (E$)	% Total Loans Defaulted or Late
1967-68	189	15,700	85	n.a.
1968-69	868	157,620	183	10
1969-70	4,769	502,874	105	6
1970-71	14,164	1,442,979	102	8
1971-72	12,624	1,124,011	89	10
1972-73	13,302	1,703,491	72	2

Source: CADU annual reports 1967-68 to 1972-73.
Note: There are slight differences in these numbers in most reports.

gram.[78] The revolution prevented experimentation with this recommendation.

Table 4 also shows that despite the expansion of area covered by the CADU, the number of loans declined after the 1970-71 fiscal year, notwithstanding CADU projections of 20,000 credit takers by 1971-72.[79] A number of explanations for this were offered:[80] (1) the decline in wheat prices in 1970-71 led farmers to withdraw from purchasing inputs with credit until grain prices rose; (2) the extension system was ineffective in conveying to farmers the calculations on returns from given inputs; (3) credit down payment requirements limited participation by smaller farmers; (4) farmers feared indebtedness and viewed their margin of profitability as narrowing because of increased rents or unstable grain prices; (5) some landlords were discouraging participation by their tenants by refusing to pay their share of inputs; and (6) eviction patterns led tenants to be insecure and apathetic about production-increasing opportunities.

Clearly wheat prices have been critical to project success. A close look at wheat prices and indicators of project success, such as sales of fertilizer and seed, support this. This relationship is discussed elsewhere in this chapter. But tenancy constraints and credit procedures were also critical to the rise and fall of project success indicators. Tenants appear to have found the adoption of CADU promoted inputs less attractive as sharecropping rates increased from one-third of gross output to one-half. Drawing on CADU generated data, Tesfai Tecle argues that a tenant paying one-half his gross output in rent had little incentive to adopt the new package of practices that was costly even if procured on credit, because under the existing sharecropping arrangements, landlords were assured of some greater reward no matter what the field performance of the "package," whereas tenants realized

Table 5: *Comparison of Benefits per Hectare to Tenants and Landlords by Using Improved Wheat Seed and Chemical Fertilizer in 1970*

Wheat Yield Increases	Tenant Paying One-third of His Gross Output and Bearing All Costs		Tenant Paying One-half of His Gross Output and Bearing All Costs	
(%)	Net Return to Tenant (E$)	Net Return to Landlord (E$)	Net Return to Tenant (E$)	Net Return to Landlord (E$)
20	-50.00	13.33	-70.00	20.00
40	-36.67	26.67	-50.00	40.00
60	-10.00	40.00	-30.00	60.00
80	16.67	53.33	-10.00	80.00
100	43.33	66.67	10.00	100.00

Source: Tesfai Tecle, *Evolution of Rural Strategies*, p. 21.
Note: For this analysis the average yield for unfertilized local wheat is assumed to be 10 quintals per hectare and the farm gate price is assumed to be E$ 20 per quintal.

benefits only if rather substantial increases in production were achieved.[81] That this was the case is demonstrated in Table 5. Chapter 5 documents that with CADU success came rapidly increasing rents for tenant farmers.

In the first years, CADU extended credit and inputs to any farmer willing to innovate. When it became clear that the uneven distribution of land and the patterns of tenancy or sharecropping were leading to undesired skewing of participation in project benefits, the criteria for giving credit were altered. Analysis of credit statistics for 1967-68 suggested that a large proportion had gone to farmers holding more than 40 hectares. Recognizing that a major revision in credit policy was required, the project staff decided in 1969 to limit credit to its original target population, then defined as tenants with less than 40 hectares and landowners with less than 25 hectares. This ceiling was again lowered in 1972 to 30 hectares for tenants and 20 hectares for landowners. At that time, some CADU staff argued for lowering the ceiling further, to 20 and 10 hectares respectively. The dramatic turnabout in credit distribution that resulted from these decisions is set forth in Table 6.

As suggested by Table 4, CADU's credit repayment rates have been high, particularly by African standards. The project's internal studies demonstrated that larger, richer farmers tended to default. Others repaid on time.[82] The reasons for this are found in CADU's policies that required a partial down payment for inputs, a guarantor, loan collection at the time of crop sales, and group disqualification from credit access if the annual repayment rate for a model farmer area was below 90 percent.[83] High repayment rates also resulted from the fact that the Marketing Division was well run and had good management information records.[84]

Table 6: *Distribution of Credit by Type of Farmer*

Type of Farmer % of	1967-68		1968-70		1971-72	
	% of Credit Takers	% of Credit Vol.	% of Credit Takers	% of Credit Vol.	% of Credit Takers	Credit Vol.
Tenants	9	4	32	28	30	30
Landowners 1-10 ha	43	17	40	39	62	56
11-20 ha	19	19	9	14	7	10
21-40 ha	11	24	4	6	2	4
>40 ha	10	33	1	2	-	-
Unknown Status	9	4	14	12	-	-

Source: Henock Kifle, *An Analysis of the CADU Credit Program 1968/69-1970/71 and its Impact on Income Distribution.* (Asella: CADU, Publication No. 66, 1971); Michael Beyene, *An Analysis of CADU Credit Program 1971/72- 1972/73* (Asella: CADU, Publication No. 92, 1974).

Table 7: *CADU Sales of Inputs 1967/68-1972/73*

Year	Quantity of Fertilizer (Qts)	Quantity of Improved Seeds (Qts)
1967-68	42	189
1968-69	2,822	4,540
1969-70	18,700	11,300
1970-71	41,955	14,239
1971-72	45,325	15,316
1972-73	40,129	5,404

Source: CADU Annual Reports 1967/68 to 1972/73
Note: There are slight differences in these numbers in most reports.

Because credit was in kind, CADU's trade center activities expanded rapidly. By 1972 they were handling large quantities of seeds, fertilizer, farm implements, insecticides, herbicides, knapsack sprayers, and plastic milk pots and buckets. But their major "sales" were of improved seeds and fertilizer, sales which are documented in Table 7. If the 4,000 farmers making cash purchases in 1972-73 are added to credit takers, some 17,000 farmers, then approximately one-fourth of Chilalo farmers, were being reached by the marketing program.[85]

Table 7 suggests the same pattern identified and discussed in regard to Table 4's documentation of credit expansion. Among the reasons for the leveling off of fertilizer sales were: (1) low and unstable wheat prices in 1971-72; (2) farmer inclination to resist the purchase of inputs, even on credit terms, until a high benefit/cost ratio existed; (3) local belief that fertilizer had residual effects beyond a single season; and (4) changes in CADU's loan policies.[86] The precipitous decline in seed purchases that marked 1972-73 were thought to be the result of farmers saving their own seed from previous purchases or harvests and the emergence of a local private market for seeds.[87]

When the project began, a quintal of diammonium phosphate was E$ 28 per quintal, rapidly rising to E$ 37 in 1969.[88] By 1973 the price reached E$ 40 per quintal. CADU believed demand for fertilizer would fall by a higher increase than that marking the rise in price; hence, it had subsidized the cost above E$ 38 after 1971. However, when it became clear in late 1973 that world-wide shortages, industry production costs, and rising freight rates from western ports would raise the price of this key component of CADU success to E$ 53, senior officers of the project and the Ministry of Agriculture became very worried. A decision was made to subsidize the price at E$ 44 on the assumption that small-scale landowners probably could absorb the increase and with the realization that the project was not designed to support a larger subsidy. This reluctant decision was made with the realization that tenants would be likely to find fertilizer uneconomical at that higher price and that the growing commercial farmers of the region probably could absorb it and continue to expand their mechanized fields in the process.

CADU was subsequently saved from these unfortunate results by the steep rise in world wheat prices and the unfolding of the revolution, which at least stopped the expansion of large-scale farms. But the rise in fertilizer prices reveals how integrated rural development projects are affected by external factors beyond the control of project officers. CADU's major tool for reversing these trends and promoting greater use of production increasing inputs was its extension service. It, however, needed improvement, a 1974 project evaluation report concluding that it was the weakest link in CADU's production increasing strategy.[89] Towards using that tool more effectively the report urged "the development of a vigorous extension method aimed at transforming attitudes of farmers and converting them from subsistence to business farmers, so that they would more readily adopt innovations at a lower benefit/cost ratio than that which seems to be acceptable at present."[90] Success here would not be enough, for two major policy changes were obviously needed to allow the project to reach its full potential: (1) the establishment of a price stabilization policy for the region's most important crop, wheat; and (2) the implementation of effective tenancy laws that would protect many potential credit and input takers from eviction or exploitation. By late 1973 it was clear that neither policy was likely to be forthcoming in the near term.

Credit and input sales tended to lag one year behind shifts in wheat prices.[91] Therefore, project officials hoped for a turn around in project participation when wheat prices began to rise in 1973. Indeed, some CADU officers believed the 1973-74 agricultural season would undermine the land tenure-tenancy thesis and establish that local participation in project activities was primarily determined by wheat prices and farmer perceptions of improved seed-fertilizer package yields. Initial support for their view emerged in 1973-74 when rising prices and a more aggressive extension effort appeared to correlate with the dramatic increase in the number of loans to 25,205 and the rise of fertilizer sales by some 60 percent to 70,604 quintals.[92] However, the emergence of peasant mobilization and rural unrest in 1974 introduced new and confounding factors that made testing of this thesis impossible.

Just prior to the revolution there was some discussion about having the Social Development Section work with the Marketing Division to promote savings mobilization. Based on initial consumption studies, it was argued that rising incomes generated by the project created the potential for promoting savings through the provision of safe local banking services.[93] The object was a project run system that would undermine the money lender and stimulate savings for future productive farm investment. Initial proposals were to offer a modest interest as an incentive and eventually create a non-profit cooperative bank for small-scale savers. However, concrete steps in this direction were not taken because of the revolution.

The Marketing Division also experimented with cooperative formation in the early 1970s. Discussion of these efforts will be made in Chapter 5.

v. Supporting Development Services

The CADU project promoted water development, forestry and soil conservation, road construction, and improved health for Chilalo's inhabitants.

The development of water resources for human and livestock consumption was given high priority. The objective was to promote long range improvements in human health and increased dairy production. Towards this end experts undertook comprehensive surveys of surface and ground water resources, recorded run-off flows and siltation patterns, investigated irrigation potential of area rivers, carried out detailed studies of well drilling costs and results, and tested such community water supply systems as earthen dams, ponds, and bore wells with hand driven pumps.[94] As a result of this accumulating evidence, CADU was able to produce comprehensive master water plans in 1970 and 1973.[95] Importantly, these plans were to be implemented by Chilalo inhabitants rather than by CADU, whose role in water development was to organize community self-help activities, oversee local cost contributions, aid in long term financial loans, make available detailed plans, and provide technical services where required. Overall, this was a successful activity, the only criticism of it being that perhaps the *awraja* had been overstudied and that drinking water was in such short supply that community systems probably should have been promoted concurrently with the Section's extensive investigations.[96]

In response to such criticisms, the Section spent the last few prerevolution years experimenting with earth dams and water pumps that could improve community water supplies. Some 75 wells were drilled but their cost precluded adoption of the technology by communities, much less households. Forestry resource activities were centered on solving deforestation and soil erosion problems and trying to inventory forest resources, formulate plans for their management, offer programs for better forest resource utilization, and develop nurseries for introducing improved tree varieties to farmers.[97] The Forestry Section succeeded by 1973 in planting over 100 species of trees throughout the region, identifying with reasonable precision which eucalyptus species were suitable for various sites, developing successful nursery and planting techniques, distributing thousands of potted seedlings to local farmers chosen to plant quarter hectare forestry demonstration plots, reafforesting several hundred hectares of government land, and testing the potential for local saw mill operations.[98] However, the Section had great difficulty protecting the government forest at Munessa.

There, under project plans, CADU's forestry unit was to have jurisdiction over the forest, preventing excisions by timber cutters or squatters, settling boundary problems, and promoting industrial development of the resource through conservation practices, afforestation, and selective timbering. However, CADU staff received little support from local officials and judges in its efforts to carry out these tasks, largely because of the interests of provincial elites in opening up these valuable timber lands for private exploitation. This lack of government cooperation created a serious question for the 1974 evaluation team, which while recognizing the threat of deforestation in Chilalo and the potential of a managed forest for creating needed jobs, felt the activities of the project in Munessa were probably beyond its jurisdiction (as well as too costly for the project budget) and should be transferred to the State Forest Development Authority – even if it were not fully capable of carrying out the task.[99]

CADU was actively involved in improving the health of Chilalo's inhabitants.[100] At the time of the project's inception the purpose of health activities was to determine how health and nutritional factors limited economic growth, as well as to relate increased population growth to rural problems and experiment with possibilities of introducing family planning. As a result of this undertaking, CADU was able to contribute to the basis of knowledge on rural health. This stimulated the government to strengthen provincial health services and strengthen nutritional and family-planning components in household extension programs.

In the early stages of the project CADU ran several health clinics and satellite health stations. However, this led to conflict with provincial health officers. So in 1970 CADU phased out of health activities and turned over those health services it was performing to a separate Arussi health program under the control of the Ministry of Public Health. SIDA supported this program through a separate funding arrangement. CADU's road construction program began with the initial objective of expanding the area's local road network to connect major marketing centers.[101] Initial studies proposed the building of five stretches of road totalling 154 kilometers.[102] Project success in its credit lending and input supply activities led to expanded efforts in 1971 to construct or maintain up to 330 kilometers of feeder roads. Substantial progress was made toward these goals despite problems in obtaining spare parts for equipment and difficulties recruiting and retaining a Swedish engineer and trained heavy equipment operators.

The Road Section's major achievement was the construction of 46.5 kilometers of gravelled road between Bilalo and the Bekoji road.[103] That road was built with capital intensive methods. Although its E$ 20,000/km cost was reasonable, growing tenant evictions forced the Road Section in 1972 to add the additional objectives of creating alternative employment opportunities and developing techniques for low cost, labor intensive road construction. This led to the employment of 250-350 laborers by late 1973. Overall, the Road Section's 1973 capacity for construction and repair was approximately 50 km per year. However, this was not viewed as adequate by the 1974 project review which recommended the Section expand its activities by opening up more dry weather roads and improving existing ones so that the effectiveness of extension and marketing agents could be enhanced.[104]

CADU's experience established the importance of transport and infrastructure to the success of a large integrated rural development project. One study clearly documented this by finding that 1972 transport charges ran from E$ 2.40 per ton/km in areas where only animal and human porterage was available, to E$ 0.10 per ton/km between points connected by all weather roads and assured backhaul loads.[105] By building roads, CADU made it easier to disseminate project innovations, to efficiently transport inputs and the increased market surpluses resulting from them, and to lower marketing margins by reducing the costs of transport and handling by intermediary markets. But as demonstrated in Chapter 5, roads increased the penetration of tractors and harvesters, leading to evictions in areas of land concentration and tenancy.

CADU's Common Services Department and the auditing and legal units under the Project Director demonstrated that a well established internal administrative system can be set up in a large integrated rural development project in a relatively short period of time. This Department effectively controlled the use of all funds and project property, prepared and monitored project unit budgets, assisted units to draft annual work plans, maintained records and accounts, purchased and cleared imported project goods, and managed the personnel system.[106] Aside from expected legal services on contracts and general questions, the Legal Unit brought cases against credit defaulters and towards 1972 began trying to protect tenants from eviction.

Perhaps the major achievements of the administrative cadre were: (1) the 1972 job description, evaluation, and salary scale system; (2) the efficiency with which the Equipment and Stores Section managed and maintained over 100 vehicles running up nearly two million kilometers in 1973; and (3) the Building Section, organizationally located in the Infrastructure Department, which contributed greatly to the good living conditions and high morale of project staff through the construction of residential houses, staff and extension offices, and marketing and seed stores.[107]

Finally, a summary of the activities of the Planning and Evaluation Section is essential, for its work product included a unique body of knowledge that was instrumental in giving flexibility to CADU strategies and activities and contributing to the development of national policies and programs. Importantly, the changing focus of the Section over the 1967-73 period contributes to understanding of a monitoring and evaluation unit in a comprehensive project. The initial objectives of the Section were to monitor and evaluate activities outlined in the project's annual work programs, as well as to undertake general surveys and case studies. Given CADU's wide ranging activities and the manpower resources of the Section, these objectives proved overly ambitious. They also appeared less relevant than other kinds of evaluative work. Hence, a more realistic set of objectives was formulated in 1970 after a review of the unit's work product and problems.[108]

It led to less singular unit reviews and increased study of aggregate project impact, generating a more useful management information system. This was achieved through the preparation of progress reports linked to established CADU goals, the measurement of project impact based on key selected indicators, the carrying out of special studies related to identified problems or policy issues, and the establishment of a data bank on the project area and CADU activities. Examples of such studies include the evaluation of agricultural extension methods and results, studies of employment effects on consumption changes, and analyses of cost-benefit impact.

More than 100 general reports and special studies were produced and distributed in CADU's distinctive monograph format.[109] Most studies were focused on technical agriculture and economic issues closely linked to project activities. Several, such as the studies on mechanization and credit, contributed to project policy formulation and expanded general understanding of important development questions in Chilalo and Ethiopia generally. Because of political sensitivities most studies glossed over the task environment's substantial constraints, and those that did not, such as the 1972 mechanization study, were produced in limited numbers and given restricted circulation.[110] Local cultural, social, and political structures and behavioral patterns were particularly understudied. Certainly there is little mention in these reports of the kinds of issues addressed in Chapter 5. But issues glossed over were, as shown elsewhere, actively discussed at CADU and in Addis Ababa.

By 1973 the Section was too understaffed to meet the emerging research, reporting, and monitoring functions it had pioneered.[111] A number of very important studies thus were not undertaken.[112] Still, the Section's successes are sufficient to demonstrate the importance of having such a unit in a large-scale project, and designers of integrated rural development projects would be well served by reviewing the organization and activities of this section, particularly the revised evaluation program of April 1972, which emphasized management information for steering purposes and aggregate evaluation of project activities.

Notes

1. Bengt Nekby, *CADU: An Ethiopian Experiment in Developing Peasant Farming* (Stockholm: Prisma Publishers, 1971), pp. 7-8.
2. Because Swedish critics of CADU asked why should a socialist country aid a reactionary semi-feudal one, it is useful to review: V. Halldin Norberg, *Swedes in Haile Selassie's Ethiopia, 1924-1952: A Study in Early Development Cooperation* (Uppsala: Scandinavian Institute of African Studies, 1977). See also: Seleshi Sisaye, "Swedish Development Aid Policy: A Discussion with Reference to Ethiopia," *Public Administration and Development,* II (1982), pp. 147-67; and his "Swedish Aid to Ethiopia, 1954-67," *Journal of African Studies,* VIII, 2 (1981), pp. 85-90.
3. Tesfai Tecle, *The Evolution of Alternative Rural Development Strategies in Ethiopia: Implications for Employment and Income Distribution* (East Lansing: Michigan State University, African Rural Employment Paper No. 12, 1975), pp. 6-7.
4. Nekby, *CADU*, pp. 9-10. This was a tactical error given the project's second major goal of increasing local participation. Writes Betru Grebregziabher: "No Ethiopian directly participated in the actual field investigation or in the technical aspects of project design, although the plan was reviewed by government bureaucrats." Betru Gebregziabher, *Integrated Rural Development in Rural Ethiopia: An Evaluative Study of the Chilalo Agricultural Development Unit* (Bloomington: University of Indiana, International Development Research Center, 1975), p. 17. The mission was dominated by Swedish academics from the University of Agriculture at Uppsala. On the mission see: Thomas Bergendal, "Ethio-Swedish Regional Development Project: Program No. 7, 1966" (Internal Memorandum, Stockholm, May 18, 1966).
5. Swedish International Development Agency, *Report No. I on the Establishment of Regional Development Project in Ethiopia* (Addis Ababa: SIDA, Project Preparation Team, 1966), p. 128.
6. Nekby, *CADU*, pp. 8-9.
7. SIDA, *Report No. 1.*
8. Michael Ståhl, *Ethiopia: Political Contradictions in Agricultural Development* (Stockholm: Liber Tryck, 1974), p. 96.
9. Planned budget and finance shares for the project's first phase are set forth in Swedish International Development Authority, *Plans of Operation for the Chilalo Agricultural Development Unit (CADU) 1971-1974/75* (Addis Ababa: SIDA, 1971). In brief, Sweden paid 67 percent of investment and operating costs as well as Swedish staff salaries, special studies, and staff scholarships. Ethiopia covered the cost of land needed

by the project, major roads, and salaries of Ethiopian personnel. The budget for the first contract period was E$ 15.7 million, of which E$ 1.4 million for roads was not utilized and was to be spent in the second contract period. The costs of the 5 year second contract period were estimated to run about E$ 27.5 million. The overall project estimated a 13 year period of expenditures amounting to E$ 50,700,000. The E$ 37 million figure is for the first seven years of operation. SIDA and government funds were deposited twice a year into a special account controlled by the project director, the Swedes waiting until the Ethiopian contribution was paid.

10. Members included the Ministers of Finance, Planning, Land Reform and Administration, Community Development and Social Affairs, a representative of the Prime Minister's office, and the Governor of Arussi Province. Betru Gebregziabher, *Integrated Rural Development*, p. 27.
11. The operation of these ministries and agencies during the 1960s and early 1970s is described in: John M. Cohen and Peter H. Koehn, *Ethiopian Provincial and Municipal Government: Imperial Patterns and Post-revolutionary Changes* (East Lansing: Michigan State University, African Studies Center, 1980), pp. 214-75.
12. Betru Gebregziabher, *Integrated Rural Development*, pp. 30-6.
13. EPID and the MPP are briefly described in Chapter 5.
14. SIDA, *Report No. I*, p. 189. In regard to these goals, the report stated: "...it must be underlined that the project not only aims at an increased production. This could probably be achieved most easily through large-scale farming and big industrial ventures often under foreign management. The most important aspect of this project is, however, to develop the ability of local people to deal with their own problems and to completely lead the progress of their society."
15. Nekby, *CADU*, p. 47.
16. CADU, *CADU Annual Report 1970/71* (Addis Ababa: CADU, Publication No. 65, 1971), pp. 1-2. Note the Ethiopian budget year runs from July 8 to July 7. This is what is meant, for example, by such notations as 1970-71 or 1971-72, which appear throughout this study.
17. That "social development" could have been specified is illustrated by the lengthy operationalization of CADU's "participation" objective in: John M. Cohen and Norman T. Uphoff, *Rural Development Participation: Concepts and Measures for Project Design, Implementation and Evaluation* (Ithaca: Cornell University, Rural Development Monograph No. 2, 1977), pp. 176-302.
18. This organization chart is from: CADU, *Annual Report 1970/71* , p. iv. The description of the goals and various organizational units which follows is taken from *Ibid.*, pp. 8-55.
19. This organization chart is from: *Ibid.*, p. iii.
20. The description which follows is taken from: CADU, *CADU Annual Reports 1971/72 & 1972/73* (Asella: CADU, Publication No. 77, n.d.), pp. 2-58.
21. This Department was reorganized subsequently into three Development District Sections (Asella, Bekoji and Kofele), a Training Center Section, and an Information and Public Relations Section. But the functions remained the same as described above. See the organization chart in: CADU, *Annual Reports 1971/72 & 1972/73*, p. ix.
22. Betru Gebregziabher, *Integrated Rural Development*, p. 41.
23. Richard O. Niehoff and Bernard D. Wilder, *Non-Formal Education for Ethiopia* (East Lansing: Michigan State University, Institute for International Studies on Education, 1974), p. 258.
24. Betru Gebregziabher, *Integrated Rural Development*, p. 44. Ato Paulos is an example of the caliber of Ethiopian civil servant CADU attracted and the role the project played in helping advance professional skills. Born in 1940 in Asmara, he completed his

batchelor's degree in economics at Addis Ababa's University College. In addition, he received advanced training at Manchester University in the U.K. and Williams College in the U.S.A. Aside from service with CADU, he worked for the Ministry of Finance, the Development Bank and the World Bank. During the Michael Imru government of 1974 he served as Minister of Public Works and Housing. After leaving Ethiopia he took up a position with the World Bank in Washington, D.C.

25. These groups were formed to deal with such topics as management of personnel, transport, credit, research, appropriate technology, livestock, and road building.
26. Hunter, et al., *Final Report on the Appraisal of CADU and EPID* (Report by the Evaluation Team appointed by the Imperial Ethiopian Government and the Swedish International Development Authority, Asella, May 1974), p. 26.
27. These zones were established in 1968. Their boundaries were slightly changed in 1969 when the zones were renamed as development districts. See Figure 2.
28. Background marketing studies by CADU include: Lars Leander, *Grain Marketing Experiment in Arussi* (Addis Ababa: SIDA, Project Preparation Report No. 11, 1967); *Lars Leander, Feasibility Study on Local Roads and Market Places in Chilalo Awraja* (Addis Ababa: CADU, Report No. 33, 1969); Mehari Tesfai, *Feasibility Study on the Establishment of a Rural General Store in Kentere* (Asella: CADU, Report No. 72, 1971); Lars Haglund, *The Grain Marketing System of Chilalo* (Asella: CADU, Minor Research Study No. 12, 1974).
29. Studies in Chilalo and nearby Ada *Awraja* are described in: Gene Ellis, "Cheating by Grain Traders in Ethiopia," *Northeast African Studies*, IV, 1 (1982), pp. 27-32.
30. Average local market wheat prices per quintal were: 1957/67 E$ 20.60; 1967/8 E$ 23.20; 1968/9 E$ 24.30; 1969/70 E$ 32.30; 1970/71 E$ 28.10. From late 1971 to mid-1973 there was a drop to E$ 22.00-E$ 20.00. Prices began to rise significantly by early 1974. Hunter, et al., *Final Report*, p. 11.
31. CADU was buying other crops as well. For example, in 1971/72 the project purchased 1,068 quintals of peas, 904 quintals of rape seed, and 1,900 quintals of maize.
32. The following is based on analysis in: Tesfai Tecle, *Evolution of Rural Strategies*, pp. 22-23.
33. In 1972 CADU bought wheat at E$ 0.50 to E$ 1.50 per quintal higher than local prices. On average it paid E$ 23.50 per quintal and sold it for $E 27.50. CADU, *Annual Report 1970/71*, p. 46.
34. Price setting procedures began with a market survey and price forecast for the coming year by the Planning and Evaluation Section. The Board of the Marketing Section then set the price. In the 1971/72 season, it was decided to pay farmers the difference between the peak price (less a margin for risk) and the anticipated cost per unit to the Division. This generated a price expected to be above that of local merchants. *Ibid.*
35. In 1971/72 the Marketing Division lost E$ 576,599. This was reduced to E$ 74,000 in 1972/73. Hunter et al., *Final Report*, p. 25.
36. Tesfai Tecle, *Evolution of Rural Strategies*, p. 42.
37. CADU designers borrowed the "model farmer" approach from the Comilla Project. Akhter Hameed Khan, the first director of Comilla, noted many differences between the model farmer strategy in both projects during an April 1975 visit to CADU. For example, CADU had no weekly training meetings for model farmers as was the case at Comilla. *Ibid.*, fn. 12, p. 14.
38. Only two studies shed light on this question. One 1972 study found 25% of model farmers in the Iteya region to be tenants. The second in 1970 found some model farmers selected in 1968 had expanded their holdings by as much as three times, ceasing to be average farmers for their areas. Göran Bergman, *Training of Model Farmers (Baseline Study)* (Asella: CADU, Report No. 60, 1970), pp. 12-13.

39. CADU publications on model farmers include: Göran Nyberg, *Training of Model Farmers (Baseline Study)* (Asella: CADU, Report No. 31, 1969); Bergman, *Training of Model Farmers* ; Susanne Bergholtz, *Farm Management Studies of Model Farmers in the CADU Project Area* (Asella: CADU, Minor Research Tasks Report No. 1, 1969).
40. CADU, Extension and Education Department, *Descriptions of Agricultural Demonstrations* (Asella: CADU, Report No. 16, 1968) and its *Results of Demonstrations* 1968 (Asella: CADU, Report No. 24, 1969).
41. Only one CADU study looked at the reasons why various types of participants enlist in programs or adopt new innovations. Interestingly, it was done by a Swedish student and considered rather off-beat by the CADU staff. This study was a typical diffusion of innovation inquiry and it brought some useful data to those making project strategy. It studied some background characteristics of participants and non-participants and contained some generalized opinions as to how individuals came to participate. Johan Toborn, *The Innovation-Diffusion Process* (Asella: CADU, Special Study No. 3, 1971).
42. CADU, *1970 Project Description* (Asella: CADU, 1970), p. 7; CADU, *Annual Report 1970/71*, p. 2.
43. Hunter, et al., *Final Report*, p. 9.
44. CADU, *Annual Report 1970-71*, pp. 2-4.
45. Tesfai Tecle, *Evolution of Rural Strategies*, pp. 82-3; Hunter, et al., *Final Report*, p. 54.
46. Indeed, actual studies came later: CADU, Planning and Evaluation Unit, *Case Study on Farm Households in the Asella Area* (Asella: CADU, Publication No. 78, 1972); Pia Bergman, *Decision Making in the Family* (Asella: CADU, Special Study No. 2, 1971).
47. Initial staff was composed of three Ethiopians with high school degrees, a Swedish home demonstration agent and an FAO adviser. Extension Agents typically had an 8th to 11th grade education. They were given a course of 6 and one-half months and three week refresher courses each year. The content induced substantive materials to focus on practical training in household activites. Provided with a kit of kitchen equipment and gardening tools, agents were changed with promoting four groups of 15-20 women in each of 6 villages. Niehoff and Wilder, *Non-Formal Education in Ethiopia*, pp. 254-5.
48. Solomon Bekure, et al., *Evaluation of the Arssi Regional Development Unit (ARDU) June-July 1981* (Uppsala: International Rural Development Center, Swedish University of Agricultural Sciences, September 1981), p. IV-2.
49. The only available studies are: CADU, Planning and Evaluation Section, *Women's Extension* (Asella: CADU, Publication No. 58, 1970); Hanna Kebede, *Home Economics Extension Study* (Asella: CADU, Publication No. 107, 1974). See also, Solomon Bekure, et al., *Evaluation*, pp. IV, 2-4.
50. Betru Gebregziabher, *Integrated Rural Development*, p. 53.
51. The 1974 evaluation report expressly noted 409 agents were trained for CADU and EPID. These were broken down for CADU as 94 assistant marketing agents, 74 assistant extension agents, and 34 home economics agents. Hunter, et al., *Final Report*, p. 13. During 1971/72 the Training Section reported running a six month course for 32 assistant extension agents, 22 assistant marketing foremen, 22 women's extension agents, and 6 cooperative agents; a two month course for 30 marketing foremen; short courses for 50 model farmers from new extension areas; and a variety of short inservice courses. CADU, *Annual Reports 1971/72 & 1972/73*, p. 23.
52. Hunter, et al., *Final Report*, p. 14. Betru Gebregziabher, who served in the Information Unit describes a different program of 6 months initial training, including two

months practical work on CADU's 20 hectare demonstration farm, one year of supervised field experience, and a four month refresher course aimed at synthesizing theory and field experiences. *Integrated Rural Development*, p. 40.

53. Useful background papers produced by CADU include: Bo Bengtsson, *Cultivation Practices and the Weed, Pest and Disease Situation in Some Parts of the Chilalo Awraja* (Asella: CADU, Publication No. 10, 1968); Planning and Evaluation Section, *A Case Study of Peasant Farming in Dighelu and Yeloma Areas, Chilalo Awraja, Ethiopia* (Asella: CADU, Publication No. 22, 1969). CADU produced numerous reports on the results of soil inventories, agrobotanical investigations, pasture studies, variety and fertilizer trials, observation and demonstration plot surveys, plant protection studies, crop sampling surveys, and general agricultural surveys. Many of these are usefully summed up in Harald Linder, *Crop Protection Improvement: Activities in Chilalo Agricultural Development Unit in Ethiopia, 1966-1970* (Uppsala: Swedish University of Agriculture, Forestry and Veterinary Medicine, Rural Development Study No. 5, 1976).
54. These are: (1) Rift Valley slope on altitude of 1500-2000 meters with annual rainfall of 692 mm. and silty, loam grey clay soil, good drainage capacity but grave erosion; (2) Iteya-Kulumsa terrace on altitude 2000-2250 meters with annual rainfall of 877 mm. and black clay soil, good drainage capacity, erosion tendency, and rich to poor phosphorus; (3) Chilalo Mountain slope on altitude of 2250-2500 meters with annual rainfall of 1,481 mm. and reddish to dark clay soil, poor drainage capacity, some erosion tendency, and poor phosphorus content; and (4) Sagure-Kofele area on altitude of 2400-2700 with annual rainfall unrecorded and dark clay soil, poor drainage capacity, and poor phosphorus content. As for natural vegetation and crops by zones: (1) acacia savanna grassland, maize 40%, barley 28%, Teff 15%, wheat 12%, (2) grassland with scattered acacia, wheat 49%, barley 26%; (3) grassland with some forest, wheat 49%, barley 26%; and (4) grassland and some woodland, barley 59%, wheat 18%.
55. For example, in the extension areas of Asella North, Gonde, Iteya, and Huruta, total cultivated area under wheat increased from 36% in 1968 to 49% in 1970, while the percent of farmers growing wheat increased from 72% in 1968 to 92% in 1970. Importantly, landowners with less than 20 hectares and tenants with less than 30 hectares derived 76% of their cash incomes from wheat sales. Yields in the area increased from a 1968 average of 9.8 quintals per hectare to 19.2. See CADU publications No. 78 (p. 33); 64 (p. 32); 77 (p. 8), 14 (pp. 19-20), and 71 (pp. 23-4).
56. Hunter, et al., *Final Report*, pp. 17-18.
57. This was said to be true of research results with wheat, pasture and fodder crops, and upgraded dairy stock. *Ibid.*, p. 17.
58. CADU, *Annual Reports 1971/72 & 1972/73*, pp. 54-6.
59. In 1971 the Seed Division reported total net revenues of E$ 332,955 against aggregate costs of E$ 255,2765. *Ibid.*, p. 55.
60. Among the most useful CADU publications on livestock activities are: CADU, Planning and Evaluation Section, *Feasibility Study on a Farm for Breeding of Grade Cattle at Gobe, Arussi Province* (Asella: CADU, Publication No. 18, 1968); CADU Research and Livestock Section, *Animals Husbandry Activities 1968/69* (Asella: CADU, Publication No. 56, 1970); C. Tillaeus and P. O. Nilsson, *CADU Veterinary Service, A Summary of Experiences* (Asella: CADU, Publication No. 101, 1974); Sven Persson, *Animal Husbandry Activities 1970-1973* (Asella: CADU, Publication No. 102, 1974).
61. CADU, *Annual Reports 1971/72 & 1972/73*, pp. 57-8.
62. Hunter, et al., *Final Report*, p. 18.

63. *Ibid.*
64. Solomon Bekure, et al., *Evaluation*, p. VI, 2.
65. CADU, *Annual Reports 1971/72 & 1972/73*, pp. 16-18.
66. Experiments were done on fodder beets, Rhodes grass, Coloured Guinea, and Nandi Setaria, and legumes such as Desmodium Uncinatum and alfalfa.
67. The program is described in CADU's annual reports, the Agricultural Engineering Section's progress reports of 1969, 1970, and 1971, and its *Progress Report No. IV, 1971/72-1972/73* (Asella: CADU Publication No. 96, 1974).
68. The 1974 evaluation team noted that: "Since the traditional plow is effective on steep slopes, stony land and heavy wet soils, some effort should be made to improve it." Hunter, et al., *Final Report*, p. 18.
69. The production-sales problem is demonstrated by 1971/72 figures. In total 1,300 harrows were produced and 333 were delivered to CADU's Marketing Division. CADU, *Annual Reports 1971/72 & 1972/73*, p. 11. But only 139 harrows were sold in 1971/72 and 145 in 1972/73. Hunter, et al., *Final Report*, p. 17.
70. Tesfai Tecle, *Evolution of Rural Strategies*, pp. 11-12.
71. Local lending interest rates could go as high as 100 percent, with rates as high as 400 percent recorded, see: Göran Bergman and Håkan Lindquist, *Credit Situation in Chilalo Awraja* (Asella: Chilalo Agricultural Development Unit, Minor Research Task, No. 2, 1969).
72. In 1971/72 CADU received funds to support input purchases through the Agricultural Inputs and Marketing Services, a subsidiary of the Agro-Industrial Development Bank (AIDB). AIDB was set up in 1970 to provide credit for large and small-scale farms. In 1971/72 interest charged CADU rose from 8 to 10 percent. CADU continued to maintain a lending rate of 12 percent using the margin to cover the cost of credit supervision and administration. Tesfai Tecle argues that in reality the actual interest that farmers needed to pay for CADU to break even was much higher. His calculations suggest that in 1974 CADU's distribution fee, actual interest rate, and bad debts required an interest rate of 25 percent to break even. *Evolution of Rural Strategies* , fn. 13, p. 18.
73. The basic source on credit in Chilalo are: Henock Kifle, *An Analysis of the CADU Credit Program 1968/69-1970/71 and Its Impact on Income Distribution* (Asella: CADU, Publication No. 92, 1974).
74. Owners with less than 5 hectares and tenants with less than 8 hectares had to provide a down payment of 25% on fertilizer and 50% on seeds. All other tenants and farmers had to cover 50% of these inputs.
75. The basic credit process was as follows: Farmer indicates need, agent visits farm, decides if it is suitable, prepares farm plan and loan application with farmer, and then recommends credit: Commerce and Industry Department considers loan and reaches decision with aid of Executive Director: If approved, loan agreement between farmer and project is signed at trade center: A borrower's file and account are opened: Down payment is collected at trade center: Delivery order for inputs is issued by Commerce and Industry Department section to trade center foreman who supplies them: Crop is delivered and repayment of credit is made, with continual supervision by agent at farm throughout interim period. The average loan ran between E$ 120 and E$ 200.
76. Hunter, et al., *Final Report*, p. 53.
77. *Ibid.*, pp. 23-4.
78. A 1972 consumption study supported this recommendation by suggesting farmers in the project area had an increasing capacity and propensity to save. Johan Holmberg, *Survey of Consumption Patterns in Etheya Extension Area* (Asella: CADU, Publication No. 90, 1973).

79. CADU, *Annual Reports 1971/72 & 1972/73*, p. vii.
80. These are summarized in: Hunter, et al., *Final Report*, p. 12.
81. Tesfai Tecle, *Evolution of Rural Strategies*, p. 15.
82. Exclusion of large landowners from credit early in the program gave them no reason not to default. This led to the high default rate of 10 percent for the 1968/69 fiscal year. Otherwise, as Table 4 demonstrates, repayment rates have always been 90 percent or higher, a figure court collections might have improved upon. Henock Kifle, *Analysis of CADU Credit*; Beyene, *Analysis of CADU Credit.*
83. 1974 evaluation report found this practice inequitable. Recommending that group punishment be discontinued, the report noted "borrowers are not conscious of being a 'group' in any real sense with mutual obligations. Default by a few larger borrowers can penalize smaller men who have honestly repaid." Hunter, et al., *Final Report*, p. 23.
84. In 1971/72 a computerized data processing system was contracted out to the Addis Ababa based Bouroughs Company. But the system initially worked far below expectation and merits review in the difficulties of using computers.
85. Hunter, et al., *Final Report*, p. 10.
86. *Ibid.*, pp. 12-13.
87. CADU, *Annual Reports 1971/72 & 1972/73*, p. 48.
88. The government review of the 1973-74 fertilizer crisis is set forth in: Ministry of Agriculture, "Memorandum for Minister of Agriculture on the Pricing of Fertilizers to be Sold by the Package Program in 1974" (Internal Memorandum, EPID, December 10, 1973).
89. Among the problems identified were: (1) slow progress in promoting other crops which compete favorably with wheat, such as maize, haricot beans, and teff; (2) problems convincing farmers of the importance of clean, certified seed; (3) difficulties getting farmers to adopt improved husbandry practices, such as crop rotation and weed control; (4) failure to teach farmers how to calculate benefits of improved inputs; and (5) lack of experimentation with extension techniques to address such problems. Hunter, et al., *Final Report*, p. 10.
90. *Ibid.*, p. 13.
91. Tesfai Tecle, *Evolution of Rural Strategies*, p. 15.
92. *Ibid.*, p. 15.
93. Johan Holmberg, *The Credit Programme of the Chilalo Agricultural Development Unit (CADU) in Ethiopia* (Washington, D.C.: USAID Spring Review of Small Farm Credit, Vol. VIII, 1973), pp. 57, 80.
94. Among the helpful water studies produced by CADU are: Carl-Gösta Wenner, *Reconnointering Survey of Water Resources in Chilalo Awraja* (Addis Ababa: SIDA, Project Preparation Report No. 4, 1967); Olle Schonbeck, *Trials With Experimental Household Wells* (Asella: CADU Publication No. 85, 1973). For details of the Section's activities in the early 1970s see: CADU, *Annual Reports, 1971/72 & 1972/73*, pp. 31-5.
95. Carl-Gösta Wenner, *A Master Plan for Water Resources and Supplies within CADU's First Project Area* (Asella: CADU, Publication No. 53, 1970); Carl-Gösta Wenner, *A Master Plan for Water Resources and Supplies in the Chilalo Awraja* (Asella: CADU, Publication No. 89, 1973).
96. Hunter, et al., *Final Report*, p. 19.
97. The forestry program produced a number of studies, the most significant of which are: Gunnar Poulsen, *Creation of a Forestry Administration in Arussi Province* (Addis Ababa: SIDA, Project Preparation Report No. 5, 1967); Gunnar Poulsen, *CADU Forestry Activities* (Asella: CADU, Publication No. 84, 1973); Johan Holmberg,

Feasibility Study on the Utilization of the Munessa Forest (Asella: CADU, Publication No. 86, 1973). Useful conservation studies produced by CADU staff include: Gunnar Poulsen, *Some Reflections of Water Erosion in Chilalo Awraja* (Asella: CADU, Publication No. 2, 1969); Kebede Tato, *A Preliminary Survey of Soil Erosion in the Chilalo Awraja* (Asella: CADU, Special Study No. 1, 1976).

98. The section's activities were last described prior to the revolution in: CADU, *Annual Reports 1971/72 & 1972/73*, pp. 12-15.

99. Hunter, et al., *Final Report*, pp. 27-8.

100. On health activities see the CADU annual reports and such studies as: Göran Nyberg, *Health Education (Base-line Study)* (Asella: CADU, Publication No. 29, 1969); Stig Lundin, *Survey of Health Facilities of Arussi: 1969-1970* (Asella: CADU Publication No. 57, 1970); Gunnar Arhammar, *Report on a Combined Food and Health Survey on Yeloma Farming District (Asella*: CADU, Publication No. 41, 1969); Stig Lundin, *Sanitation Survey of Bekoji* (Asella: CADU, Publication No. 61, 1970); Stig Lundin, *Family Guidance in the CADU Programme 1970* (Asella: CADU, Publication No. 62, 1971); Gunnar Arhammar, *Assessment of Status of Health in an Ethiopian Rural Community (Experience of Two Years' Public Health Work in Chilalo Awraja)*, Arussi (Asella: CADU, Publication No. 69, 1970); Stig Lundin, *CADU Health Programme, Report of the Period 71-73* (Asella: CADU Publication No. 93, 1974); Stig Lundin, *The Consumption of Household Water in Sagure: An Appraisal of Five Years Work on Water Sanitation* (Asella: CADU, Publication No. 98, 1974).

101. The basic CADU study, aside from annual work plans and reports, is: Leander, *Feasibility Study on Local Roads.*

102. These plans called for the expenditure of E$ 4.2 million on roads between Asella and Kersa, Iteya and Huruta, Sagure and Tijo, Meraro and Huruta, Sagure and Tijo, Merara, Kere and Goge, and from Gonde to Arata Mission to Zeway & Dugda *Woreda*. Leander, *Feasibility Study*, pp. 5, 53-5.

103. See also: SIDA, *Plan of Operation for the Chilalo Agricultural Development Unit (CADU) 1971-1974/5* (Addis Ababa: SIDA, 1971), p. 11.

104. Hunter, et al., *Final Report*, p. 20.

105. Tesfai Tecle, *Evolution of Rural Strategies*, p. 74.

106. For details see: CADU, *Annual Reports 1971/72 & 1972/73*, pp. 35-45.

107. For a set of photographs illustrating the quality of CADU site facilities and suggesting their importance to attracting good Swedish and Ethiopian staff, see: Nekby, *CADU*, pp. 90-9, 112-13.

108. Johan Holmberg, *Master Plan for the Evaluation of CADU* (Asella: CADU, Publication No. 81, 1972).

109. These publications are available in such major research libraries as Cornell's Mann Library or Israel's Rehovot Rural Development Center. In Ethiopia they are found at the SIDA mission headquarters and the Institute for Ethiopian Studies.

110. Henock Kifle, *Investigations on Mechanized Farming.*

111. The wide range of studies and reports the Section undertook or advised on is demonstrated by: CADU, *Annual Reports 1971/71 & 1972/73*, pp. 1-5.

112. Topics identified in the 1974 review are: (1) analysis of relative stagnation in the expansion of credit/fertilizer program, taking into account the participation of different peasant groups; (2) analysis of land tenure, traditional institutions, household expenditures and incomes; (3) research on local marketing patterns and their linkages with the national system; (4) comparative research on diffusion of innovation; and (5) studies of farm systems management. Hunter, et al., *Final Report*, p. 27.

CHAPTER 5

CADU's Economic and Social Impact Prior to the Revolution

> By encouraging a capitalist mode of production in the feudal regions, the Imperial Government has rendered new features to the age-old exploitation of the peasants. The southern highlands are being drawn into the modern, dynamic process of underdevelopment.
>
> Michael Ståhl (1974)

By 1973 it was obvious to experienced observers that after six years of CADU presence Chilalo was rapidly becoming one of the most productive farming areas in the country, small-holders and tenants participating in the project were prospering, and large-scale commercial farms were expanding. Signs of agricultural productivity, rising incomes, and economic development were everywhere: Asella had a new bank, hotel, and cinema, tin roofed farm houses were more numerous, tractors and combines were commonplace, Land Rover taxis were penetrating farther into the countryside, and local markets were handling larger volumes of trade. But it was also common knowledge in the towns that CADU's activities had brought increased tenant eviction, rising land rents and prices, and expanded government and elite's capacity to profit from benefits intended for the target population.

Moving beyond observation to a systematic analysis of CADU's successes and its harmful effects on the Chilalo region is no easy task. First, the CADU case demonstrates how difficult it is to separate an integrated rural development project's technical and administrative design from the task environment in which it is implemented. Second, evaluation of the achievements of the CADU period are clouded by the project's unintended consequences for many tenant farmers and the use of those consequences by opponents of Haile Selassie's regime to argue for economic and political reforms. Third, only limited and highly generalized data exist on the economic benefits generated by the project and the social costs that resulted.[1]

Balancing between qualitative and quantitative data, this chapter will attempt to evaluate the success of CADU in reaching its two principal objectives: (1) bringing economic benefits to its target population; and (2) increasing their participation in the development process. Given the question this case study seeks to address; namely, "is integrated rural development an appropriate intervention strategy for poverty stricken agrarian countries?," every effort will be made to separate the design and management of CADU from the difficult land tenure, provincial government, and local elite constraints that hampered its success. Even if this can be done, the review of the constraints the project faced, and the land tenure issues and green revolution questions that review raises, overshadows the important design and implementation lessons the case study offers. Indeed, the image that emerges is a negative one. Yet, despite this image, the conclusion reached at the end of this chapter and in Chapter 7 is that the CADU case establishes the utility of integrated rural development as an intervention strategy and offers valuable insights on how to design and implement such a project.

Economic Impact

The concluding section of Chapter 6, "Seventeen Years of Integrated Rural Development," demonstrates that over the 1968-85 period in general and CADU's first 6 years in particular, the project made substantial progress in achieving its objectives of verifying methods of agricultural development and raising agricultural productivity by the target population. The question addressed here is the extent to which tenants and small-holders shared in the economic growth generated by the project in the Chilalo region.

This is not an easy question to answer because the objectives of the CADU project were never operationalized with clear indicators suitable for quantification. As a result there is little systematic data on increase and distribution of benefits. Piecing together a number of monitoring and evaluation studies, project economists concluded in 1973 that the average annual income of farmers in Chilalo had increased between 50 and 100 percent.[2] This claim is supported by a study done in the original project area. It suggests that farm households adopting only improved wheat seeds increased their average annual income from approximately E$ 313 in 1966 to E$ 883 in 1971.[3] Such data led many CADU officers to argue that it was reasonable to assume that cash incomes of participating households had roughly doubled in those areas where the project had operated for several years. It was also used to conclude that by 1971, after an initial period of heavy investment, total minimum benefits from the project were approaching the gross costs of the enterprise and promised to exceed them over the next few years.[4] Assuming these conclusions are valid, by 1973 CADU had made considerable progress toward reaching its major economic objectives.

Distribution of benefits among different rural classes and types of farmers in Chilalo is more difficult to document. The only helpful data come from credit, tax, and consumption studies.

Analyzing credit figures, Tesfai Tecle concluded that distribution of benefits paralleled the distribution of credit.[5] Using data summarized in

Table 6, he argued that landowners and tenants with above average holdings accounted for larger proportions of benefits in CADU's early years, despite the fact that they comprised a smaller proportion of the target population. This pattern he attributed to the greater purchasing power of large farmers and CADU's initial policy of providing inputs on credit to all farmers regardless of the size of their holdings. By 1969 it became clear that many tenants were discouraged from obtaining inputs because of high rents based on their gross output, and all small-holders were constrained from obtaining inputs because of the project's 25 percent downpayment requirement. In response to this pattern, CADU set ceilings on those eligible to receive inputs on credit. As a result of this policy change, Tesfai found a significant difference in the distribution of benefits between eligible tenants and landowners by 1972. At the same time he noted that the incomes of large farmers were expanding at a rapid pace, largely because they were now obtaining from the private sector the package of green revolution inputs CADU had introduced in Chilalo.

Tax records support the view that farmers with large holdings benefitted disproportionately from CADU's presence. While the data reported cannot be used to generate income gains, since the assessment formulas were set just as the project began and cannot be trusted because of uneven record keeping, they can be used to give some evidence as to income gains by taxpayer-landholding size. This is done in Table 8, which suggests that while income for small and medium-scale farmers increased substantially in a four year period, incomes for large-scale farmers went up many times faster: tax collections went up three to four times for the first group and ten times for the latter. This does not mean incomes rose in these proportions, since taxes were not a fixed proportion of income, but there is a substantial enough difference that even allowing for the data's failings suggested above, it gives some idea of differential distribution of benefits generated by CADU programs.

Qualitative observations over the project's first seven years clearly support the view that the consumption by tenants, small-scale land-holders, and large farmers increased substantially. However, only one empirical study confirms such observations.[6] Undertaken in the Iteya region and based on four interviews with each of 124 farmers over a nine month period, it showed a remarkable rise in economic prosperity. Personal consumption from food to clothing and radios had increased, investment in farm production assets (such as wells, implements and buildings) was beginning, savings and investment in the local capital markets were rising, and expenditures on education and improved family health care were increasing.

Table 8: *Agricultural Income Tax Revenues In Chilalo Awraja* (E$ 1000)

Type of Taxpayer	1967/68	1968/69	1969/70	1970/71	1971/72	1972/73
Small and Middlefarmers	246	895	953	858	782	894
Large farmers	16	65	99	47	160	?
Total	262	960	1,052	905	942	-

Source: Treasury Office, Ministry of Finance in Asella. Reported in Hunter et al., *Final Report*, p. 58.

But the Iteya area was an original project area, relatively well off prior to 1967, and marked by heavy tenant eviction since then. This fact led the study's author to warn that many of Iteya's poorest farmers had disappeared and the findings on consumption by income groups could be applied to other areas of Chilalo only with great caution.[7] Still, the study found that: (1) all farmers in the area had experienced rapid and substantial income increases since 1967; (2) in absolute terms all households had raised their overall standard of living through increased purchases of food, clothing, and household goods; (3) all income groups preferred productive and educational investments to luxury goods purchases and were increasing such expenditures; and (4) while richer farmers had a significant surplus of income over expenditure at least half the farmers in the area were saving some of their increased cash earnings.

Stimulation of Local Participation

SIDA's project design called on CADU "to give the population increased awareness and responsibility for development" by ensuring their "participation" in project activities.[8] Yet, both designers and project administrators were uncertain what the objective meant or how it might be reached. To a large extent this was because the project was ahead of the development community, which did not begin to conceptualize the strategy of "rural development participation" until the early 1970s.[9] Not surprisingly, CADU professionals tended to define "participation" as a sharing in project generated benefits by the target population.

The only experiments in promoting a broader form of participation were the model farmer, cooperative formation, self-help, and farmer committee programs. These, however, were forged from above and limited in their effects by a task environment hostile to participation and by senior Swedish staff made indifferent to participation by their own technocratic biases.[10]

Those biases, strengthened by the lack of support for participation by the government and distrust of CADU mobilization efforts by local elites, led to a 1970 policy statement that "the achievement of economic development should be the ultimate goal with which the others should not be allowed to interfere."[11] The shortsightedness of this position, as well as its contradiction of initial project objectives, was quickly pointed out by the first evaluation report, which stated, "the project is not likely to contribute significantly to economic development unless the active participation of the local population is obtained."[12] Specifically disagreeing with the position of project managers, one evaluator pointedly argued that:

> ...participation is more than...merely taking advantage, as individual farmers, of the services that the project offered (but meant) the inhabitants of Chilalo should be more involved in, and eventually responsible for, the making of decisions governing events and activities beyond their own farm boundaries...[13]

These views of the evaluation team prevailed in Stockholm, in part because of growing public awareness of the irony of socialist-inclined Sweden aiding semi-feudal Ethiopia. But doing something to promote them proved extremely difficult.

One of the few concrete attempts to engage in local participation and dialogue was the *Awraja* Development Committee, which was intended to serve an information and coordination function. It met only once, on January 16, 1969, to discuss an agenda covering an introduction to CADU, marketing and credit programs, industrial and commercial possibilities, extension programs, identification of model farming activity, cooperative formation strategies, experimental land adjudication issues, rural science teaching, the Asella water system, and water and road development programs. Attending were the *awraja* governor, the mayor of Asella, the governors of *woredas* in the project area, the provincial education officer, health officer, agriculture officer, and land reform officer, the executive and assistant executive directors of CADU, representatives of farmers in each of the six extension areas, and representatives of the major area businessmen and landowners. The problem with the meeting was that its members varied considerably in terms of status and power, which inhibited discussion. The meeting was static and accomplished little. Thus as a channel for participation in implementation it was quite limited. Both sides recognized this and held no more meetings.

Senior CADU officers and middle level staff distrusted Chilalo's local government system and the men who staffed it. Their views are well summed up in a project document:

> The lower echelons of the local administration are generally of low quality and distrusted by farmers. It has, therefore, not been possible and would even have been dangerous to co-operate too closely. In connection with field days and other occasions

> this level of the administration has shown very little interest and even opposition to the development work. The relation may thus be described by the word neutrality. The efforts would...have benefitted from a more positive relation...It is thus of great importance to upgrade the local administration. Not until then would it be worthwhile to try to achieve a good co-operation through the establishment of a liaison committee for officials.[14]

Despite such cynicism, the 1971-1974/75 project plan of operation called for the establishment of a "Local Officials Committee" composed of the governors and representatives of government agencies and aimed at promoting exchange of information and promotion of coordination. It was never formed.

By 1972, as CADU staff came under increased pressure from Swedish critics of the project to build more participation into it, the idea of Farmer's Committees based on the model farmer emerged.[15] Naively, project documents expressed hope that the committees would "become forums for deliberations on local issues and development ... and the foundations for a viable and vigorous co-operative movement."[16]

The scheme aimed at setting up 600 Model Farmer Area Development Committees. The committees were to include the area's model farmer, a local government representative, the *golmassa* (a local-level representative of the people to the sub-district governor), three elders, and the area's extension agent. The committee was to be charged with increasing cooperation, coordination, and exchange of information, providing a forum for transmission of CADU's program to farmers and for feedback on the project, undertaking credit screening, and creating a nucleus for collective credit repayment responsibility. All these functions were to be performed in an advisory fashion as part of the implementation process. If they had been extensively formed, these committees would have involved 3,000 to 4,000 local people, local leaders, and government officials.

Above this level were to have been 40 Extension Area Development Committees with the same objectives. Membership on these committees was to have included an elected model farmer, an elected *golmassa*, three tenants and two landowning farmers (these seven to have been elected from their respective nominal constituencies within the extension area) plus the agricultural extension agent, the trade center foreman, the marketing supervisor, and the agricultural extension district supervisor for the extension area.

Serving the same purposes but over a wider geographic area were to have been four District (Zone) Center Development Committees, each having a representative farmer elected by the ten constituent Extension Area Committees, all *woreda* governors in that development zone, the agricultural extension supervisor, and the marketing supervisor of the district. Finally, with the same objectives and seeking to insure greater integration of development work with local administration, there was to have been a 21-member

Awraja Development Committee, composed of the *awraja* governor, the executive director of CADU, a representative of the provincial governor, a farmer representing each of the four districts, field agents of all *awraja* ministries, the head of CADU's Information Unit, and others who might be appointed from time to time. Above all this was to have been a ministerial committee aimed at coordinating CADU with other activities of the Ethiopian government.

This cumbersome scheme was never implemented as planned. As of late 1973, some 250 Model Farmer Area Development Committees were organized, but rather than being used toward the ends described, they served largely as screening bodies in the credit approval process and as an aid in collecting defaulted loans.[17] None of the higher level committees was functioning when the revolution began.

Another major channel for participation in the project and larger processes of development was the cooperative. Some CADU staff contended that cooperatives were the chief mechanism for promoting participation by the area's residents. But CADU's senior officers were hesitant to promote them because of their knowledge of failed cooperative formation in other countries and the political and social constraints that marked the CADU area. Among these were status differences between tenants and landlords, patterns of client-patron relationships, fears by provincial elites of possible mobilization of peasants through cooperatives, the hostile attitude of the Ministry of National Community Development, which protected large landowner interests while overseeing the registration of cooperatives, and high levels of illiteracy among the target population. For these reasons CADU decided to move cautiously in forming organizations that were so critical to achieving its social and participation objectives.

CADU's strategy for cooperative promotion was to build successful project-run trade centers which would at a future point be converted into primary cooperative societies. Under this plan the project's Marketing Division would eventually be transformed into a secondary union for the area's cooperatives.[18] This purported strategy was in reality a fiction which emerged when project staff realized how difficult it would be to form cooperatives and discovered that giving credit and marketing services without charge reduced interests in cooperatives, which had membership fees and other service expenses. Long range CADU projections envisioned the primary cooperatives it hoped to form administering credit applications of members, selling inputs, constructing storage facilities, collecting members' surplus production and selling it to CADU's marketing division and distributing profits to its members.

Cooperative formation was also slowed by CADU's top-down, overly complex system for cooperative establishment and operation. Promotion began with CADU staff assembling participants at trade centers on several occasions and informing them about coops and what they could do for the rural population. After such elementary instruction, farmers were encouraged to raise funds through contributing shares and to elect trustees who would undergo more intensive training courses on the economic advantages of group over individual purchases, sales and credit, and the daily management activities of cooperatives. Pre-cooperative societies were then to be formed in which the trustees participated in all the activities of the trade centers, which continued to be run by CADU. When the time was ripe, the trustees and farmer members would inherit the trade center as a cooperative. Such meetings were held in four areas and attended by an average of 200 to 300 farmers. The major obstacle CADU had to overcome in these meetings was farmer distrust of its intentions, a distrust generated by elites who argued the cooperatives were being created to squeeze profits out of rural people. Despite such concerns, CADU studies suggested farmers were interested in gaining the benefits of cooperative membership but were realistic about their lack of management skills, the real risk of big farmer domination of decisions, the cost of membership fees relative to promised benefits, and the difficulties of meeting and running cooperative activities during the rainy seasons.[19]

By 1971 there was a registered cooperative in Bilalo and three unregistered ones in Kechema, Gonde, and Sagure. Total membership at that time stood at 1,027.[20] Recognizing that more progress in creating cooperatives was needed, CADU transferred the unit responsible for their formation from the Extension to the Marketing Division in 1972 and set a goal of establishing five new cooperatives a year. But while the Bilalo society grew,[21] CADU efforts to form new ones or register the other three pre-cooperatives failed, largely because of local elite resistance and the ability of Ministry of National Community Development field staff to protect the interests of large-scale farmers and landlords against the perceived small-holder biases of CADU organizers.

This stand-off occurred because by law only one cooperative could be formed in a given area. Project studies documented that bigger farmers and landowners were more likely to join cooperatives, that they would use their status and power to control management decisions, and that peasants feared that control would lead to exclusion of small-holders, abuse of responsibility, and misappropriation of assets.[22] CADU had the power to prevent larger farmers from dominating pre-registered cooperatives formed around its trade centers. But this protection of small-holder and tenant interests ended once the cooperative was registered. Project officers were deeply concerned about local elite domination of cooperatives, a concern justified by efforts of larger commercial farmers to block the emergence of a smallholder cooperative in the Gonde area by forming one of their own.[23] Such concerns held back staff efforts to move cooperatives to the registration stage.

CADU attempted two other "participatory" innovations. First, farmers were organized by extension areas and made collectively responsible for credit defaults in their area. That is, if credit takers in their area reached a default level of 10 percent or more, the entire group of credit takers in the area would no longer be eligible for future CADU credit. The 1974 evaluation team termed this kind of participation "group punishment" and urged CADU staff to stop this practice. What inquiry was made on defaulters indicated they tended to be large-scale farmers. No information is available as to how such groups attempted to induce defaulters to repay their production loans. A second participation initiative centered on efforts to form groups of tenants who could contract with a landowner to rent a large block of land for a fixed period, thereby competing with outside businessmen seeking such land for large-scale mechanization. This group effort will be described when the chapter turns to tenant eviction issues.

One missed participatory opportunity was CADU's failure to promote savings clubs. The success of the project's seed-fertilizer package created considerable potential for the mobilization of savings, a potential confirmed by a CADU study.[24] It noted the need of small-holders for an institution where they could obtain credit for consumer goods and protect their earnings until needed. The small-scale borrowing opportunity appeared most attractive because CADU studies showed interest charged by lenders other than CADU commonly ran 10 percent per month. The credit study argued that if a fair interest rate were paid depositors, it would provide a good incentive for savings. Ideally, this could have been built into the emerging trade center activities. But no progress was made on this proposal prior to the revolution.

CADU planned to stimulate self-help efforts in improving water supplies, roads, health services, educational facilities, and housing. Yet CADU never directly studied any traditional associations that could have been the basis of self-help programs or past experience with self-help efforts in the project area.[25] Nor did it make any strong effort to stimulate a self-help movement, a failure clearly noted by the second evaluation team which in 1974 recommended: "More vigorous efforts should be made to promote...self-help activities...There should be a more positive attitude towards those traditional institutions which could be encouraged to meet development needs."[26]

Given the difficulties CADU had in using local government officials to facilitate contact with the people of Chilalo, the project relied increasingly on its Information and Public Relations Section. By 1973 it was actively informing the local population about CADU activities and promoting popular interest in development and social questions.[27] It used portable audio and video equipment as well as pamphlets in Amharic to reach rural people at markets, religious gatherings, and public meetings with messages about the project's objectives, activities, and achievements. There the unit's staff promoted local awareness of special CADU activities, such as cattle vaccination campaigns, organized meetings aimed at increasing public knowledge of major project innovations, such as the development committee program, handed out pamphlets on project innovations, represented the project at national expositions, and guided the increasing number of visitors through the project site. But most significantly, it worked hard to inform rural people about their rights under existing laws and proposed tenancy reforms, so that CADU's achievements might survive should the Swedish presence or the project end.

CONSTRAINTS ON PROJECT SUCCESS

Despite the rapid increase in participating farmers, rise in agricultural productivity, and expansion of area covered, a number of constraints prevented CADU from reaching its full potential. Indeed, these constraints caused the project to have adverse effects on some of the tenants and small-scale landowners it sought to reach. By 1973 it was clear that they could not be removed without government implementation of progressive policy, administrative, and land tenure reforms. Yet, despite six years of effort, SIDA and CADU were unable to obtain such government actions. As a result, the achievements of the project were overlooked and the negative consequences of its activities set CADU's general reputation in the development community.

The inability of the government to promulgate such reforms was closely connected to the political and economic structures on which Haile Selassie's empire rested. Substantial insight into them, as well as the constraints which held back CADU's potential and led to harmful consequences for its target population, can be gained by reviewing Chilalo's exploitive land tenure systems, the history of Ethiopia's land reform movement, and the area's inefficient, corrupt provincial government system.

i. Land Tenure System

Ethiopia's complex land tenure history and patterns are well described in other studies and need not be reviewed here.[28] Of the 1,010,000 hectares in Chilalo in 1966, around 625 to 650,000 were registered and probably arable. At the start of the CADU project, the notoriously deficient local land tax registers[29] indicated that there were 482,500 hectares of private land, 53,600 hectares of church land, and 112,000 hectares of government land, some 43,400 hectares of which were already held by grantees either in lieu of salary for a local government post or for life as a substitute for pension.[30] Sizes of holdings ranged from less than one to thousands of hectares. Large farms were quite common in the Hetosa area north of Asella, smallholdings prevailed in the middle regions, and tenancy rates were particularly high in southern *woredas*.[31]

Perhaps 150,000 hectares of land were cultivated in 1966, the rest held in pasture and woodlands. Government reports suggest that the average area cultivated per holding ranged from 2.5 to 3.0 hectares and that 45 to 55 percent of Chilalo's farmers were tenants when the CADU project began.[32] According to such official data more than 90 percent of them were share-croppers, of whom 84 percent paid one-third or more of their production to landowners, 40 percent of whom were absentees holding an estimated 40 percent of Chilalo's measured arable lands.

The SIDA design team had all these statistics on land tenure. The record shows that although they recognized the threat posed to the project by these tenancy levels, they did not appreciate fully the extent to which Ethiopia was a blocked society incapable of providing the land reforms needed to protect the target population from the negative effects of the green revolution strategy. This was so largely because the literature on Ethiopian development was poorly developed and the design team was dominated by technical specialists insensitive to the subtle variables of imperial government policies and semi-feudal rural society. But it was also due to the fact that the Swedish government wished to move the project forward without unsettling diplomatic relationships with tough questions or threatening conditions precedent. If there were any strong concerns or objections within SIDA they were tempered by the Ethiopian government's assurance that a land reform bill would be submitted to Parliament during the first contract period and implemented in the project area within two years of the project's commencement. SIDA's reliance on this assurance was to cost the project's reputation dearly.

In 1970, as the first project phase was ending and CADU was struggling with the land tenure-generated problems described later in this chapter, SIDA demanded progress in land reform before it would finance the second phase. During the negotiations that followed, the two governments gave considerable attention to this constraint. A six-month project extension was signed, but SIDA discussed the question further in Stockholm, implying that cancellation of the project was possible. Indeed, the issue was debated in the Swedish Parliament and press.[33] When the Emperor resubmitted the agricultural tenancy proclamation to his Parliament in late 1970, however, it was taken as an act of good faith, and a second agreement was signed extending the project from January 1971 to July 1975. The degree of Swedish pressure is reflected in the agreement, which boldly stated:

> Implementation of legislation on agricultural tenancy relationships shall start throughout the project area not later than one year after the promulgation of such legislation. Proposals on nation-wide legislation on cadastral survey, land registration and measures aiming at optimal utilization of land shall be submitted to Parliament not later than two years after the signature of the agreement. The CADU area shall have priority in the implementation of such legislation.[34]

Beneath this agreement was the recognition that the CADU project made Chilalo a good laboratory for developing procedures for administering and implementing difficult reforms. In fact, CADU staff proposed developing the aerial photography and topographical mapping techniques needed to produce the land use maps such legislation would require. But by 1974 no such legislation had appeared and the 1970 agreement remained unhonored.

Clearly, land tenure reform was a major political issue throughout CADU's history, as it was for most donors during the last few years of Haile Selassie's reign.[35] A review of the land reform movement reveals why they had so little influence. Briefly, arguments for land tenure reform had been made in Ethiopia's political circles since the 1920s, but it took the abortive *coup d'état* attempt of 1960 to stimulate government awareness of the need to consider the land question more carefully. By 1961 a Committee on land reform had been established and in 1962 the Second Five Year Plan outlined a land policy aimed at improving landlord-tenant relations, instituting progressive land taxation, abolishing out-of-date holdings and undertaking cadastral surveys and land registration.[36] The Committee also initiated a number of studies and policy formulations that opened the land reform process to foreign involvement and created channels for frustrated Ethiopian and Swedish officials of CADU to carry the emerging Chilalo experience to friendly, progressive government technicians and officers.[37]

In 1964 tenant protection legislation was presented to Parliament but rejected in both houses.[38] However, it brought the issues of land reform to the larger community through demonstrations by progressive MPs and students before Parliament in 1965 during the discussion of the bill. Despite this setback, the government established a Ministry of Land Reform and Administration in 1966.[39] Based on its provincial land tenure studies and land reform policy papers, as well as growing domestic political and donor pressure, the Third Five Year Plan spelled out in 1968 a clear strategy for moderate reforms. It envisaged no redistribution, but incorporated vigorous land reform policies and spelled out in detail the measures, setting deadlines for the submission of the legislation to Parliament.[40] Three pieces of legislation were prepared: regulation of agricultural tenancy relationships, registration of immovable property, and taxation of under-utilized land. As drafted this legislation probably would not have solved the eviction problems CADU was increasingly facing.[41] Still, SIDA continued to press for the three reform bills, arguing that progressive agricultural development could not occur without them.[42] But only the tenancy reform draft was approved by the Council of Ministers and formally submitted to Parliament, in 1971. Despite some debate that body adjourned without action on it. It failed because of strong reaction by church officials, landowners, provincial elites, government administrators worried about enforcement, and progressives who opposed the bill because it did not go far enough.

During the Parliamentary recess, observers expected the Emperor to issue the legislation by decree. Instead, the Emperor maintained the constitutional position that Parliament must first issue such legislation, since it would affect the property of the Ethiopian citizens, and returned all legislation to the Ministry of Land Reform and Administration for redrafting. Despite the efforts of committed reformers in the Ministry to draft progressive but acceptable legislation on tenancy, land taxation, adjudication and registration, government land grants, ceilings on land holdings, and resettlement, only a single landlord-tenant bill was approved by the Council of Ministers for submission to the 1972-73 parliamentary session.[43] No vote was taken and the fourth parliament was dissolved for new elections.[44]

The elections of the fifth Ethiopian Parliament in 1973 led to the defeat of incumbents who had supported land reform bills and the election of outspoken opponents of such legislation. Moreover, the concept paper prepared for the Fourth Five Year Development Plan (1974/75-1978/79) referred only weakly to land tenure, a departure from the strong position that had been building in earlier plans.[45] It therefore seemed doubtful in late 1973 that anything other than a weak tenancy bill, difficult to implement, would be forthcoming. The events of 1974 led to the abolition of the Parliament, the rejection of the legislation which had been developed by the MLRA, and the end of this era of land reform history.

ii. Local Government System

In 1967 the local officials, judges, ministry field agents, clerks, and police of Chilalo *Awraja* were governed by the Ministry of Interior under an unintegrated prefectural system that was established at the end of the Italian occupation.[46] Goals of the system were set by central elites who controlled the ministries, but there was substantial room for local administrators to interpret, resist or even suppress orders from above. In operating local government on a daily basis, these officials acted according to the perceived needs of the provincial elite (of which they were members) and the promotion of their own interests. Provincial, *awraja* and *woreda* governors focused their activities narrowly on the maintenance of order, had little inclination to promote development for or participation by the majority of the population who were small-holders, and showed little concern for the great percentage of Ethiopians who were poor, unhealthy, and illiterate. Low salaries encouraged corrupt behavior, such as the misappropriation of government funds, theft of self-help contributions, acceptance of bribes in return for government services or favors.

Better educated civil servants did not want to live in rural or outlying urban locales, so progressive persons were rarely found in the provinces. Educated people who did enter the system were frequently isolated and those who idealistically sought to serve the urban poor or the peasant, who fought corruption and criticized the inefficiency of government, rarely advanced. They eventually came into conflict with traditional elements and were usually transferred as a result of local bureaucratic pressure. If they were field agents of development ministries, their positions and uncertain lines of authority often prevented them from being able to promote reforms. Other educated and initially idealistic progressives never faced such problems because they were co-opted by the rewards of the system.

Most local government officials had few qualifications for office. Their outlook was traditional and they lacked the education necessary to fully understand the economic strategies behind the government's development plans. These characteristics also led to excessive formalism, delay, and chaotic record keeping. Moreover, they rarely had budgets beyond their salary and overhead requirements. Supervision of these employees was usually minimal, and they were often shifted to positions without respect for their experience. These factors lowered morale and led to outside interests in land buying and farming. As a result, many employees worked only a few hours a day and eschewed innovation.

Despite the need for increased government activities resulting from Chilalo's establishment as a development center, the senior officials in Addis Ababa made no effort to improve local government performance through redeployment of better officers, salary increases, or training programs. Nor did CADU make a sustained effort to enlighten local governors or grass-roots officials about development, the new Third Five Year Plan, or the project. For these and other reasons, local government hostility to CADU was as strong or stronger in 1973 than in 1967.

For example, the head of the Information Unit reported after a 1973 development seminar for area governors that they "expressed a clear dissatisfaction with and strong resistance to some of the project activities."[47] This was particularly the case with *woreda* governors who wanted rural people crowding their offices seeking intermediation with development ministry field agents, rather than attending crop demonstrations and development meetings directly sponsored and run by CADU staff or sending delegations direct to project headquarters when they wanted to voice demands.

Surely, critics note, a strategy could have been developed that would have involved such officials in the project, satisfying their need to exercise authority and maintain prestige without undermining the project. However, the matter was not this simple. The involvement of local government officials in some or all aspects of project design, implementation, and evaluation was perceived by those who had conceived the project as very risky. Not only were these officials seen as exploiters of the target population and supporters of the provincial elite,[48] but they were viewed as incompetent administrators whose bureaucracies would hamper speedy implementation of the project. To a great extent these observations were correct. So from the very beginning the project bypassed local government units, at most allowing officials to participate indirectly in project benefits.[49]

CADU also failed to establish strong cooperative linkages with line ministry field agents working in the *awraja* or province. Indeed, even the provincial representative of the Ministry of Agriculture in Arussi was not well connected to the project. Rather, as pointed out in Chapter 4, CADU's linkages were to the central ministry, most notably after 1971 to a vice minister of Agriculture who headed up EPID and was assisted by a deputy funded by SIDA.[50] Although support from above was invaluable, the lack of it at the local level proved to be a major constraint, for there were certain complex local issues CADU could not solve alone and the hostility CADU's independence generated in the provincial development ministries hampered local cooperation in efforts to resolve them.[51]

CADU's mandate and diverse activities worried the staff of the major ministries operating in Chilalo. Field officers of such ministries perceived CADU as an expanding organization seeking to take over their assigned tasks, reducing their office's responsibility or forcing them to spend more time in the more difficult to work in *awrajas* of Arussi Province. As a result, some were hostile to the project, a response reinforced by jealousy over the housing and other benefits CADU staff had.

The initial CADU plan of operation called for the establishment of functional linkages with line ministries.[52] These were to be facilitated by coordination at the national level through the ministerial committee described in Chapter 4 and locally in coordination with the Ministry of Interior's governors and the various development ministries' field agents. However, many of these supportive linkages did not work in practice even after the 1971 reform establishing EPID. Not only did CADU have difficulties getting supporting instructions to development ministries from the coordination committee, but it had problems obtaining the cooperation of the provincial governor and ministry field agents in executing those instructions that did reach Asella. Hence, CADU contacts at the national center did not necessarily ensure cooperation by local government officials.

Examples of local government blockages will be presented shortly. These led the 1974 evaluation team to state:

> ... we recommend (by CADU) a whole-hearted and persistent effort be made to build up positive and cooperative relationships (with) the administrative authorities and Department staffs of the (area).[53]

Yet, to do so was not easy, for CADU lacked knowledge of and a strategy for involving local officials in project activities.[54] Moreover, to work with them would have been to identify CADU with the target population's negative perception of government, for the peasant approached CADU's innovations with a suspicion born of many years of government contact.

One possibility for such cooperation emerged in 1973 with the ill-fated *Awraja* Self-Government Reform.[55] Responding to pressure for local government reform from liberal Ethiopians and development experts who argued that centralization held back development by stifling local innovation, the government proposed to try decentralization on a pilot basis in 18 *awrajas*, one of which was Chilalo. CADU supported this innovation and the 1974 evaluation team welcomed it as an important step toward overcoming a number of problems hampering the project.[56] The events of early 1974, however, kept the government from testing this decentralization effort in Chilalo.

GREEN REVOLUTION AND SOCIAL EFFECTS

The CADU project demonstrates that an integrated rural development project centered on the introduction of green revolution inputs can bring dramatic increases in agricultural productivity and income to a rural area. But it also reveals how structural constraints in the task environment can cause a well designed and implemented project to have harmful effects on an area and prevent the project from reaching its full potential. This latter point is illustrated by a review of how CADU's target population was hurt by the interaction between the project's activities and land holding patterns, tenant exploitation, government policies, and local government corruption.

i. Government Policy on Mechanization

As shown in Chapter 3, until the early 1970s the Ethiopian government's strategy for increasing agricultural production centered on the promotion of large commercial farms and the use of capital intensive machinery. It was promoted by government policies, such as the provision of duty-free import of machinery and parts, credit, and foreign exchange for buying such equipment with government subsidized loans at 7 percent, and fuel tax waivers.[57] When these inducements were combined with green revolution production increases, commercial farming could be a profitable venture. This was the case in Chilalo, it being estimated that the use of new seeds, fertilizer, and mechanical equipment on a 40-hectare plot could produce a return of E$ 19,000 on an investment of E$ 9,000 – or 111 percent per year.[58]

Despite these inducements, in 1967 there were not more than 30 tractors and several thousand hectares of large-scale commercial farms in the Chilalo region.[59] However, by 1973 mechanized commercial farming had expanded dramatically, largely at the expense of evicted tenant farmers. This was documented by a 1971 CADU study in four northern *woredas* that found the area under tractor cultivation increased 41 percent in 1968, 54 percent in 1969, and 65 percent in 1970.[60] CADU investigated this trend in these *woredas* but suppressed the report for some time because of its political implications. No subsequent study of mechanization rates throughout the project area was carried out and available government figures conflict. But in 1971 there were probably some 150 large-scale farmers working an average of 180-200 hectares each and operating more than 250 tractors and 50 combines.[61] In all, perhaps 30,000 hectares were under mechanized production. No figures are available for early 1974, but it is clear that the rapid rate of mechanization continued right up to the beginning of the revolution.

Government policies supporting mechanized farming were reinforced by CADU's demonstration effect and the absence of tenant protection from eviction. There is no doubt that CADU's assistance to commercial farmers in the early days of the project and its large mechanized seed farm operations at Kulumsa stimulated local awareness of the potential of commercial farming. With hindsight, it seems remarkable that CADU provided machinery services until 1970 to large farmers interested in mechanization and took so long to recognize the need to set ceilings limiting access to project fertilizer and credit to smaller-scale landowners and tenants. More important was the diffusion of the CADU's green revolution message to landowners and provincial elites holding blocks of land of 20 hectares or larger. This message, together with the lack of tenant legislation, lured merchants, government officials, military officers, lawyers, and other elites into commercial exploitation of Chilalo's agrarian promise. Landowners, now convinced of the success of a mechanized venture, removed their tenants and either farmed commercially themselves or rented their land on long-term leases with fixed, high rent schedules to other commercial farmers or elite investors whose primary profession was not farming. These latter contractors frequently lived in Addis Ababa where they joined with friends and hired farm managers out of the nation's agricultural schools. Although accurate data are lacking, it is estimated that approximately 40 percent of total mechanized land in Chilalo was worked by contract farmers in 1973. Their major crop was wheat, which was generally marketed at commercial prices in Addis Ababa.

The only hope CADU officials had for stopping these trends came in May 1973 when, after prolonged discussion and pressure from aid agencies (most notably SIDA), the government ended the tax free gasoline benefits, and in December 1973 when the Arab-Israeli war led to a 60 percent increase in fuel costs. Unfortunately, this constraint on commercial agriculture also led to a dramatic increase in fertilizer prices for small-holders. Before CADU could predict the effects of increased fuel and fertilizer costs on the area's expansion-oriented commercial farmers, the instability of the creeping *coup d'état* of 1974 changed all assumptions on the economics of mechanized production.

Given the speed at which mechanized agricultural production and tenant evictions spread in Chilalo, it seems remarkable that the trend was not anticipated by project designers and those who directed the initial years of project operations. However, to the project's credit, its officers and staff tried hard to slow mechanization and promote tenancy protection laws once the eviction patterns became clear.

ii. Tenant Insecurity and Eviction

Evictions continued until the revolution. However, despite the fact that the poorest and most vulnerable of the local population were being evicted on a large scale, no systematic study was undertaken to document the extent of the problem in the Chilalo Region. There were several reasons for this.

First, baseline data on tenancy patterns prior to the arrival of CADU were based on limited sampling of government land registers and unreliable. A 1966 study by the central government found 44 percent of holdings owned, 8 percent partly owned, and 48 percent rented.[62] Importantly, the study suggested those renting held only 20 percent of the *awraja's* total cultivated area. A less rigorous survey by the Arussi governor in 1971 set tenancy at 63 percent.[63] CADU never did an area survey; however, its 1970 and 1972 general agricultural surveys in selected *woredas* confirmed that there were wide variations in tenancy rates when data was disaggregated by subdistricts or compared over time, largely because of land consolidation and eviction generated by the project.[64] Reviewing such data, Swedish and Ethiopian statisticians at CADU took the position that the tenancy rate was approximately 45 percent in 1968.

Secondly, *awraja*-wide studies of evictions were not undertaken because of formidable data collection problems. Most tenancies were not recorded, local records on household movements kept by grassroots headmen were difficult to analyze, evicted tenants generally left the area to seek land in other provinces, and local elites and their allies in the provincial administration discouraged systematic inquiry. As a result empirical evidence was drawn from studies confined to a few areas.

One study in the northern part of Chilalo, where the project operated the longest, estimated that as of 1971, 500 to 550 tenant households had been evicted.[65] A study of the Iteya extension area, where land was suitable for mechanization, documented a decline in the percentage of tenants to all farmers from 46 percent in 1968 to 12 percent in 1972.[66] Of those evicted, it is thought that about 45 percent were displaced for owner operator cultivation and 55 percent for farming by outsiders on a contract basis.

Third, not all those losing their land were tenants. Some owner cultivators lost their holdings to local elites through default on mortgage contracts known as "antichresis". Under this system lenders had the right to use pledged land for an agreed loan period. If the debtor failed to repay the loan the lender gained the land. Special CADU studies found lenders were often merchants and civil servants who were using the system to consolidate holdings for subsequent mechanization.[67] No data is available on what portion of the evicted households resulted from this practice or the link between defaults and CADU intervention.

Fourth, there is disagreement among outsiders estimating the size of evictions. For example, one Ethiopian expert concluded in 1974 that an estimated 2,000 tenant households might have been evicted in Chilalo as a result of CADU, a figure raised to 5,000 by the Commercial Bank of Ethiopia in 1975.[68] Another, more dispassionate Ethiopian specialist concluded that evictions were much lower, and that in any case project activities had generated 2,000 jobs, providing in the process offsetting employment gains in the region.[69] It appears, however, that evictions were larger than 2,000 households and CADU's efforts to avoid adverse employment effects were less successful than they might have been.

A review of available studies, interviews, and observations,[70] suggests that total evictions between 1967 and 1974 ranged between 2,500-5,000 tenant households, a figure used by the government 15 years later.[71] Such figures were the basis of predictions in 1973 by knowledgeable observers that eventually 15,000 farm households would be evicted to make way for large-scale commercialized farming.

Evidence also suggests that aside from increased labor requirements in the peasant sector resulting from its seed-fertilizer package,[72] CADU's efforts to provide employment opportunities to offset evictions were inadequate. As noted in Chapter 4, CADU hired those evicted tenants who did not move on as daily laborers, particularly for labor intensive road construction. But given the risk of temporary daily employment, tenancy was more secure. Ironically, labor intensive road construction led to further evictions; for example, a 1973 road project in the Kersa area opened up access for tractors and combines, threatening by their presence thousands of tenant households working land suitable for large farm operations. CADU also made little progress promoting local industries, such as oil and flour mills, weaving, honey processing, and furniture fabrication, despite having begun to explore their possibilities as early as 1967. Clearly, evictions were high and arguments that they were offset by non-farm employment misleading.

As the previous section demonstrated, despite CADU and SIDA pressure, efforts for land reform in general, and tenant protection in particular, failed throughout the 1967-73 period. Hence, Chilalo tenants had no effective legal protection against eviction.[73] Evicted tenants were typically told to leave after the harvest and paid no compensation for improvements. Because of the possibility of eviction and excessive rent level, CADU policy makers concluded that lack of protective leases limited tenant participation in project programs and held back productivity gains in the area.

To overcome this constraint, CADU attempted to introduce tenant protection by requiring landlords to enter into CADU leases prepared in order for their tenants to obtain project credit. These leases stipulated tenancy periods during which eviction was precluded and rent fixed, so that the tenant benefitted from yield and income generated by his adoption of the projects package. But the simple model lease of CADU's lawyers proved ineffective and, at times, counter-productive. Some landowners, believing it a disguised first step to seizing their land, refused to sign. Others did so but insisted their signature had no validity, making the exercise an open sham. Importantly, CADU found tenant participation declined in areas where it insisted on the leases while continuing to increase where leases were not pushed.[74] Such landlord resistance was given political support. For example, when CADU tried to enforce tenant protection in local Chilalo courts, it was condemned publicly by the judges for disturbing the peace. Clearly, CADU could not easily circumvent the land tenure system.

iii. Tenant Rents and Land Costs

CADU's success in raising agricultural production profits led to increased tenancy rents. While economists would expect rents to rise as land use and productivity increased, higher rents absorb income benefits which are important to inducing peasants to take innovation risks. Peasants realized that the income promised by the project would be absorbed by others and calculated their risks accordingly. This was acknowledged by the second Ethiopian director of CADU who wrote while a member of the Planning and Evaluation Unit:

> Depending on the tenancy relationship from one third to a half of this increased income of the tenants has gone to the landlords. Thus, as long as share-cropping exists, it will not be possible to bring about a more even distribution of income between these two groups of farmers...[75]

Prior to CADU's arrival only a few tenants used cash for rent payment. For the rest the 1966 data suggested that after collection of a 10 percent tithe by the landowner on the total production, 25 percent of the sharecroppers providing their own oxen and inputs passed one-third to one-half of the remaining produce on to landlords, 44 percent passed one-fourth to one-half, and 6 percent passed one-tenth to one-fourth.[76] A smaller number of tenants who had no oxen and used those of the landlord generally paid between one-half and two-thirds of their production as rent.[77] Under the impact of green revolution inputs, increasing mechanization, and land pressure, the percentage of tenants paying one-half or more rose steeply, and the number of farmers paying cash rents rose to 25 percent.[78] After noting the difficulty of comparing different studies and conflicting statistics, CADU statisticians concluded there was "a clear trend towards more onerous agreements for the tenants."[79]

The rise in cash payments was due to investment by provincial or national elites who contracted land from the owner for a certain number of years at an annually increasing rate and either mechanized it or rented it to their own subtenants. The assurance of rent, irrespective of harvest, was attractive to landowners with large holdings. This was particularly true of those who did not live in communities near their land and were not subject to the kinds of social measures that constrain tenant exploitation and eviction. For such absentee owners, tenants vs. mechanization was a choice between two systems of administration and profit making. Not surprisingly, as green revolution profitability spread, they were attracted by rent offers from private contractors that provided fixed annual incomes, advance payment, easy administration, and incomes up to three times what were currently received from tenants.[80] While making up their minds on contractors, some landowners asked their tenants for annual financial or production "gifts" to guarantee each additional one year tenure. In short, tenancy relationships became more rather than less exploitive with agricultural progress.

In 1972 CADU launched a pilot program to protect tenants from contract farmers by organizing them into groups capable of contracting for larger holdings. While one farm household could at most farm only 6 hectares, 5 to 6 households could work the 40 hectare minimum size outsiders were bidding for. The program began after CADU economists determined that with their advice and the project's production package, the venture was economically sound. Three year written leases were prepared with the full rent for the period paid in advance. This payment was made possible by CADU credit to the farmers on commercial terms. Twenty-six farmers benefitted from the program the first year and another 30 were added in 1973, so that some 200 hectares were worked by 56 households as the events of 1974 ended the need to develop such approaches for protecting tenants.[81]

CADU's study of areas mechanized in northern *woredas* found an increase in the area farmed and a 30 percent rise in land prices between 1968 and 1970. Government officers identified the magnitude of price increases per hectare as ranging from E$ 2,000 in dry lowland to E$ 13,000 in the most fertile sections.[82] These price increases and the expansion of farming reduced the pasture available for livestock and blocked traditional easements used by peasants to herd their cattle to market, pasture, and water. Since the peasant used oxen for plowing, his operations were jeopardized by the decline of grazing areas. Moreover, mechanization was converting pastures to wheat fields, taking areas rented by small-holders for raising livestock to supplement income and provide a hedge against drought or crop failure. Importantly, even though CADU increased the incomes of participating tenants, the rise in land prices prevented them from moving toward the status of land ownership.

iv. Government Land Grants and Tenants

Haile Selassie's government had significant land holdings in Chilalo from which it granted land to gentry, civil servants, and the military or police under a series of imperial orders. One of these was a 1952 Order which entitled landless and unemployed Ethiopian nationals to up to 20 hectares of land in freehold. But since the government used such land to reduce opposition and secure loyalty, it had rarely gone to tenant farmers. This was true in Chilalo, for its fertility and the success of CADU had driven up land prices, leading to demands by acquisitive elites for patronage grants.

As mechanization and tenant eviction increased, CADU officials argued for the identification of government land and its distribution to evicted tenants under the 1952 order. Letters in CADU's archives document that central and local government officials resisted this demand by claiming there was more government land. But this was not the case.

There were two principal types of government tenures in the Chilalo area, *mengist* and *maderia*.[83] That substantial blocks of each type were found in Chilalo could be documented from the land reform ministry's local field office and the Treasury's tax offices. A published 1967 survey by the Ministry of Land Reform and Administration identified 26,480 hectares of *maderia* and 46,640 of *mengist* in 1967.[84] CADU's 1969 review of the records found 43,500 hectares of *maderia* and 67,000 of *mengist*.[85] Beyond this, it was common knowledge that government land existed and was being granted. This author identified a grant of 700 hectares to a leading commercial farmer and 400 hectares to a high church official in 1971-72. Moreover, the Arussi provincial governor's office records indicated that between 1967 and 1971, the period of CADU's presence, some 19,000 hectares of government land was granted. Even CADU knew this, for when it needed to move tenants from project land to be used for cattle production, the government had no difficulty in locating 2,400 hectares for them.[86]

Despite such evidence, CADU made no sustained effort to identify and claim government land for evicted tenants.[87] Apparently the project's staff recognized the lack of government interest in helping the landless and realized they could not combat the existing system of patronage.

v. Markets and Farm Gate Prices

Prior to the arrival of CADU the Chilalo area had a grain marketing system that kept small-scale farmers from receiving fair prices. Local traders served as agents for a few buyers in the larger towns. Using unpublicized market information supplied by buyers in Asella, these traders colluded to set low prices. This was relatively easy to do because small-holders and tenants generally lacked knowledge of how commercial markets worked and had fewer bargaining skills than petty merchants. They also cheated peasants on weighing, calculating payments, and payment.[88] Because of the absence of local storage capacity, both farmers and traders had to dispose of their grain soon after harvest. Pressure to sell during harvest also came from farmers' need to pay taxes, meet debts, and resupply their households with basic consumption goods. A pattern of sales when supply was high depressed prices to farmers and benefitted grain merchants in the main towns.

Despite a decade of evidence that the commodity marketing system in Ethiopia was inefficient and marked by high costs and exploitive practices, the government did little to stabilize prices, propagate market information in smaller towns, prevent trader price collusion, regulate the chain of marketing middlemen, promote quality and measure standards, increase rural storage capacity, or improve the network of rural roads.[89] In particular, the local government representatives of central ministries did not prevent price collusion and cheating of peasants even though it legally controlled local market operations.[90]

Chapter 4 describes how CADU used a market-led strategy to stimulate adoption of the project's production technologies. This program forced traders to offer higher prices, but the 1972 wheat purchasing experience described earlier demonstrates how difficult it was for CADU unilaterally to attempt to offset the absence of price incentives from the national government. At a more direct level CADU tried to introduce preweigh scales on roads leading to markets, an act initially resisted by local officials and traders. In addition, CADU promoted trade centers and cooperatives to provide a stimulus to better, more stable prices. But local merchants worked with government officials and other elites to block or hinder the formation of cooperative societies that could offer farmers alternative outlets for production. Despite CADU's efforts to the contrary, a major result of these market conditions was that small-holders lost benefits generated by their hard work, risk taking, and innovation. Such losses discouraged innovation and affected the distribution of benefits and multiplier effects the project had on the national economy.

vi. Local Government and Distribution of Benefits

As with most integrated rural development projects funded by international donors, the central government at times failed to get various agencies of the government to perform actions agreed upon in the project document. For example, in 1970 it was agreed that the Imperial Highway Authority would asphalt the primary road from Dodota through Asella to Asasa and Bale Province.[91] Yet, by 1974 the road was still in poor condition because the Authority steadily excluded funding for that activity from its IBRD highway loan program, trying to force SIDA to use its own funds to upgrade the road. CADU did spend E$ 120,000 on such efforts, but they were insufficient to maintain this main project artery, particularly south of Asella. Other examples could be given. However, the focus of this section is on the role of local government, a topic often neglected by project designers and managers already overwhelmed by the task of working out central government relationships such as the one just described.

Local government officials assisted Chilalo's elites to capture the income gains of small-holders generated by CADU's green revolution packages. For example, the courts refused to protect tenants from eviction or to enforce their legal rights against landowners; treasury officials stepped up revenue collections from target population farmers but allowed major landowners and mechanized farmers to evade taxes; land reform officials blocked requests to grant government land to evicted tenants; education and health personnel made no real efforts to extend their services to peasant families; and, most importantly, many governors increased the required levels of "voluntary contributions" by peasants to self-help funds for projects from which they rarely benefitted. Several examples substantiate this broad charge. Before production increases, a poor farmer who earned less than E$300 per year was required under the agricultural income law of 1967 to pay a minimum tax of E$1.50 at the district treasury.[92] It was expensive for peasants to go to the district capital and most wanted to pay and leave quickly. Treasurers knew this and created delays unless the farmers paid extorted fees of E$1 for service for that day, E$1 for the use of the table in preparing the receipts, and E$1 for the official seal or stamp. These personal fees (known generally as *yeterapeza* or "for the table") often amounted to more than the tax. As production increased revenue, officials began asking for more than double the past *yeterapeza* rates with the simple explanation that the farmer had raised his production and could afford the increase.

Governors at all local levels developed projects and collected self-help donations from rural inhabitants. Not infrequently the collected funds disappeared and the project was never completed. Such embezzlement was viewed by the governor as a perquisite of office, and the peasant naturally viewed such development activities as contrary to his interest. For example, after the collection of funds (which nearby poor farmers claimed were coerced) to cap a spring and pipe water into one Chilalo town, the peasants were charged at the town tap for water formerly free. The peasants contributed money, provided the labor, and lost a free resource.[93] With increased production and income, governors stepped up their self-help fund raising activities and demanded higher donations on the grounds that the peasants could now afford them.

The majority of taxpayers in pre-revolutionary Chilalo were tenants and small-scale landowners. Because of the interrelation of corrupt local government officials and provincial elites, wealthy and powerful individuals did not pay their fair share or were exempt, while the poorer man bore the major burden of taxation.[94] Because of CADU awareness that increased production should lead to increased government tax revenues for *awraja* development, local treasury officials were pressured to collect more taxes.

Revenue collection was increased in the early 1970s but the target population farmers paid more while the elites retained their tax advantages.[95] Government expenditures of these revenues largely benefitted the local government officials, merchants, and other townsmen. The few schools, health stations, water systems, and electrification schemes paid for by the government rarely touched the lives of peasant families. It was the town elites who had access to such facilities. Whatever other government revenues were expended in the *awraja* were consumed primarily in salaries for government employees and security forces, which generally passed to landlords, merchants, and tradesmen, or to owners of bars, bus lines, and hotels.

The tax rates that led to the government revenues reported at the beginning of this chapter in Table 8 were based on assessments made prior to the establishment of CADU. The next assessment for the 1975-79 period was to have been carried out in 1974. CADU officials were clearly worried in early 1974 about under-assessment for large-scale commercial producers and full assessment for small-holders. Indeed, the 1974 evaluation team went beyond political niceties to recommend that the government recognize the potential tax benefits generated by CADU-led development, fully but fairly capture it, stop evasion by large commercial farmers, and return tax revenues to Chilalo through increased government developmental expenditures.[96] Had there been no revolution those recommendations probably would have been ignored.

Evaluation of the Project in 1973

Just before the Ethiopian revolution began, a joint Ethiopian-Swedish evaluation team found the CADU project to be effectively and efficiently managed.[97] Their review noted that participating farmers and the rural community had benefitted from the project's introduction of improved crop and livestock technology, provision of production inputs and credit, expansion of market and cooperative opportunities, construction of roads, development of water resources, identification of local industry opportunities, protection of soils and forests, and promotion of improved health and nutrition. Beyond this, senior government policy makers, expatriate advisers, and foreign aid officers believed the CADU experience had: (1) developed and verified a methodology for rural development that had influenced the design of other integrated rural development projects;[98] (2) generated evidence that small-scale farmers and tenants were economic men who could contribute to national growth if given yield-increasing technologies and equitable economic opportunities; (3) promoted a shift in agricultural policies from the Third Five Year Plan's emphasis on large-scale commercial farming to the Fourth plan's proposed focus on developing peasant agriculture;[99] (4) provided the experience and insight underlying the design of the country wide, small-holder focused Minimum Package Project that began in 1971;[100] (5) influenced the reorganization of the Ministry of Agriculture;[101] (6) produced a group of well-trained Ethiopian staff who appeared destined to play an important role in other agricultural projects; and (7) shaped the direction and content of tenancy reform legislation prior to the revolution and the 1975 land tenure reform.[102] More generally, it was clear that CADU had converted Chilalo into the richest wheat growing area in Ethiopia and project participants into some of the country's better off peasants. Nevertheless, by 1973 the project was widely viewed by those outside the project, SIDA, and the Ministry of Agriculture as an unsuccessful rural development intervention.

The reason can be found in the reflections of the project's first director, Bengt Nekby:

> The working party had, of course, neither instructions nor competence to judge the political situation in Ethiopia. The Swedish Parliament had already confirmed the choice of Ethiopia as one of the main receivers of Swedish assistance. The difficult conditions with respect to ownership registration and tenancy, at least in certain parts of the country, were noted. The working party thought, however, that, if these conditions were taken into account in the selection of an area for a future project, it should be possible to find conditions that were conducive to the implementation of the project.[103]

The design team's lack of "competence to judge the political situation" and over-confidence that an area could be found to implement the project led to a number of negative effects on the target population that overshadowed the project's successes. To a large extent, these resulted from constraints generated by the history of Abyssinian colonialism, a tenure system that concentrated land in the hands of a powerful provincial elite, a local government system supportive of elite interests, and a central government unwilling or unable to commit itself to economic policies and agrarian reforms supportive of small-scale agriculture.

Critics of the project argued that while aimed at peasant producers it succeeded in convincing absentee and surplus land-holders that improved seeds, fertilizer, and mechanization could return attractive profits. The result was that land prices nearly doubled, tenant rents rapidly rose to one-half of crop production, pressure increased to convert pasture land into cultivated areas, large-scale mechanization arrived in force, and outsiders tried to profit from the infrastructural production advantages in the area created by the project. Most importantly, they argued that the price of development was paid by the landless who were evicted to make way for tractors, a price easily extracted because of the lack of legal protection for tenants. Economic growth was seen as principally benefitting larger farmers, tradesmen, and other provincial elites of the towns. The government was accused of insensitivity to the eviction problem, lack of interest in making the local government system responsive to CADU's needs and problems, and lack of support for project objectives when they collided with the vested interests of the local notables. In this regard it is important to note that the critics recognized that only the determined efforts of the CADU staff prevented the project from becoming subservient to traditional forces and that the staff's leadership and hard work was a major factor in achieving increases in the standard of living and production levels of small-scale landowners and tenants.

From a national perspective, critics of CADU argued that it created inequality by making Chilalo farmers more productive under the fiction that it was a pilot project eventually to be replicated elsewhere in the empire. They asserted the project was far too expensive to be repeated elsewhere in the country, thereby preserving the new advantages of the *awraja*. In addition, critics argued that the project's contribution to the national economy's development was not justified by its costs. Finally, they held that the major reason for green revolution strategies rested on the proposition that increased food grain production can promote growth-inducing linkages with other sectors of the economy.[104] To be effective, they argued, these growth linkages must generate demand for labor intensive goods produced in Ethiopia, thereby allowing urban labor to share in economic growth and raise the demand for food grains. Since Chilalo's land ownership patterns and social system allowed a high proportion of the increased income to flow to elites, they concluded links were weakened, for such persons tended to demand capital intensive, imported goods, particularly when moving into mechanized farming.

Based on these arguments, the critics concluded that as of 1973: (1) the major change generated by the project was a shift toward an early form of capitalist based agriculture; (2) the eviction of peasants by the combination of green revolution and mechanization would continue; (3) Haile Selassie's government or its successor would not carry out the governmental and agrarian reforms needed to remove the constraints hampering the project; (4) the cooperatives, if established, would eventually be seized by provincial elites as a vehicle for advancing their interests and stemming social mobilization among peasants; and (5) when the SIDA turned the project over to local government officials and cooperatives it would in effect surrender the target population to the greedy self-interests of the provincial elite. At a more general level, they concluded that the project proved there was an obvious ceiling on mechanization without reform, for, given the limited capacity of Ethiopia to absorb Chilalo levels of tenant eviction on a nation wide scale, the country could not afford very many integrated rural development projects in highland areas marked by high tenancy rates.

The critics included western academic researchers, Ethiopian intellectuals, Haile Selassie University faculty and students, professionals in donor agencies, and members of the international press. The cumulative weight of their written evaluations, structured debate, and open public criticism damaged the project's reputation, overshadowing its innovative design, impressive implementation successes, and influence on agricultural development strategies in the country.

However, from the perspective of agricultural production specialists, economists, and project management experts, CADU had achieved many of its objectives. The criteria they used centered on numbers of farmers reached, adoption of innovation rates, increased crop and livestock yields, average household income, project cost/benefit ratios, and so on. Such criteria, reviewed for the 1967-84 period at the end of Chapter 6, clearly justify their conclusion that CADU was a successful project. Unfortunately, such criteria could not be considered dispassionately until the economic, political, and social constraints of semi-feudal Ethiopia were removed. This was to happen with dramatic speed in the next few years.

Notes

1. The lack of systematic empirical data, particularly on employment, income, and tax generation effects, was criticized by the 1974 evaluation team: Guy Hunter, et al., *Final Report of the Appraisal of CADU and EPID* (Report by Evaluation Team Appointed by the Imperial Ethiopian Government and Swedish International Development Authority, Asella, May 1974), p. 57.
2. CADU, *Annual Reports 1971/72 and 1972/73* (Asella: CADU, Publication No. 77, n.d.), p. viii.
3. Johan Holmberg, *Survey of Consumption Patterns in Etheya Extension Area* (Asella: Chilalo Agricultural Development Unit, Publication No. 90, 1973), pp. 1-2. See his footnote 5, p. 122 for qualifications on this figure. The only other calculated income change study suggests that those members of the target population who adopted project inputs had a real increase in their household income of E$ 200 to E$ 300 per year, the pre-CADU household income for a family of five from a six hectare farm being approximately E$ 800 per year. CADU, *Annual Report 1970/71* (Asella: CADU, Publication No. 65, 1971), p. 4.
4. On the cost/benefit and internal rate of return of CADU from 1967/68 to 1970/71 see: CADU, Planning and Evaluation Section, *Cost/Benefit Analysis on CADU for the Period 1967/68-1974/75* (Asella: CADU, 1971), p. 5, and CADU, *Annual Report 1970/71*, p. 7.
5. Tesfai Tecle, "An Economic Evaluation of Agricultural Package Programmes in Ethiopia" (Unpublished Ph.D. diss., Cornell University, 1973) and his *Evolution of Alternative Rural Development Strategies in Ethiopia: Implications for Employment and Income Distribution* (East Lansing: Michigan State University, African Rural Employment Paper No. 12, 1975), p. 58.
6. Holmberg, *Survey of Consumption*, pp. 117-21.
7. *Ibid.*, p. 121.
8. "...it must be underlined that the project not only aims at increased production. This could probably be achieved most easily through large scale farming and big industrial

ventures, often under foreign management. The more important aspect of this project is, however, to develop the ability of the local people to deal with their own problems and to competently lead the progress of their society. This may perhaps be a slower but more secure and long-lasting approach,which will encompass and benefit the whole population and not just a fraction of it." SIDA, *Report Number I on the Establishment of a Regional Development Project in Ethiopia* (Addis Ababa: Swedish International Development Authority, October 1966), Part II, p. 189.

9. On the background to the "popular participation movement" in the 1970s and the concept of participation as used in this section, see: John M. Cohen and Norman T. Uphoff, "Participation's Place in Rural Development: Seeking Clarity Through Specificity," *World Development*, VIII, 3 (1980), pp. 213-35.
10. Professor Milosavljevic of the first project evaluation team noted the absence of participation, suggesting it was because "CADU is a production oriented project under paternalistic control of technicians and cannot contribute to this goal." CADU, *Final Report on the Appraisal Team on the Chilalo Agricultural Development Unit* (Asella: CADU, 1970), p. 32. The senior CADU staff in mid-1972 was dominated by economists and included no sociologist, anthropologist, political scientist, or social worker.
11. CADU, *Tentative CADU Programme 1970-1975* (Asella: CADU, Publication No. 26, 1969), p. 12.
12. CADU, *Final Report on the Appraisal*, p. 3.
13. *Ibid.*, p. 32.
14. CADU, *Preliminary Report for the Period 1967-70* (Asella: CADU, Publication No. 43, n.d.), p. 10.
15. The following is drawn from an internal memorandum: CADU, Planning and Evaluation Section, "Framework for Formation of Farmers' Committees" (Internal Memorandum for Planning and Evaluation Section, Asella, 1972).
16. CADU, "A Brief Description" (Paper Prepared for the Development From Below Workshop, Addis Ababa, October 12-20, 1973), p. 16.
17. CADU, "Memorandum Prepared for the Council of Ministers on the CADU System and Procedure of Credit Provision" (Internal Memorandum, December 1971).
18. Bengt Nekby, *CADU: An Ethiopian Experiment in Developing Peasant Farming* (Stockholm: Prisma Publishers, 1971), pp. 28-9.
19. Arne Flodh, *Cooperative Activities Before Measurement* (Asella: CADU, Publication No. 79, 1971); CADU, *Annual Report 1970/71*, p. 40.
20. CADU, *Annual Reports 1971/72 & 1972/73*, p. 52.
21. With strong leadership the 700 member Bilalo cooperative obtained and distributed fertilizer to members, bought land for evicted farmers from profits on member grain marketing, and showed potential for promoting development. It was assisted, however, by two full time CADU staff. Hunter et al., *Final Report*, p. 29.
22. Flodh, *Cooperative Activities*.
23. In order to block CADU activities about 12-20 big commercial farmers attempted to form their own cooperative society and wanted to exclude tenants or small landowners from membership for voting reasons. If they registered a society, it would prevent smaller farmers from forming their own, since by law two cooperative societies could not be formed in the same area.
24. Martin Lundquist, *Mobilizing Savings in Chilalo* (Asella: CADU, Minor Research Task No. 8, 1973); Johan Holmberg, *The Credit Programme of the Chilalo Agricultural Development Unit (CADU) in Ethiopia* (Washington, D.C.: USAID Spring Review of Small Farm Credit, Vol. VIII, 1973), pp. 57, 80.

25. The anthropological study of Arne Lexander lent insight into these but no feasibility study was done relative to their potential role in the development process. *The Changing Rural Society in Arussiland: Some Findings from a Field Study* (Addis Ababa: CADU, Publication No. 50, 1970).
26. Hunter et al., *Final Report*, pp. 79-80.
27. CADU, *Annual Reports 1971/72 & 1972/73*, pp. 24-7.
28. The principal studies on Ethiopian land tenure are summarized by: H. C. Dunning, "Land Reform in Ethiopia: A Case Study in Non-Development," U.C.L.A. *Law Review*, 18 (1970), pp. 271-307; John M. Cohen and Dov Weintraub, *Land and Peasant in Imperial Ethiopia: The Social Background to a Revolution* (Assen: Van Gorcum and Co., 1974), pp. 28-75. For an insider's view of the land reform movement relative to Chilalo see: Hans Wetterhall, *A Case Study in Contemporary Changes in Agrarian Structure, Ethiopia: Chilalo Sub-Province* (Stockholm: Report to the Agrarian Reform Service, Human Resources and Institution Division, Food and Agricultural Organization, May 1974), pp. 114-25.
29. Chilalo's land tax records were neither complete nor up-to-date. Official measurement units varied considerably in size, only recently registered land using standard measurement rules. Fraud to evade taxes, innaccurate book-keping, and lost files further hampered efforts to determine the amount of land by size and tenure. Sample surveys to get suggested patterns tended to be biased by respondents qualifying their answers depending on whether they thought the interviewer interested in taxes, redistribution of land, credit, and so on.
30. Tentative figures by type of tenure were: (1) private-*gebar* 338,800, *rist gult* 41,000, *siso gult* 102,600; (2) church-*sermon* 53,600; (3) government-*maderia* 43,400, *mengist* 67,000, *gebretel* 1,600; and (4) urban 4,854 hectares. Planning and Evaluation Section, *Tentative CADU Program 1970/75* (Addis Ababa: CADU, Publication No. 26, 1969), p. 33. By the early 1970s all *rist gult* and *siso gult* were transformed to *geber* by a law abolishing their status. The characteristics and tax implications of these typical southern tenures are described in Dunning, "Land Reform in Ethiopia."
31. Central Statistical Office, *Report on a Survey of Arussi* (Addis Ababa: Central Statistical Office, 1966), p. 17.
32. Ministry of Land Reform and Administration, *Report on Land Tenure Survey in Arussi Province* (Addis Ababa: Department of Land Tenure, 1967), pp. 10, 21.
33. In late 1970 and early 1971, heated political discussion occurred in the Swedish press on the country's assistance to Ethiopia, and particularly the CADU project. Critical voices argued that Swedish aid should be given to more progressive regimes and should be conditional on actual political and social reforms. The *Ethiopian Herald* ran an angry editorial on February 13, 1971, stating: "What is happening in Sweden...aid should be given on the basis of understanding and mutual respect. A patronizing attitude is totally out of place. There is a limit to the price one has to pay for help offered. There is also a limit beyond which friendship cannot be strained without breaking." The Swedish newspaper *Dagens Nyheter* responded in an editorial on February 17 that criticized the SIDA decision to approve the extension of the CADU agreement and harshly criticized the Ethiopian government and its land tenure policies. This prompted Mr. Anders Forsse, the Deputy Director-General of SIDA, to write an article published on February 23. Forsse first explained that the Ethiopian government had in the CADU agreement committed itself to start implementation of the tenancy reform in the entire CADU area within one year after Parliament's resolution to pass the proposed legislation. The Ethiopian government could not agree with Sweden that Parliament would actually pass the legislation, Forsse noted. He also pointed out that Sweden had made a unilateral statement that it would review the CADU agreement if

the implementation of tenant legislation did not begin within two years. By this, he pointed out, Sweden had declared its willingness to use, if necessary, the general cancellation clause included in all SIDA technical assistance agreements. Forsse then concluded by noting: "It is actually not a matter of 'bargaining' in the conventional sense of the word, nor of 'conditions' that the Swedish development assistance donor enforces upon the receiver. It is rather a joint concern to reach an agreement on the goals of a mutual program and to analyze together the prerequisites – personnel, equipment, financing, organization, legislation, etc. – necessary to achieve the goals set. It is in such a context, and not on the basis of Swedish development assistance or colonial pressures, that the Imperial Ethiopian Government has committed itself with respect to the extensive tenancy land reform recently proposed by the Government to the Parliament of Ethiopia. Swedish mass media have presented a distorted view of the negotiations and the transactions of the parties concerned."

34. SIDA, "Plan of Operation of the Chilalo Agricultural Development Unit (CADU) 1971-1974/75" (Mimeographed, Addis Ababa, 1971), p. 10.

35. For a review of this pressure see: John M. Cohen, "Foreign Involvement in the Formulation of Ethiopia's Land Tenure Policies", *Northeast African Studies*, VII, 2 (1985), pp. 23-50; VII, 3 (1985), pp. 1-20.

36. Ethiopia, *Second Five Year Development Plan* (Addis Ababa: Berhanena Selam Printing Press, 1962), p. 327.

37. The report of this project was published by J. C. D. Lawrence and H. S. Mann, "F.A.O. Land Policy Project (Ethiopia)," *Ethiopia Observer*, IX, 4 (1966), pp. 286-336.

38. The content of the bill aimed at limiting share tenancy rents for rates dependent on the inputs provided by the landlord. It also prohibited personal services performed by tenants for landlords and assured the tenant a minimum of four years tenure. See: Dunning, "Land Reform in Ethiopia," pp. 280-1.

39. Article 18 of the Ministers Definition of Powers Order, "Order No. 46 of 1966," *Negarit Gazeta*, 25th yr., no 23 (27 July 1966), pp. 133-4. The new ministry was specifically charged with: (1) preparing, recommending and implementing reforms related to land tenure and tenancy; (2) administering most government land holdings; (3) distributing government land under approved reform schemes; (4) developing resettlement programs on government land and administering the transfer of land to implementing agencies; (5) establishing and maintaining land registers; (6) conducting cadastral and land surveys; (7) expediting the settlement of land claims through cadastral surveys and land registers; and (8) classifying land for tax purposes and recommending land tax policies to the Ministry of Finance.

40. The Third Five Year Plan envisaged no redistribution. It proposed protection of tenants from arbitrary eviction, the establishment of fixed rent system and the end of sharecropping, written leases with compensation for improvements made by the tenants, pre-emption rights for the tenant on sale by landlord, tithe registration and adjudication procedures, solution of the problems of sale and credit caused by communal tenure systems in the northern provinces, as well as cadastral survey, progressive land tax to force unutilized land into production and the use of land grants for development purposes. Ethiopia, *Third Five Year Development Plan (1968-1973)* (Addis Ababa: Behanena Selam Printing Press, 1968), pp. 195-7.

41. For a critique of emerging tenancy legislation see: Gene Ellis, "Land Tenancy Reform in Ethiopia: A Retrospective Analysis," *Economic Development and Cultural Change*, XXVIII, 3 (1980), pp. 523-45. The 1971 tenancy bill was quite similar to the 1968 bill. The under-utilized land proposal was deemed inappropriate because (1) the penalty tax could be availed by bogus transfers to relatives, which would generate little land

for sale to small-holders or (2) owners could contract holdings to commercial farmers, driving landless tenants who work part of the holding out through consolidation for mechanization. Hence, the law as drafted might have contributed to the problems CADU faced.Critics argued that a better method was to expropriate with compensation land exceeding a ceiling and to re-allocate it for development purposes.

42. This is the conclusion reached by: International Bank for Reconstruction and Development, *Agricultural Sector Survey Ethiopia*, III (Washington, D.C.: Agricultural Projects Department, Report No. PA-143a, 1973), p. 1; and Doreen Warriner, "A Report on Land Reform in Ethiopia" (Addis Ababa: Economic Commission for Africa, March-April 1970).

43. The specific content of the proposed tenancy regulations of 1972 was set forth in: Ministry of Land Reform and Administration, "Agricultural Tenancy Relationship Proclamation Explanation" (White Paper distributed for Internal Government Information, 1972). Important details were the limitations on share tenancy rates and attempts to secure tenant rights to land and improvements. The bill is described in: Wetterhall, *Case Study*. pp. 114-8; appendix pp. 1-3; pp. 159-68. In general, it provided for indefinite security of tenure so long as the tenant fulfilled his lease conditions; rent was limited to one third of normal main crop obtained without purchased inputs; leases were to be put in writing and rent to be fixed in cash if either party or the Minister demanded it; and tenancy tribunals independent of the elite dominated local court system were to be established.

44. Intensive debate in 1973 showed the issue was very controversial but just might pass. In May 1973 a vote was called. Reportedly, opponents knew they were in the minority and stalled the vote by walking out of the chambers. Intensive negotiations followed over the next few days. Observers believe a compromise was reached that won over enough votes to provide a quorum. However, on the day of the scheduled vote the speaker announced it would not be held. The politics behind this are still known only to the Ethiopians involved. Given the tendency of MPs to act independently only when the central government was divided or not committed to an issue, Parliament probably failed to consider the bill because many of the Emperor's advisors were against the bill on the grounds that if it passed tenants would believe they "own" the land and rural conflict would occur. This view was held by a number of traditional governors, military and police officers and some members of the royal family. It was supported by the then current threat on the Somali border, the increase of guerrilla activity in Eritrea, and the historical fears of separatism that have plagued attempts to build a centralized nation state. All these factors probably induced the Emperor to withhold support for the bill.

45. Imperial Ethiopian Government, "A General Frame-Work for the Fourth Five Year Development Plan (1974/75-1978/79)" (Addis Ababa: Prepared for Second Meeting of the Consultative Group for Ethiopia, June 1973), p. 5, 7.

46. The little studied local government system is described in John M. Cohen and Peter H. Koehn, *Ethiopian Provincial and Municipal Government: Imperial Patterns and Postrevolutionary Changes* (East Lansing: Michigan State University, Ethiopian Monograph No. 9, 1980). For a review of the unintegrated prefectional system see: Brian C. Smith, *Field Administration: An Aspect of Decentralization* (London: Routledge and Kegan Paul, 1967), p. 79.

47. Betru Gebregziabher, *Integrated Rural Development in Rural Ethiopia: An Evaluative Study of the Chilalo Agriculture Development Unit* (Bloomington, Ind.: University of Indiana, International Development Research Center, 1975), pp. 34-5.

48. For example Betru Gebregziabher writes of a local governor who "was a part-time farmer who usually operated large plots through contributions of labor and other inputs from his subjects." *Ibid.*,p. 34.
49. Many were farmers and bought seed, fertilizers and other inputs from trade centers. Generally, however, they felt excluded from benefits, criticizing CADU for not providing them with Land Rovers when CADU employees had access to them and for not giving them interest-free credit or for precluding them from credit.
50. EPID is described in footnotes 100-101 below.
51. This problem was summarized by the second evaluation team chaired by Guy Hunter. "It was perhaps felt expedient at the time, although unfortunate in the long run, that CADU should initially launch its program almost without reference to the provincial administration. The view seems to have been taken: (a) that since CADU had a degree of 'autonomy', it was not necessary and might be frustrating, to work through the local administration; and (b) that CADU's concern for small farmers might not be shared by the Governors at various levels...This isolation of CADU, so easily moving into hostility, could be serious in the shorter term, and impossible to maintain in the long run." Hunter, et al., *Final Report*, p. 50.
52. The Imperial Highway Authority was to construct major roads, Education was to increase grade school enrollments, Public Health was to maintain health services, Land Reform was to implement reforms when passed by Parliament, Water Resources was to develop the area's resources, Telecommunications was to promote telephone and radio links, Interior was to implement *awraja* self government, Electric Light and Power Authority was to promote electrification, and so on.
53. Hunter, *Final Report*, p. 51.
54. In the view of René Dumont and others on the first evaluation team: "...prior to launching another project, local officials should be not only *informed* but also *educated* in the importance of such schemes. In particular it would be desirable to bring in a few key officials...who have been well prepared for the *administration* of such a scheme and who are, at the very least, development conscious." (emphasis added). CADU, *Final Report on the Appraisal*, p. 38.
55. The reform is described in detail in: Cohen and Koehn, *Ethiopian Provincial and Municipal Government*, pp. 52-65.
56. Hunter, et al., *Final Report*, pp. 49-51, 74-5.
57. James T. Goering, "Some Thoughts on Future Strategies for Agricultural Development" (Paper presented to Seminar on Development Administration, Institute of Public Administration, Addis Ababa, 1971), pp. 6-7, 16. The fuel tax benefit alone provided an annual income benefit of approximately E$ 1,600 per tractor, and a study near Chilalo estimates that abolition of fuel subsidies would raise tractor costs per work hour by one-third.
58. CADU, Planning and Evaluation Section, "Preliminary Investigation on Mechanized Farming and Its Effects" (Internal Mimeographed Draft, CADU, Asella, 1971), p. 1.
59. Henock Kifle, *Investigations on Mechanized Farming and Its Effects on Peasant Agriculture* (Asella: CADU, Publication No. 74, 1972), Table 2.1.
60. See: Haile Wolde, "Problems of Land Tenure in the Implementation of the CADU Project" (Addis Ababa, mimeographed, 1973). Commercial farms were largely found in Northern Asella, Gonde, Iteya, and Huruta *Woredas*. Henock Kifle, *Investigations*, pp. 5-6.
61. Based on author's figures on mechanization in Arussi provincial Ministry of Agriculture's fuel tax records. Another study puts the 1972 figures at 184 tractors and 37 combines cultivating 23,000 hectares, with an average farm size of 183 hectares.

CADU, *General Agricultural Survey 1972* (Asella: CADU, Publication No. 82, 1973), pp. 24-6.

62. MLRA, *Land Tenure Survey in Arussi*, p. 22.
63. This study defined tenant as any person renting land however small, which probably inflated tenancy rates.
64. One CADU study prior to the onset of mechanization estimated that in northern Chilalo 53 percent of farmers were landowners, 29 percent tenants, and 17 percent other non-owners; and in the southern part 40 percent landowners, 39 percent tenants, and 21 percent other non-owners. CADU, Planning and Evaluation Section, *General Agricultural Survey 1970* (Asella: CADU, Publication No. 71, 1971), p. 62. An excellent comparative statistical study of rural changes from the mid-1960s to 1973 is set forth in CADU, *General Agricultural Survey 1972*, pp. 22-3.
65. CADU, "Preliminary Investigation on Mechanized Farming," p. 12.
66. CADU, *General Agricultural Survey 1972*, p. 23.
67. A 1972 study found 25% of holders of land rights in northern districts under antichresis contracts. Average holdings were 5 hectares and worth E$ 1000 to E$ 2000. Loans averaged E$ 100 to E$ 500. Wetterhall, *Case Study*, p. x, footnote 95.
68. Solomon Bekure, "A Perspective on Ethiopia's Approaches to Rural Development: Implications for Socio-Economic Researchers" (Speech at 1974 Conference on African Rural Employment Research, Debre Zeit, Ethiopia, September 29–October 4, 1974). Commercial Bank of Ethiopia, *Market Report Jan-Feb* (Addis Ababa: CBE, 1975), p. 38. Working with similar rough figures and observations, Michael Ståhl estimated that between 1966 and 1972, peasant holdings in Chilalo *Awraja* decreased by 2,300, most of which were tenant holdings. *Ethiopia: Political Contradictions in Agricultural Development* (Stockholm: Libertryck, 1974), p. 105.
69. Tesfai Tecle, *Evolution of Rural Strategies*, footnote 23, p. 59.
70. For example: CADU, *General Agricultural Survey 1972*, pp. 23-4. One example of observation or the use of "unobtrusive measures" was counting the number of stands of large trees in the middle of tractor-ploughed fields. These usually marked former tenant homesteads, as trees had been previously planted around farmsteads and had not been cut down when the tenant was evicted so that the trees might continue to grow. When driving through the countryside, one could spot quite easily such "remains" of tenant households.
71. It claimed "3,500 peasants were evicted from 38,390 hectares by 171 landlords in the heyday of Haile Selassie's oligarchic rule." "Arsi Peasants Recall Nationalization With Deep Feeling," *Ethiopian Herald* (February 28, 1980), p. 6.
72. Estimates are that on non-mechanized farms each additional quintal of grain produced by the package required an additional input of 3.5 man days work. Improved implements developed by CADU could have reduced this somewhat if used. J. Goering, "Agricultural Technology in Ethiopia: Development, Diffusion, Results and Implications" (Discussion Paper, Ethiopia Government Planning Commission, September 1972), p. 17.
73. The Civil Code of Ethiopia (Arts. 2975-3018) provided some legal rights; however, the code assumed the right of the tenant to challenge the landlord. This right did not exist. Government of Ethiopia, *Civil Code* (Addis Ababa: Berhanena Selam Printing Press, 1960), pp. 494-502.
74. The 1974 evaluation recommended abandonment of the leases, arguing they constrained tenant participation. Hunter, et al., *Final Report*, pp. 42-3.
75. Henock Kifle, *An Analysis of the CADU Credit Programme 1968/69-1970/71 and Its Impact on Income Distribution* (Asella: CADU, Publication No. 66, 1971), p. 15.
76. MLRA, *Land Tenure Survey in Arussi*, pp. 10, 21.

77. This was the case for 14% of the tenants surveyed. Three percent, probably relatives renting land and oxen, paid one-tenth to one-fourth. *Ibid.*
78. CADU, *General Agricultural Survey 1972*, p. 28.
79. *Ibid.*
80. For example: "A landlord may be offered E$ 1000-E$ 1500 paid in advance, for land from which his present rents bring in E$ 400-E$ 600 per annum." Hunter, et al., *Final Report*, p. 43.
81. Wetterhall, *Case Study*, p. 69.
82. From *Awraja* Governor to *Woreda* Governors, Reg. No 142112 (1970), *Awraja* Governor's Office, Archives, with replies.
83. For details on these tenures and on government land grants see: John M. Cohen, "Ethiopia after Haile Selassie: The Government Land Factor," *African Affairs*, LXXII, 289 (1973), pp. 371-9.
84. MLRA, *Land Tenure Survey in Arussi*, p. 5.
85. CADU, *Tentative CADU Programs 1970/75*, p. 33.
86. See Henock Kifle, "A Plan for the Resettlement of Tenants at Assassa from Gobe: First Phase" (Internal Memorandum, CADU, Asella, 1970), p. 4.
87. Plans were made to survey government land but CADU engineers gave priority to road and resettlement surveys. One study of registers was commissioned. It also identified government holdings. See: Wetterhall, *Case Study*, p. 27. See also: "Inventory of Government Land in Arussi Province by Wereda in 1971/72," appendix to H. Wetterhall, "Government Land in Ethiopia" (MLRA Internal Memorandum, June 1972).
88. CADU studies found "...traders underestimated the true weight of grains by an estimated 8.55%...farmers were sometimes shortchanged, receiving a sum less than the trader's estimated weight and the market price...on average paid 12% less than they should have been had they been paid the market price for the for the correct weight." Gene Ellis, "Cheating by Grain Traders in Ethiopia," *Northeast African Studies* , IV, 1 (1982), p. 28.
89. See the Stanford Research Institute's studies, particularly A. R. Thodey, *Marketing of Grain Pulses in Ethiopia* (Palo Alto: SRI, Report No. 16, 1969). For a detailed study in well linked rural area see: Winfried Manig, *Marketing of Selected Agricultural Commodities in the Baco Area, Ethiopia* (Ithaca: Cornell University, Department of Agricultural Economics, Occasional Paper No. 66, 1973), especially pp. 63-70.
90. Personnel of the Ministry of Commerce and Industry were located in Asella and generally charged with registering traders, inspecting business firms, ensuring fair prices for consumers, checking weights and measures, preventing adulteration of products, and supervising regulated industries, such as flour mills. Cohen and Koehn, *Ethiopian Provincial and Municipal Government*, p. 270, footnote 200.
91. In mid-1972 it was announced that the 125 km Asella to Dodola road would be part of the IDA-IEG loan for E$ 60 million to build feeder roads and asphalt existing ones. "IHA Acquires Loan for Feeder Roads from IDA and AID," *Ethiopian Herald* (June 24, 1972), p. 1.
92. A study in northern project districts found 50% of tenants had taxable income below E$ 300 and 40% between E$ 300 and E$ 400. Wetterhall, *Case Study*, p. 89.
93. "Bekoji Water Supply," USAID Ethiopia Mission, Archives, Self-Help & Development File No. 663-11-993-120.
94. See: Lawrence and Mann, "FAO Land Policy," pp. 319-24.
95. Holmberg, *The Credit Programme*, p. 56.
96. Hunter, et al., *Final Report*, pp. 57-9.
97. *Ibid.*

98. Subsequent large scale integrated rural development projects include the Wolamo Agricultural Development Project begun in 1970 with World Bank funding and the ADA Development Project started in 1972 by USAID. Summaries of these are found in: Tesfai Tecle, *Evolution of Rural Strategies*, pp. 24-44. Other such projects included the Southern Regional Agricultural Development Project, the Tach Adiabo and Hedekti Agricultural Development Unit, and the Humera Agricultural Development Project.

99. IEG, "A General Framework for the Fourth Five Year Development Plan (1974/75-1978/79)." This plan stated the government's intention to push agriculture as the key to the country's development, and to invest in peasant agriculture as the key to agriculture productivity increases.

100. The Minimum Package Project (MPP) provided improved seed, fertilizer, and credit in program areas 3-5 kms either side of a 75 km stretch of all weather road. The first phase ran from 1971/72 to 1975/76 and was funded principally by an IDA credit. As of 1973/74 the project had established 28 program areas divided into 207 extension areas and marketing centers. These were located in all provinces except Arussi, which was served by CADU. In 1973/74, 43,143 farmers borrowed E$ 1,906,077 in credit and purchased 1,232 quintals of seed and 67,239 quintals of fertilizer. Only 8.2% of these farmers were tenants but 57% were small-holders with less than 5 hectares (90% less than 10 hectares). The overall design was influenced by CADU innovations and the MPP's implementation guided by Ethiopians and Swedes with CADU experience. This first phase is reviewed in: Ministry of Agriculture, "The Agricultural Minimum Package Program: Phase II 1977/78-1979/80 Project Proposal" (Addis Ababa: Extension and Project Implementation Department, EPID Publication No. 37, December 1976), Annex 2, pp. 1-25; Tesfai Tecle, *Evolution of Alternative Strategies*, pp. 44-63; and Hunter, et al., *Final Report*, pp. 34-6. the MPP experience in specific areas is well analyzed in: Michael Ståhl, *Contradictions in Agricultural Development: A Study of Three Minimum Package Projects in Southern Ethiopia* (Uppsala: Scandinavian Institute of African Studies, Research Report No. 14, 1973).

101. In 1971 the government reorganized the Ministry of Agriculture with the objective of establishing a unit responsible for all national agricultural development projects. Titled the Extension and Project Implementation Department (EPID), the Department was made responsible for administering and improving agricultural extension, incorporating and supervising formerly semi-autonomous integrated rural development projects, and implementing the new Minimum Package Program. The jurisdiction, objectives, and work plan of the Division were influenced by Swedish experience in Arussi. SIDA provided funding for EPID headquarters operations and Swedish advisers. The creation of EPID allowed the government to better monitor the activities of CADU type projects. Specifically, EPID was charged with responsibility for compiling and analyzing work programs and budgets for comprehensive projects, appraising their progress reports, coordinating their activities with other units of the Ministry, and facilitating their funding and relationships with supporting donors. For an evaluation of EPID as of 1974 see: Eileen Stommes and Seleshi Sisaye, "The Administration of Agricultural Development Programs: A Look at the Ethiopian Approach – Part II," *Agricultural Administration*, VI, 3 (1979), pp. 221-39; and Hunter, et al., *Final Report*, pp. 37-40.

102. The 1975 reform was influenced in several ways: (1) debate over CADU generated evictions generated greater awareness for reform among intellectuals and government officials; (2) senior or ex-CADU staff testified before the land reform drafting committee; (3) elements from Chilalo shaped terms in the legislation, for example, the 800 hectare peasant association size is directly related to the golmassa area, the

peasant associations to the Model Farmer Area Development Committees, and the service cooperatives related to trade center programs. Cohen, "Foreign Involvement," pp. 33-43.

103. Nekby, *CADU*, p. 9.

104. See John W. Mellor and Uma J. Lele, "Growth Linkages of the New Foodgrain Technologies," *Indian Journal of Agricultural Economics*, 28 (January-March 1973), pp. 35-55; in the Ethiopian context, see John W. Mellor, "Report on Rural Development Issues in Ethiopia – Problems and Prescriptions with Special Reference to EPID and the ADA Project" (Internal Memorandum, USAID, Addis Ababa, 24 July 1974).

CHAPTER 6

Revolution and Development: ARDU 1974-84

> The gin-and-tonic radicals who sit on their behinds criticizing us are abysmally naive. Stop CADU, they urge. Wait for the revolution instead. But do they really believe that the day there's a new man at the top, an Ethiopian cow will suddenly give more than 150 liters of milk a year? Or that our poor farmers will suddenly know how to use fertilizer, how to combat disease, how to form cooperatives...? No, it's not social change they believe in but magic.
>
> CADU Extension Agent in Asella (January 1974)

In 1974, Ethiopia's agrarian stagnation and blocked development combined with the simultaneous occurrence of military stalemate in Eritrea, drought, famine, world-wide inflation, urban unrest, and military pay mutinies to create conditions which eventually bred a *coup d'état* and the emergence of a strong, radical military government. The development policies and agrarian reforms introduced by this new regime had a profound and far reaching impact on the people of the Chilalo region and the CADU project.

EXPANSION FROM CADU TO ARDU

CADU was always under pressure from the government to expand into adjacent areas. This was expected by the project's designers because it was conceived as a pilot exercise aimed at testing a methodology before expanding it. CADU's area doubled between 1967 and 1971, largely in response to demands by local communities outside the project's boundaries who wanted to secure its benefits. By 1972, pressure to expand to the entire province came from central level planners who argued that the concentration of the project's significant resources in a small area promoted regional disparity. It was most strongly manifest in the decision of the Government to exclude Arussi Province from the nationwide Minimum Package Programs generated by the CADU experience and launched with donor funding in 1971. Despite the fact that the project's rapid expansion had spread CADU resources and manpower thin, staff planners and SIDA officers bowed to such pressure and prepared in 1973 a proposal that would be the basis for the project's third phase (1975-80) and would extend the project into Ticho and Arbagugu *Awrajas*.[1]

The proposal was never explicitly implemented. Briefly, CADU activities were to remain unchanged in Chilalo. Expansion into the new *awrajas* was to occur gradually, aiming at establishing 17 development districts by 1980. The proposal identified lack of roads and agronomical knowledge as the major constraints in the new areas. To deal with these it outlined a two-phase strategy for each *awraja*. First, roads were to be constructed while extensive agricultural research was carried out.[2] Then, in a second phase, tested varieties would be released and inputs made available to farmers through the established CADU marketing system.[3] Drawing on lessons learned in Chilalo about marketing and social formation, the proposal presented a strategy for building stronger, more effective cooperatives.

The issuance of the proposal came at the same time as the SIDA evaluation of CADU described in the previous chapter. The evaluation report supported the proposal's strategy for expansion into the two new *awrajas*. Further, it recommended the transition of CADU from a semi-autonomous project under the supervision of the Ministry of Agriculture to a national center of experimentation comprised of operating units directly under the divisions of the Ministry of Agriculture and serving first Arussi Province and later the entire nation.[4] The evaluation made no specific recommendations on how to effect such a transition without a loss in development efficiency. The absence of specificity proved unimportant, for by the time the report was issued the 1974 creeping *coup d'état* was well advanced. The events surrounding this upheaval precluded systematic deliberation of either the 1973 proposal for expansion or the Phase III evaluation. Rather, the Government simply extended the project to cover all three *awrajas* and renamed the project area as Arssi Region,[5] reflecting this expansion in a new project name: the Arssi Rural Development Unit (ARDU).

Covering an estimated 23,500 km^2, the region was populated by 892,700 people, some 93 percent of whom lived on scattered farms or in very small settlements.[6] Arssi's three districts, 22 subdistricts, major towns, and roads are presented in Figure 5.

The history and land tenure system of Arbagugu and Ticho *Awrajas* were quite similar to those of Chilalo. Both were conquest areas colonized by northerners. However, because of the poorer quality of soils in Arbagugu and Ticho, and the lack of roads, there were fewer absentee owners and less exploitive rent arrangements than in Chilalo.[7] More importantly, holdings were generally small and of relatively equal size, a quite different situation from that faced by CADU when it began operations in Chilalo in 1967. There is no need to dwell on the patterns of mechanization, tenancy, land grants, and exploitation in Arbagugu and Ticho, as was done for Chilalo in

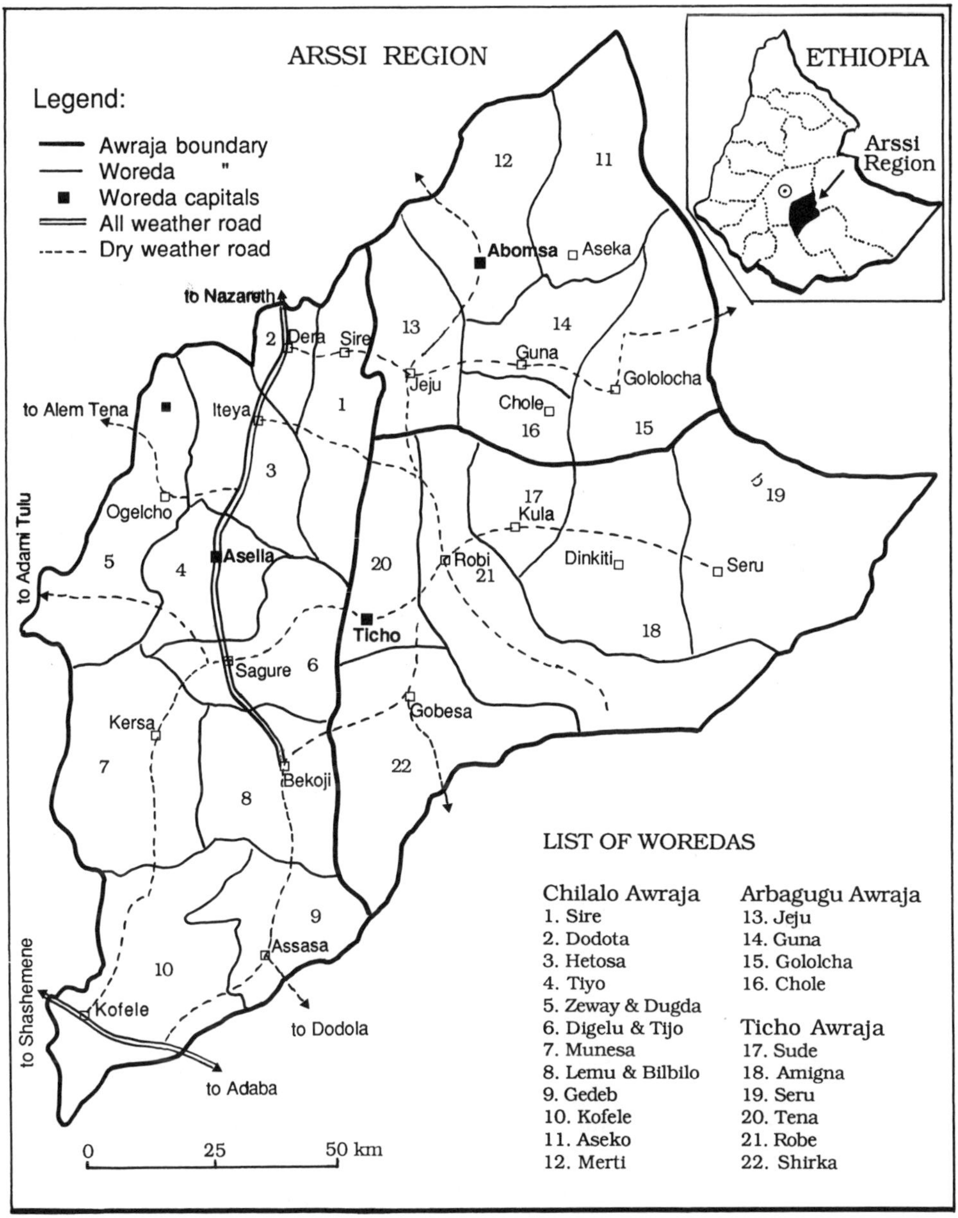

Figure 5: *Map of Administrative and Development Divisions of Arssi Region*

Chapter 5, because land reform was declared shortly after CADU expanded to cover those two *awrajas*.

The major difference between Chilalo and the two new *awrajas* lay in ethnicity and religion. The majority of the rural population in Arbagugu and Ticho were Oromo and Muslim.[8] Such was not the case in the northern part of Chilalo or in the towns of Arssi, for there the numbers of Christians and Amharas were much higher. These patterns of ethnicity and religion were important because ARDU faced different language and social trust barriers as its staff moved beyond the CADU areas to reach the more culturally different and scattered farmsteads of the new *awrajas*. Unfortunately, the rush of revolutionary events precluded ARDU from undertaking community level studies, such as those carried out by CADU in Chilalo, that might have enlightened project staff about the complexities of rural social and institutional structures in these new areas.

A final difference centered on the absence of government services and development infrastructure in the new areas. Arbagugu and Ticho's principal towns were less developed than Chilalo's, for none had electricity and few the public service facilities of Asella. At best they were market towns with a few grain merchants, some retail traders and a handful of government offices. Because of their isolation, Arbagugu and Ticho had fewer schools, health centers, markets, mills, and other facilities. Such under-development, coupled with the lack of agronomical and physical data on the two *awrajas*, created serious technical and logistical problems for ARDU staff as they sought to comply with the mandate to expand.

EFFECTS OF THE REVOLUTION ON CHILALO

In September of 1974, the Emperor was arrested and a provisional military government was formed to replace his rule.[9] With the execution of some 60 aristocrats, high government officials, and military officers in November, and declaration of far-reaching rural and urban land reforms in 1975, it became clear that the military rebellions, strikes, and general urban unrest that began in early 1974 had given way to a process of profound social transformation. The new military leaders proclaimed an official policy of socialism, allowed the Soviet Union to gain a strong foothold on their soil, fought a war against the Somali Republic, battled a separatist movement in Eritrea, and engaged in a bloody power struggle in major urban areas that killed or drove into exile many of the skilled people needed for Ethiopia to profit from the development opportunities created by the reforms.[10]

The agrarian reforms and rural development policies introduced by the emerging regime had far reaching impact on the project and those it served.[11] Briefly, the land reform of March 1975 abolished without compensation all private ownership, making land the collective property of the

Ethiopian people. Any person who cultivated land himself was to be allotted up to 10 hectares. Tenancy was, in effect, abolished by a prohibition against hired labor. While a holder was forbidden to sell, mortgage, or lease the land, incentives were maintained by the law's recognition of family succession to a deceased's holding if they continued personally to cultivate it. Tenants and hired laborers were granted possessory rights over the land they tilled when the law was announced, and rents or other obligations they owed landowners were abolished.

After declaring the reform, the military moved toward implementing it with the help of students on national service and field agents of development ministries. At the same time Ethiopia's new military leaders purged elites and officials in the towns and countryside while assigning progressive, often militantly socialist administrative officers and civilians to the local level. They also began to politicize the peasantry in July 1975 through laws stimulating the formation of peasant associations and local revolutionary and development committees. Nowhere were these reforms more quickly implemented than in Chilalo.

Among the first rural disturbances to flow from the instability in Addis Ababa were those in the project area.[12] More than 7 years of CADU presence had made the region's peasantry more open to rapid mobilization. The project had tied the area into the national center with improved roads, attempted to activate the tenant and small-scale landowners through most of its activities, stimulated a wave of rising expectations, and raised peasant anger through the thousands of tenant evictions that followed the expansion of mechanization stimulated by its presence. Chilalo peasants also had more experience with political organization as a result of CADU's efforts to promote among the local population an increased awareness of and responsibility for development work.

As the military mutiny expanded into a revolution, tenants influenced by CADU began to resist eviction and high rents, project staff called frequent strikes to protest government action to control the rising unrest, and leaders of factions within CADU joined other outspoken forces in the community, such as secondary school students, in calls for the removal of corrupt local officials.[13] There were also intense internal struggles within CADU over the project's strategy, organization, and leadership. Some of the project's more radical staff members became involved in national debates, greatly influencing the drafting of the land tenure reform law.[14]

In effect, 1974 was a year of expanding conflict between CADU and Chilalo's provincial elites, between CADU's leadership and senior officers within the Ministry of Agriculture, and between various groups within the project's staff. These disputes remained strong up to 1978 and continued to plague the project throughout the early 1980s. Despite this upheaval and internal debate, the project continued to operate and expand, albeit with much less efficiency and effectiveness.

With the declaration of the land reform in 1975, internal political activity in ARDU temporarily declined, for the staff needed all the energy it could muster to implement the new law and mobilize farmers into peasant organizations. The project assisted students and reform officers sent from Addis Ababa, allowing them to used ARDU's established extension and market center networks to mobilize the peasantry and advising them on organizing tactics. Project staff and outside reformers successfully used ARDU's structures for calling peasant meetings, spreading information about the reforms, and combatting disruptive rumors propagated by fleeing landowners.

Chilalo peasants accepted the proclamation with enthusiasm.[15] Together with them, ARDU staff, students, and reform officers moved to dispossess large landowners. Despite the cumulative cleavages of Oromo ethnicity and tenant status, the peasants did not to any significant degree attack Amhara townsmen. Isolated and without effective organization, the big landowners retreated to the towns or to Addis Ababa. There occurred no notable case of major landlords or commercial farmers moving to Arssi's hills to establish an opposition movement, as was the case in other parts of the country.[16]

Because of the absence of bloodshed the reforms were rapidly implemented, because the military junta had made its commitment quite clear, traditional local officials and the police were effectively neutralized, and the active posture of the students and ARDU made it difficult for the provincial elite to develop strategies to block or cripple the changes that had been decreed. Violence was minimized by the fact that those seizing land were generally its occupants. The fact that traditional landowners and local nobility were ineffective in defending their interests suggests that their domination of wealth, status, and power was built on decayed foundations, that they had transferred their interests elsewhere, particularly into urban investments, that they feared the commitment of the military and abandoned their land on the assumption they were vastly outnumbered, or that they knew the imperial power would no longer back them and recognized how crucial it was to any organized resistance. Probably all of these reasons were involved in the collapse of the landed class in Chilalo and Arssi.[17]

ARDU played an important role in the reform process by making sure large commercial holdings were efficiently transferred to tenants, experimentally organized as group farms, or taken over on a temporary basis by ARDU to ensure production was maintained. The efforts of project staff to assist government officials and idealistic students to establish group farms as a prelude to producer cooperatives merits attention for their general failure clearly indicated that Arssi's small-holders favored individual holdings.

Only peasants with little or no land and limited resources were attracted to group farms carved out of former commercial holdings. ARDU plowed the land, planted it with improved seeds, and aided the settlers with housing and food supplies. Weeding and harvesting were left to members of the group farm. A year later it was obvious that farmers who participated in these cooperatives did so mainly because they lacked oxen and inputs. In was also clear that these farmers were uncomfortable with the rough accounting procedures worked out to measure the resources and labor contributed to the group enterprise and the distribution of produce and income.[18] In most cases, therefore, when the first year was over, many members of group farms demanded the land be divided into smaller units so they could be individually worked. Still, the overall effect of these early efforts to promote group farms was an increase in peasant awareness of the advantages and disadvantages of producer cooperatives, a fact which helps explain peasant lack of interest in ARDU campaigns for producer cooperatives in the 1980s.

The largest commercial farms were taken over by ARDU and managed by project staff until they could be transferred to state farms or subdivided for peasants. In addition to this large unexpected operational task, ARDU's technical staff responded to increased demands for oxen, production inputs, and basic services that came from former tenants and small-holders who were previously dependent on landed elites swept away by the reforms. Finally, the project demonstrated substantial flexibility to move beyond its mandate. For example, it kept large farms in operation for the state in neighboring Bale Region, resettled over 1000 urban unemployed in the Arssi area, and carried out a wide range of relief and rehabilitation work.[19]

In summary, within two years of the commencement of the revolution the major constraints hampering the success of CADU had been removed. By 1976 the local government system was in the hands of younger, reform oriented military men, the initial phase of land redistribution was complete, and 1,104 peasant associations with a membership of 256,384 households had been organized in Arssi.[20] Although stronger in Chilalo than in the other two *awrajas*, these organizations were in the control of their areas, implementing the land reform's provisions, setting up their own courts, organizing their own militia, and otherwise acting to constrain and limit the influence of former landed gentry.

There is no systematic ARDU study of the effects of the land tenure reform on the pre-revolutionary holdings of small-scale owner-cultivators and tenants in Arssi.[21] Preliminary evidence suggests that during the initial redistribution stage the peasant associations, through locally determined and differing allocation rules, succeeded in providing holdings for the landless and narrowing the range of land size held by farming households. While some studies argue that peasant associations are facing land pressure and land fragmentation as land is reallocated to younger members of the association coming of age and needing land,[22] this does not appear to be the case in Arssi. There peasant associations appear to be much larger than the 800 hectare ideal size and still have substantial blocks of grazing land to allocate to their members.[23] Data on average holding size is inadequate but limited studies suggest that by the late 1970s more than 95 percent of farm households held between one to six hectares, the average size of holding being 2.1 to 2.5 hectares, significantly below the reform law's 10 hectares ceiling.[24]

The political and social turmoil of the 1970s made it difficult for ARDU to assist Arssi's peasants to seize on development opportunities unfrozen by the revolution and its reforms. Because of the staff's emphasis on activism and the re-emergence of disruptive internal strikes protesting the objectives and strategy of the project,[25] technical innovation declined.[26] Replacement of project directors,[27] purges of militant radicals,[28] departures of experienced staff,[29] and declines in administrative performance and equipment maintenance limited ARDU's capacity to be effective. What was once a well knit project team of committed and qualified personnel became an inexperienced group of new recruits with limited technical experience and managerial training. So by 1976 the project found it difficult to extend the established CADU model throughout Arssi, manage commercial farms under state control, and construct feeder roads, market centers, and water points in the two new *awrajas* within its jurisdiction. ARDU clearly needed revitalization.

DEBATE OVER ARDU DESIGN

Considerable internal debate took place between 1974 and 1976 over what the strategy and organization of ARDU would be in the post-Haile Selassie era.[30] Two factions emerged, labeled by staff themselves as "reformers" and "radicals". Located in the research, extension, and technical service wings of ARDU, the "reformers" argued the major objective should be increased production, favored technically specialized extension agents under the hierarchical supervision of their departments and divisions, believed CADU's model farmer approach should be continued, thought social development should be confined to activities directly connected to agricultural production – such as home economics and youth training – and resisted arguments of the radicals that ARDU promote revolutionary objectives the government had not yet decreed.

Based largely in ARDU's marketing and cooperative units, the "radicals" favored concentrating ARDU activities on raising the political consciousness of rural people and promoting their struggle against landlords, middlemen, and reactionary government officials, delegating more authority to ARDU's District Development Officers, training multipurpose extension workers to replace specialized agents, and focusing project resources on promoting group farming and collective self-reliance throughout the region. The arguments for these changes in project strategies were based on the belief that the model farmer system created local elites and as such was incompatible with Ethiopia's new social realities, that narrow field agent specialization confused farmers seeking services and hampered effective coordination of project activities, and that decentralization and participation would force the project's agricultural production professionals to be more aware of the need to balance seed-fertilizer programs with social development and off-farm employment intervention.[31]

Formal deliberation over the direction of the project took place in the Social Development Committee, a body of key officers created to manage the emerging debate between the two factions. But the debate spilled into the work place and the community. It created politicized factions that outlasted the proponents of different views, divided project staff over the next decade, and hampered important coordination functions within and between ARDU's administrative and program units. Ultimately both groups compromised around a design that maintained past ARDU activities and promoted new social objectives, largely through a strategy based on the radical position.

The agreed aim of the project's next phase was to continue increasing agricultural productivity while:

> ...creating a conscious and self-reliant co-operative community instead of being limited to only increasing individual economic productivity ... every effort will be made to induce collective action for self-reliance in each and every rural community of the project.[32]

Towards these ends the Phase III draftsmen were directed to formulate a methodology that continued CADU's success in achieving economic development throughout the region and developing integrated rural development strategies for application throughout the country while promoting the revolution-generated goals of: (1) organizing the target population on the basis of equality; (2) mobilizing their potential productive forces and ensuring equal opportunity in sharing the fruits of collective development efforts; (3) promoting self-reliance through increased participation of the rural people in the planning programing, implementation and evaluation of political, economic and cultural activities in their communities; and (4) building local capacity to take responsibility for development processes.

The compromise on these objectives and a specific strategy for achieving them were facilitated by the pressing need to prepare a document for SIDA-Government negotiations over foreign aid financing of the project. Forged out of the internal debates just described, growing recognition that the political context of Ethiopia had greatly changed, and specific awareness of emerging ARDU practice over the first two revolutionary years, a paper was produced by the project's senior staff in early 1976 that outlined a strategy for the 1976-80 period.[33]

Before describing that strategy, it is important to note that despite the strikes, purges and turnover of professional staff described earlier, the

Table 9: *Participation in Program in Selected Years*

Year	Number of farmers	Fertilizer (quintals)	Improved Seed (quintals)
1967/68	189	42	189
1972/73	13,302	40,129	5,404
1975/76	57,000	64,553	19,572

Source: ARDU, "Objectives-1984", pp. 9-10.

momentum established by CADU carried the project through the early years of the revolution and the uncertainty of the Phase II negotiations. During the 1974-76 period the project had an annual budget of US$ 2.5 to 3.0 million and was reaching more rural people than ever before, albeit with less efficiency. By mid-1976 ARDU employed a direct staff of 1,300 to serve some 1,000 peasant associations farming nearly 400,000 hectares, several times the number and area CADU was designed to reach.[34] Despite the rhetoric of social mobilization, the provision of direct farmer services remained the project's principal objective. These were delivered by 150 rural development agents through 7 project field offices. The increase in farmer participation stimulated by the revolution is shown in Table 9's summary of input services. Finally, while no basic agricultural research was undertaken, technical departments carried out applied experimentation aimed at improving crop and pasture varieties, upgrading livestock breeds, producing more certified high yielding seeds, establishing tree nurseries, and fabricating better farm implements.

Proposals for ARDU's Third Phase

The government document submitted to SIDA reaffirmed the major objectives negotiated by the Social Development Committee and reflected the enthusiasm of ARDU staff for the revolution reforms of the military. Towards these ends it proposed a technical package quite similar to that outlined in the 1973 CADU expansion to ARDU document. But it declared bold social development objectives that were unthinkable in the Haile Selassie era and outlined a quite different extension and marketing methodology designed to provide both social and economic development. The principal differences between the new project design and the two previous CADU phases centered on the proposal's: (1) mobilizing focus on promoting popular participation, self-reliance and social justice;[35] (2) restructuring of the extension and marketing system; and (3) down grading of emphasis on technical research.[36]

Phase III's emphasis on social mobilization and equity was based on channelling the project's extension and marketing operations through the fledgling peasant associations and a hierarchy of primary and secondary cooperatives created from them. Designing a strategy for doing this was no easy task, for the legislation establishing such organizations and committees was vague on their objectives, structures, and functions.[37] This was particularly the case with service cooperatives, about which the Peasant Association Proclamation defined only general functions and was silent about their operations.[38] Still, the proposal managed to present a strategy whereby ARDU's field personnel strengthened the organization and management of the peasant associations while combining groups of them into primary service cooperatives to be further organized ultimately into secondary associations at the *woreda* level. In addition, the proposal outlined steps whereby ARDU staff would also help the government establish a hierarchy of "revolutionary administrative and development committees"[39] at the *woreda*, *awraja*, and regional level that would ensure local participation in the operation of government development activities in Arssi, particularly by linking them to the proposed hierarchy of service cooperatives. Finally, the proposal called for specific efforts to establish women's associations, youth groups, and cooperative associations of producers such as basket makers and poultry-egg producers.[40]

In order to strengthen peasant organizations and decentralize extension and marketing operations, Phase II's design made major changes in the system developed under CADU. First, the model farmer strategy was abandoned.[41] Instead, ARDU field agents were to reach farmers through a new approach based on decentralization of project management, redefinition of field staff roles, and creation of local centers in direct contact with the new peasant organizations. This approach to extension aimed at working directly with peasant associations through the promotion of cooperatives and self-help efforts. Two major changes in project design were made to facilitate this. First the old specialized extension agent system used by CADU was abandoned to end farmer confusion over who provided what services, lack of coordination between specialized agents, and unnecessary administrative complexity and costly service overlaps. The place of specialized agents was to be taken by "multipurpose rural development agents" (RDAs) broadly trained in extension, marketing, and cooperative management skills.[42] Second, an Extension, Education and Cooperative Promotion Department was formed to consolidate the extension activities of these multifunctional agents and to decentralize its operations to several District Development Offices (DDO) that would administer Rural Development Centers (RDC). Each DDO coordinator was to formulate his own plans, supervise the activities of the RDAs, and control all project resources allocated his area, from agricultural inputs to vehicles. Here the purpose was to move decisions closer to the field level, promote increased grassroots participation in ARDU activities, and facilitate greater accountability of extension agents to the newly emerging peasant organizations.

Working closely with peasant associations in their jurisdiction, the RDAs were to help them draft plans that would identify the needs and priorities of their members and forward them to the DDO. To build such grassroots capacity, the RDAs were to mount extensive literacy and political education campaigns in all peasant associations, women's groups, and youth organizations.

The DDO was to work with RDAs jointly to plan, coordinate, and oversee activities in the 5 to 8 RDCs within their jurisdiction. All activities of the Animal Health and Breeding, Plant Husbandry and Agri-Engineering, Infrastructure, and Industry Promotion units of ARDU were to be required to channel their technical research, production, and service activities through the DDOs. In bringing ARDU activities to their areas, DDOs were to work in close collaboration with the *Woreda* Revolutionary Administrative and Development Committee and the Cooperative Coordinating Committee to promote ARDU's objectives, giving particular attention to preparing comprehensive development plans for the whole *woreda* based on the local plans produced by the RDCs. Here the objective was to stimulate the pace of development, to minimize the ability of distant officials in Addis Ababa to impose development initiatives on local officials, and to increase the participation of rural people in the development of their areas.

This "planning from below" strategy was to culminate in a regional development plan produced by senior ARDU headquarters staff in collaboration with regional government officers and development committees. Once formulated, the Phase III document envisioned the plan being carried out through self-help efforts generated and implemented by the new peasant organizations created by the revolution's legislation.

The extension system, functioning through and interacting with the complex organization system just described, was to promote four major agricultural development activities during the 1976-80 phase. First, agricultural diversification was to be advanced by reducing excessive reliance on single cash crops, such as wheat, and stimulating a mix of crop and livestock activities. Each community was to be provided with a crop production package tailored to its needs. Special efforts were to be made to develop viable crop packages for low altitude areas. A second program was to be pushed to raise skill levels, create jobs for those unable to find land, and diversify economic development in the region. Called an "industrial crafts program," it was to be aimed at training carpenters, weavers or metal workers and establishing small firms to process the region's food, fiber, and forestry products. Third, Phase III was to attempt to expand existing measures aimed at maintaining soil fertility, preventing erosion, and reducing destruction of forests. Towards this end, ARDU staff were to stimulate collective self-help endeavors aimed at conservation and tree planting.

The Phase II design envisioned ARDU assisting the government to promote the establishment of agricultural collectives.[43] However, since the government's objectives for these new structures were not yet well elaborated, the document vaguely referred to RDAs assisting "mutual aid teams" and "producer cooperatives" while reaffirming that extension agent activities, such as demonstration plots, verification trials, and field days, would continue to benefit both individual and group farmers.

Phase III's design assumed service cooperatives needed simple, inexpensive structures. Project staff were to use their pre-revolution cooperative experience to provide designs for low cost stores and storage facilities, to formulate simple but effective inventory and financial management systems, and to define an upward reaching hierarchy of service cooperatives that promoted economies of scale and effective services. The proposal briefly outlined the major tasks for three cooperative levels,[44] manpower needs for project performance,[45] and basic rules for accounting and financing.[46] It also set forth procedures for the election of primary coordinating and union level boards[47] and sketched out rough plans for how the secondary cooperative union would be formed out of ARDU's pre-existing Marketing Division.[48] The design outlined procedures for working with the government to establish a region-wide secondary union to deal directly with the national Agricultural Marketing Corporation (AMC) for inputs and marketing and the central Agricultural Industrial Development Bank (AIDB) for credit provision and repayment.[49] Here the objective was to institutionalize ties to credit, supply, and sales markets independent of ARDU. Finally, the proposal outlined a time table for the rapid establishment of service cooperatives, providing for lagging areas to have their marketing handled by DDOs until they could be organized.

The strategy for ARDU during Phase III is reflected in Figure 6.

The 1976 project paper concluded with a plan for expansion of activities in Arbagugu and Ticho *Awrajas*.[50] It envisioned an initial preparatory phase lasting one year and focused on: carrying out social-economic studies; preparing demonstration plots; acquainting the target population with the project; organizing cooperatives, women's groups and youth groups; and demonstrating seed, fertilizer, and implements. The first stage of the implementation phase was to last one to three years, depending on progress with road construction. During this stage emphasis would be on: forming service cooperatives and training their managers; introducing credit programs and providing inputs; increasing social development activities; and beginning forest and industrial promotion programs. The second implementation stage was to center on providing the following additional activities: sale of improved cattle, sheep, and poultry; artificial insemination and veterinary services; land development; and industrial development.

Assuming road construction would move forward as planned and that manpower could be trained and deployed, the Phase III paper anticipated

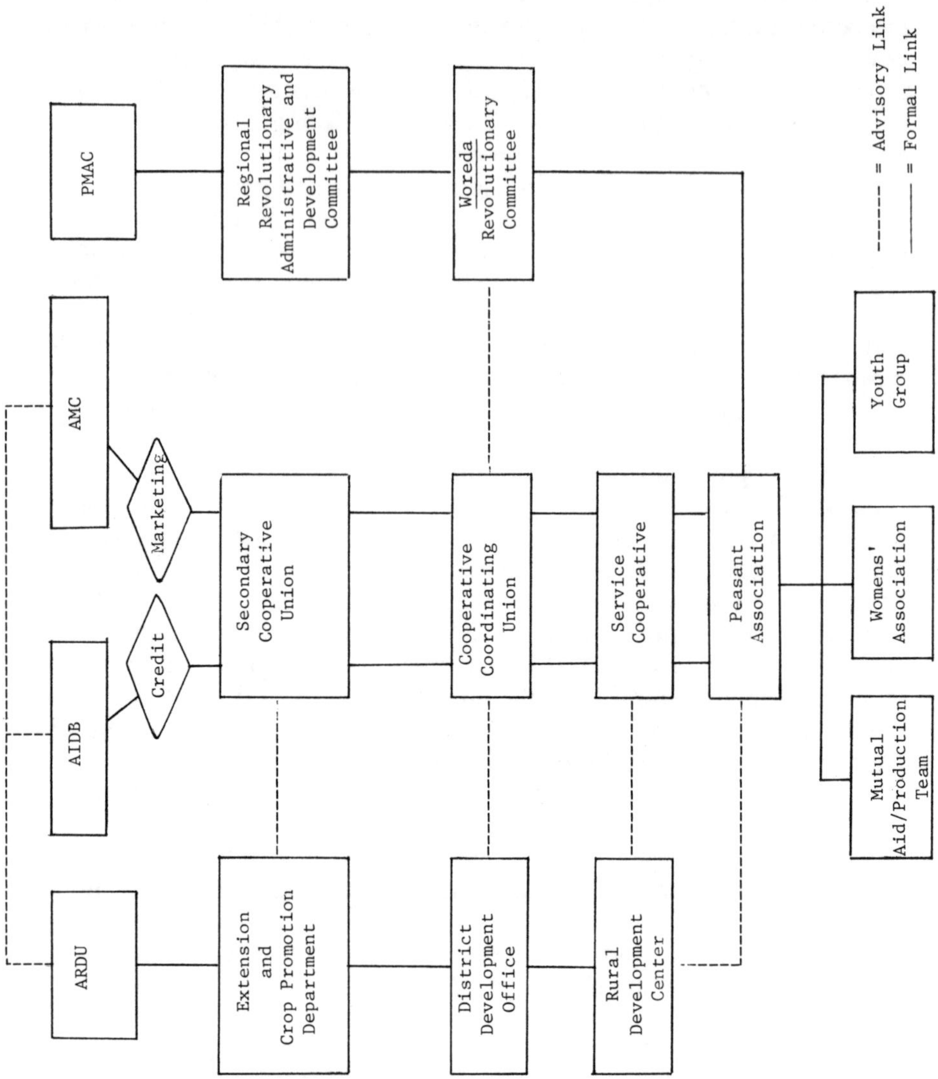

Figure 6: *Proposed ARDU Strategy for Linking Project with New Revolutionary Organizations*

establishment of a fifth DDO in Robe in 1976 or 1977 and a sixth one in Arbagugu sometime during 1977 or 1978. In the meantime some reorganization of the existing four DDOs in Chilalo was proposed as part of the ARDU expansion from CADU to ARDU.

The project paper concluded with cost-benefit projections. It estimated expenditures of US$ 15.2 million for the 1975-80 period with net expenditure per fiscal year averaging US$ 2.9 million.[51] Benefits were estimated to increase from US$ 3.4 million in 1975-76 to US$ 5.3 million in 1979-80, with participants in the projects' various production programs increasing their annual household income over the period by US$ 243.[52]

Three major problems hampered the project's capacity to carry out its strategy. First, project managers were uncertain about SIDA's continued support and financing. However, through creative contract finance and extensions, SIDA kept ARDU funded and operating from 1976 through 1985. Officially, Phase III began in July 1976 and was carried forward through a series of short term extensions of six months to three years. Second, and more significantly, the continued promulgation of agrarian and market reforms by an increasingly dictatorial and socialist regime steadily changed the task environment Phase III was designed to address. Finally, often violent revolutionary debate throughout the country[53] and the reformer-radical split within ARDU contributed to high turnover of project managers, loss of professional staff, and increased use of RDAs with limited technical and managerial training.[54]

AGRARIAN SOCIALISM IN ARSSI: 1976-84

The major alterations in the 1976 Phase II strategy came from the 1977 proclamation creating the All Ethiopian Peasant Association (AEPA) and 1978 and 1981 proclamations outlining guidelines for service and producer cooperatives. Both are intended to increase government control over peasant associations and use them as vehicles to promote the regime's socialist objectives.[55]

The AEPA proclamation outlined a hierarchy of committees that culminate at a national general assembly.[56] These committees are to oversee peasant association defense squads, coordinate activities of peasant organizations with government bodies, increase self-reliance, improve peasant organization performance, and promote higher productivity and social mobilization. More specifically, these committees are directed to organize and oversee revolutionary women's associations, youth groups, production and self-help committees, and service cooperatives.

Progress toward building the AEPA's upper level was hampered by the government's internal disputes over the form and direction of a mobilizing political party.[57] But at the lower levels, the AEPA and supporting legislation[58] led to more disciplined peasant associations with stronger ties to the activities of ministries operating in their areas. This was particularly the case in Arssi, where a series of governors were appointed who had strong inclinations to promote a hierarchy of peasant associations.[59]

Local government reform began with the removal of corrupt and conservative senior officials. In November 1974 Sahlu Diffayei, the provincial governor who had hampered CADU's project, was executed.[60] For the next two years the region was administered by professional appointees supportive of the project if not sympathetic to the position of its radical staff members.[61] The rise of Oromo and Somali secessionist movements[62] brought insecurity to Arssi, so after 1977 the region's senior government post was filled by military men.[63] By the early 1980s, Arssi was relatively peaceful again.

Below the regional administrator, the government appointed *awraja* administrators with progressive inclinations, and replaced landowning local officials with peasant association leaders. However, poorly trained petty officials of the Ministry of Interior and the permanent field staff of the operating ministries were not widely replaced. Nor did the new governors find it easy to instill in such government personnel a new spirit and discipline of public service. So throughout the 1974-84 period local administration resembled that under the Emperor, mainly because it continued to be highly centralized and difficult to motivate for development objectives.[64] The absence of disciplined and committed personnel to replace Haile Selassie's provincial bureaucrats and field agents is reflected in ARDU reports. They note excessive Ministry of Interior interference in project personnel administration, communications problems between project staff and local government officials working with peasant organizations, and poor coordination between ARDU and other field ministries.[65] Still, throughout the ARDU period, local government was far less a constraint than it had been before the revolution.

Since 1976, Ethiopia's major rural policy objective has been the conversion of peasant associations into agricultural collectives, called locally "producer cooperatives". Major steps toward this goal were taken with the issuance of proclamations in 1978 and 1979.[66] This legislation outlines procedures for organizing and operating service and producer cooperatives.

Service cooperatives are defined as interim stage organizations engaged in the purchase and sale of agricultural inputs and the retail of consumer goods.[67] They are formed by at least three but not more than ten peasant associations. Until the mid-1980s, when the provincial governor effectively repressed private grain traders in Arssi, most concentrated on the rental functions because the government-set prices they paid for grain were below those in parallel markets, limiting their purchases, and because local demand was high for such basic commodities as sugar, salt, cooking oil, matches, clothing, and farm tools. Proponents of service cooperatives originally conceived of them as joining together into secondary unions that would have the economic scale to increase their input supply and agricultural marketing capacity through the acquisition of storage, transport, credit, and other facilities. However, by 1984 no legal framework existed for establishing vertical integration of cooperatives, a constraint that hampered the ARDU strategy substantially.

Believing that small farms are inefficient and group farms provide the most optimal use of land and manpower,[68] Ethiopian planners have steadily promoted "producer cooperatives." By law only one producer cooperative can exist in a peasant association area. When established, the producer cooperative chairman generally becomes head of the association, thus strengthening the cooperative's influence in peasant association affairs. Cooperatives are formed in three stages once members of a peasant association decide to form a group farm by merging their plots or demanding a block of land from associations.[69] In the first stage, *malba*, land is pooled but members retain their own oxen, implements, and a small piece of land for household production. Income is based on the share of labor and resources contributed by the member. At the second stage, *welba*, members transfer all their resources to the cooperative, receiving the right to farm a one-tenth hectare kitchen plot and an income based on socialist principles, with work points given for time worked and difficulty of work. The highest stage, *weland*, results from merging several *welbas* to achieve an ideal size farm of 4000 hectares and 500 households. Here mechanized production and scientific management is to prevail, with members organized into production brigades and their income based on labor contributions.

The official goal of the government is to have half the country's cultivated land worked by producer cooperatives in 1994. However, despite a number of inducements,[70] Arssi's small-holders are reluctant to move in this direction.[71] Such resistance led in part to the villagization campaign of 1984-86. It altered major agrarian patterns in Arssi by moving 80 percent of the region's population into villages as a prelude to the eventual decree of universal agricultural collective formation.[72] This campaign will be described shortly. For now it need only be noted that it and the government's continual pressure to form collectives steadily eroded SIDA's support for the still evolving ARDU project.

By 1982, the Arssi Region had 1085 peasant associations with a membership of 235,378 farm families.[73] These associations ranged considerably in size and membership from the legislation's model of 800 hectare units with 200 households.[74] Firmly established as the lowest level of government administration, the associations carried out local arbitration through their grassroots tribunals, promoted security through their rural defense squads, collected taxes, raised self-help funds, and, most importantly, provided a channel for administrative and technical officials of the government to reach the peasantry. Depending on their resources and leadership, these associations mobilized labor and other contributions to provide primary schools for their members, build and maintain roads and water systems in their areas, and promote soil conservation projects.[75]

ARDU reached peasant associations through service cooperatives. In 1982, Arssi had 142 of them, membership in these organizations being mandatory for peasant association members.[76] These organizations proved popular, largely because of their retail activities.[77] Through the Ethiopian Domestic Distribution Corporation (EDDC), Arssi service cooperatives could obtain scarce consumer items often not on the shelves of private shops. Building on this retail function, the service cooperatives were expanded into centers for the provision of inputs and purchase of farm production. As service cooperatives learned how to estimate input demand, mobilize credit for input sales, purchase grain from members according to government quotas and rules, and recover loans at the end of the harvest, they provided attractive institutions for reaching local farmers.[78]

ARDU staff tried to use them as channels for providing extension services, introducing project-led innovations, and mobilizing local resources for development purposes. These objectives were facilitated by the profits service cooperatives made selling grain purchased from farmers to the AMC. Under government regulations such profits were to be distributed as follows: 25 percent for investment in business activities, 25 percent for interest free loans to producer cooperatives, 25 percent held in reserve, and the rest allocated for social purposes, such as school or clinic construction, assistance to local families whose members serve in the military, and so on. A number of service cooperatives used their profits to expand into income generating activities, such as dairy farming, bee-keeping, tractor rental, and grain milling. Arssi cooperatives also built schools and clinics, the operation of which were usually taken over by field ministries. Registered service cooperatives, of which there were 57 in Arssi in 1982 did particularly well in promoting development activities because they could obtain additional credit in support of their activities directly from the Agricultural Industrial Development Bank (AIDB).

But many cooperatives, particularly those in less developed areas of Arssi, had difficulty making profits. First, the EDDC did not always provide sufficient quantities of consumer goods, a failure that became more serious as time passed and the government faced increasingly severe economic constraints. Second, the government parastatals providing farm inputs and picking up grain purchases provided unreliable services, which led to loss of profits. Third, many service cooperatives lacked the management capacity to carry out their functions efficiently.

Sketchy data suggest the average net annual profit for Chilalo service cooperatives in 1980 was EthB. 35-40,000. Service cooperatives in the lesser developed *awrajas* of Arbagugu and Ticho probably averaged EthB.

3-6,000 annually. ARDU sought to raise these profit levels by assisting service cooperatives to improve the management and accounting capacity of their executive committee members and contract employees. In addition, it pressed the government either to increase the size of service cooperatives or authorize the formation of secondary cooperative societies so that primary ones could more easily deal with complicated order procedures and lower heavy acquisition and transport costs for both supply and marketing activities. Finally, ARDU argued that the government must increase its capacity to audit and register service cooperatives so as to facilitate the access of these organizations to formal credit markets.

Arssi in 1982 also had 168 producer cooperatives (92 *malba* and 76 *welb*a) with 14,161 farm households cultivating 46,204 hectares of group farms covering 64,945 hectares.[79] While producer cooperatives comprised only six percent of the region's rural households and cultivated only 9.8 percent of the farmed land, this progress was far above the national average.[80] Clearly, ARDU seized the opportunity for social mobilization made possible by the new legislation, shifting the project's emphasis and altering its patterns of achievement in the process.[81] In this regard, ARDU was swimming upstream. Evidence of this is suggested by a 1984 survey that found only 25 percent of the 150 Arssi farmers interviewed had any interest in joining group farms.[82] In fact, this survey revealed that ARDU mobilization of producer cooperatives created production threatening insecurity, some 37 percent of those interviewed stating they felt their land rights were insecure and a large number, 55 percent, saying they had made no investment in farm improvement since the land reform.[83]

There was good reason for farmers to prefer individual holdings. Producer cooperative experience in Arssi between 1976 and 1982 showed that small farms were more productive than producer cooperatives. To some extent this was because ARDU did not develop an extension package that fit the field preparation, weeding, crop protection, and pasture rotation requirements of larger farms, particularly those which were mechanized. It was also due to the inability of producer cooperatives to manage their land, labor, and machinery efficiently and ARDU's failure to set up training programs that addressed this incapacity. But to most observers, producer cooperatives simply could not generate the individual incentives that have made small-scale farms successful world wide.

The 1976 Phase III strategy was affected by the government's low investment in the agricultural sector, neglect of small-scale farmers, promotion of resettlement schemes organized as producer cooperatives, and decision to seek control of grain marketing.

In 1980 agriculture continued to account for half Ethiopia's GDP and 90 to 95 percent of the country's exports. Some 80 to 85 percent of the population worked 94 percent of cultivated land on an individual basis.[84] Significant opportunities existed for expanding small-holder production. But funds needed to undertake research, improve extension, and remove input constraints were held back, the FAO estimating that only 8 percent of an already inadequate Ministry of Agriculture budget went to the peasant sector.[85] Rather, the government allocated its limited agricultural expenditures to resettlement schemes, producer cooperatives, and state farms. Further, it adopted price, marketing, and tax policies designed to pressure small-holders to join group farm schemes.

Of the estimated 750,000 hectares of former commercial farm land seized by the military, one-third was set aside for resettlement of rural and urban landless or the formation of collectives by peasant associations, some 67,000 hectares were converted to state farms, and the rest taken over by small-holders. Early in the land reform process several large commercial farms formed by tenant eviction during the CADU years were converted into state farms. After the 1976 harvest, however, peasant associations demanded that some of this land be returned to them for redistribution to former tenants who wanted to resettle in their home areas. The pressure was so intense that the government returned several thousand hectares, particularly in northern areas of Chilalo *Awraja*.[86]

By 1983 the Ministry of State Farms oversaw one-quarter million hectares of farmland. Of these 44,600 hectares were in Arssi, up from 6,200 hectares in 1978. These were largely located along the region's southern and eastern borders, at Diksis, Adela, Lola, Geradela, Timela, and Kofelle.[87] ARDU's policy was to avoid involvement with state farms, particularly because small-holders were evicted to establish them and they had potential to absorb project resources wastefully. While ARDU was successful in limiting the use of its equipment and manpower by state farms in its region,[88] it was not able to avoid assistance to resettlement schemes.

ARDU assisted the government in implementing two types of resettlement schemes. The first was generated by the revolution's agrarian reforms and the second by state farm evictions. Initial resettlement schemes in Arssi were established to provide relief for landless urban unemployed and peasants from environmentally degraded areas.[89] The project also assisted the government to settle landless people found in the region's towns into groups of 50 to 100 on producer cooperatives ranging from 40 to 300 hectares.[90]

The second type of resettlement activity in Arssi took far more project resources. Between 1978 and 1984, ARDU assisted the government to establish 18 villages for 9,000 households evicted in southern and eastern Arssi to make way for state farms. Known as "the Wabe Villages," these resettlement schemes are based on producer cooperatives organized around large villages. The extent to which ARDU's involvement in dealing with this state farm formation problem affected project performance is revealed by the 1981/82 *Annual Report*, which attributes the failure of ARDU to reach a number of work plan objectives to the diversion of its manpower and resources to the establishment of the Wabe villages.

To avoid urban unrest, as well as gain control over private traders, the government introduced price regulations for food grains in 1975. The next step in controlling the private grain trade came in 1976 when the Agricultural Marketing Corporation (AMC) was established.[91] It soon introduced a system of grain sale restrictions and quotas that considerably advanced the government toward its goal of ending all private trade in food grains by 1995.

Forced deliveries were introduced during the 1977/78 agricultural season. First, the AMC required state farms to sell all their output to its agents. Then, in 1980, the government decreed that service cooperatives must sell all their purchases to the AMC and private wholesalers must deliver half their purchases to the corporation. Prices were fixed at the start of each agricultural season and the services cooperatives and private traders paid only a small gazetted margin over the fixed farm gate price.

Soon service cooperatives were made agents of the AMC. Producer cooperatives were required to sell all their output to them while small-holders were required to deliver an annually set quota. Small-holder quotas were determined by the Grain Purchase Task Force, an agency established in 1977 and organized around a hierarchy of committees extending from Addis Ababa to the *woredas*. These committees allocated grain delivery quotas to peasant associations, as well as enforced regional rules established to regulate the private grain trade. Ministers sat on the highest committee, while at the *woreda* level chairmen of the peasant associations were among the members. In Arssi the *woreda* committees were chaired by the administrator, with the AMC representative serving as secretary. At the peasant association level the quota received by the service cooperative was distributed among individual members.

In principal, individual farm quotas were determined by: (1) the size of the holding and the number of household members dependent on it for subsistence; (2) the yields of the holding as determined by its fertility classification, weather for the particular season, the farmer's husbandry practices, and past patterns of production; and (3) the economic well being of the holder, including livestock and marketed cash crop sales. But quotas were also fixed for political reasons.

In Arssi, some peasant association chairman used quota allocations to reward or punish those who supported or fought his actions in leading the PA. Also some peasant associations allocated higher quotas to better farmers. Given the low prices paid on quota grain, this created a disincentive to farmers who had adopted CADU-ARDU packages and raised their productivity.

Arssi's quota has been heavy as CADU-ARDU made it one of the three major grain producing areas of the country and the government needed its output. In general, farmers and peasant associations in Arssi have found it difficult to meet quotas, particularly during the 1983-85 period of poor rainfall.

The government had problems enforcing the AMC purchase and quota guidelines in Arssi because small-holders received EthB. 5 per quintal less than producer cooperatives for their grain, official prices were well below parallel market prices,[92] and private traders too strong and numerous. To promote compliance with AMC rules, Arssi's regional administrator initially restricted the private sector by prohibiting traders from moving their stock to other regions and requiring them to sell 100 percent of their purchases to the marketing parastatal or its agents. But price differentials between the parallel market and fixed AMC rates were so great that this decree did not substantially increase AMC procurement or reduce trading in private markets.[93] So restrictions on private traders were increased. In 1984 grain merchants were banned from Asella, their stocks confiscated and facilities transferred to service cooperatives. Elsewhere in Arssi, petty traders were denied licences or harassed, in part through political pressures from service cooperatives who wanted to increase the profit they made through sales to the AMC. Angry farmers and high profit margins, however, made it difficult to drive private traders entirely out of business. Throughout early 1985 there were active, illegal "night markets" and smuggling operations in Arssi. This led to concerted government efforts to put private traders out of business by restricting their activities and fining or imprisoning farmers who sold to them.

By 1984 low fixed prices, burdensome quotas, suppression of parallel markets, and AMC practices of refusing deliveries when overextended,[94] proved to be powerful disincentives to Arssi's small-holders. These disincentives were reinforced by the absence of consumer goods and rising fertilizer and seed prices.

Government limitations on private retail traders and the inability of the EDDC to supply service cooperatives with sufficient quantities of basic consumer commodities lowered small-holder incentives to produce for the market, particularly because the prices of consumer products were rising while the AMC's grain procurement prices remained low. To promote productivity, Arssi's governor decreed that farmers who failed to deliver their grain quotas were precluded from buying goods at service cooperatives. Since basic goods such as salt and sugar could not be sold in the private market this put pressure on farmers to meet quotes or be forced to go without these goods or pay high black market prices.

Incentives to increase production were also affected by the inability of the Ministry of Agriculture's AMC and AIDB, and the Ministry of Domestic Trade's Ethiopian Seed Corporation, to serve as reliable suppliers of fertilizer, credit, and improved seed. This was because improved seeds, fertilizer and credit went mostly to state farms. For comparative purposes it should be noted that state farms received 82 percent of imported fertilizer in 1980-83 while small-scale farmers not in producer cooperatives were allocated at most three percent.[95] ARDU's size and political influence facilitated the project's capacity to gain a significant share of the limited inputs available to small-holders and to ensure that per capita fertilizer use remained stable after 1979, although at a level below that of the 1970-78 period. However, ARDU often had to use its own input supplies and transport because the AMC tended to underestimate demand or have difficulty delivering on time.

The result of government disincentives was lower peasant income, reduced further by a large increase in "indirect taxes" after the revolution. While nominal taxes have remained reasonably stable for small-holders, levies for national defense, famine, local self-help, party office construction, and other campaigns increased. By 1984 they were to run 15 percent of an average peasant household's cash income. The AMC's low prices could be considered an indirect tax as well. Clearly, these direct and indirect taxes reduced the potential for Arssi's farmers to buy consumer goods and stimulate small-scale enterprises in the region's towns, limiting agriculture's potential to promote economic development.

Through these agrarian policies and other reforms in the economy and polity, Ethiopia's leaders moved closer to the Soviet model.[96] But the policies and programs borrowed from that model showed little evidence of promoting agricultural and rural development. As a result, a decade after the revolution its economic promise was largely unfulfilled. Reform alone could not change rapidly the subsistence character of Ethiopian agriculture. Because of government policies and investment neglect, the agricultural sector in 1984 was as subsistence based as it had been during Haile Selassie's reign, the basic factor proportions, production units, and farming methods largely untouched by the revolution and its land reform.[97] Because of its slow growth the agricultural sector was unable to contribute greatly to earning the foreign exchange needed for development, the marketed surplus necessary to provide national food self-sufficiency or the output required to raise per capita nutritional levels.

Despite low agricultural growth the standard of living of peasants in former tenancy areas had improved, in part because farm families retained food previously paid in rent. But rural Ethiopians still had one of the lowest per capita incomes in the world.[98] Lack of agricultural development promised to continue until the government created policies and programs that seized the opportunity created by the land tenure reform.

By 1985 many Ethiopian development professionals, and most western experts recognized that the key to agricultural development is the small-holder sector. Approximately 86 percent of the total population of 41.1 million live in rural areas and depend on agriculture for livelihood, the number of individual small-holders having increased from 6.5 million in 1974 to 7 million in 1982. Of the total cultivated land in 1982, individual small-holders held 94 percent, state farms 4 percent, collective farms 1.3 percent, and agricultural settlements 0.7 percent.[99] Overall the small-holder sector produced 90 to 95 percent of agricultural output and generated 80 to 85 percent of national employment. Making explicit reference to the CADU-ARDU model and accepting the 1975 observations of an experienced Ethiopianist that "the dream of most Ethiopian cultivators seems to become a Kulak,"[100] critics of the government's agrarian reform strategy made strong arguments for promoting individual farm production.[101] Yet, ideological rhetoric grew stronger, led by clear anti-small-holder statements by the head of state[102] and timid arguments by intimidated Ethiopian professionals.[103] The absence of internal criticism of the emerging model is reflected in the 10 year plan presented at the September 1984 ceremony establishing a Workers' Party and celebrating the 10th anniversary of the revolution.[104] There Colonel Mengistu set his government's goal as having half the rural population in producer cooperatives or state farms by 1994. Towards this end, the government stepped up its press attacks on small-holders, called for the formation of group farms, and accelerated the country's movement toward a form of agrarian socialism that had generally failed in Eastern Europe and the Third World.

The results of such policies were clearly visible by 1985. In the words of a long time Ethiopia observer, Paul B. Henze, after a recent visit:

> ...it is hard to escape the impression of economic stagnation here. Soviet-style socialism has produced no economic boom. Many farmers in fertile central and south Ethiopia are not cooperating with a government drive to raise productivity. The leadership's investment in state farms is not paying off; the projects are highly inefficient. Nationalized industry is performing haphazardly.[105]

Perhaps the most devastating indicator that social revolution had out-paced economic revolution was the tragic famine of 1984. To be sure, its roots lay in two years of failed rain, leading to a shortfall of some 1.5 million tons of grain, affecting some 7.7 million people, forcing 2.2 million from their farms and villages, and threatening 5.5 million with starvation.[106] But like all modern famines, inappropriate government agricultural policies contributed to it.[107] Government decisions to ignore the productive potential of the dominant small-holder sector, promote ideological objectives through producer cooperatives and state farms, and gain control of peasant grain production through price and market mechanisms greatly contributed to suffering and starvation for millions of Ethiopians. So too did its failure to act after it and the World Bank had concluded more than a year earlier, in March 1983, that, "For some 5 million rural people drought has removed their capacity to sustain their own lives."[108] Arssi is evidence that small-holder programs like ARDU could have made a difference. While the region suffered a 25 percent decline in production during the drought, it had no starvation and was the only region in the country with marketable surplus.[109]

1982 ARDU Performance

Throughout its history, the project's organization was altered to improve performance. The 1982 chart is presented in Figure 7. A comparison with the 1971 organization chart[110] shows similarity of structure but a pattern of steady adjustment to revolutionary reforms and the need to improve performance in specific units. The most significant organizational changes during this 10 year period were: (1) the termination of the project's status as a semi-independent government unit and its transfer to the Ministry of Agriculture's jurisdiction; (2) the reform of the extension program to reflect Phase III's priorities and strategy; (3) the reorganization of various departments in an effort to make them financially self supporting, such as the Seed Multiplication and Animal Breeding Sections, or to ensure they operated more efficiently, such as the Road and Industry Sections;[111] and (4) divestment of some units to other ministries.[112]

The first change had minor impact, the Ministry generally ignoring supervision responsibility during the 1976-84 period and confining its activities to reviews of budget and staffing documents. The third change was unsuccessful, leading SIDA to recognize that its assumption the government would gradually take over financing of the project was ill-founded.[113] While seeking to devise a "disengagement strategy" and insisting on earmarking its ARDU allocations to promote fiscal integrity and SIDA priorities, the Swedes increased their financial support until it reached 50 percent of the project's budget, some of which went for recurrent cost support.[114]

Several documents published in 1981-82 provide a portrait of a project generally carrying out the strategy presented for Phase III but plagued by weak management, mechanistic use of administrative structures and systems introduced by CADU prior to the revolution, decaying physical plant and equipment resources, and ineffective staff performance.[115] A brief review of the major departments and sections will be presented, followed by an overall evaluation of the project.

First, the Plant Husbandry Department's sections conducted trials on a wide range of cereal, pulse, oil seed, vegetable, forage, and pasture grass varieties.[116] But, despite a staff of 9 high and 8 middle level professionals, no research break-throughs were achieved in 1982 reporting year, a pattern which had prevailed since the revolution. This was the case despite new project links with the National Institute of Agricultural Research. Progress was needed because some seed varieties were becoming vulnerable to disease and pests, peasants continuing to multiply them even when ARDU

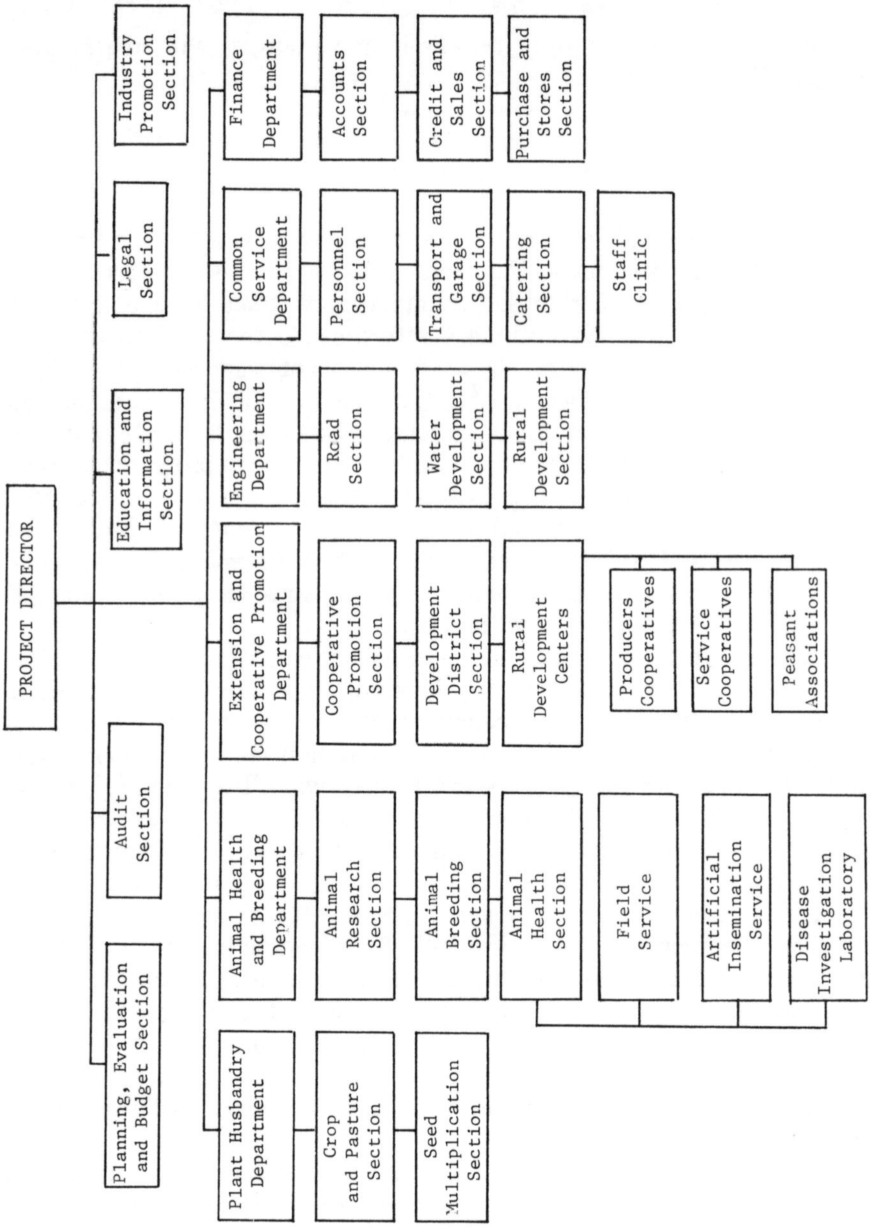

Figure 7: *ARDU Organization Chart in 1982*

withdrew them from production. Still, the surveys and trials conducted by the Department continued to contribute to building knowledge about the agricultural potential and constraints in Arssi.

In 1982 the Seed Multiplication Section produced some 29,000 quintals of certified seed on 1570 hectares of project land while contracting with cooperative societies for an additional 11,500 quintals.[117] Eighty percent of this output was high yielding wheat and barley seed, but an increasing amount of teff, maize, pulses, and forage crop seeds were also grown. The Section had problems keeping up seed quality, mainly because project research units had not been upgrading the varieties produced and seed farmer managers were careless about maintaining quality standards.

The three sections of the Animal Health and Breeding Department continued past activities aimed at improving the quality of livestock and dairy products. They experimented to upgrade local cattle and sheep varieties for milk and mutton production and identify optimal feeding levels for cross-bred cattle, studied growth rates of local and cross-bred calves, analyzed milk yields of cross-bred cattle to facilitate better breeding bull selection, raised cross-bred heifers and bull calves for sale in the region, conducted research on parasitic infection in sheep, studied performance of different breeds of sheep, worked with dairy associations to raise their milk yields, operated a pure Frisian bull semen collection program that produced sufficient doses to service 4,274 animals for farmers, and provided veterinary services aimed at preventing and controlling a number of animal diseases, including vaccinating 788,000 head and treating 79,300 animals. Overall the performance of the department was marginal relative to its targets; shortages of staff, inadequate transport, and poor laboratory facilities hampered its efforts.

Roads, water systems, dams, and buildings, stores, and sheds were constructed by the Engineering Department, many of them linked to self-help efforts mobilized by ARDU's extension agents. The goals of the Road Section continued to be connecting the main towns of Arssi with all-weather roads, creating employment opportunities, and developing techniques for construction of cheap rural roads. Under the 1976-80 plan, ARDU was to finance fully first class penetration roads and peasant associations to finance 50 percent of second class feeder roads and 100 percent of village roads. Maintenance was to be shared equally by ARDU and peasant associations. However, peasants held back contributions needed to construct and maintain routes. So only four of the 76 kilometers built in 1982 were partly self-help financed. This led to underutilization of staff and equipment.

The Water Development Section emphasized the organization of self-help schemes in communities, the construction of irrigation systems, dams and spring water facilities, and the development of ground water supplies through drilling programs and pump installations. Resources of the Rural Development Section were used to assist peasant organizations through 57

RDCs located in ARDU's 6 decentralized DDOs.[118] Based in these centers, ARDU's 138 extension and social mobilization agents worked with peasant associations, service cooperatives and producer cooperatives. Probably 80 percent of field agent time went into social mobilization.

Technical performance of these multipurpose RDAs was overseen by six ARDU headquarter committees composed of specialists in agronomy, crop protection, farm management, animal husbandry, home economics, and cooperative promotion. Similar, though fewer, subject matter committees were formed at the DDO level as well. On the technical side, few targets were reached in 1981-82. Little progress was made in increasing the number of demonstration fields or constructing cooperative village infrastructure, assembly halls, clinics, classrooms, grain stores and mills, and other facilities.

The 1982 objectives of the Extension and Cooperative Promotion Department were to: (1) assist the consolidation of peasant, youth, and women's organizations; (2) promote the formation and success of service and producer cooperatives; (3) introduce non-formal education that included social, political, and economic content; (4) promote local self-help schemes; (5) facilitate villagization and resettlement programs; (6) manage extension trials and farmer demonstration plots; (7) advise farmers on crop, livestock, and improved farm implements; (8) assist the AMC and AIDB to provide inputs, credit and marketing services; and (9) ensure the provision of adequate veterinary and artificial insemination services. Although such activities were carried out, extension trials were limited, crop protection trials inadequate, improved livestock sales below expected levels, and farm implements sales marginal. Offsetting this, RDA's did assist the AMC and AIDB to allocate 66,623 quintals of fertilizer, 11,861 quintals of improved seed and US$ 3.2 million in credit to some 80,000 farmers.[119] This was an increase over the 1975-76 figure.

In 1982, ARDU provided improved seed and the government distributed credit and fertilizer. Both used the service cooperatives to distribute these inputs to peasant associations and producer cooperatives. Peasant associations and producer cooperatives had estimated their needs for this growing season nearly a year earlier, forwarding their estimates through the service cooperatives. On receipt of inputs for the 1982/83 growing season, they paid 15 to 25 percent down and committed themselves to pay interest on the remaining value at a rate of 12 percent per annum. While credit repayment levels declined in the turbulent early years of land reform, area farmers were back to the high repayment rates of the CADU era by 1982.[120] Generally, there were sufficient quantities to meet local demand, in part because farmers were applying at levels far below those recommended by CADU and extension agents were too focused on producer cooperative formation to address this problem. The AMC had difficulty distributing fertilizer on a timely basis. Producer cooperatives received proportionally more fertilizer than small-holders. Improved seed was scarce, most of what was available being distributed to producer cooperatives. The shortage of improved seed was due largely to inefficiencies in the operation of ARDU's seed multiplication program. Service cooperatives were not able to provide adequate supplies of hand tools, pesticides, acaricides, and other needed inputs.

Crop production was reasonably good in 1982/83, ARDU estimating that some 550,000 metric tons of cereals and pulses were produced. Of this, the AMC procured only 15 percent. Farmers were reluctant to sell because they had little confidence the AMC would make grain available for retail sale later in the year. More importantly, the parallel markets offered much higher prices. These were particularly attractive given the cost of inputs. Only producer cooperatives were required to sell all production to the AMC. While it was not clear the AMC could handle more than one-fourth of total production, the government was beginning a program to drive the private sector out of grain markets.

A *methodological* point is in order here that has important implications for this chapter in general and its concluding section in particular. After the revolution project data on such indicators as hectares under cereals and pulses, amounts of inputs provided associations and cooperatives, yields per hectare in terms of kilograms or other weight measures, number of households, or average size of land holding became increasingly unreliable. Indeed, figures on particular indicators often differed for the same year in SIDA consultant reports, ARDU project documents, World Bank reports related to the project, and so on. For example, an ARDU report for 1984 claims that the AMC procured 40 percent of the 1982/83 Arssi cereals and pulses crop while a more authoritative SIDA consulting report issued in January 1985 put the procurement rate at 15 percent. Another example of confused data found in a December 1985 consulting report, which put area under production in 1984 in Arssi at 504,500 hectares and a January 1985 SIDA consultant report that put area under production in 1982 at 377,000 hectares, a difference too great to be explained by a mere increase in area farmed between the two years. Hence, it must be recognized that attempts to calculate productivity and yield on the basis of data set forth in this chapter can produce misleading or contradictory results. In this sense, this chapter is guilty of hyper-quantification for different figures come from different and at times conflicting reports. Still, as the last section shows, *the trends are clear even if they cannot be precisely quantified or the data made internally consistent.*

As for self-help schemes, Department agents, with substantial support from Engineering Department sections, mobilized local associations to build roads, construct or expand grain stores, schools, meeting halls and clinics, electrify towns, install flour mills and oil seed presses, improve markets, survey and lay out producer cooperative villages, and build bridges. Little progress was made in soil conservation, especially in terracing hillsides, although dams were constructed, springs protected, and seedling nurseries established. Self-help activities had clearly intensified since the revolution.[121] Yet, despite these results, the promotion of self-help efforts was well below the targets set for the reporting period.[122]

In the early 1980s, the Cooperative Promotion Section's agents sought to: (1) help organize service and producer cooperatives; (2) train farmer representatives in simple financial management systems; (3) advise on the plans and budgets of cooperatives and audit their financial records; (4) improve input and credit management systems; and (5) assist cooperatives to meet provisions required for legal registration. By 1982 the 1,086 peasant associations in Arssi provided the base for 142 service cooperatives with 235,400 members and 168 producer cooperatives with 14,161 members.[123]

Agents of this Section were charged with helping service cooperatives to provide inputs on credits, collect repayments, make loans to producer cooperatives, and assist smaller cooperatives to begin such activities as seed multiplication, bee-keeping, and fabrication. But too much staff time went into forming producer cooperatives and facilitating their transition form *malba* to *welba* stages given the fact their membership represented only 1.1 percent of the region's established population and 4.5 percent of the 470,869 cultivated hectares estimated for the Region in 1982.[124] Indeed, a considerable amount of time was spent by the Section's staff assisting in the establishment of 18 producer cooperative based "Wabe Villages" in Chilalo and Ticho *Awrajas*.[125] Because of this tendency to allocate scarce manpower for ideological purposes, ARDU's multipurpose extension agents reached only a small percentage of Arssi's farm population. If the project had direct effects on peasant production and welfare, it was primarily through the provision of inputs by the service cooperatives it advised.

Rural people were also reached through the activities of the Education and Information Section, a unit responsible for conducting short-term training programs and seminars for project field staff and rural organization representatives and promoting public awareness of the project and its objectives. By 1982 it was training 4000 farmer representatives a year in 10- to 15-day programs focused on crop production, plant disease, soil and water conservation, home science, skin and hides, bee-keeping, and cooperative management. A small number of additional people were also trained in 2-3 month metal and woodwork courses for the cooperative skills centers.[126] But the project staff's major interest was to promote social mobilization. Hence, an additional 2000 representatives of peasant, women and youth organizations were trained in leadership techniques. As with other sections, ARDU annual reports show this unit's inability to achieve its work plan targets.

ARDU's Project Training Center ran specific courses for multipurpose RDAs, livestock technicians (vaccinators and AI agents), and cooperative marketing specialists. Between 1969 and 1981, the Center trained 700 extension, marketing, cooperatives, and home economics agents,[127] but nearly 70 percent of these were trained before 1975, demonstrating the decline in training since CADU days.

The project also sought to promote economic growth through an Industrial Promotion Section aimed at: (1) designing and fabricating farm implements and equipment; (2) establishing rural skills centers and local industrial cooperatives; (3) training local people in industrial arts; and, (4) promoting improved bee-keeping. Towards these ends, it supervised in 1982 some 10 skills centers staffed by ARDU trained artisans, built an oil press and used it to train cooperative members on its operation and maintenance, established a cooperative brick factory, and promoted the formulation of cooperative bee farms, giving training in honey production, processing, and marketing. Its headquarters' facilities also produced preassembly materials that were dispatched to skills centers for final fabrication. Sale was made to local farmers only when the demand of cooperatives was met.

A major problem affecting all ARDU staff was the lack of transport. By 1982 the Common Services Department was managing a fleet of 100 ageing vehicles and trucks. While these covered 1.6 million kilometers that year, this was inadequate given ARDU's work plan, largely because the fleet had not been expanded despite the extension of the project's jurisdiction to all three Arssi *awrajas*.

One of the most innovative aspects of the CADU project was the Planning, Evaluation and Budget Section. As of 1982, its responsibilities were to: (1) conduct research on the project area; (2) undertake feasibility studies for proposed activities and evaluation exercises for established ones; and (3) promote improved efficiency and effectiveness of ARDU units through analysis of project performance and supervision of work plans and budget formulation processes. Unfortunately, its staff of five senior and two middle level officers proved unable to carry out the research proposed by the Phase III project paper or gather more than rudimentary performance data on ARDU's departments and sectors.[128] Continuing the pattern that had emerged since 1974, the Section gave low priority to undertaking studies documenting structural and behavioral patterns of the rural society the project proposed to develop or the effects of ARDU on the region's rural population and townsmen. Rather, its activities centered on mechanistically carrying out evaluation and monitoring exercises established in the CADU days, such as preparing project work plans and budget documents, reviewing expenditure reports, and evaluating quarterly and monthly work progress reports. This was certainly not the Planning and Evaluation Unit of the CADU era. To a large extent this was because it was politically safer to avoid studies on topics related to yields, income, and social development, particularly because of the inevitable comparison they would generate between the smaller-holder model and agrarian socialism.

ARDU's activities were carried out by an establishment plagued by high turnover and inexperienced recruits. In mid-1982, ARDU's staff included 45 professionals, 198 sub-professionals, 1677 permanent low level employees, and a large number of casual workers. This staff was not a drain on the country's national extension manpower resources, the project employing only 8.1 percent of the total Ministry of Agriculture staff with certificate degrees or higher.[129] At this time no high or middle level foreign experts worked for ARDU, a significant difference from 1967 when there were 36 or 1973 when there were 15.

EVALUATION OF ARDU

Despite the optimism and reforms of the 1976 Phase III document and the positive statements of annual reports, the 1974-85 period saw a gradual decline in ARDU's performance, as documented in a 1981 evaluation by a team of experienced specialists.[130] Their report identified six major problems that hampered ARDU's effectiveness.

First, a major cause of poor project performance was the project's limited professional and administrative capacity to carry out the range of research, extension, and social mobilization activities outlined in the Phase III design. Few of those trained at ARDU remained with the project because: (1) the revolution had forced many Ethiopian experts into exile; (2) the project's decline prevented it from attracting the dedicated and innovative individuals who had run CADU at a level that allowed it to influence national development policies; (3) the government transferred ARDU staff with little prior consultation; and (4) the ideological debates and political factions generated in the 1974-76 period contributed to disruptive internal competition for power and rapid turnover by staff. Frequently, it was the best, most experienced senior project officers who departed.

Retention problems led to high turnover of project directors, eight between 1977 and 1981 and four in 1981 alone.[131] The result was delayed project decision making, absence of clear project directions among core ARDU staff, uncreative problem solving, and general in-attention to setting and reviewing project objectives and strategies, analyzing in detail project investment proposals, collecting adequate data on project activities, and reporting accurately on project work plans, budgets, and activities. As a result of the retention problem, ARDU was forced to appoint junior officers with limited qualifications to leadership posts in the project's major units. Even if these officers were dedicated to their jobs, commitment was no substitute for adequate training and experience.

Second, poor project performance was the result of the Ministry of Agriculture's failure to administer ARDU in a coherent, supportive way. With the reorganization of the Ministry in 1979, ARDU became one of 14 regional offices and its employees members of Ministry staff and subject to Central Personnel Agency rules.[132] This was a move in the right direction, for one of the major criticisms of CADU had been its status as an semi-autonomous agency operating outside the ministerial system and unlikely to survive the end of SIDA financial assistance. But this incorporation had effects that hampered ARDU's capacity to be the dynamic, achievement-directed organization it had been before the revolution.

There are several reasons for this. First, the incorporation of ARDU staff into the civil service ended the project's capacity to hire experts on contract, to pay salaries and wages above parastatal rates, or to promote on the basis of performance. This, plus the freeze on civil service salaries after 1974, lowered morale. Second, senior ministry officers let ARDU run itself while making arbitrary decisions from time to time that threatened project objectives. For example, without prior consultation, the Ministry's Permanent Secretary transferred ARDU's milk pasteurizing plant to the Dairy Development Enterprise, Munessa forest tasks to the Forest and Wildlife Development Agency, and the project's responsibility for maintaining feeder roads to the Ethiopian Transport and Construction Authority.[133] Third, and perhaps most importantly, the liaison between the Ministry of Agriculture and the project was so weak that ARDU's major purpose of developing innovations of national utility was compromised. ARDU could not be the spearhead of national significance it was during CADU's first two phases if its personnel were not attuned to Ministry policies and programs and senior Ministry officers were poorly informed about the project's strategy and activities.

Third, ARDU performance was affected by the lack of a government policy on decentralization that would allow it to take advantage of its unique history and region-wide obligations. To be sure, decentralization in a period of revolutionary upheaval and insecure military control was difficult. But without clear policy, ARDU officers at times found their activities in conflict with central directives.[134] Lack of clear policy also made it difficult for them to build effective links between the project and the regional local government administration in general and the *awraja* and *woreda* revolutionary and administrative development committees in particular. The absence of such links hampered coordination and, at times, led to disputes that disrupted project performance.

Fourth, excessive focus on cooperative formation led to limited demands for scientists in the crop and livestock departments. Agents rarely informed researchers of the problems, needs, or ideas of farmers, and carried few innovations aside from CADU-generated seed and fertilizer recommendations. Nor did ARDU's senior officers demand research results. Consequently, a number of important tasks were neglected,[135] so that Phase III did not succeed in moving beyond CADU's emphasis on cereal and fertilizer to new crops essential for better farming or family nutrition. This was the case despite the fact that productive farmers' organizations and meaningful social development could not be achieved without income increases generated by research-based rises in agricultural output.[136]

Fifth, although well articulated on paper, the extension program reached few farmers with production advice, in part because the messages were haphazardly delivered and poorly communicated and in part because the incentive signals to agents were to facilitate social mobilization rather than to promote agricultural productivity.[137] The multipurpose agent concept had not proven appropriate, no RDAs having the ability, training, or physical capacity to carry out the range of assigned duties. Staff morale was low because of insufficient training, rapid turnover, and high expectations that could not be met. As a result, agricultural productivity was below what an effective extension program could have generated. Clearly what was needed was a return to the specialized agent model of CADU, particularly if ARDU was to serve cooperative organizations rather than individual farmers. But internal project rhetoric prevented this.[138]

Sixth, and finally, lack of properly maintained equipment, limited supplies, and inadequate transport hampered the activities of ARDU staff in all project sections.[139] More funds, and more efficient and effective use of them, were a prerequisite to improving project performance.

RECOMMENDATIONS FOR ARDU PHASE IV

The central question addressed during the 1981 evaluation was whether SIDA should support a fourth phase.[140] Despite the changed task environment and the problems identified, the evaluation team answered yes. Their report recommended that the Swedish and Ethiopian governments invest in rehabilitating the project's existing facilities and equipment while altering its strategy so as to increase the productivity of Arssi's small-scale farmers. Briefly, the report concentrated its recommendations on strengthening programs weakened by post-revolution emphasis on social mobilization. It called for: (1) renewed emphasis on research;[141] (2) return to an extension system staffed by technical specialists who reach farmers directly;[142] (3) improvement in the operation of service cooperatives;[143] (4) stronger project financing and staffing;[144] and (5) return of project responsibilities inappropriately transferred to other government units.[145] The evaluation mission further recommended the government meet certain conditions before a fourth phase was begun. These included: (1) improving salaries and terms of services for ARDU officers; (2) formulating a regional administration experiment to test ways to integrate the project with established structures of provincial government; and (3) increasing the exchange of information between ARDU and the Ministry of Agriculture, as well as improving the Ministry's technical backstopping for the project. In addition, the mission recommended that SIDA funds be earmarked to ensure that certain activities, such as livestock promotion, not be neglected by the zeal of staff members for other activities, such as cooperative formation.

These Phase IV recommendations attempted to return ARDU to the technical and economic focus of CADU and stood in contrast to the government's policy on the formation of producer cooperatives and the 1976 Phase III design emphasis on collective formation and social mobilization. They also conflicted with the views of some senior SIDA professionals in Stockholm that the project had run its course and could not be effective in Ethiopia's current policy environment. But the strength of the evaluation mission's recommendations kept Swedish funding flowing to ARDU on a limited, interim basis despite the fact that five years later no formal SIDA-Ethiopian agreement had been signed for Phase IV.

ARDU AND PADEP

During the period of uncertainty over Phase IV, an initiative emerged that would expand ARDU to cover large parts of Bale Region as well as extend the project model to all of Ethiopia's highland areas. Known as the Peasant Agriculture Development Extension Program (PADEP), it represented the attempt of donors to induce the government to support small-holder production.

Despite acceptable rates of return, ARDU was the only large IRD project to survive the first decade of agrarian socialism. Outside of Arssi, the major activity aimed at increasing small-holder productivity was the CADU influenced MPP.[146] When its first phase ended in 1981, the World Bank and the International Fund for Agricultural Development (IFAD) proposed financing a second phase that would expand the program from 155 to 440 *woredas*, provided the government altered its policy biases against small-holders and private grain traders. This the government was reluctant to do, partly because of ideological reasons and partly because it benefitted from the current price and quota system and preferred to use the country's limited number of extension agents to promote cooperatives rather than extend technical messages. Still, the shape of a new program emerged as the MPP extension discussions took place. Just as the MPP was a scaled down version of CADU, this new initiative, intensified as the PADEP program,[147] was based on ARDU's strategy and its initial experiments with the innovative Training and Visit System of research and extension.[148]

PADEP aimed at establishing four zonal projects in eight regions[149] to promote increased small-holder farm production and resource conservation through a design based on: (1) integration of all research, extension and other Ministry of Agriculture programs through regional headquarters having responsibility for overseeing plan formulation, budget operation, and work plan implementation; (2) organization of *woredas* within regions to function similarly to the DDOs in ARDU;[150] (3) creation of additional field posts and recruitment or redeployment of staff to them; (4) division of *woredas* into service cooperatives staffed by multipurpose RDAs as in ARDU;[151] (5) promotion of stronger institutions for providing agricultural inputs and extension services to farmers; (6) revitalization of extension staff and facilities through improved training, reporting systems, and evaluation activities based on the introduction of the Training and Visit System; (7) development of reliable, financially viable, cereal and export crop recommendations specifically tailored to regions and their administrative subdivisions; (8) concentration of extension resources in high potential areas of special promise; and (9) provision of finance to meet small-farm fertilizer requirements.[152] Under PADEP a regional director would integrate and implement all Ministry of Agriculture activities through an ARDU strategy-based system linking extension programs with service cooperatives, the AMC, and the AIDB. The World Bank also proposed providing funds to central government agencies that would help implement the price and market policies it saw as a prerequisite to a successful PADEP program.

PADEP's funding was to be dependent on Western aid because the Soviet Bloc was unwilling to provide assistance to projects targeted on individual small-scale producers. But the World Bank, PADEP's pivotal donor, remained unable to reach agreement with the Ministry of Agriculture during the 1983-86 period because there was little evidence that its conditions precedent on policy reforms needed to provide incentives to small-holders and private traders, would be met by a government increasingly dominated by Marxist central planners.[153] As of late-1986, the one program aimed at the massive small-holder sector hung in limbo.[154]

Beyond ARDU to BARDU

Under PADEP, Arssi and Bale Regions were to be consolidated, with ARDU becoming the Bale-Arssi Rural Development Unit (BARDU).[155] A large region of 124,600 square kilometers of rolling plains, Bale's 5 *awrajas* and 25 *woredas* covered three ecological zones: highlands dominated by barley, wheat, sorghum and teff; midlands where haricot beans and coffee, as well as food grains, were important crops; and lowlands suitable for livestock production but inhospitable to food crops, although maize and sorghum were grown.[156] Only four percent of the region, or 500,000 hectares, was under crops. The major ones were barley, growing on 58 percent of this land, and wheat, occupying 32 percent. Crop yields were low, running 700 to 1000 kilograms per hectare for wheat, barley, and sorghum and 1000 to 1200 kilograms per hectare for maize. In part, low productivity resulted from the absence of crop protection defenses against a number of weeds, diseases, and pests, as well as husbandry practices less advanced than those found in CADU-ARDU influenced Arssi. But the most significant reason for low yields was the limited penetration of appropriate higher yielding seeds and low levels of fertilizer utilization.

The effectiveness of the Ministry of Agriculture in Bale was limited by excessive staffing rates at regional and district offices, inexperienced field agents, bad roads, and inadequate transport. Very little research was being carried out, making the development of production-increasing packages difficult. A number of environmental problems, such as overgrazing and fuel wood shortages, were not being addressed. And the government had failed to extend the AMC's marketing services into most Bale *woredas* while restricting private trade. As a result service cooperatives had insufficient incentives to operate effectively and expand their activities as they had done in Chilalo, Arbagugu, and Ticho.

Unlike Arssi, more than 90 percent of Bale's estimated 900,000 people lived in villages, most of which had been settled in response to insecurity related to the Somali war and Oromo secessionist movements. Other villages had been formed by northerners from drought stricken areas. Averaging 250 households, Bale's villages provided the basis for peasant association and service cooperative formation. At the time of the BARDU evaluation mission, Bale had 561 peasant associations, most of which were based in villages, and 133 service cooperatives.[157] Most villages had an office for the peasant association and an assembly hall. Many service cooperatives had a building, so the infrastructure for the extension system planned for ARDU at the service cooperative level existed in Bale. This advanced social organization created interesting opportunities for effective extension and cooperative promotion activities.

The joint government-SIDA mission proposed strengthening ARDU so it could provide improved services to Arssi farmers and extend basic components of its program into 12 *woredas* in western Bale. There the project would concentrate primarily on crop production and supportive programs[158] in the middle altitude mixed farming areas, largely because little research was available on livestock and no animal production extension package was yet tailored to Bale's conditions. Crop programs were viewed as possible because of the similarity of Bale to some parts of Arssi and the fact that major crops in the expansion area were wheat and barley.

A project design paper for BARDU was completed in December 1983.[159] It outlined a zonal project based in Asella. The ARDU organization described for 1981 would oversee operations in Arssi, except for one major change: the project would return to CADU's concept of specialized agents by dividing the Extension and Cooperative Promotion Department into a Rural Development Department and a Peasant Association and Cooperative Promotion Department.[160] Bale was to be administered by a Deputy Director and a simpler organization consisting of four departments: Rural Development, Engineering, Finance, and Common Services. The Rural Development Department was to be the key to Bale's program, consisting of four teams specialized in crop production, animal resources, cooperatives promotion, and forest, soil, and water conservation. These would work downward to the *awraja*, *woreda*, and service cooperative level as proposed in the general PADEP strategy.

Under BARDU, the existing Arssi organization and activities would be strengthened and Bale would gradually evolve to match them. For this to happen it was deemed essential that the project return to the practice of preparing the kinds of operational plans that had made CADU successful, the BARDU proposal noting that no applied planning documents had been drafted throughout the project's third phase.[161] The design was tentative for several reasons. First, the administrative, financial, and technical aspects of the link between the two regions and the project needed to be elaborated.[162] Second, the multipurpose extension agent issue needed attention, for political cadres in Arssi felt the Training and Visit System experiment in Arssi was undermining socialist objectives, and Bale already had a multipurpose training center at Agarfa that the government argued should be used to train up to 20,000 farmers a year. Third, the problem of increasing government finance for recurrent costs needed to be resolved, for there was no sign the government was prepared to give substantial funds to ARDU or BARDU. SIDA was opposed to providing recurrent budget support for staffing – and reluctant to fund the replacement or repair of deteriorating capital investments it had made since the late 1960s.[163] Fourth, more attention needed to be given to the transfer of the project's Arssi-based resources to Bale.

Assuming these and other technical design issues could be worked out, SIDA proposed a 10 year project of three phases: Phase IV of two years, Phase V of three years, and Phase VI of five years. Before elaborating and completing the BARDU design, the government's Central Planning Supreme Council needed to approve the PADEP program as well as agree to two sets of conditions outlined in a 1983 SIDA *Aide Mémoire*.[164] The first repeated World Bank conditions that the government adopt in the project area a supportive small-farm policy that guaranteed fair and reasonable prices to farmers, promoted access to private traders, and facilitated the transport of agricultural production to and between markets.[165] The marketing constraint was particularly important because at best the AMC could not organize the procurement of more than one quarter of the surplus grain Arssi and northern Bale would produce in a good year, despite the fact that 1982-83 parallel market prices for grain ran up to three times those of the AMC. SIDA concluded that present government steps to treat private grain trade as a criminal activity would lead peasants to avoid the risk of selling outside AMC channels and lower their farm production. The second set of conditions required the government to agree to correct some of the problems identified in the 1981 ARDU evaluation.[166]

Prompt resolution of these conditions was essential, for the ARDU agreement, already in a 6 month extension, was scheduled to end December 31, 1983. Unfortunately the politics of the 10th anniversary of the revolution and the strong ideological views of important officials and policy planners in the government made 1984 a difficult year to negotiate conditions aimed at improving the productive capacity of small-holders and private traders in high potential farming areas. These political and policy constraints were compounded by a strong World Bank position that demanded major market liberation and price policy changes prior to its support for agricultural programs in Ethiopia.[167]

Recognizing that delays were inevitable, SIDA committed itself to ARDU for two or three years until a longer term agreement could be signed for a fourth project phase. This was a wise decision, for by March 1984 it had received no request from the government to move forward with an agreement for continuing ARDU and preparing BARDU. Throughout the year, SIDA had coupled its negotiations to break this deadlock with the World Bank's larger efforts to create a policy environment consistent with the private sector enhancing objectives outlined in its 1981 paper on accelerating development in sub-Saharan Africa.[168] But Bank insistence on government compliance with its proposed conditions precedent, and Ethiopian reversals on agreements with visiting missions to comply with some of these conditions, frustrated Swedish efforts to launch BARDU.

The deadlock was finally broken in late 1984 when a mission from Stockholm declared itself reasonably satisfied with the government's response to the conditions outlined in the 1983 *Aide Mémoire* . That mission's report on its November 26 to December 3 negotiations recommended SIDA proceed on its own to prepare BARDU as part of the PADEP program. The timetable proposed required a mid-1985 ARDU evaluation, a project paper based on its recommendations by September, and an aid agreement supporting BARDU for two or possibly five years signed by January 1986.

SEAD AND VILLAGIZATION

In early 1985, the Ministry of Agriculture was reorganized and its activities deconcentrated to eight zones comprised of regional offices. One of these, the South-Eastern Area Development Zone (SEAD), combined the Arssi and Bale Regions. In April 1985 SIDA and the government agreed to prepare a detailed appraisal document that would identify ways Swedish aid could help the Ministry of Agriculture establish zonal operations consistent with its new policies and structures while building on CADU/ARDU's heritage.

As of early 1986 this restructuring was continuing to evolve and staff were being transferred from headquarters to these zones. Therefore, the description that follows and SIDA's views on the SEAD format are tentative.

Under the reorganization, ARDU ceased to exist and the operations of all its activities were revised to fit those followed by all other regional offices of the Ministry of Agriculture as defined by the national PADEP program. So, by virtue of this reorganization, CADU-ARDU completed its gradual transition from a semi-autonomous unit to a fully integrated regional office of the Ministry. As a result, SIDA would no longer fund a time-bound IRD project. Rather, it would provide financial and technical assistance to one of several PADEP zones responsible for carrying out a wide range of IRD type activities through the Ministry of Agriculture's field operations.

To assist this significant institutional reorganization, and to continue its long term commitment to the Arssi area, a SIDA mission prepared a paper outlining in some detail a three year US$ 13 million foreign aid-supported program for SEAD. Since the PADEP initiative was strongly influenced by the CADU-ARDU experience, and since the two governments agreed that SEAD's activities would be based on CADU-ARDU tested initiatives, the SIDA document, released in December 1985, outlined a strategy quite similar to that proposed for BARDU.[169]

Briefly, under the SIDA design, SEAD would focus primarily on increasing the productivity of small-holders and building up their service cooperatives.[170] This was because nearly all farmers in the SEAD zone worked small farms and there was substantial evidence that such units had untapped potential to increase productivity as well as out-perform mechanized producer cooperatives.[171] Rather than concentrating on organizing producers cooperatives at the rate called for by the new ten-year plan,[172] the mission recommended consolidating and strengthening those already established.[173] Carrying out the activities outlined for SEAD would be no easy task since the zone comprised 58,000 square kilometers containing an estimated 450,000 households cultivating 613,000 hectares of crops.[174] In order to comply with the national PADEP structure for decentralized Ministry of Agriculture zonal units, SEAD's organization differed from the evolved but rather consistent format that marked CADU and ARDU.

Under the PADEP model, zonal offices were given greater autonomy in planning, budgeting and evaluation within a general framework determined at ministry headquarters. As planned, ARDU's project director becomes a zonal chief based in the former project's Asella offices. In theory he has complete authority over the deployment of zonal resources. But in practice his management is constrained by decisions of senior ministry and party officials in Addis Ababa. The zonal chief has a broad span of authority that reaches 3,600 employees through two regional deputies, eight *awraja* or District Development Offices (DDOs), five departments, and four service units.

Unlike ARDU, the DDOs report directly to the zonal head. The departments provide technical support to field officers in the DDOs rather than directing them. Regional deputies are largely confined to liaison functions, the most important of which is ensuring that budget allocations and zonal resources reach field officers.

Ministry activities in the SEAD zone reach rural producers through DAs in service cooperatives. Under a 1985 government directive they are "the major force for implementing and executing all directives concerning cooperatives at the grass-root level."[175] This essentially political function conflicts with the SIDA proposal's emphasis on using DAs to channel production-increasing messages to the zone's farmers, particularly since there are not enough DAs to reach more than a small fraction of the total farming community and who speak the local Oromo language.[176] Available evidence suggests that producer cooperative formation and technical support monopolize the DAs.

The 1985 reform aimed at more than decentralization and regional uniformity. In the words of the SIDA design team it was essentially political:

> The objectives of the cooperative and agricultural development administration of the CADU/ARDU era were to assist producers to overcome their production and marketing problems. However, the objectives now handed down by (the government) and the party are more specific. They aim to consolidate the socialist production and distribution system guided by Marxism-Leninism. A radical change is considered necessary to break the habits of the past. To achieve this, (the government) aims to regulate all six functions of the agricultural system: production, research, extension, marketing, input supply, and, most important, access to land. These ideological objectives pervade all official policy statements and directives on the subject of agricultural production and marketing. The purpose is to mobilize the development administration in the revolutionary struggle.[177]

Despite these organizational changes and political realities, the December 1985 SIDA proposal for SEAD zone support was grounded on the CADU strategy. That is, it stressed the provision of production enhancing services to farmers while downplaying ARDU's emphasis on mass mobilization. In outlining its technical recommendations, the SIDA team revealed the extent to which the services and infrastructure built up by CADU-ARDU had deteriorated since the revolution. But unlike the 1983 BARDU report, SIDA's SEAD proposal recognized the need to use Swedish aid to rebuild them. This was largely because they concluded that incorporation of the former project into the Ministry of Agriculture had not destroyed the CADU-ARDU organizational structure and because they believed present services and infrastructure could be revitalized by the injection of funds to rehabilitate facilities, purchase new equipment, and strengthen staff training. More importantly, the proposal was optimistic because the strategy it recommended was based on proven components of the CADU model: applied agricultural research, technical extension, master plans based on careful studies, administrative and financial management systems, and expatriate advisory and consultant services.

The SIDA proposal gave top priority to rebuilding crop and pasture research in the zone. Making prescriptions was not easy because no research reports had been published since 1980. Fragmented and unimaginative trials continued to take place but there was no effort to consider the farm system as a whole. Such variables as farmer risk or the role of livestock on the farm were ignored. The research that occurred was insensitive to small-holder needs. Despite the emphasis on group farms little research had been directed to the special problems faced by large mechanized farms under Arssi-Bale conditions. Moreover small-holder recommendations had changed little in the past 10 years, remaining brief and limited to fertilizer use, seeding rates, and weeding schedules.

In addition, the livestock program developed by CADU-ARDU needed to be rehabilitated, for draft power, milk, meat, manure, and hides contributed to 35 percent of the SEAD zone's agricultural output. The proposal expected this contribution to increase because the government set no prices for livestock products and allowed private traders to operate in the sector. This made livestock an attractive alternative to small-holders facing low government grain prices and burdensome quotas.

Over the previous decade livestock disease investigation programs had declined and veterinary laboratories had been so poorly funded that research activities and clinic services could not be adequately provided. Importantly, the artificial insemination and animal breeding program was not achieving high enough calving rates, and programs aimed at increasing milk yields and upgrading sheep and poultry stock were not productive.

To some extent this decline in the crop and livestock research programs was due to the failure of the Ministry to provide funds to purchase or maintain the stations and their research equipment. More importantly, it was due to the lack of qualified research staff and the failure of the national Institute for Agricultural Research or the ministry to set priorities, methodologies, and standards. For these reasons, SIDA proposed assisting SEAD to reequip or establish research stations in the zone, to provide field trial supplies, and to facilitate zonal staff to forge a coherent research strategy. As for livestock, SIDA offered to rehabilitate animal research laboratories, train more research technicians, and provide technical assistance to help revitalize and better manage essential livestock promotion programs.

The CADU-ARDU project was more successful at linking research and extension than most other development agencies in Ethiopia or abroad, but that link had steadily deteriorated since the revolution. Before the link could be reestablished the staffing and support of the extension service needed to be improved.

By 1986 it was clear that strengthening agricultural extension would be a difficult task for SEAD, even if the problems of adaptive research and limited field trials could be solved. The demands of producer cooperatives for extension services increasingly absorbed the time and energy of field agents. Extension agents were too few on the ground and too ill-equipped. SIDA proposed dealing with this problem by strengthening the zone's capacity to train field staff to extend the Training and Visit System beyond pilot *woredas* in Arssi. Particular attention was to be given to increasing the number of qualified subject matter specialists through in-service training and strengthening the research-extension link by rebuilding the CADU system of adaptive research and demonstration trials. In addition SIDA was to fund the construction of buildings and purchase of transport for Bale, which lacked the agricultural administration infrastructure built by CADU-ARDU in Arssi.

The SIDA proposal team recognized that even if research and extension activities of the ministry could be improved in the SEAD zone the government's policy of emphasizing the promotion of agrarian socialism to the detriment of agricultural productivity would make it difficult to use zonal field agents to link technical staff with farmers. In an effort to gloss over the problem they recommended slowing the formation of producer cooperatives while seeking to strengthen those already formed, using service cooperatives as the base of research-extension-farmer interaction, and strengthening performance of service cooperatives.

SIDA's recommendations on group farm mobilization were unlikely to be followed, a fact recognized by most team members. But the proposal did contain an innovative strategy for building the capacity of service cooperatives to promote agricultural productivity. It argued that these institutions had to be strengthened given the government's continued efforts to drive private traders out of the Arssi-Bale area and demand more economic and social development activities from service cooperatives, as well as its failure to improve the operational capacity of the AMC. Given these trends, SIDA proposed strengthening the capacity of service cooperatives to manage their marketing systems through improved information systems, training programs, and the establishment of a Cooperative Development Fund.[178] The Fund was envisioned as a source of revolving credit for the SEAD zone that would assist service cooperatives to purchase grain mills, trucks, scales, and other facilities to support the commercial operations demanded of these organizations.

The proposal recognized that promoting improved extension services and more efficient service cooperatives would be a formidable task. There were not enough DAs in 1985 to serve the zone's service cooperatives as planned. Nor did all the existing DAs have the requisite skills. Training of extension staff at Asella had been discontinued several years earlier and the former CADU-ARDU facilities were converted into administrative offices. This left SEAD dependent on national training centers which lacked the capacity to produce the number of production and cooperative extension personnel needed throughout the country. Nor did Arssi or Bale have adequate farm training centers to increase local farmer knowledge or strengthen management of service cooperatives.

Beyond core improvements in research, extension, and cooperative formation activities, the SIDA proposal offered concrete recommendations for strengthening SEAD's programs to build rural infrastructure and conserve the zone's soil and forest resources. Here emphasis was put on: (1) rehabilitating the seed multiplication section's capacity to produce high quality seed;[179] (2) promoting the establishment of tree nurseries and protecting existing tree plantations;[180] (3) promoting soil conservation practices in threatened areas;[181] (4) constructing rural roads to open up areas with agricultural potential while solving maintenance problems that threaten the established network;[182] (5) expanding water supplies for small towns on the basis of a comprehensive master plan;[183] (6) strengthening the small-scale irrigation program through improvements in design, construction, and water application methods;[184] and (7) revitalizing the rural industry and technical skill training program.[185] Underlying all the findings and recommendations of the SIDA proposal team was the recognition that management had deteriorated during the 10 year transition from CADU's semi-independent position to SEAD's full integration into the Ministry of Agriculture. To a great extent this was due to the steady expansion of area covered during a revolutionary period that hampered the training and retention of qualified administrators. But it was also due to the administrative format adopted by the Ministry of Agriculture for the SEAD zone, the decline in morale caused by limited recurrent budget allocations for equipment and supplies, the bureaucratic indiscipline generated by a 10 year freeze on government salaries, and the politicization of even the lowest clerical service units.

As organized, the span of control of the zonal chief and his support officers was too broad. Inadequate gate keeping focused their attention on a myriad of routine matters such as a faltering personnel and financial control system, an inadequate stores and property management operation, and the absence of effective radio-telephone links covering the zone.[186] This administrative burden and the absence of useful monitoring and evaluation data of the type once generated by CADU's Planning and Evaluation Section, limited the capacity of SEAD's Senior Staff to engage in strategic thinking, to promote effective planning and budgeting, or to practice anticipatory management.

Incorporation of SEAD into the Ministry of Agriculture and the expansion of other government agencies and ministries into the Arssi and Bale Regions created coordination problems far greater than those ever faced by CADU or ARDU. The reorganization of the Ministry of Agriculture and the relationships between its departments and SEAD's administrative and technical units, as well as to the evolving system of DDOs, RDCs and RDAs, is covered in great detail in the SIDA proposal for support for rural development in Arssi and Bale for 1986-89.[187] So too are the range of agencies outside the Ministry of Agriculture's control that increasingly operate within the geographical area covered by SEAD.[188] Suffice to say this early in SEAD's history, there is a substantial probability that organizational complexity, jurisdictional conflict, and bureaucratic infighting will make it very difficult for SEAD to carry out its annual work programs or reach its full potential.

Despite the problems reviewed here, SIDA officials in Stockholm generally accepted the proposal's recommendations. But substantial questions remained as to whether the government would comply with the policy and activity conditions precedent SIDA tabled during discussions over BARDU. Indeed, Stockholm concluded that unless the current policy biases against small-holders and private grain traders were removed, and long festering management and institutional problems in ARDU addressed, SEAD would not realize its potential for promoting agricultural productivity and improved quality of rural life in Arssi.

By January 1986 SIDA recognized that it was unlikely the government would address these conditions. As Sweden contemplated withdrawing support from SEAD over this lack of progress, the Ethiopians implemented a powerful new policy aimed at destroying free-holders and the private sector: villagization.[189]

The most controversial proposal in the 1976 Phase III documentation was a call for promoting social services through a scheme "whereby the scattered rural homesteads and villages will be attached to a central location to facilitate the provisions of basic services," such as water supply, medical care, education, and marketing facilities.[190] Clearly the draftsmen had in mind the then ongoing program of villagization in Tanzania, a program that was to have disastrous results for that country's agricultural production and rural development.[191] While ARDU's Phase III did not promote villagization it kept the strategy being discussed through the late 1970s and early 1980s, particularly through ARDU's role in the construction of the Wabe Villages.

Insecurity had led to gradual villagization in Bale and Hararghe between 1979 and 1984.[192] In addition, the resettlement of farmers evicted to make way for state farms in the Wabe Shebelli Valley had provided a model for the establishment of producer cooperative based villages. These experiences led the government to decree in 1985 a villagization campaign aimed at moving 33 million people into villages by the mid-1990s.[193]

Arssi was one of the first regions to be villagized.[194] During the December 1985-March 1986 campaign, nearly one million Arssi farm families were moved into 850 villages. In support of this move, the government argued villagization would: (1) enhance extension services aimed at increasing agricultural productivity; (2) promote more rational land use patterns and conserve natural resources; (3) facilitate access of rural people to schools, clinics, water supplies, and service cooperatives; and (4) strengthen security and self-defense. Such gains notwithstanding, the Swedes viewed the implementation of this program in the Arssi area as an indefensible disruption of small-holder productivity in a major grain producing area of the country at a time when Ethiopia was dangerously short of food.[195] SIDA also concluded that the more important, and unstated objective of villagization was to strengthen political control at the grassroots level so as to reinforce government agrarian policies and use the new villages as a foundation for establishing agricultural collectives.

Believing that villagization would lead to decreased agricultural production in Arssi for the next few years, and recognizing that the adoption of this policy demonstrated that ideological goals prevailed over economic rationality, SIDA suspended progress toward full support of SEAD. In a strongly worded statement in January 1986, the Swedish government declared it impossible to disregard Ethiopia's policies toward small-holders any longer, even in a project specific context.[196] While believing that eventually Ethiopia would recognize that its promotion of agrarian socialism would not raise productivity, SIDA reluctantly concluded that it could not agree to support SEAD as planned. So, in a June 1986 bilateral aid agreement, the Swedes substantially reduced their financial aid below an initially proposed US$ 4.3 million per year and targeted its use over a three year period on policy-neutral investments in SEAD's agricultural research, training, road construction, and soil conservation activities. Then in early 1987 SIDA began internal discussions as to whether SEAD funding should be suspended and aid reallocated to agroforestry projects elsewhere in Ethiopia. In essence, after years of CADU-ARDU support, SIDA was beginning to adopt a strategy of hibernation, waiting for the agricultural disaster Ethiopia was moving toward to break across the political system and force national decision makers to recognize that the country's economic future had to be built on the dominant small-holder sector.

The CADU-ARDU project lasted 17 years. There is no question that the overall heritage of Swedish aid, flexible project design, staff dedication, and land reform has increased productivity, improved diets, raised gross rural income, and extended quality of life-enhancing infrastructure and services. But data proving this is problematic (see page 175).

In the initial CADU area yield per hectare has doubled since 1967, and good gains were made in areas to which the project was later extended. So widespread were these gains that by the late 1970s national crop samples suggested Arssi led Ethiopia's administrative regions in crop production per capita and yields per hectare.[197] As a result, Arssi became the major wheat producing area, the second largest cereal producing area (behind Shoa), and the third largest pulse producing area (behind Shoa and Gojjam) in Ethiopia. Importantly, CADU-ARDU's presence had changed Arssi from a subsistence region in the 1960s to the third largest regional contributor to the national commercial cereal market, behind Shoa and Gojjam. Indeed, all three of Arssi's *awrajas* are now surplus generating areas.

It is estimated by ARDU that total production of food grains by Arssi's small-holders averaged 478,000 metric tons between 1980/81 and 1983/84. Arssi's 198 producer cooperatives averaged an additional 11,000 metric tons of food grain production during this period. Marketed surplus probably averaged 175,000 metric tons, of which the AMC purchased an annual average of 57,250 metric tons, or 19 percent of total national AMC purchases from peasants during this period. If the increased restrictions on private traders introduced in 1984 are successful, and if villagization makes it more difficult for Arssi farmers to circumvent AMC agents, Arssi is likely to increase its share of contributions to the AMC. Importantly, these gains in marketed sales were made despite the disincentives to production discussed earlier and a large population increase over the 1967-84 period.

The draft 1984 census for Arssi puts the population at 1,662,223,[199] more than double the 1965 government estimate of 722,500.[200] This increase was well above the national annual population growth rate for the 1965-1983 period,[201] suggesting large migration into the project area stimulated by the production-increasing effect of CADU-ARDU.

The increase in Arssi households and cultivated farm land served by CADU in 1967 and ARDU in 1984 is given in Table 10. If the households and land in Bale served by the project are added to Arssi totals, SEAD covered some 320,000 farms cultivating 613,000 hectares of land.[202] Just before the creation of SEAD, ARDU reached Arssi's farm households through a complex hierarchy of 6 DDOs, 58 RDCs and 175 RDAs serving 1,085 peasant associations through 143 service cooperatives and with 283 producer cooperatives.[203] Bale's households were served by 42 RDCs and

Table 10: *Arssi Households and Cultivated Area Served by Project: 1967-84*

Year	Households	Cultivated area
1967	60,000	150,000
1974	143,000	415,000
1984	235,600	504,500

Source: SIDA, *Proposal for SIDA Support*, pp. 223-6.

82 RDAs working through 139 service cooperatives and with 108 producer cooperatives.[204] The increase in population and cultivated area provided more livelihood for rural people and food for national markets, but it also increased environmental problems. Expanded production came at the expense of the region's grazing land. The resulting conversion of pasture to farm land led to an increase in soil erosion throughout the region and new conservation problems for ARDU's staff. It also led to problems for smaller households in the more densely populated peasant associations. They had little pasture to maintain a pair of plow oxen, much less take advantage of ARDU's livestock programs. As demonstrated, the project addressed these problems as they emerged but limited funds and emphasis on social mobilization made progress difficult.

Over its 17 year period CADU-ARDU significantly increased the amount of credit, fertilizer, and improved seed available to farmers in the project area. This was the case even after the government began giving state farms and producer cooperatives throughout Ethiopia priority access to production inputs. The increase in the distribution of credit and inputs over this period is summarized by Table 11. The 1981 evaluation teams attributed the slow increase in fertilizer sales since the mid-1970s to deteriorating wheat to fertilizer price-ratios.[205] Seed sales also declined from the 1977-78 high because farmers increasingly saved their own from previous harvests. However, despite these factors, ARDU reported in 1985 that if the government did not limit input supplies because of policies supporting state farms and producer cooperatives, it could be selling 133,000 quintals of fertilizer and 65,000 quintals of seed to Arssi's farmers.[206] In interpreting data in Table 11, it should be noted that focused studies in areas of strong project presence show higher participation rates. For example, one survey of 2500 households found 70 percent of them regularly participated in ARDU's credit program.[207]

The spread of higher yielding seeds, supporting production inputs, and better husbandry techniques by the project over the 1967-82 period should have led to considerable increases in the Arssi region's agricultural output. Certainly this was the trend suggested by pre-revolutionary crop samples carried out by CADU. However, the absence of such studies since 1973 makes it very difficult empirically to demonstrate such a trend.[208]

Table 11: *Increase in Project Distribution of Credit and Inputs 1967-84*

Fiscal Year	Credit Volume '000 Birr	Number of Credit Participants	Input Sold (Quintals)	
			Fertilizer	Seed
1967/68	-	189	42	189
1968/69	158	869	2,822	4,540
1969/70	503	4,760	18,700	11,300
1970/71	4,442	14,146	41,955	14,239
1971/72	1,124	12,624	45,325	15,316
1972/73	1,703	13,302	40,129	5,404
1973/74	2,260	25,201	70,604	2,253
1974/75	2,734	42,000	50,705	11,976
1975/76	-	57,000	64,553	19,572
1976/77	3,226	50,157	87,357	15,815
1977/78	4,211	65,000	68,006	29,745
1978/79	3,844	61,062	71,236	18,960
1979/80	3,343	70,000* (57,272)	88,697	18,694
1980/81	6,920	70,000* (54,272)	73,176	18,755
1981/82	6,560	80,000* (65,453)	66,623	11,861
1982/83	-	90,000* (73,635)	83,091	16,503

Source: ARDU, "Objectives-1984," pp. 9-10; S. Bekure, et al., *Evaluation*, p. 3, 9.
Note: * = Includes credit participants organized under producer cooperatives.
( ) = Estimated independent small-holders.

ARDU plant breeders identified seed varieties capable of significantly increasing cereal production in the region.[209] They also demonstrated the potential of these varieties on the project's seed multiplication farms. However, in 1985 these potential yields were not yet achieved by Arssi farmers. Progress toward higher yields in Arssi was occurring, particularly by farmers who adopted recommended ARDU packages. This can be demonstrated for wheat and barley: traditional growers achieve 700 and 1000 kilograms per hectare respectively, while adopting Chilalo farmers are achieving 1600 kilograms per hectare for wheat and barley. ARDU, however, produces both crops at 4,000 kilograms per hectare.[210] Some of the contact farmers in the 1983 pilot Training and Visit System program claimed to reach yields of 3,000 kilograms of wheat per hectare when they followed ARDU advice.[211] These potential yield increases are significant since in 1983 an estimated 41 percent of Arssi's cropped farm land was under barley and 31 percent under wheat. The success of CADU-ARDU in increasing

Table 12: *Average Crop Yields by Awraja in 1981*
(Kilograms per Hectare ('00) in 1981)

Crop	1966 Estimate	ARDU Seed Farm	Chilalo *Awraja*	Arbagugu *Awraja*	Ticho *Awraja*
Wheat	5-9.0	40.0	16.3	13.3	12.8
Barley	9-10.0	40.0	16.3	11.6	14.1
Teff	3.0	15.0	11.0	10.0	9.3
Maize	n.a	60.0	27.1	18.0	24.1

Source: ARDU, "Objectives-1984," p. 5; Solomon Bekure, et al., *Evaluation*, p. v, iv; Bengtsson, *Rural Development Research*, p. 111.

agricultural yields and productivity in the project area is demonstrated by Table 12.

Yield increases are also suggested by two other studies. The first, undertaken by the Ministry of Agriculture of 20 highland peasant associations in all 10 regions, showed that the two Arssi associations had significantly more yield per hectare than the average of the other 18.[212] Chilalo's Bilbilo Royeha association in Limu *Woreda* and Bedi Damota association in Bilbilo *Woreda* reported average yields as 1150 kg./ha. and 1930 kg./ha. respectively for wheat and barley. Neither was classified as occupying fertile land. The sample average was 738 kg./ha.

The second study was carried out in Chilalo by an independent researcher in 1980.[213] He revisited 25 farmers studied in 1967 and an additional 25 new farmers. The conclusion of the study was that the average yield increases for sample farmers were up because of increased use of fertilizer, adoption of higher yielding seeds, increased planting densities, and adoption of herbicides. Basic data from this study are presented in Table 13.

The livestock program also increased the output of draft power, milk, meat, manure, and hides in the region. But the benefits generated are even less well documented than those from crops. It is estimated there are now at least 5000 dairy cows in Arssi producing a surplus of five million liters per annum, most of which is consumed in the region's towns, enhancing farm income and local nutrition.[214] It is also clear that years of research and experimentation with livestock breeding (dairy cows, sheep, and poultry), disease prevention, artificial insemination, and milk processing and marketing provide a solid base for further grains in livestock production. All that is required is for the Ministry of Agriculture to commit itself to promoting livestock productivity in the SEAD zone.

Given these yield increases the income of Arssi's small-holders should have risen considerably. Indeed, the region's farmers should be the richest in the country. However, ARDU has not generated data that establishes that increased yields have led to higher incomes.

Table 13: *Adoption of Innovation and Yield Increases for Sample of Chilalo Farmers: 1967-80*

Item	1967 Visited Farmers (N=43)	1980	
		Revisited Farmers Farmers (N=25)	Newly Visited Farmers (N=25)
Use of Fertilizer	4%	100%	60%
Average Amount of Fertilizer/farm	0	120 kg.	80 kg.
Use of Improved Seeds			
Wheat	16%	88%	68%
Barley	0%	44%	20%
Maize	0%	67%	22%
Average Yields in Dry Matter (kg./ha.)			
Wheat	908	1230	1170
Barley	1130	1520	1760
Maize	1610	1530	2860
Average Plant Population/ha.			
Wheat	1.5×10^6	3.1×10^6	
Barley	1.5×10^6	2.2×10^6	
Adoption of Herbicides			
Tried in fields	9%	40%	24%
In use 1980	-	12%	12%

Source: Bengtsson, *Rural Development Research*, pp. 183-4.

CADU data demonstrate rising income in the project area between 1967 and 1971. ARDU reports household income continued to rise between 1974 and 1984, but has only sketchy data to support its claims. Specifically, pre-revolution data for Chilalo *Awraja* approximates 1971 CADU estimates that farm households adopting project seed-fertilizer packages raised their real income from a 1966 figure of EthB. 313 to EthB. 883.[215] ARDU data suggest a doubling of income between 1974 and 1980, with former tenants having higher increases because of the abolition of rent payments by the land reform legislation.[216] Data by *awraja* in support of this assertion are set forth in Table 14.

Yet, there are important reasons to challenge claims that Arssi's farmers have had substantial increases in real net income since 1974. Low government prices and enforced delivery quotas discussed earlier have kept farm profits low, particularly since the regional administrator began to suppress private grain traders. Profits have also been eroded by rising costs for production inputs, micro-economists estimating that between 1974 and 1980 terms of trade moved substantially against grain producers.[217] Household income also has been reduced by taxation and mandatory contributions to

Table 14: *Average Income Distribution per Household Before and After Land Tenure Reform*

Awraja	Pre 1975 (EthB.)	1980 (EthB.)
Chilalo	875	1,647
Arbagugu	639	1,352
Ticho	765	1,378

Source: ARDU, *Investigations on Impact*, p. 59.

national campaigns for defense, drought, party office construction, and so on. Finally, inflation and rising prices for consumer goods have eroded the value of peasant's remaining disposable income. Still ARDU and SIDA claimed in 1981 that incomes of Arssi's farmers were much higher than in 1966, that they varied across the region despite clear evidence of greater economic equality since the revolution began, and that they were "considerable as compared to national figures."[218] ARDU also claimed that the land tenure reform and project efforts to promote widespread economic equality led to a reduced income gap; project statisticians asserted that the Gini coefficient measuring the area between the diagonal of perfect equality and the Lorenz curve of inequality had declined in Arssi from 22 to 9 percent.[219] Finally, based on analysis of consumption and savings data drawn from the 1980 survey, ARDU's economists estimated that consumption and savings were much higher than those found elsewhere in rural Ethiopia.[220]

Overall consumption data for the 1980 survey suggest that most household expenditures went for food and beverage, clothing and footware, social fees, and taxes or contributions.[221] The survey found a high correlation between sample farmers with tin roofed houses and radios and areas where CADU-ARDU had operated the longest.[222] These data also suggest farmers were beginning to increase their savings, particularly in the project's main grain growing areas. [223] Still, because of the government's extractive price, marketing, and taxation policies described earlier, many farmers have little net disposable income to save or expend. Despite higher yields, many farmers appear to knowledgeable observers to be no better housed or clothed than they were 20 years ago. For political reasons, ARDU has not investigated this obvious contradiction between yields and disposable income.

Per capita consumption of wheat and barley had increased since the arrival of the project and the implementation of land reform. Overall it rose from 41 kilograms of wheat and 98 kilograms of barley per person to 85 kilograms and 143 kilograms respectively.[224] Another study focusing on all food grains found per capita consumption of Arssi farmers to be 184 kilograms per capita as opposed to a national average for rural people of 146 kilograms per person.[225] The people of Arssi were better nourished in 1982 than in the mid-1960s.

The increased yields, potentially higher income, and improved household food consumption reviewed here, as well as the improved physical infrastructure and increased human services reported elsewhere in this book, testify to the potential of an integrated rural development project to address problems of agrarian stagnation and rural poverty in Third World countries. This is particularly the case given the strong influence the project had on land reform, the organization of the Ministry of Agriculture, and the design of the nationwide MPP and PADEP programs.

To be sure the project has problems as well as successes. These were reviewed in Chapters 5 and 6. In summary, the most important of these were: (1) the inability of the Ethiopian government to assume financial responsibility for the CADU-ARDU operation or to address recurrent cost issues; (2) the unwillingness of the government to alter policies that undermine the capacity of CADU-ARDU to promote small-holder productivity and income; (3) the difficulty of recruiting and retaining qualified managers and technical professionals; (4) the ineffective and mechanistic use of CADU-introduced organizational structures and systems by project personnel, as well as the decay of the project's physical plant and equipment; and (5) the excessive politicization of the project strategy after the revolution and its effect on the technical direction and successes of the project. All but the first of these major problems can be attributed to the revolution, a force no project design could have anticipated and one that affected all projects in Ethiopia – not just those of the integrated rural development type. The first is a serious problem for all donor-funded interventions, and particularly those that are large and costly such as CADU-ARDU. The implications of this problem will be discussed in the next chapter.

Surprisingly, SIDA has commissioned no cost-benefit study of the project since 1971, when such an exercise revealed benefits were rapidly exceeding total costs.[226] To be sure, ARDU's failure to collect systematic data after 1974, and the inconsistencies in available data discussed earlier, contributed to a reluctance to attempt such an exercise. But according to SIDA officials, by the late 1970s the internal rate of return was so clearly in excess of 100 percent that a technical effort to obtain accurate data needed to do a cost-benefit analysis was not merited.[227] In support of the position that it was not necessary to quantify the obvious, they offered two lines of argument. First, they pointed out that the project is primarily interested in higher yields for small-holders. Since success in promoting this objective is well established, there is no need to consider macro-level internal rates of return, particularly because the assumptions and data needed to carry out such a difficult exercise are questionable. Second, they provide discrete examples of obvious and substantial national benefits. For example, they note that the incremental gains from wheat production during the 1980-83 period alone easily cover the 1967-83 SIDA-Ethiopian investment of US$ 41.5 million (EthB. 85 million) in the project.[228]

Against the charge that the project was too expensive a drain on limited national resources and contributed to regional inequality, it is important to note that external evaluators concluded in 1974 that CADU did not make excessive demands on scarce national manpower and budget resources and generated important benefits for the entire country. Analyzing costs by expenditure categories, they argued that 40 percent of CADU expenditures had benefits beyond project boundaries.[229] These related to services with wider benefits (e.g. agricultural and livestock research, training for EPID, advances in general administration systems) and investments that substituted for government services that would normally have been funded through the budgets of field ministries and state agencies (e.g. agricultural extension, road construction, water development, cooperative formation).

As for special investments the project made in Chilalo and Arssi, it can be argued that they too had wider benefits, the most important being the stimulation of policy debates within the government on the appropriate rural development strategy for Ethiopia. In particular, the CADU experience established that the critical mass of investments and activities needed to promote agricultural growth was higher than the government supposed. If this message and the success of the project in stimulating economic growth influenced the government's allocation of development expenditures toward greater investment in peasant agriculture, then even the distinctly local costs would have had a larger national impact. The drafts of the Fourth Five Year Development Plan proposed in the final months of Haile Selassie's reign demonstrated that this was the case.[230] Since the revolution it is the CADU-ARDU model that has provided, mainly through the PADAP initiative, the only viable alternative to the strategy of agrarian socialism pushed by the government. Finally, had CADU-ARDU not turned Arssi from a deficit to a surplus food producing region it would not be able to make its presently critical contribution to national food supplies.

While the charge of excessive investment in one area is too simplistic, it is true that CADU-ARDU made Chilalo one of the most productive farming areas in Ethiopia. However, as Chapters 5 and 6 have demonstrated, the project's experience influenced the design of the land tenure reform and created one of the most change-oriented peasantries in the country. To a large extent Chilalo's progressiveness set an example for the rest of rural Ethiopia during the early days of the revolution. Since such progressiveness was clearly related to the rise of economic status of the *awraja*, the fact that regional inequality resulted is less undesirable than critics believe.

Given this performance, it is not surprising that SIDA continued to support integrated rural development despite the problems that have plagued the project since the revolution. Clearly, substantial constraints needed to be overcome to make SEAD work effectively for the advance of hundreds of thousands of small-holder households in the combined regions. But whether the critic is optimistic or pessimistic about the possibilities of success, the experience of this project between 1967 and 1984 has much to offer to the debate over whether integrated rural development is an ill-conceived fad of the 1970s or a strategy that merits application when conditions are appropriate.

Notes

1. The initial 1972 proposal is found in: Lars Leander, "A Proposal for the Extension of the CADU Program into Arbagugu and Ticho" (Internal Memorandum, Asella, July 9,1973).
2. Two types of roads were proposed: (1) penetration roads; and (2) feeder roads. Priority was to be given to penetration roads linking commercial and administrative centers to Asella, the northern highway in Shoa from Addis Ababa to Dire Dawa, and the southern highway linking Shasemene with Bale Province. A number of smaller feeder roads were to be extended off these penetration roads. In all some 495 kilometers of roads were to be built between 1974 and 1980 by labor intensive methods and according to methods tested in Chilalo *Awraja*. The 68 kilometers of primary road were to be fully financed by the project and the 427 kilometers of feeder roads to be jointly funded on a fifty–fifty basis by the project and local contributions. Research efforts were to focus on agronomy trials (cereals, legumes, oil-crops, cultural practices), fertilizer experimentation, forage crop studies (observation of fodder beets, grasses, oats, local grasses),crop protection survey (diseases, insects, weeds), soil sampling, climate observation, and seed collection. In the second phase tested varieties would be released, foreign crops tested, crop protection trials carried out, erosion studied, and seed farms established.
3. One extension agent would be assigned to each development district. During the preparation phase he would: (1) inform farmers about the project, its objectives and methods; (2) identify target groups for certain activities; (3) assist in the technical trials and surveys; and (4) carry out demonstrations on promising crop production innovation, seeds and fertilizer. When the second phase began he would be joined by a marketing specialist. In their first implementation year they would: (5) run demonstration plots on a full scale; (6) organize model farmer areas and select model farmers; (7) introduce and sell improved seeds of cereal, pulse and oil crops; (8) establish a credit program on a limited scale; and (9) begin the provision and sale of improved seeds, fertilizer and implements. The second implementation year would consolidate those activities and carry out initial studies on forestry and livestock. In the third year of the implementation phase, a second extension agent would join the team, allowing activities to expand further to include: (10) introduction of soil conservation and afforestation on a limited scale; (11) establishment of forest nurseries; and (12) initiation of livestock extension activities for cattle and sheep.

4. Guy Hunter, et al., *Final Report on the Appraisal of CADU and EPID* (Report by the Evaluation team appointed by the Imperial Ethiopian Government and the Swedish International Development Authority, Asella, May 1974), pp. 68-71.
5. The term "province" (*Teklay Ghizat*) was changed to "administrative region" (*Kifle Hager*) to imply division of land rather than area governed. The title "governor" was changed to "administrator." The name "Arussi" was altered to "Arssi" to assuage the rising ethnic resentment of the Oromo majority: P.T. Baxter, "Ethiopia's Unacknowledged Problem: The Oromo," *African Affairs*, LXXVII, 308 (1978), pp. 283-96.
6. Imperial Ethiopian Government, *Statistical Abstract of Ethiopia*, 1975 (Addis Ababa: Central Statistical Office, 1976), p. 24.
7. Comparative data are found in: Ministry of Land Reform and Administration, *Report on Land Tenure Survey in Arussi Province* (Addis Ababa: Department of Land Tenure, 1967), pp. 5-8, 10-11, 22; Central Statistical Office, *Report on Survey of Arussi* (Addis Ababa: Central Statistical Office, 1966), p. 19.
8. Haile Selassie's government carefully avoided gathering data on religion and ethnicity for it feared they would demonstrate the domination of the Christian Amhara in southern provinces. The waves of Islam that moved across parts of Arssi, and the attraction of the religion to the conquered people are described in: J. Spencer Trimingham, *Islam in Ethiopia* (London: Frank Cass & Co., 1965), pp. 207-9; Baxter, "Ethiopia's Unacknowledged Problem," pp. 283-96.
9. The revolution is described in: Marina and David Ottaway, *Ethiopia: Empire in Revolution* (New York: Africana Publishing Co., 1975); Fred Halliday and Maxine Molyneux, *The Ethiopian Revolution* (London: Verso, 1981). The large literature that has emerged since the revolution is reviewed in: John M. Cohen, "Revolution and Publication: Ethiopia Since 1974," *African Studies Association Review of Books*, V (1980), pp. 154-63.
10. Paul B. Henze, "Communism and Ethiopia," *Problems of Communism*, XXX (1981), pp. 55-74; Edmond J. Keller, "The Ethiopian Revolution: How Socialist Is It?", *Journal of African Studies*, XI, 2 (1984), pp. 52-65.
11. On the reforms and their implementation see: John M. Cohen and Peter H. Koehn, "Rural and Urban Land Reform in Ethiopia," *African Law Studies*, XIV (1977), pp. 3-61; Dessalegn Rahmato, *Agrarian Reform in Ethiopia* (Uppsala: Scandinavian Institute of African Studies, 1984); Alula Abate and Fassil G. Kiros, "Agrarian Reform, Structural Changes and Rural Development in Ethiopia," in *Agrarian Reform in Contemporary Developing Countries*, edited by Ajit Kumar Ghose (New York: St. Martin's Press, 1983); Adrian P. Wood, "Rural Development and National Integration in Ethiopia," *African Affairs*, LXXXI, 329 (1983), pp. 509-39.
12. Because of the instability in Chilalo and the sensitivity of CADU and SIDA staff to repercussions for political reporting, no detailed study is available on the processes of change in Chilalo between 1974 and March 1975. The following tentative review is based on interviews in Ethiopia and abroad with ARDU staff members, SIDA officers, Peace Corps Volunteers, and *Zemecha* participants.
13. The events of 1974-75 in Chilalo are described in: John M. Cohen, "Green Revolution in Ethiopia: The Politics of Rural Development in a Blocked and Inequitable Society," in *Analyzing Political Change in Africa*, edited by James R. Scarritt (Boulder: Westview Press, 1980), pp.133-8.
14. Based on project experience, members of ARDU's staff submitted to the military's coordinating committee a proposal for reforms quite similar to those ultimately issued in 1975. See the August-September 1984 ARDU staff journal, *Limat*. Betru Gebregziabher, *Integrated Rural Development in Rural Ethiopia : An Evaluative Study*

of the Chilalo Agricultural Development Unit (Bloomington: University of Indiana, International Research Center, 1975), p. 60.

15. For example, 25,000 Chilalo residents met a visiting Derg mission with great enthusiasm shortly after the reform was announced: "Peasants in Chilalo Hail the Nationalization of Rural Land," *The Ethiopian Herald* (March 18, 1975), p.1.
16. The Ethiopian press, eager to report such resistance, noted only one case of a local aristocrat jailed in Arssi for resisting the reform. This case occurred in October when the former governor of Ticho *Awraja*, Fitawari Bekele Ogato, and 16 supporters were killed trying to flee to Bale Region. This once powerful Arssi landowner was charged with "banditry" and efforts to sabotage the revolution. "81 Fugitives Killed in Wollo Arussi Region," *The Ethiopian Herald* (October 9, 1975), p. 1. One other Chilalo landowner carried on a substantial resistance effort in another province but did not fight for his holdings near Asella. He was an heir of Ras Biru, who held large tracts of land in Chilalo, particularly in Hetosa Woreda. His sons, one a particularly successful commercial farmer in Chilalo, maintained a resistance in the Menz district of Shoa Province for 10 months, where they became a rallying point for some 3,000 Shoan dissidents and royalists. The PMAC announced that they had been killed in mid-1975. Colin Legum, "Fighting on Three Fronts in Ethiopia," *The Observer* (October 12, 1975), p. 8.
17. It should be noted that a superficial study of the implementation of land reform in Arssi Region found the 1975-76 period marked by local officials hampering efforts of reform officers and students to meet with peasants, landlords making threatening night visits to peasants, rural elites and their police allies imprisoning or even murdering outspoken former tenants or newly elected peasant association leaders, and landowners returning to reclaim expropriated holdings at gun point. Unfortunately, this report by Aster Akalu fails to provide any dates or location for such events, nor does it give any indication of the frequency or pervasiveness of them. *The Process of Land Nationalization in Ethiopia: Land Nationalization and the Peasants* (Lund: Gleerup, LXXVI, 1982). To be sure such things happened, but there is no evidence that during the 1975-76 period they were as common or disrupting as she implies. A lengthy review of *Ethiopian Herald* reveals efforts to mobilize class consciousness and form of a people's militia. But only a few reports can be found of social unrest and conflict despite the government policy of reporting them as part of its efforts to promote political awareness. In reviewing the *Zemetcha* in Arssi the government reported "...it did not take us long to mobilize the farmers ... Our main headache was the local bureaucratic establishment (which)...had been keeping up a campaign to smear the *Zemetcha* participants in a bid to poison their relations with the farmers." "Campaigners' Achievements Hailed", *Ethiopian Herald* (July 15, 1976), p. 5. This lengthy review of the 1975-76 campaign had nothing in it on bloodshed or excessive conflict. Other reports included: "26 Merchants Charged with Sabotage to Appear in Arussi Court", *Ethiopian Herald* (July 15,1976), p. 6. (They were charged with hording grain and pepper.); "Arssi People's Militia Liquidates 14 Outlaws Stealing Cattle from Working Masses," *Ethiopian Herald* (March 11, 1977), p. 1. (They were thieves not anti-revolutionary forces); "Anti-People Clergymen exposed in Arssi," *Ethiopian Herald* (August 29, 1979, p. 5. (Anti-revolutionaries charged with hiding weapons in a church and trying to use clergy to help them regain lost land). Armed conflict did occur in lowland areas of Arbagugu and Ticho *Awrajas* from mid-1977 until early 1978; however, the evidence is that those killed or captured were involved in Somali and Oromo successionist movements connected with the Ogaden War rather than proponents of Haile Selassie or his land tenure system. For example, in March 1977 troops and local militia launched a campaign in Ticho *Awraja's* Chole *Woreda* to stamp out alleged

counter revolutionaries. Eighty-four were killed but their alleged activities were not spelled out in the press. "84 Assassins in Chole District Liquidated," *Ethiopian Herald* (March 22, 1977), p. 1. Then in May the press claimed 9 bandits charged with "misleading and suppressing peasants" were captured in Ticho *Awraja*. "Militiamen in Arssi Capture Nine Bandits," *Ethiopian Herald* (May 29, 1977), p. 1. Later that month 42 outlaws with 52 firearms were captured in Aminia *Woreda*. They were said to have forced 600 persons "to flee their homes and join the contra-revolutionary camp." "Militiamen in Arssi Capture 42 Outlaws," *Ethiopian Herald* (May 31, 1977), p. 1. By July the government claimed to have captured 480 arms, 41 automatic weapons and 10,793 rounds of ammunition. "PMAC Member in Arssi Inspects Captured Arms," *Ethiopian Herald* (July 9, 1977), p. 1. While not admitted to in the press, it seems clear these were men that Somalia, the Western Somali Liberation Front, and the Oromo Liberation Front were infiltrating into Arssi: Ottaways, *Ethiopia*, p. 164 and Halliday and Molyneux, *Ethiopian Revolution*, pp. 196-205. See also "Misled Individuals Are Returning Home," *Ethiopian Herald* (August 30, 1977), p. 3 (They had been "trained by fascist ruling classes in Mogadisho to sabotage in Ethiopia.)"; "Begiled Persons in Arssi join Revolution Camp," *Ethiopian Herald* (April 1, 1978), p. 1. These areas were not effected by the previous years of CADU presence that so facilitated the process of land reform in Chilalo. However, Aster Akalu's view raises a major point: until historians are allowed again to undertake studies in rural Ethiopia the events and processes of land reform will never be accurately understood.

18. For an example of one group farm effort in Chilalo, see: Alula Abate and Fassil G. Kiros, "Agrarian Reform," p. 61; David B. Ottaway, "Ethiopia's Rush From Feudalism," *The Washington Post* (June 8, 1975), p. C1. Based on 1976 interviews in Arssi, Aster Akalu concluded: "...the peasants are still in favour of individual holding rather than collective holdings. They say that they are willing to work on their own holdings and produce more for their own households. It seems very difficult for them to co-ordinate their activities on (individual and communal plots). Therefore, until effective association leaders emerge who can help the peasant co-ordinate their work, the question of collective farming will not be solved properly." *Process of Land Nationalization*, p. 165.
19. ARDU, *Plans for 1976-80* (Asella: ARDU, Publication No. 1, 1976), p. 25.
20. The breakdown was 599 associations with 133,351 members in Chilalo District, 286 with 75,166 in Ticho District, and 219 with 47,867 in Arbagugu District. Ministry of Land Reform and Administration, "Number of Farmers Associations and their Members Established" (Internal Memorandum, MLRA, Addis Ababa, 1976), p.2.
21. The only attempt is: Negussie Woldemichael, *A Review of Agrarian Reform and Rural Development in Ethiopia* (Asella: ARDU Publication No. 25, 1984). It sheds little light on the reform effects on land holdings, productivity, or income.
22. For example, Fassil Gebre Kiros, "Agricultural Land Fragmentation: A Problem of Land Distribution Observed in Some Ethiopian Peasant Associations," *Ethiopian Journal of Development Research*, IV, 2 (1980), pp. 1-12. The effect of fragmentation on government policy is reviewed in: Marina Ottaway, "Drought and Development in Ethiopia," *Current History*, LXXXV, 511 (1986), p. 220.
23. See: John M. Cohen and Ingvar Jonsson, "Size of Peasant Association Holdings and Government Policies: Questions Raised by Recent Research in Ethiopia's Arssi Region," *Northeast African Studies*, IX, 1 (1987).
24. Changes in distribution of land since 1974 are described in: Planning, Evaluation and Budget Section, *Investigations on the Impact of the Agrarian Reform on Peasant's Income and Expenditure Patterns, 1980* (Asella: ARDU Publication No. 18, 1981), p. 10; Tesfaye Teklu, *Socio-Economic Conditions in Dodota – 1977* (Addis Ababa: Insti-

tute of Development Research, Report No. 27, August 1979), pp. 23-31, 69-77. See also: Bo M. I. Bengtsson's 1980 restudy of 43 Chilalo farmers interviewed in 1967: *Rural Development Research and Agricultural Innovations* (Uppsala: Swedish University of Agriculture, Department of Plant Husbandry, Report No. 115, 1983), pp. 113-4, 185; and Alemneh Dejene's study of 150 farmers throughout Arssi Region, *Smallholder Perceptions of Rural Development and Emerging Institutions in Arssi Region Since the Ethiopian Revolution* (Cambridge: Harvard Institute for International Development, Development Discussion Paper No. 192, 1985), pp. 37-50. For comparative purposes see: Dessalegn Rahmato, *Agrarian Reform*, pp. 37-73.

25. Despite government bans on strikes, ARDU remained a hot bed of radical demonstrations and union organization throughout 1975. These strikes ranged from protests against social conditions to demands for dismissal of unpopular supervisors. Their pitch and consistency increased the government's distrust of the project. This led to police raids, such as one in May 1975 in which six staff members were arrested for subversive activity. Another labor issue in late September revealed the continued hostilities between conservative local forces and the project. When the military government responded to new Confederation of Ethiopian Labour Union demands with shootings and arrests in Addis Ababa, the Asella police sought the authority to apply the same treatment to the project, which was affiliated with the union. Had authority to arrest and shoot been granted, much blood would have been spilled, for the provincial elites were allies of the police and both had old scores to settle with project staff.
26. A telling indicator of this was the termination of the large flow of reports that characterized the project between 1968 and 1973. During this period more than 100 reports were issued. But by 1975 the 1973/74 annual report had still not been written.
27. Henock Kifle resigned in mid-1975 to take a Ministry of Agriculture post in Addis Ababa. From then until November, the project was run by his deputy, a Swede with considerable sympathy for the objectives of more radical ARDU staff members. His replacement struggled to depoliticize the project, reestablish the professional discipline that had marked the 1967-73 period, and overcome the conditions created by two years of lax management, but he ran headlong into an antagonized staff. Overreacting to staff resistance, he fired a large number of those who opposed him. This bought the project to a halt, necessitating the intervention of the Ministry of Agriculture. When it was clear that senior decision makers at headquarters would not back him, he resigned.
28. In 1976 the military directed a purge of militant radicals in ARDU. This did not improve the situation, since it led to the removal of experienced and energetic staff members who proved difficult to replace. Reportedly, the purge was stimulated by the refusal of some 60 new development workers trained at ARDU headquarters to take their final exams, largely because of the urging of a radical ARDU cooperatives officer who wanted to create a crisis supportive of his own political objectives. In effect, this was simply the straw that broke the camel's back.
29. The 1981 project review team found that only 8 of the 32 key headquarters staff had been with ARDU more than three years, that 30 percent of staff had been with the project less than one year, that the project had eight directors between 1974 and 1981, and that only 3 staff members had MSc. degrees. Solomon Bekure, et al., *Evaluation of the Arssi Regional Development Unit (ARDU) June-July 1981* (Uppsala: International Rural Development Centre, Swedish University of Agricultural Sciences, September 1981), p. XI, 1.
30. This description of the two factions is found in a case study prepared by: Hanna Kabede and Robert E. Klitgaard, "Managing Integrated Rural Development in Ethiopia" (Case Study Prepared for Harvard University, Kennedy School of Government, 1982), Parts A and B. It is also drawn from interviews.

31. The critique of the radicals was presented in neutral language in: Planning and Evaluation Section, "A Brief Description of the ARDU Project" (Asella: ARDU, November 30, 1976), pp. 1-11.
32. Planning and Evaluation Section, "A Brief Description of the ARDU Project," p. 2.
33. ARDU, *Plan for 1976-1980* (Asella: Arusi Rural Development Unit, Publication No. 1, 1976).
34. A. G. Betru, "Fact Sheet on the Arsi Rural Development Unit (ARDU)" (Internal Data Sheet, ARDU, September 9, 1976).
35. The rhetoric of the proposal ran high on this point, the document calling for: (1) organizing the target population on the basis of democratic principles, allowing equality of opportunity to participate in or lead peasant associations and cooperatives; (2) promoting self-reliance of rural people by increasing their ability to identify, plan, finance, and implement social and development activities in their communities; and (3) decentralizing ARDU activities so project staff and leadership would be more responsible and accountable to the "broad masses."
36. The document incorrectly assumed away technical concerns arguing: "The use and benefits of improved seed varieties and fertilizer is now effectively spread among Chilalo farmers, and it is the belief of the project that this aspect of this agricultural extension work is now completed." ARDU, *Plan for 1976-80*, p. 34.
37. *Peasant Associations Organization and Consolidated Proclamation*, Proclamation No. 71 of 1975, *Negarit Gazeta*, 35th yr., no. 15 (14 December 1975), pp. 107-118. It covers peasant associations established by the land reform proclamation earlier in the year.
38. Article 7 of Proclamation No. 71 identified: distributing fertilizer, seeds, and farm implements; providing and managing credit; marketing and storing grain produced by members; improving farm implements; running flour mills, stimulating cottage industry; providing extension services; supplying consumer goods; teaching members the principles of socialism; promoting better health services and public welfare; fighting against corruption; and educating the population for political activity.
39. Articles 41-54 of Proclamation No. 71. The functions of these committees were to help integrate the activities of different ministries and their field agents so they better served the people of the area where they operated, and to insure that peasants participated in the policy decisions of such ministries when those decisions affected local interests. The proclamation attempted to minimize conflict between local, regional, and central interests by building a hierarchical set of committees which were to facilitate two-way channels of communication on development and governance issues.
40. ARDU's work with women's associations was to center on bringing them more political awareness and involving them in the development process through specific income generating projects that raised family income and increased female stature in the household. As for youth groups, the Phase III paper proposed education programs that helped young people develop a cooperative spirit, discipline, appreciation for the dignity of labor and rural life, and skills to help them earn income off the farm.
41. CADU reached its target population through model farmers representing 800 hectare areas. Part of their land was used for demonstration and field days. Project extension agents gave them some training as well as inputs. Most were progressive, experienced farmers. In 1974 there were 414 of them in Chilalo, and considered "...suitable information-disseminators... a relatively cheap method for reaching the grass-root levels." CADU, *Annual Report 1970/71* (Asella: CADU, Publication No. 65, 1971), pp. 1-4.
42. The proposal outlined an extensive training strategy managed from the project's training center but decentralized by Local Training Centers (LTC) and Mobile Training Centers charged with raising literacy and numeracy as a preclude to more substantive

courses, leadership, civics, management practices, and book keeping. LTCs were to reach rural people through their new organizations. Asella's center was to train RDAs in: (1) economics and farm management; (2) methods and approach of extension; (3) plant husbandry; (4) animal husbandry; and (5) social analysis and communications. ARDU, *Plans for 1976-78*, pp. 8-16. Peasant association representatives were to receive training in class analysis, democratic rights and responsibilities, functions of PAs, and leadership. Cooperative representatives were to learn principles of collective action, laws on cooperatives, leadership skills, and basic management and administration techniques. Women's group representatives were to receive training in civics, home economics, health, and hygiene, bookkeeping and home improvement. Youth were to be trained in the new revolutionary organizations, civics, and home economics. Finally, local development committee members were to learn how to mobilize local revenue, identify community needs, and meet them. *Ibid.*, III, pp. 8-10.

43. Their objective was to make the group farm (called mutual aid team or production cooperative in the Phase III paper) the focus of all extension efforts. Under the guidance of the RDA workers, each group farm was to design a detailed production plan and work program. Demonstration of new innovations were to be carried out on these group farms. Here the emphasis was to be on "learning by doing," a strategy envisioning farmers operating demonstration plots themselves and being involved in the evaluation of trial results.

44. Primary cooperatives were to engage in sales of farm inputs, purchase of agricultural production, provision and collection of credit, and establishment of consumer shops. Co-operative Coordinating Committees were only to have a "policy formulating function," whatever that meant, and not be involved in sales, credit, or purchase activities. Apparently, their function was to be as reviewers of activities, procedures, and rules introduced by ARDU for primary societies. The secondary union was to arrange credit and cash payments for primary society inputs. It also was to be involved in wholesale handling of agricultural and livestock produce, storage, transport and terminal marketing services, and audit or otherwise supervise primary society activities. At a later stage the secondary union was envisioned as selling local agro-industry products and helping finance their establishment and operations.

45. An ARDU trained cooperative manager was to assist each service cooperative. The manager was to provide on the job training to two members who would succeed him in two years. The secondary union was to be served by two senior managers, four middle-level staff (accountant, sales/purchase, manager/inspector, and field operation coordinator) and 12 book keepers, store keepers, office clerks, and field clerks.

46. ARDU's budget was to finance the cost of the cooperative managers of primary societies. All other costs were to be born by society members. The manager was to keep one account per peasant association and the associations were to keep one account per individual member. The secondary union was to keep one account per primary society. It was expected to finance its recurrent cost on the margin between purchases and sales.

47. Few details were given, a paper on these and other operational activities was promised in several months. The paper contained no outline of election or by-law procedures for primary cooperatives. Cooperative Coordinating Committees were to be formed at the District Development Center level from representatives elected by the primary societies. The secondary union was to be governed by a board of elected members of primary societies but ARDU was to keep a strong influence on the board so long as the union needed subsidies from the project's budget.

48. The fixed assets of the division, largely stores and offices in Asella, were to be transferred to the secondary union on grant and loan terms. Employees transferred left the

ARDU payroll. The paper promised a detailed plan for the transition within several months.

49. CADU's Marketing Division was abolished, its fertilizer and purchase activities largely taken over by the AMC and its credit provision for fertilizer and seed taken over by the AIDB. These independent parastatals coordinated their activities with ARDU but supplied inputs and purchased farm produce directly from peasant organizations. ARDU's milk marketing system had been taken over by the Dairy Development Authority, though it relied on the project's processing system. But the project did continue to supply high yielding seeds through its Seed Multiplication Section.
50. Referring to the map in Figure 5, it should be noted that Gololcha *Woreda* and parts of Seru and Shirka *Woredas* were not to be included in ARDU. Rather, they were to be served by EPID programs in the adjacent regions because there was no road system that linked them adequately to Arssi's towns and ARDU's DDOs. Since Aseko *Woreda* was difficult to reach from any direction, it was to be largely excluded from both ARDU and EPID programs.
51. ARDU, *Plan for 1976-80*, p. 59.
52. *Ibid.*, pp. 65-70.
53. Throughout 1975-76 urban political violence, particularly in Addis Ababa, created a period of terror. It centered on members of the Ethiopian Peoples' Revolutionary Party, members of which were on ARDU's staff. See: John Markakis and Nega Ayele, *Class and Revolution in Ethiopia* (London: Spokesman, 1978), pp. 146-77.
54. See footnote 29.
55. The military both trusted and was suspicious of these new organizations, which it needed to achieve control and promote revolutionary development objectives but recognized were learning to defend their own interests. Henze, "Communism and Ethiopia," p. 71.
56. *All Ethiopian Peasant Association Proclamation*, Proclamation No. 130 of 1977 (July 7, 1977). The AEPA is described in: Tirfe Mammo, "Ethiopia: A Brief Survey of the Various Proclamations Dealing with Agrarian Transformation" (Stockholm: Agricultural Division, SIDA, 1983), pp. 22-3; Björn Genberg, Michael Ståhl, and Edvard Taube, "Report on Peasant Associations and Agricultural Cooperatives in Ethiopia" (Report Prepared for SIDA, Addis Ababa, November 1982).
57. The struggle to create a political organization is described in: Ottaways, *Ethiopia*, pp. 99-127; Halliday and Molyneux, *Ethiopian Revolution*, pp. 96-135.
58. For example, *Peasant Associations Organization and Consolidated Proclamation*, Proclamation No. 71 of 1975 (December 14, 1975). See: Cohen and Koehn, "Rural and Urban Land Reform," pp. 16-19.
59. Chapter 4 describes CADU's attempted to organize such a hierarchy prior to the revolution. Two early regional administrators had supported such efforts as Ministry of Agriculture Officials (Tesfa Bushen 1974-76) or CADU staff (Girma Tolossa 1976). A military officer, Lt. Sileshi Mengesha, who served from 1977-81, strongly favored the formation of a peoples' party in Arssi and saw the AEPA as a vehicle for doing so, although the AEPA and the Working Peoples' Control Committee of Arssi Region, formed in 1983, are separate organizations.
60. He was openly charged in Parliament and the press with collecting money illegally from people, embezzlement of self-help funds, corrupting judicial processes, and squandering public funds during his nine year term. For example, charges were made against him in the Chamber of Deputies in mid-February, *Addis Zemen* (February 12, 1974) and the general press *Ethiopian Herald* (April 27, 1974 and December 25, 1974). By April he was removed and an inquiry was being undertaken by central inspectors in

Asella. Full investigations of these charges never occurred because the military executed him in November 1974.

61. In 1974 a senior Ministry of Agriculture official, Tesfa Bushen, the Vice Minister in charge of EPID described in Chapters 4 and 5, was appointed governor of Arssi. This was a positive sign for he knew the project well and in his previous post was responsible for the operation of all integrated rural development projects carried out by the Ministry of Agriculture. However, throughout 1975 he was increasingly viewed with distrust by more radical members of ARDU and by the military. So in February 1976 he was dismissed and replaced by a man who six months earlier had been head of ARDU's extension division, Dr. Girma Tolossa. Since he proved to be weaker than the previous governor, the hands of the still to be replaced *woreda* governors and minor officials were strengthened. These were the same men who were hostile to CADU before 1974. Still, by 1976 their power to resist or alter ARDU initiatives had been greatly reduced and the new governor obviously knew the project and the region well from his earlier work.
62. For background on the Oromo Liberation Front see: Lubie Birru, "Abbyssinian Colonialism as the Genesis of the Crisis in the Horn: Oromo Resistance (1855-1913)," *Northeast African Studies*, II, 3 (1980-81), pp. 93-8; Richard Greenfield and Mohammed Hassan, "Interpretation of Oromo Nationality," *Horn of Africa*, III, 3 (1980), pp. 3-14.
63. In 1977 the PMAC filled the administrative post with a member of the military's inner ruling circle, Lt. Sileshi Mengesha. He served in this post from November 1977 to late 1981. A non-commissioned officer when the revolution began, he rose rapidly through the ranks of the *Derg*. Sent to Tigre to organize the "Red Terror" against counter revolutionaries, he proved tougher than his predecessor and as a reward he was made administrator of Arssi. An unsophisticated man of limited education, he threw his support behind the growth of state farms in the region while promoting the formation of a people's party in Arssi. "The lives and Times of the Dergue", *Northeast African Studies*, V, 3 (1984), pp. 23-4. In mid-1978 the military sent one of its most ruthless trouble shooters, Lt. Negussie Wolde, to Arssi to deal with OLM activity: *Ibid*, pp. 35-36.
64. On local government reforms and prospects after the revolution see: Cohen and Koehn, *Ethiopian Provincial Administration*, pp. 276-317.
65. Solomon Bekure, et al., *Evaluation*, p. XI, 2. Problems of field level integration were identified by Fassil G. Kiros, who held interviews with ARDU and local government officials. Based on this inquiry, he concluded that as of 1983 there was a need to reorient the still traditional regional administration in Arssi toward the role of development planning, to increase communication and interaction between ARDU staff and local government officials working with peasant associations and cooperatives, and to promote increased coordination of project plans with those of development ministry field offices in the region. "Learning From ARDU: Toward a Regional System of Rural Development in Ethiopia" (Paper Presented to Seminar on Regional Planning and Development in Ethiopia, Ambo, April 1983), pp. 24-7, 31-2.
66. *Cooperative Societies Proclamation*, Proclamation No.138 of 1978 (March 3, 1978). The June 1979 Amharic *Producers Cooperative Guide* is summarized in: Fassil G. Kiros,"Mobilizing the Peasantry for Rural Development – The Ethiopian Experiment in Progress" (Paper Presented at 7th International Conference of Ethiopian Studies, Lund, 1982).
67. The functions identified in the legislation are: (1) providing crop purchase service; (2) marketing the produce at fair prices; (3) giving loans at fair interest rates; (4) providing

storage and savings services; (5) supplying consumer goods to members according to their needs; (6) educating members in socialist philosophy and raising political consciousness; (7) supplying improved agricultural inputs and providing tractor hire services; (8) collecting self-help contributions; (9) providing flour-mill services; (10) promoting cottage industries; and (11) expanding into producer cooperatives. See: Alemayehu Lirenso, "Rural Service Cooperatives in Ethiopia: Tasks and Performance," *Northeast African Studies*, VII, 2 (1985), pp. 51-8.

68. Wood, "Rural Development," p. 537. For a critique of this view see: Bruce F. Johnston and William C. Clark, *Redesigning Rural Development: A Strategic Perspective* (Baltimore: The Johns Hopkins University Press, 1982).

69. Procedures for establishing producer cooperatives under the 1981 "Agricultural Producers Cooperative Directive" are described in: Genberg, et al., "Report on Peasant Associations," pp. 11-17.

70. The government has allowed producer cooperatives to: (1) receive allocation of fertile land in the peasant association; (2) obtain agricultural inputs at concessionary prices; (3) receive interest free credits and loans from service cooperatives of which they are members; (4) receive priority access to extension agents and new innovations such as cross-bred cattle; (5) sell produce directly to the AMC for a price higher than that service cooperatives are allowed to pay; and (6) obtain priority access to consumer goods, building materials, and training opportunities.

71. No detailed studies of producer cooperatives are yet available, but observers report many early joiners came from the ranks of the landless or those without oxen or resources who were settled on former commercial farms of pre-revolutionary days. They also contend peasants dislike the work point system. See, for example: David B. Ottaway, "Ethiopia Tests Collectives," *The Washington Post* (December 5, 1980).

72. John M. Cohen and Nils-Ivar Isaksson, *Villagization in the Arssi Region of Ethiopia* (Uppsala: Swedish University of Agricultural Sciences, International Rural Development Centre, Rural Development Study No. 19, 1987).

73. Comparative figures were 641 PAs in Chilalo with 19,716 male and 16,571 female household representatives; 231 PAs in Arbagugu with 47,754 male and 3,688 female representatives; and 214 PAs in Ticho with 44,748 male and 2,901 female representatives. ARDU, *Annual Report 1981/82*, p. 18.

74. A comparative study of 18 highland PAs included two from Arssi, Bilbilo Rogecha and Bedi Damota, located in more sparsely populated areas of Chilalo's mountainous hill chains and marked by some swampy land needing drainage. Against a sample average of 982 hectares containing 576 households with an average of 1.89 hectares/household Bilbilo Rogecha covered 640 hectares and had 205 households averaging 2.1 hectares/households. Bedi Damota's figures were 800 hectares with 290 households averaging 2.8 hectares each. Yeraswork Admassie, Mulugetta Abebe and Markos Ezra, *Ethiopian Highlands Reclamation Study: Report on the Sociological Survey and Sociological Considerations in Preparing a Development Strategy* (Addis Ababa: Ministry of Agriculture, Land Use Planning and Regulatory Department, December 1983), Annex IV. In another study of 150 sample households, Alemneh Dejene found PAs to range in size from 437 to 1200 hectares, with the larger ones tending to be in dryer lowland areas. Likewise, the number of households per association ranged from 170 to 402 and the density of households per hectare from 2 to 7.8. In general, the most densely populated associations were in fertile highland areas. But the difficulty of finding patterns is revealed by the study's observation that the most sparsely populated and densely populated associations in the sample, with 102 and 402 households each, had 800 total hectares each. *Smallholders Perceptions* , p. 147. However, a study based on detailed SEAD maps and interviews in 16 Arssi peasant associ-

ations, generated evidence that the PAs hold substantially larger blocks of land and average 1500 to 2000 hectares: Cohen and Jonsson, "Size of Peasant Associations."

75. Profiles on Arssi peasant associations are found in: Alula Abate, "Peasant Associations and Collective Agriculture in Ethiopia: Promise and Performance," *Journal of African Studies*, X, 3 (1983), p. 100; Dessalegn Rahmato, *Agrarian Reform*, pp. 74-96; Alemneh Dejene, *Smallholder Perceptions*, pp. 146-55.
76. ARDU, *Annual Report 1981/82* (Asella: ARDU, Publication No. 22, 1982), p. 20. In 1982 Chilalo had 81 SCs with 136,287 member house-holds, Arbagugu 27 SCs with 51,442 member households, and Ticho had 34 SCs with 47,649 member households. ARDU, "Amharic Description of Project" (September, 1982). The growth in turnover capital for service cooperatives has been rapid, increasing from EthB. 5.17 million in 1978-79 to EthB. 14.15 million in 1982-83. ARDU, "Objectives, Activities, Impact, Prospect and Problems" (Mimeographed Project Description, Asella, February 1984), p. 8.
77. The popularity of these organizations is qualified by Alemneh Dejene's survey of 150 rural heads of household in Arssi Region, 44 percent of whom found their performance to be unsatisfactory. Among the reasons given were shortages of consumer goods, low quality products, favoritism in distribution of scarce items, and untimely availability of agricultural inputs. Dissatisfied farmers preferred the private traders to service cooperatives. *Smallholder Perceptions*, pp. 157-60.
78. ARDU, *Annual Report 1981/82*, pp. 19-20 of the 142 SCs, 90 of them sold fertilizer and seed and 88 engaged in grain marketing for the AMC. *Ibid.*
79. ARDU, "Objectives – 1984," p. 5. For a profile of ARDU's model producer cooperative at Dixis, see: ARDU, *Annual Report 1979/80* (Asella: ARDU, Publication No. 17, 1981), p. 6.
80. Two-thirds of Arssi's producer cooperatives were in Chilalo, reflecting the progressive effects of the CADU period. ARDU, Planning, Evaluation, and Budget Section, "Short Description" (Amharic, Asella, September 1982). The major constraints were lack of funds for productive investment and trained management personnel: Genberg, et al., "Report on Peasant Associations," p. 15.
81. This pattern reflected the national trend, it being estimated that the Ministry of Agriculture expended 80% of its resources in support of producer cooperatives in 1982 when only 2% of the country's farm households were in them, they farmed less than 1% of the cultivated land, and contributed only 3% of total cereal, pulse, and oil seed output.
82. Alemneh Dejene, *Smallholders Perceptions*, p. 167.
83. *Ibid.*, pp. 80-85.
84. IBRD, *Agricultural Development in Ethiopia (with Particular Reference to the Highlands)*, 2 vols., (Washington D.C.: Eastern Africa Projects Department, Northern African Division, Report No. 3956-ET, May 28, 1982), p. 41.
85. FAO, *Ethiopia: Report of the High-Level WCAARD Follow up Mission, May 3-9, 1982* (Rome: FAO, WCAARD Mission No. 7, 1982), p. 2. For a review, of government agricultural policy, see: IBRD, *Agricultural Development*, I, p. 38 and *passim*.
86. Aster Akalu reports the return in 1977 of 880 hectares in Tijo and Hetosa *Woredas* and 3,480 hectares in Ziway and Dugda *Woreda*. *Process of Land Nationalization*, p. 154.
87. "State Co-op Farms in Arsi Being Expanded," *Ethiopian Herald* (March 29, 1983). Most were not financially viable, being plagued by overmechanization, uneconomic use of inputs, undisciplined labor, and scarcity of competent managers. Wood, "Rural Development," p. 526.
88. ARDU annual reports from 1975 to 1982 contain no references to state farm linkages, a pattern confirmed by Fassil G. Kiros who found no formal linkages or coordination

of activities between the project and the Ministry of State Farms. "Learning From ARDU", pp. 25-6.

89. Early in the revolution the government established a land settlement authority and placed all pre-reform settlement activities under it. The initial Settlement Development Authority was located in the Ministry of Agriculture and Settlement. In 1979 it was withdrawn from the Ministry and merged with the Relief and Rehabilitation Commission. Five million people, roughly 20% of the rural population, needed public assistance to regain their capacity to earn a living. This effort alone constituted a heavy financial burden on the economy and a drain on scarce administrative manpower needed to promote development. In 1983 the Commission oversaw 20 low cost settlement schemes and 65 special schemes. Eshetu Chole and Teshome Mulat, "Land Settlement in Ethiopia: A Review of Developments" (Paper Presented at International Ethiopian Studies Conference, Addis Ababa, December 1984), p. 12.

90. For example, Aster Akalu reports 2 schemes for 115 people on 120 hectares in Gedeb Asasa, 5 schemes for 182 people on 292 hectares in Sere, 4 schemes for 296 people on 476 hectares in Dotota, and 3 schemes for 347 people on 900 hectares in Hetosa. *Process of Land Nationalization*, p. 156.

91. *Agricultural Marketing Corporation Establishment Proclamation*, Proclamation No. 105, November 11, 1976. By 1985 it operated 5 regional zone centers, 104 market centers, and 1768 collection centers.

92. In 1981 the official AMC price was EthB 34 per quintal and market price EthB 50 for wheat. Wholesale prices in Addis Ababa's private sector were about EthB 90. IBRD, "Ethiopia: The Agricultural Sector - An Interim Report" (Washington, D.C.: East Africa Region, Report No. ET 3956a-ET, January 26, 1983), pp. 22-5, 29.

93. Evidence on procurement is conflicting. Cf. ARDU, "Objectives – 1984," p. 1 with M.E. Adams, "SIDA/ARDU Review Report of 1/1985" (unpublished memorandum, 1985), p. 7.

94. A 1981 review of the AMC found it overextended, suffering from high staff turnover, and so inefficient that it lost an estimated 25% of stocks prior to sale in urban areas. This required high price markups to cover costs. More serious criticism is found in the report: Johan Toborn, "Marketing and Distribution in Ethiopia" (SIDA/ARDU Consulting Report, October 1985), pp. 2-15.

95. FAO, *Ethiopia Highlands Reclamation Study*, p. 17.

96. On these policies and reforms relative to communist ideology see: Keller, "The Ethiopian Revolution," pp. 52-65; John Harbeson, "Socialist Politics in Ethiopia," in *African Socialism*, edited by C. Rosberg, 2nd ed. (Berkeley: Institute for International Studies, 1979), pp. 345-72; Paul B. Henze, *Communist Ethiopia – Is It Succeeding?* (Santa Monica: The Rand Corporation, Paper Series P. 7054, 1985).

97. Annual growth in GNP for 1970-82 was 2.2% per annum, as compared to 4.4% annually during the 1960-70 period. Average annual growth rate in agriculture fell from 2.2% during 1960-70 period to 0.9% for the 1970-82 years. This serious decline in productivity was compounded by a population growth rate that increased from a 1960-70 average of 2.0% per annum to a 1970-82 average of 3.0%. World Bank, *Toward Sustained Development in Sub-Saharian Africa: A Joint Program of Action* (Washington, D.C.: World Bank, 1984), p. 58, 77, 82. Per capita agricultural output in 1981 was only 85% the 1970 level and food production per capita 84%. IBRD, *Economic Memorandum on Ethiopia* (Washington, D.C.: East Africa Region, Report No. ET 3956, May 28, 1982), p. 4, 69.

98. National accounts for 1980 indicate a per capital income of US$ 140 and analysts generally concluded that after tax rural family incomes had risen since the land reform

in absolute terms and relative to urban income, which appeared to have fallen significantly since 1974.

99. State farms and collectives are more important than these figures indicate because they contribute more to wholesale market output, have higher use of government resources and farm inputs, and produce higher value crops. IBRD, *Agricultural Development in Ethiopia (with Particular Reference to the Highlands)*, 2 vols., (Washington, D.C.: Eastern Africa Projects Department, Northern Agricultural Division, Report No. 3956-ET, May 28, 1982), p. 41.

100. Allan Hoben, "Perspectives on Land Reform in Ethiopia: The Political Role of the Peasantry," *Journal of Modern African Studies*, XII, 4 (1975), p. 68.

101. This model is described in: John M. Cohen, Arthur A. Goldsmith, and John W. Mellor, "Rural Development Issues Following Ethiopian Land Reform," *Africa Today*, XXIII, 2 (1976), pp. 7-28. For an example of a small-holder program recommended by a donor see: FAO, *Ethiopia Highlands Reclamation Study: Macro-Economic Review* (Rome: Food and Agriculture Organization of the United Nations, Report No. UTF/ETH/037/ETH, Working Paper No. 9, 1984). Other examples include the MPP and PADEP initiatives discussed below.

102. In response to economic stagnation and charges it neglected the small-holder sector, Lt. Col. Mengistu Haile-Mariam said: "When we planned our country's economic development, we had the strategic objective of our Revolution in mind. It was not planned for economic development (to be) solely an end in itself... There are some who have forgotten that the sole basis of our revolutionary struggle was the ideology and politics which we follow..." Colin Legum, ed., *African Contemporary Record: 1981-82* (New York: Africana Publishing Co., 1981), p. B152. Further, Mengistu has warned that rampant individualism and petty bourgeois tendencies of the peasantry could lead to capitalism and must be curbed. Ottaways, *Afrocommunism*, p. 141.

103. Government pressure on professionals to support this policy was significant. See the conclusions of two leading Ethiopian experts who despite the evidence in their case studies of post reform rural areas were forced to conclude in 1983 that: "Left to their own devices, the peasants, in the early post distribution situation, are particulary vulnerable to alienation from socialist aims ....Petty subsistence production continues to dominate in Ethiopian agriculture, and is likely to impede the immediate government efforts to promote technological change and to provide essential services to the peasant sector....Petty production needs to be replaced by relatively large-scale production so as to realize the full potential of modern technology." Alula Abate and Fassil G. Kiros, "Agrarian Reforms," pp. 179-80. They knew, however, their data spoke for itself. Such a conclusion runs against the accumulated literature on agrarian socialism and strong evidence that small-scale farmers can be a major engine for agricultural and economic development, as has been the case in Taiwan, South Korea, and Kenya. David Morawetz, "Economic Lessons from Small Socialist Developing Countries," *World Development*, VIII (1980), pp. 337-69; Michael Ellman, "Agricultural Productivity Under Socialism," *World Development*, 9/10 (1981), pp. 979-89.

104. The plan is set forth in: IBRD, *Economic Memorandum on Ethiopia* (Washington, D.C.: East Africa Region, Report No. 3552b-ET, December 15, 1981) pp. 2-25.

105 Paul B. Henze, "Ethiopia Marches to Marxist Drummer but with Western Flair," *The Christian Science Monitor* (May 24, 1984).

106. Judith Miller, "Famine Engulfs Ethiopia Again: Death Toll Rises," *The New York Times* (September 18, 1984), p. 1. The short fall was estimated at 25% of expected 1984 production by the FAO and 50% by the Ministry of Agriculture. Estimates at

the time were that one million will die famine related deaths. "Ethiopia: The Death Stakes," *Africa Confidential*, XXXVI, 1 (January 1985), pp. 1-3.

107. See generally: Nicole Ball, *World Hunger: A Guide to the Economic and Political Dimensions* (Oxford: Clio Press, 1981); Michael F. Lofchie, "Political and Economic Origins of African Hunger," *Journal of Modern African Studies*, XIII, 4 (1975), pp. 551-67; Nicole Ball, "Understanding the Causes of African Famine," *Journal of Modern African Studies*, XIV, 3 (1976), pp. 517-22.

108. Government of Ethiopia and World Bank, "Review of Farmer's Incentives and Agricultural Marketing and Distribution Efficiency" (Confidential Report of Joint Mission, Addis Ababa, March 17, 1983), p. 12. The steps the government claims to have taken are reviewed by the head of the Relief and Rehabilitation Commission in: Dawit Wolde Giorgis, "Institutional and Practical Responses to Drought in Ethiopia" (Paper Presented to International Ethiopian Studies Conference, Addis Ababa, November 1984).

109. Confidential FAO report and "Ethiopia: The Death Stakes," p. 3, which noted that of the three exporting regions, Gojjam and Shoa stood no chance of producing a surplus in a bad year.

110. Set forth in: John M. Cohen, "Rural Change in Ethiopia: the Chilalo Agricultural Development Unit," *Economic Development and Cultural Change*, XXII, 4 (1974), p. 589.

111. The purpose of this was to increase the probability of the project surviving the end of SIDA funding. During Phase I of CADU, SIDA assumed rising agricultural tax revenue from project induced production gains would allow the IEG to increase its contribution. It also assumed seed multiplication and livestock production units would become self-financing while cooperatives grew strong enough to take over marketing and credit functions. The revolution, among other factors, negated these expected outcomes.

112. Principal changes from the organization described in Cohen, "Rural Change in Ethiopia," pp. 588-608 were: (1) management of the Munessa forest was granted to the State Forest Development Agency; (2) the maintenance of feeder roads was awarded to the Ethiopian Transport and Construction Authority; (3) the milk collection and processing program developed in the first phase was transferred to the Diary Development Enterprise; and (4) the AMC and AIDB gradually took over the input distribution and marketing functions of the project. In addition: (5) the seed and cattle breeding boards ceased to be self-financing and were reintegrated into their respective crop and livestock departments in order to strengthen their programs; and (6) the financial management section of the Common Services Department were hived off to promote better budgeting and accounting performance.

113. In 1970 SIDA established ceilings for CADU support and a strategy for phase out. By 1975, SIDA stated that MPP rather than ARDU would get priority. However, the revolution's effects on government investment priorities and revenue collection led to severe underfunding of the Ministry of Agriculture and ARDU, so that in 1982 SIDA decided to cease MPP funding and give priority to ARDU. The 1982 SIDA report stated SIDA's commitment to provide financial support for the project for a decade more if certain conditions supportive of small-holder development could be met and a strategy for successful disengagement forged.

114. The 1982-83 budget ran US$ 7.95 million. Since the Ethiopian currency was fixed to the value of the US dollar, which had appreciated rapidly since 1979, the value of SIDA support had declined. Of this budget 10% went for professional staff, 21% for low level staff, 10% for transport, 10% for services and 49% for materials. The Extension and Cooperative Promotion Department took 36% of this budget while

Plant Husbandry received 3.5%, suggesting where project priorities were. Evaluation and Budget Section, *Work Program and Budget 1982/83* (Asella: ARDU, Publication No. 23, December 1982), p. 258.

115. ARDU, *Annual Report 1981/82* (Asella: Arssi Rural Development Unit, Publication No. 22, 1982); Solomon Bekure, et al., Evaluation; Planning, Evaluation and Budget Section, *Evaluation of the Extension, Education and Crop Production Department (1976-1980)* (Asella: ARDU, 1981).

116. Its tasks were to: (1) undertake meteorological, crop, weed, and pest surveys; (2) test and screen different crops to identify varieties best adapted to different ecologies; (3) determine optimal growing techniques for different crop varieties; (4) establish and improve pastures; (5) study methods of controlling weeds, insects, and diseases; (6) improve knowledge of soil conditions; and (7) study nutrient value of food and forage crops.

117. The objects of this unit were to: (1) produce clean seeds of improved varieties; (2) operate ARDU farms efficiently; (3) supervise and assist cooperatives producing improved seeds; (4) make ARDU machinery available to such cooperatives; and (5) clean seeds for the project, government agencies, and peasant organizations.

118. ARDU, "Objectives, Activities, Impact, Prospect and Problems" (Mimeographed Project Description, Asella, November 1982), p. 11.

119. ARDU, "Objectives – 1984," pp. 9-10; Solomon Bekure, et al., *Evaluation*, p. 3, 9. The 80,000 include independent small-holders (65,453) and peasants organized into producer cooperatives.

120. Solomon Bekure, et al., *Evaluation*, I, p. 3. ARDU received credit each year from the Agricultural Industrial Development Bank and repaid from collections. In the early 1980s repayment rates were high, averaging 98%.

121. Cumulative ARDU annual reports for 1979/80, 1980/81, and 1981/82 report: 6,333 km of new terracing laid, 1,303 km of rural roads cleared, 114 offices and 104 km stores constructed, 113 low-cost bridges and 74 schools built, 98 small dams and 16 check dams constructed, 36 flour mills and 8 seedling nurseries established, 34 skills centers built, 21 farmers villages constructed, and 35 springs protected.

122. Major constraints on self-help promotion in Arssi were: (1) the Government's requirement that 75% of the cost of roads and 50% of the cost of water projects be raised locally; (2) lack of consciousness about the importance of group activities; (3) difficulties organizing scattered villages in rough terrain for collective ventures; and (4) the lack of institutionalized credit sources that communities could borrow from. Planning, Evaluation and Budget Section, *Evaluation of Extension*, pp. 56-7.

123. ARDU, "Annual Report 1981/82," p.18; ARDU "Objectives – 1984," p. 5.

124. Government of Ethiopia and World Bank, "Review of Farmers Incentives and Agricultural Marketing and Distribution Efficiency" (Joint Mission Team Report, Addis Ababa, March 17, 1983), p. 88.

125. These resettlement villages were identified by Col. Mengistu as failing during an ARDU tour, so considerable project resources were devoted to them in 1981-82, leading to failure of the Section to achieve its work plan objectives.

126. CADU's Agricultural Engineering Section was expanded in 1976 into an Industrial Promotion Section that sought to design improved farm implements and rural products (e.g. furniture and candles), train artisans to produce them, and establish financially viable rural industries (e.g. brick making, ropemaking, door and window frame-construction, tailoring, grain and oil milling). Working with Service Cooperatives, the section established Skills Centers. Some 6 of these operated in 1982. They employed 2 to 8 workers each and produced only a few trained craftsmen, perhaps 20

by 1982. Aside from a high cost per trainee, the products, particularly the farm implements, appear to have been inappropriate and/or poorly marketed.

127. Solomon Bekure, et al., *Evaluation*, p. II, 10. Not all those trained joined ARDU staff. Of the 200 trained after 1975, half went to EPID.

128. Between 1966 and 1974 the project produced 95 technical reports on agronomy, forestry, farm implements, livestock, extension, social development, water resources and so on. But during the 1975-81 period, ARDU staff published only 12 technical studies, 6 of which were on very general social development topics and none of which were on livestock development, extension, water resources, or forestry topics.

129. 1983 estimates put certificate degree holders or higher at 5,758, with 468 of them in the Arssi Region. According to these figures Arssi had no Ph.D.s, 8.4% of MSc, 7.7% of BAs, 8.7% of diploma and 7.7% of certificate holders. GOE/IEG, "Review of Farmers," p. 96.

130. Serving on the team were the mission leader, Solomon Bekure of the International Livestock Center for Africa and formerly head of EPID in the mid-1970s and Bengt Nekby of the World Bank and the first director of CADU. Four other Swedish experts made up the rest of the team.

131. Solomon Bekure, et al., *Evaluation*, XI, p. 1.

132. The Ministry in 1981 had a set of administrative, technical, legal, and financial sections that allowed the Permanent Secretary to oversee six departments (Peasant Association and Cooperatives, Agricultural Extension, Animal Resources Development, Fishery Resources, Forestry and Wildlife Conservation, and Land Use Planning). These provided coordinated services to the Regional Offices of Agriculture, which reported directly to the Permanent Secretary and oversaw 80 *awraja* offices and 440 *woreda* offices. *Ibid.*, p. vii.

133. The transfer of the milk pasteurizing plant in 1976/77 was viewed by evaluators as unwise, for the receiving agency was unable to collect milk as efficiently as ARDU from farmers who had taken project staff advice and upgraded their dairy herd, as a result threatening the project's important dairy development and livestock breeding programs. Penetration of the Forest and Wildlife Development Agency into ARDU's jurisdiction threatened the project's programs aimed at developing forest plantations that could provide firewood, pole, and fence materials to Arssi farmers on a sustainable basis and generated jurisdictional disputes over the direction and control of forest protection, nursery, and seedling planting programs essential to conserve the region's soil and water resources. Finally, the road authority was given responsibility to maintain feeder roads but had no budget to do so, leading to a decay of the infrastructure critical to project success.

134. The evaluation stated: "The Government faces a choice in rural development programmes between maintaining strong sectoral national institutions for the planning and implementation of a comprehensive development scheme with better possibilities for integration and local participation. ARDU has shown the viability of decentralization ... If the Government elects to promote rural development through central sectoral institutions, the regional integrated organization of ARDU loses some of its significance." *Ibid.*, p. I, 5.

135. These included: (1) development of crop protection packages to cope with the threat of plant disease and pests generated by the project induced trend toward monocropping by area farmers; (2) breeding of drought resistant grain crops for Arssi's lowland areas; (3) field testing of tree species suitable for the area's different ecological zones; (4) formulation of production strategies for the acidic, heavy clay soil of Arbagugu and Ticho *Awraja's* water-logged highland area; (5) analysis of soil conservation methods suitable for use in Arssi's highly variable topography; (6) collection of soil profile

data suitable for giving a better picture of general plant nutrients in the project's different zones; (7) study of fertilizer application to determine reliable rates of phosphorus application according to crop and profit returns; (8) establishment of a collection of indigenous wheat and barely strains needed for plant breeding before they are lost by land expansion and adoption of ARDU issued HYVs; (9) pasture development research centered on fodder crop development, weedgrass infestation and stocking levels; (10) oilcrop and pulse research directed toward better crop rotation and improved human nutrition; and (11) horticulture crop identification and field testing.

136. Project documents disagree with this conclusion, the 1981 evaluation justifying inattention to crop production and emphasis on social mobilization because: "The stage of development reached in self-management and administration by the various peasant's institutions has been found to be low." Planning, Evaluation and Budget Section, *Evaluation of Extension*, p. 88.

137. This is supported by: Alemneh Dejene, *Smallholder Perceptions*, pp. 177-96.

138. ARDU's internal evaluation concluded that the shift from the model farmer and specialized agent extension system to the multi-functional agent approach was a good move that should not be tampered with. Here they recommended only that agents be given more refresher courses and that decentralization at the DDO and RDA level be strengthened and made more participatory. Planning Evaluation and Budget Section, *Evaluation of Extension*, p. 81.

139. For example, the liquid nitrogen plant essential to AI's services was frequently broken, laboratories lacked functioning equipment and chemicals needed to analyze soil samples and seed quality, veterinarians lacked drugs and transport needed to prevent livestock disease, and transport was not available to get nursery seedlings to peasant associations.

140. SIDA officials considered four options. The first was for Sweden to withdraw funding from ARDU on the grounds that the project had lost its dynamic character, that further investment would promote increased regional inequality, and that SIDA aid would have generated greater marginal benefits in other areas of Ethiopia. A second alternative centered on continued subsidies for the project as presently organized, giving it more time to prove its merit now that semi-feudal constraints were removed and revolutionary reforms in place. Incorporation of the project into a larger World Bank funded national program was the third strategy considered. Here it was argued that the ARDU Model, with massive donor funding, would be established in all of Ethiopia's regions. Finally, the evaluation mission considered a fourth alternative in which a new Phase IV would be designed that would revive the project and allow it to pioneer a regional development model better matched to the post-revolutionary era. Solomon Bekure, et al., *Evaluation*, pp. 8-9.

141. The report recommended that: (1) research should be strengthened and focused on improvement of grasslands and fodder crops, trials for horticultural crops, experimentation with crop diversification and rotation, improvement of cultural practices and farm tools, and development of livestock pasture and silage systems; (2) research stations be established in every agro-ecological zone for testing research findings; (3) soil testing be expanded and better fertilizer recommendations formulated; and (4) artificial insemination facilities be improved.

142. Strong recommendations were given that: (1) the multipurpose development agent strategy be phased out, with technical specialists being separated from social mobilization agents; (2) research activities be better linked to extension agent observations and production interventions more systematically evaluated for economic and social impact; (3) artificial insemination outreach be increased by training more agents and providing them with dependable transport; and (4) extension agents give more services

to women farmers and incorporate more of them into training at skill promotion centers.

143. The report called for: (1) experimenting with ways to better manage service cooperatives, increase women's participation in income generating activities, and provide long term credit for financing local self-help schemes; and (2) organizing regional service cooperative and helping revise national legislation hampering such organizations from being effective.

144. For the first time recommendations were made for SIDA to fund some recurrent costs for a considerable period of time. The evaluation also called for the donor to: (1) provide the project with 5 to 6 foreign advisers in the fields of evaluation, plant breeding, and livestock production; and (2) fund the purchase of a new fleet of vehicles.

145. The evaluation called on the government to: (1) transfer milk collection back to ARDU so it could expand efficient milk marketing activities as the foundation of the livestock program; and (2) return to the project responsibility for road maintenance until such time as other government agencies can carry out such obligations.

146. In 1981 MPP was reaching 700,000 farmers at 155 sites located 10 kms either side of main highways through the provision of low cost inputs and limited extension advice.

147. The program proposal is outlined in: Ministry of Agriculture, "Peasant Agriculture Development Program (PADEP)" (Addis Ababa: MOA, Project Brief, March 1983). See also: IBRD, *Agricultural Sector- Interim*, pp. 38-42.

148. See: Daniel Benor and Michael Baxter, *Training and Visit Extension* (Washington, D.C.: World Bank, 1984). One ARDU experiment with T and V, which began in mid-1983, see: Alemneh Dejene, *The Training and Visit Extension for Small Farmers: Lessons in the Design of Extension Programs for High Cereal Producing Regions in Ethiopia* (Cambridge: Harvard Institute for International Development, Development Discussion Paper No.199, 1985). A national T&V program has been financed by the World Bank since June 1983. In Arssi it was tested in Hetosa and Tiyo *Woredas* where it served 20,000 households, providing comprehensive, year round advice on crop and livestock production as well as soil and water conservation. The impact was generally better than elsewhere in the World Bank program and initial studies suggest it raised production.

149. The four zones were: Shoa, Arssi/Bale, Gojjam/Gondar, Wolega/Ilubabor/Keffa. These eight regions contain 33% of the country's area, 51% of its population, and most of its high potential farm land. Over 85% of total national cereal production comes from these proposed PADEP zones.

150. The higher level *awraja* would operate similar to ARDU headquarters, being staffed by technical teams composed of crop production, livestock, and cooperative organization experts backed with research, training, construction, and transport facilities needed to supervise the performance of the *woreda* office and provide basic implementation support. Generally three teams of experts were to be available for particular areas of each *awraja*. But because of the limited number of conservation, home economics, and livestock marketing specialists, only one of each were to be assigned to the entire *awraja*.

151. Under the proposal, all farmer related services, such as extension, input supply, credit and marketing, would be handled through the service cooperative. The clear assumption was that by placing RDAs in these organizations the Ministry of Agriculture's agents would travel less, get closer to farmers through the 3 to 5 peasant associations making up the cooperative, and be more accountable to local people.

PADEP would fund the agent, the concrete base for his house, and office equipment. The service cooperative was to construct and maintain the house and provide office space in their building. Ministry of Agriculture, "PADEP," p. 34.

152. The World Bank estimated that if assumptions on T and V, incentives, and marketing policies prevailed, PADEP could raise annual growth rates for cereal production to 2.2% through yield increases of 30%, leading to internal rates of return of between 40 and 70%. The çost of the Bank's program in three zones was, US$ 50 million for 5 years. SIDA was to fund the fourth Arssi/Bale Zone.

153. The World Bank's position called for: (1) increasing the price paid farmers to a level offsetting the rise in input costs and promoting the profitability of agriculture; (2) narrowing the role of the AMC to procurement only to ensure urban supply and provide food security; (3) ending of government restrictions that hamper private traders while maintaining regulations that promote fair consumer prices; (4) rationalizing the distribution of inputs and credit so that they reach small-holders on a timely basis in the quantities needed and locating it in organizations like service cooperatives that are accountable to peasants; (5) rebuilding the faultering agricultural research system and improving its capacity to breed and upgrade HYVs tailored to specific areas; (6) upgrading training of extension agents and improving their salaries and terms of service; and (7) ending the practice of using extension agents for group farm promotion. World Bank, "PADEP Preparation Initiative Discussions: Issues for Discussion" (Internal Memorandum, Washington, D.C.: n.d.).

154. The constraints blocking PADEP in 1985 are well described in: P.K. Pohland, "Visit to Ethiopia (7/2-7/7/85) and Kenya (7/7-14/7/85)" (Internal Office Memorandum, the World Bank, July 18, 1985) and attachments.

155. "Peasant Agricultural Development Programme in Arssi-Bale" (Summary of Findings of a GOE/SIDA Mission to Arssi and Bale, Addis Ababa, September 13-22, 1983); Johan Toborn, "Report on BARDU Project Preparation" (Consultancy Report for SIDA, Addis Ababa, December 1983). The decision was based on a November 1982 SIDA report that recommended the Swedes urge the Ethiopian Government to merge Arssi with Bale Region rather than shift to the Gondar-Gojjam Region in the north or merge Arssi with Shoa, as had been recommended initially by the government. "Memorandum of Mission to Gojjam, Gondar and Arssi" (SIDA, Addis Ababa, 1982).

156. Statistics on Bale are derived from: GOE/SIDA, "Peasant Programme in Arssi-Bale," pp. 12-31.

157. *Ibid.*, pp. 1-3.

158. These included: (1) crop research and field trials based on strengthened and/or new research stations; (2) agricultural extension organized according to the general principles of the Training and Visit System; (3) tree nurseries targeted on rapidly producing seedlings for fuel woodlots, construction and windbreaks; (4) small-scale irrigation schemes aimed at testing and demonstrating water development potential; (5) stores and house construction needed to establish the ARDU development agent-service cooperative infrastructure in the new areas; (6) road construction and market upgrading required to allow the project to operate effectively; (7) animal health clinic construction and drug supply needed to begin a rudimentary vaccination and curative program; and (8) performance improvement through staff training and redeployment, rebuilding of rundown field offices, response to lack of equipment, transport and repair facilities, and establishment of more reliable radio-telephone links.

159. "Report on BARDU Preparation" (Internal Memorandum, December 1983), based on Toborn, "Report on BARDU Project Preparation."

160. In addition, a Machinery Service Section added to the Plant Husbandry Department, a Milk and Feed Processing Section added to the Animal Health and Breeding Department, the Purchase and Store Section transferred to the Common Services Department, and the Industrial promotion Section made a financially independent corporation.

161. Toborn notes: "...ARDU lacks an explicit policy on how to bring about rural development (in line with government strategies). This used to be a hallmark of the project and without it the famous ARDU spirit is bound to slowly fade away." The operational plan was also seen as essential to help bring about the kinds of changes identified as necessary "...to bring the project back to its former role as a forerunner of rural development in Ethiopia..." *Ibid.*, Annex V, p. 1.

162. Among those identified by Toborn were: (1) how ARDU's administrative routines and personnel systems would be extended to Bale; (2) how ARDU's work planning, financial management, budget and procurement systems would be operationalized in Bale; (3) how ARDU's headquarters, repair, and construction infrastructure would be used to support operations in Bale; (4) how ARDU's training program can be used to build up Bale capacity; (5) how such activities as milk purchase, nursery promotion, seed multiplication, and input marketing connections could be extended to Bale; and (6) how ARDU's research expertise can be rapidly deployed to increase knowledge about Bale. *Ibid.*, Annex IV, pp. 1-3.

163. According to Toborn: "Massive investments in the project in the late sixties and early seventies are worn out and need replacement. No allowance for accumulating depreciation to cover reinvestments has been made and the impact of this is now being felt. There is at present no procedure for handling this situation except through drastic increases in the budget when old capital is used up. The budgetary situation of the Government does not permit any major increase of the ARDU investment budget. This is the only way the recurrent cost problem manifests itself. Maintenance is neglected all through the project as a consequence of the shortage of funds. Salaries occupy an increasing share of total budget..." The budget of ARDU has remained constant or even declined in later years, and certainly so in real terms. *Ibid.*, p. 1.

164. SIDA, "Aide Mémoire" (Documents Prepared by Jan Engström, Counsellor for Development Cooperation, Swedish Embassy, Addis Ababa, October 14, 1983).

165. Specifically, the Aide Mémoire called on the government to: (1) improve prices paid to farmers for their produce and promote input supplies and prices that make farming profitable; (2) end restrictions that prevent private traders from transporting their stock beyond regional borders and result in de facto forced deliveries to the AMC; (3) issue policy guidelines for the implementation of PADEP; and (4) reorganize the Ministry of Agriculture and reorient the extension service to facilitate the successful execution of small-holder focused projects.

166. The most salient of these were outlined in a 10-6-1983 memorandum by Lars Leander. They included: (1) improving the project's accounting system, possibly through the use of computers; (2) reviewing crop promotion, credit and input supply, cross-breeding of dairy animals, and cooperative promoting activities to improve them; (3) streamlining project staffing, particularly removing redundant staff at lower levels; (4) promoting better cooperation between project seed multiplication farms and the Ethiopian Seed Corporation; (5) resolving whether ARDU or the government is responsible for access road maintenance; (6) reviewing the quality of work by the water supplies unit and replacing old equipment; (7) improving the performance of home economics activities; (8) constructing additional staff houses at Asella; (9) promoting availability of long term finance for self-help programs by the Agricultural Industrial Development Bank while securing reduction in the 75% local contribution requirement

of the government; and (10) putting the industry promotion section on a commercial footing.

167. The Bank's background paper stated: "The major source of increased production is increased yields. The main proven technical package to obtain these increases requires larger use of fertilizer and improved varieties. The adoption of this technology in Ethiopia has been slow and seems to have regressed because of: (1) deteriorating price incentives and marketing problems; (2) inadequate input distribution and credit availability; and (3) ineffective extension and research. These factors have limited the production results of the MPP II project and if not corrected would jeopardize any PADEP projects that might be prepared and appraised." "PADEP Preparation Initiative Discussions: Issues for Discussions" (Internal Memorandum, n.d.), p. 1, based on GOE/IBRD, "Review of Farmers," study.

168. World Bank, *Accelerated Development in Sub-Saharan Africa: Agenda for Action* (Washington, D.C.: The World Bank, 1981).

169. Swedish International Development Authority, *Proposal for Swedish Support to Rural Development in Arsi and Bale 1986/87 - 1988/89* (Addis Ababa: SIDA, December 1985).

170. The potential of SCs for expanded input supply and marketing was still limited in late 1985 by the absence of legislation providing a legal framework for secondary unions. Aside from obvious training programs for SC staff, SIDA proposed developing a management system for input supply and grain marketing and setting up experimental secondary unions to build the experience needed by the government to draft a legal framework for them. *Ibid.*, pp. 31-43.

171. The mission's study of family farms and PCs concluded small-holders: (1) make more efficient use of agricultural inputs; (2) use scarce land resources more intensively; (3) market a greater percentage of their production; (4) have generally higher yields despite the greater access of PCs to inputs and extension advice; and (5) match any advantage PCs are supposed to achieve through economies of scale. *Ibid.*, pp. 185-98.

172. The 1984 Plan called for 53% of the peasant population to be in PCs by 1994. This led ARDU's Cooperative Promotion staff to set a target of mobilizing 10,000 households per year to form PCs. The SIDA mission concluded such a rate could hardly be voluntary, noting most farmers were not interested in joining. Also, SEAD had no tested extension package adopted to PCs. Hence it recommended improving cropping patterns, farm management techniques, and labor organization on the PCs. *Ibid.*, pp. 253-4.

173. As of 1985 there were 283 PCs in Arssi with 25,000 members and 108 PCs in Bale with 5,500 members. The average PC in Arssi had 160 ha. of cultivated land, 170 ha. of grazing land, and 20 ha. of forest. PCs in Bale were smaller with about 90 ha. of cultivated land and 120 ha. of pasture. *Ibid.*, pp. 233-4.

174. *Ibid.*, p.3, 45.

175. The PADEP guidelines are one RDA per 1,300 to 1,700 households. But in Arssi it is 1:0.8 and Bale 1:1.7. ARDU preference for Oromo speakers will not be followed. *Ibid.*, p. 35, 45.

176. *Ibid.*

177. *Ibid.*, p. 44.

178. SIDA called for development of standardized procedures for estimating demand for consumer and production supplies, accounting for sales and credit, tracking loan recovery, budgeting, weighing and grading purchases, and analyzing investment opportunities. SIDA also called for the design of a training program to teach the executive committee and employees of service cooperatives how to use these procedures. These

management systems were to be based on extensive study of service cooperatives to be commissioned by SIDA and undertaken by the Swedish Cooperative Centre.

179. Since the 1970s yields on the Section's land had declined. For example, the yield of wheat stock seed had fallen some 20%. To a large extent the decline was due to worn out equipment and managerial inattention to variables conducive to optimal yields and quality control. By 1985, the seed produced by ARDU was largely distributed to producer cooperatives at subsidized prices, a practice that prevented the Section from making profits to cover the costs of maintaining or acquiring production and seed cleaning equipment. To assist in rehabilitating the CADU built facilities, the SIDA team recommended investment in facility maintenance and purchase of equipment if the operation was to be made profitable. It also recommended the Ethiopian Seed Corporation (which grows seeds for state farms) not be allowed to inefficiently use the Section's resources and that small-holders be given access to a fair share of the seeds produced. *Ibid.*, pp. 67-77.

180. Increased population and resulting tree cutting for land clearance, fuel, and building materials was leading to rapid deforestation. Despite efforts to establish nurseries, not enough trees were being planted because the role of trees in farm systems was ignored, farmers felt insecure in their tenure, and communities were not involved in the formation of reafforestation programs. SIDA proposed undertaking studies of trees in the farming system, extending trials of different trees, revitalizing management of existing plantations to supply wood for employment generating crafts, and to extend state forests. *Ibid.*, pp. 100-7.

181. Efforts would be made to get the diverse soil conservation efforts being undertaken in the zone focused on areas of easily recognized erosion. The construction of bench terraces would be expanded and nurseries established to supply suitable tree species and to bulk up grass seed. *Ibid.*

182. Priority was to be given to building good all-weather roads in Arbagugu and Ticho and improving maintenance of all roads. SIDA funds would be used to purchase new equipment, train road design and construction personnel, and obtain consulting services. *Ibid.*, pp. 108-22.

183. Shortage of staff and aging equipment had brought the drilling of wells and construction of water systems to a standstill. While recommending the purchase of equipment and provision of technical assistance, the SIDA proposal insisted on the need for a careful survey of zonal water resources and the preparation of a master plan for water resources available for human, livestock, and irrigation use. Further, it recommended greater attention to maintenance of existing facilities and testing of new appropriate pumping technologies. *Ibid.*, pp. 123-43.

184. While recognizing the need for irrigation to increase food production, the SIDA team argued that no new systems should be constructed until the existing ones were rehabilitated and farmers trained to use water more effectively. Too many poorly designed systems had been built without a master plan, the report noted. Hence, recommendations centered on water monitoring, preparation of a master plan, development of standard design and costing guidelines, and establishment of training programs. To facilitate the expansion of small-scale irrigation systems, the proposal recommended funding of construction equipment and provision of advisory services. *Ibid.*, pp. 144-62.

185. The team recognized the importance of zonal efforts to promote off-farm employment through the identification of products farmers could use and training local craftsmen to produce them. But it concluded that more needed to be known about choice of products, level of technology, marketing, pricing, and management of skills training centers, implement fabrication shops, and oil mill operations. A study funded by

SIDA was recommended, possibly to be followed by aid to obtain machinery and expand skills centers. *Ibid.*, pp. 163-73.

186. *Ibid.*, pp. 175-81.

187. *Ibid., passim.*

188. For example: (1) the Agricultural Input Services Corporation (AISCO) was established in 1984 to separate input delivery from AMC purchase activities, to provide inputs to farmers, and distribute credit to service cooperatives after 1986 in close collaboration with the AIDB; (2) SEAD forestry and soil conservation activities overlapped with the jurisdiction of the Forestry and Wildlife Conservation Development Authority (FAWCDA); (3) the construction and maintenance of roads requires interaction between the Ethiopian Transport and Construction Authority (ETCA) of the Ministry of Construction and the rural construction department (RCD) of the Ministry of Agriculture to construct roads in the SEAD area; (4) SEAD activities need to be coordinated with the Water Supply and Sewage Authority (WSSA) within the National Water Resources Commission (NWRC) and the Ethiopian Water Works Construction Authority (EWWCA); (5) development of irrigation projects requires collaboration of SEAD's zonal irrigation team with the Ministry of Agriculture's Irrigation Department and the National Water Resources Commission (NWRC); (6) service cooperatives must work in close collaboration with the AMC, AISCO, the AIDB, and the Ethiopian Domestic Distribution Corporation (EDDC), which services the retailing end of SC operations; and (7) SEAD seed multiplication must be coordinated with the Ministry of State Farm's Ethiopian Seed Corporation (ESC).

189. The details of the villagization program and the 1985-86 campaign in Arssi are set forth in: Cohen and Isaksson, *Villagization in Arsi Region.*

190. ARDU, *Plan for 1976-80*, p. 37.

191. See: Goran Hyden, *Beyond Ujamaa in Tanzania: Underdevelopment and an Uncaptured Peasantry* (Berkeley: University of California Press, 1980), pp. 129-55; Louise Fortmann, *Peasants, Officials and Participation in Rural Tanzania: Experience with Villagization and Decentralization* (Ithaca: Cornell University, Rural Development Committee, RLO No. 1, 1980).

192. In 1985, 95% of Bale's farmers were in 559 villages averaging 250 households. Aside from 37 resettlement villages, there were only 20 planned farmers' villages in Arssi. The late 1985 plan was to convert 815 of Arssi's 1086 PAs into farmers' villages by mid-1986. SIDA, *Proposal*, pp. 235-6.

193. The programme has been very harshly criticized in the west. See, for example: Blaine Harden, "Ethiopia's Farmers Nudged into Villages," *The Washington Post* (December 17, 1985), p. A21. Arch Puddington, "Ethiopia: the Communist Uses of Famine," *Commentary* (April 1986), pp. 30-8. The villagization program is under the control of a ministerial committee dominated by the Workers' Party of Ethiopia. It produced general directives and guidelines. Implementation was planned and coordinated at the regional level through several subcommittees: (1) planning and programming; (2) site selection and surveying; (3) materials procurement; (4) transport and logistics; (5) construction; (6) propaganda and training; (7) monitoring and evaluation; and (8) security. Similar committees operated at the *awraja* and *woreda* levels. Peasant associations had committees focused on (1) site selection and surveying; (2) materials procurement; (3) propaganda; (4) security and defense; and (5) construction. Peasant associations played a major role because the government provided no resources for the move or the establishment of village infrastructure or common services. There was also insufficient government staff to direct the process. In Arssi one village was established per peasant association. While the 1985-86 campaign did not disrupt grain production in Arssi, largely because of good rainfall and timing of the move, there are

potential long term disadvantages to agricultural productivity and community life. These include: loss of work time due to longer walks to fields and to collect fuel and water, misuse of extension agents to deal with problems of villagization, increased problems with plant diseases and pests, overgrazing close to the village and erosion in village areas, deforestation for compound and village facilities construction, high population pressure on nearby water resources, crowing and spread of communicable disease, greater government control over agricultural marketing and private traders, and use of villagization to promote less productive producer cooperatives. See: Cohen and Isaksson, *Villagization in the Arssi Region, passim.*

194. This large-scale campaign also included Shoa. In villagizing Shoa, Arssi and Hararghe, the government was disrupting densely populated highland regions that contributed 40% of national food crop production, provided 55 % of AMC cereal purchases, and contained 33% of the farming population. By April 1986, the government claimed 4.6 million peasants had moved into 8,860 villages in 8 regions. At that time plans were moving toward smaller-scale campaigns in Gojjam, Wollega, Keffa, Sidamo, and Illubabor.

195. The irony of villagization was that 15 years after the project was widely criticized for contributing to tenant evictions it was now contributing to a different kind of widespread eviction, again against the will of those moved. On the famine see: Peter Gill, *A Year in the Death of Africa: Politics, Bureaucracy and the Famine* (London: Paladin Books, 1986).

196. Based on the position that the central objective of SEAD was to raise agricultural productivity, the SIDA delegation told the government that its policies of villagization, suppression of private grain trade, maintenance of artificially low agricultural prices, and subsidization of producer cooperatives were "indefensible and difficult to explain let alone justify" given clear ARDU evidence on the agricultural potential of the SEAD zone, the productivity of small-holders, the inappropriateness of mechanized production on group farms, and the severe food shortages facing the country.

197. The crop production surveys are summarized in: Keith Griffen and Roger Hay, "Problems of Agricultural Development in Socialist Ethiopia: An Overview and a Suggested Strategy," *Journal of Peasant Studies,* XIII, 1 (1985), pp. 37-66.

198. Figures on production, surplus, and sales that generated these averages come from: Toborn, "Marketing and Distribution in Ethiopia," pp. 7, 11-13. See also, ARDU, *Investigations on Impact*, p. 26; GOPE/IBRD, "Review of Farmers," p. 88.

199. Prior to this census ARDU had estimated the 1984 population at 1,333,703. ARDU, "Objectives – 1984," p. 1.

200. Central Statistical Office, *Report on a Survey of Arssi*, p. 4.

201. Population grew a reported 2.4% per annum between 1960-70 and 2.0% per annum between 1970-81. World Bank, *World Tables* , 3rd Edition (Baltimore: Johns Hopkins University Press, 1983), I, p. 54. Recent reports put the rate at 2.9%.

202. SIDA, *Proposal for SIDA Support*, p. 225.

203. *Ibid.*, p. 55. Arssi PC membership in 1985 was 25,000 households with 73% of the 283 Arssi PCs at the *welba* stage. None had reached *weland.* Average size of membership was 85 households cultivating an average of 160 hectares of cropland, and holding 170 hectares of grazing land and 20 hectares of forest land. *Ibid.*, p. 234.

204. *Ibid.*, p. 56. Bale PC membership in 1985 was 5,500 households, with PCs averaging 50 households cultivating 90 hectares on average and holding 120 hectares of pasture. *Ibid.*, p. 234.

205. The wheat/DAP (Diammonium phosphate 18-46-0) price ratio dropped from 0.43 to 0.26 during the 1974/75 to 1980/81 period. Solomon Bekure, et al., *Evaluation*, p. I,

3. Fertilizer prices increased 70% between 1976/77 and 1979/80. Planning, Evaluation and Budget Section, *Evaluation of Extension*, p. 93.

206. Toborn, "Marketing and Distribution in Ethiopia," pp. 18-19.

207. ARDU, *Investigations on Impact*, pp. 11-13.

208. The major study was carried out in the new ARDU *awrajas* in 1977. ARDU, *Crop Sampling Survey in Arbagugu and Ticho* (Asella: Arssi Rural Development Unit, Publication No. 8, 1977). A Table suggesting higher average cereal and pulse yields between 1967/68 and 1980/81 is inadequately documented in: ARDU, "Objectives – 1984," p. 15. The major study of HYV diffusion is: Ingvar Jonsson, *Diffusion of Agricultural Innovations in Chilalo Awraja, Ethiopia* (Addis Ababa: Institute of Development Research, Addis Ababa University, Report No. 17, June 1975).

209. The three wheat, barley, and teff cultivars used by CADU-ARDU researchers are reviewed in: Solomon Bekure, et al., *Evaluation*, p. V, 10.

210. *Ibid.*, p. V, 10.

211. Alemneh Dejene, *Evaluation of the Training and Visit*, pp. 14-15.

212. Yeraswork Admassie, et al., *Ethiopian Highlands Reclamation Study*, Annex IV.

213. Bengtsson, *Rural Development Research.*

214. SIDA, *Proposal for SIDA Support*, p. 83.

215. Johan Holmberg, *Survey of Consumption Patterns in Etheya Extension Area* (Asella: CADU, Publication No. 90, 1973), pp. 1-2.

216. ARDU, "Objectives – 1984" p. 11, based on ARDU, *Investigations of Impact*, pp. 56-60. That study must, however, be treated with care. Clearly, additional research is needed on production and inputs before ARDU's success in raising incomes can be evaluated. Such research must distinguish between present income gains as constrained by government input, price, tax and marketing policies and potential income gains if small-holders received adequate inputs, extension advice, and fair prices in the market place.

217. For example, Ashwani Saith, "The Distributional Dimensions of Revolutionary Transition: Ethiopia," *Journal of Development Studies*, XXII, 1 (1985), pp. 158-60.

218. Planning, Evaluation and Budget Section, *Evaluation of Extension*, p. 59.

219. ARDU, "Objectives – 1982," p. 10, based on data presented in: ARDU, *Investigations on Impact*, p. 61.

220. ARDU's economists estimated the marginal propensity to consume and save at 0.813 and 0.187 respectively, figures much higher than those found elsewhere in rural Ethiopia. ARDU, "Objectives – 1982," p. 11.

221. ARDU, *Investigations on Impact*, p. 85.

222. *Ibid.*, pp. 19-22.

223. The mean annual savings rate per sample farmer was EthB 30.25 and 8.7% of respondents had savings. Again the highest savings rates were found in areas suitable to ARDU's crop packages and the lowest in areas dominated by livestock production. For example, the 1980 survey found 23% of farmers in the fertile Iteya RDC, one of the original CADU areas, had savings averaging EthB 60.55 each. *Ibid.*, p. 93.

224. ARDU, "Objectives – 1982," p. 11.

225. Data on the increase in per capita food grain consumption in Arssi and problems analyzing it are set forth in: Toborn, "Marketing and Distribution in Ethiopia," p. 12.

226. CADU, Planning and Evaluation Section, *Cost/Benefit Analysis on CADU for the Period 1967/68-1974/75* (Asella: CADU, 1971).

227. Interview with Deputy Director Johan Holmberg, formerly in the Planning and Evaluation Section of CADU in the early 1970s, October 23, 1986.

228. Raw data in support of this assertion include: (1) by 1980 Arssi was producing more than 200,000 tons of wheat per year; (2) international wheat prices ran $ 168/ton in

1980 to $ 137/ton in 1983; and (3) commercial and concessionary wheat imports ran from 126,526 tons in 1980 to 149,548 in 1984.

229. Hunter, et al., *Final Report*, 63-6.

230. Imperial Ethiopian Government, "A General Framework for the Fourth Five Year Development Plan (1974/75 - 1978/79)" (Addis Ababa: Prepared for the Second Meeting of the Consultative Group for Ethiopia, June 1973).

CHAPTER 7

CADU-ARDU and the Debate

> The rise and decline of IRD (1973-80) was in some ways very similar to the fate of CD in the 1950-57 period.
>
> Carl K. Eicher and John M. Staatz (1984)

The CADU-ARDU case study makes three major contributions to the literature on integrated rural development. First, it provides an example of an integrated rural development project that played a successful role in bringing economic and social development to a promising agricultural area while influencing national development policies and programs. Second, it challenges the major criticisms set forth by those who argue that integrated rural development is a strategy that should be abandoned. At the same time it highlights the lack of data underlying their analyses. Third, its detailed documentation contributes to those studying integrated rural development projects from a comparative perspective, in an effort to specify conditions under which such projects should be introduced and to identify design and implementation principles essential to a well articulated integrated rural development methodology.

The role CADU-ARDU played in promoting the economic and social development of the Arssi Region and Ethiopia has been the central focus of this book and need not be summarized here. Nor should the lessons CADU-ARDU generates be outlined in this concluding chapter, not because they are difficult to identify but because a major argument in the pages that follow is that too much of the evaluative literature is based on a single case and that little progress in the integrated rural development debate will be made until systematic comparative studies of a number of cases are carried out. Rather, the second and third contributions will be reviewed because the debate over the utility of integrated rural development projects is an important one, with proponents of the approach currently losing ground.

PROBLEMS IN COMPARATIVE ANALYSIS

Rural development experts study specific project experiences to learn more than why the one under investigation had the results it did. Rather, they seek to gain the understanding required to make generalizations and guidelines for selecting, designing, implementing, and evaluating future projects. Unfortunately, the literature on these generalizations and guidelines is larger than the body of systematic case studies on which it is based.

This is particularly true of the critical literature on integrated rural development projects. Here the growing number of conference papers, journal articles, and books that enunciate positions on the innovation are empirically thin. Moreover, they are increasingly incestuous, citing other overviews of integrated rural development, rather than turning to existing case studies and their empirical evidence.[1]

A close review of the most widely cited critiques of integrated rural development demonstrates that the authors analyzing the intervention rely on secondary studies consolidating project evaluation reports.[2] Few of these studies are as detailed as the one presented here, most being brief summaries of a particular project's experience. Yet, critics of integrated rural development rarely probe beyond these case studies, much less carry out further primary research on them. As a result, they cannot knowledgeably evaluate the findings of the secondary study, much less determine whether the documents on which it is based accurately reflect experiences reviewed.

The failure of critics to probe deeper into secondary studies is important, for often they are exercises in "negative social science," academics receiving few rewards for studying successful projects.[3] Indeed, integrated rural development projects have attracted much criticism precisely because their project papers and early press releases presented exaggerated expectations for their performance. Such critiques are relatively easy to make given the tendency of authors to synthesize overviews rather than invest research time in the broader historical, physical, or social context in which such projects are implemented. Much critical analysis rests on a handful of well known, widely cited projects. Rarely are the numerous lesser known studies reviewed. As for the well known cases, reviewers often fail to appreciate that some studies are either outdated or written too early in the period of project implementation, when trends are difficult to identify and interpret.

Nevertheless, to be fair to the generalizers, such cursory synthesizing analysis has been essential because of a curious paradox: integrated rural development is too significant an intervention not to be carefully critiqued by generalists, but the need to produce detailed case studies is too demanding in time and energy and too unrewarding a research topic to attract academics.

Having pointed out these problems in the critical literature, the chapter now turns to reviewing it. Here the object is to present only the most widely cited and influential generalizations critical of integrated rural development. Therefore selections presented here will cover the range of criticism but not all such critiques. In this regard the generalizations presented represent clusters of observations. These will be tested against the CADU-ARDU case study. Based on this exercise, the chapter will evaluate the growing argument of many comparative academic analysts and field professionals that integrated rural development interventions should be abandoned.

PROJECT EXPERIENCE AND THE LITERATURE

Critics of integrated rural development have specified more than a dozen main reasons why the intervention should not be used by Third World governments and donors. But the CADU-ARDU case challenges these, raising questions about their validity.

First, the case study demonstrates that integrated rural development projects can have a clearly articulated strategic approach and a methodology for carrying it out. As such it stands in sharp contrast to the doubts about the strategy raised by Vernon F. Ruttan in his statement:

> Integrated rural development can be described, perhaps not too inaccurately, as an ideology in search of a methodology or a technology.[4]

This widely cited point has two implications. The first is that integrated rural development has been promoted without the benefit of any systematic elaboration. To be sure, the strategy initially appeared as an operational rather than a theoretical approach. Yet, as Chapter 2 has demonstrated, there are coherent frameworks for conceptualizing and promoting integrated rural development, frameworks that have explicit theoretical foundations and offer design and implementation methodologies. Admittedly, some proponents have failed to provide the conceptual rigor, theoretical justification, and design specificity their approaches must have to qualify as a coherent "methodology or technology." But it is submitted that the framework outlined by Arthur T. Mosher in Chapter 2, and underpinned by the theoretical rationale pioneered by such analysts as John W. Mellor or Bruce F. Johnston and outlined in Chapter 1, demonstrates that there is a substantial exception to Ruttan's conclusion, one that he has come to recognize in his subsequent writing.[5]

The second implication is that no programmatic methodology exists for implementing or administering integrated rural development. This is revealed in a qualification paragraph prior to the famous "ideology in search of a methodology" statement:

> A basic weakness of the integrated rural development approach is that policy or program objectives are adopted for which no readily available closed-system technology or program methodologies are available.[6]

In essence, Ruttan raises an important question as to whether integrated rural development projects can succeed if by definition they cannot be organized around a single crop and technology, such as cotton and irrigation in the Sudan's long established Gezira Scheme. Although only a single case, it is submitted that CADU-ARDU's experience with a variety of not necessarily linked crops and technologies is substantial enough to establish that appropriate program methodologies can be forged that are based on open system technologies pursued in conjunction with a mix of agricultural and non-agricultural objectives.

Second, CADU-ARDU challenges the criticism that integrated rural development projects are too complex to be successful. A statement of William J. Siffen underlines this problem:

> The administrative problems of integrated rural development include that sometimes fatal common cold of public administration – sheer difficulty of doing ordinary things.[7]

There is no question that integration complicates administration and that this is a serious problem in bureaucratic environments marked by low administrative capacity, client elitist politics, excessive centralization, and corruption.[8] Robert Wade makes the case more specifically:

> ...the larger the number of components to be administratively integrated, the higher the cost – in time, in friction (people do not like to be integrated), in the sacrifice of performance for control. It may be suggested that the costs increase more than proportionately with the number of components, especially if the components include both the economic and the non-economic.[9]

This position is also taken by others who argue essentially that the administrative complexities of integration overwhelm designers and managers, precluding the appreciation of innovative ideas based on the analysis of past rural development experiences.[10] Such arguments also feed the general misconception that integrated rural development projects are comprehensive, a myth not supported by detailed project studies. These studies reveal that the range of project formats usually emphasizes a principal activity, such as agricultural production or physical infrastructure construction, with only a few other components added to broaden and reinforce the intervention. To imply comprehensiveness or to argue that complexity is the bundle of straw that will always break the camel's back is to mislead professionals, particularly when done with little reference to actual cases and without analyzing whether administrative constraints can be overcome.

CADU-ARDU was administratively very complex. Indeed, that complexity makes Chapters 4 and 6 so intricate. Yet, the project functioned reasonably well as an administrative unit under the burden of autocracy, the uncertainty of an unfolding revolution, and the socialist ideology of a military government. Surely it justifies the conclusion of John D. Montgomery that problems of administration are not so difficult as to require rejection of integrated approaches without an effort to find better guidelines for administration.[11]

It is concern for complexity that leads some critics to argue that integration is not necessary. This implied rejection of integrated rural development is clearly stated by Robert Wade who offers more explicit advice:

> There should be integration of planning; but not administrative integration of operations unless it can be demonstrated clearly both that simultaneous provision of factors is necessary (that the absence of one set significantly harms the effectiveness of another) and that there is no alternative way to secure simultaneous provision except through authoritative administrative integration.[12]

Observations such as those of Wade are used by others to argue that disintegrating rural development and allowing line ministries to provide services under the facilitating eye of district or provincial development authorities will ensure simultaneous performance without the burdens of achieving and maintaining administrative integration. A good example of this is found in the writing of David K. Leonard, who on the basis of a single problematic case in Kenya argues:

> It is one thing to argue that rural development requires many institutional components and that integration is therefore needed in analysis, planning and policy making. It is another to create an administratively integrated, multifunctional program in an administratively weak environment. If effective operation of each component is made dependent there is a high probability that the whole program will not work. It seem preferable to make components independent of one another – even at the cost of performance potential – in order to increase the probability that actual performance will meet minimum standards.[13]

Based on this observation, Leonard has taken a further step, one likely to become increasingly influential given donor frustration with rural development efforts, particularly those in Africa, and the trend toward using macro policy instruments and the "magic of the market" rather than projects. That step is a call for "disintegrating rural development," the principals of which Leonard describes:

> (1) Single-function organizations are less complex than multi-functional ones. (2) Small units are less complex than large ones. (3) The greater the number of hierarchial levels the larger the complexity. (4) The market is administratively simpler than a hierarchy. (5) It is much more difficult to administer benefits that are targeted for a specific clientele than those that are general. (6) When administrative capacity is in doubt, simplicity outweighs all other virtues in organizational and task design.[14]

As always, there is much merit in calls for simplicity, like Robert Chambers' maxim that "simple can be optimal."[15] The problem is that such generalizations play to the either/or inclinations of many rural development experts who are unable to think along continuums and are likely to misuse such insights to reject out of hand all administratively integrated rural development interventions.

Yet, the CADU-ARDU experience with its milk, forestry, and roads programs provides an exception to the "not necessarily administratively integrated" generalization. Briefly, the transfer of the project's successful milk production program to the separate state owned Dairy Development Enterprise led to the rapid deterioration of an important activity on whose success other project activities were predicated. Likewise the transfer of the project's responsibility for maintaining feeder roads to the Ethiopian Transport and Construction Authority, a separate agency with a limited budget and inadequate equipment, soon hampered development activities in the region, for roads began to deteriorate once the project was excluded from maintaining them. And the transfer of the project's forestry program to the ineffective Forest and Wildlife Development Agency quickly threatened years of project effort to protect the regions' forests and establish wood resource programs supportive of future generational needs. That the 1983 evaluation strongly appealed for reintegrating these services and activities back into the project testifies to the need for generating empirically grounded qualifications on Leonard's generalization. More analytically, the CADU–ARDU case suggests that under the right conditions administrative integration makes more sense and reaches preferred results, even in a task environment marked by low administrative capacity and weak institutions.

Third, CADU-ARDU demonstrates that integrated rural development project designs can avoid the rigid constructs of the blueprint model and adapt to changing conditions. This finding contradicts the conclusion of Bruce F.Johnston and William C. Clark that:

> ...integrated rural development seems incompatible with our view of rural development as a learning process...Attempts to impose a blueprint in the form of 'integrated rural development' would be counter-productive and would reduce the opportunities for learning from a more adaptive approach to the problems of organizational design and management.[16]

The notion of the distinction between blueprint and process models emerged in the 1970s and has proven to be an important concept facilitating understanding of project design and success. The major proponent of the concept is David C. Korten who argues that projects need to unfold gradually through a learning process based on evolving activities.[17] Central to the learning model idea is the observation that rural development projects of the post 1970s era cannot be designed like the highways, bridges, and hospitals of the earlier development decades. According to the argument, the blueprint mentality gained by aid agencies through experiences with physical projects is a constraint on efforts to stimulate rural productivity and progressive social change.

The learning or process approach is an important concept. The use of it by Johnston and Clark is invited because integrated rural development projects are by definition complex, requiring detailed project designs. However, the CADU-ARDU experience illustrates that a management evaluation unit that can produce timely studies of project performance and project leadership committed to progressive development can build learning and flexibility into a well articulated integrated rural development project design.

Despite its size and cost, its lengthy design documents, and detailed project agreement, CADU-ARDU has survived a social revolution that changed the nature of power and wealth in Ethiopia and Arssi. As more was learned about the difficulties of the task environment, CADU made substantial adjustments. Of all those reviewed in Chapters 4-6, perhaps the most illustrative are the altering of its mechanization and credit policies to deal with the tenant eviction problem and its shift in extension strategies to facilitate the revolution's agrarian reforms. In many ways the project has operated as if it were designed with Korten's concept in mind, for its history has been one of learning to be effective, learning how to be efficient, and learning to expand. To be sure, this argument stretches Korten's model, for he is concerned with designing projects that are people centered.[18] Nevertheless, the evidence is clear: integrated rural development as an approach should not be rejected simply because the complexities tackled require the preparation of more detailed project designs than is normally the case.

Nor should it be assumed, as it is by Johnston and Clark, that:

> Most of the proposals for integrated rural development are based on an implicit assumption that we know which activities should receive priority and how they should be integrated within organizations designed to facilitate rural development.[19]

Since the authors cite no projects in support of this charge of imperious donor rationality, it is not possible to know if they included a review of the CADU project papers. Certainly the project was designed with an explicit model in mind. But a review of the record shows that the draftsmen knew there was more to be learned and that the project would have to be adjusted as its staff came to better understand the task environment, the needs of the target population, and the advantages and disadvantages of the strategies and organization adopted. The activities of the Planning and Evaluation Section during the CADU period, plus other examples given in the case study, testify to this. So too does the plan of operation proposed for BARDU and outlined in Chapter 6, for its draftsmen framed it to be both detailed and flexible enough to allow learning and adjustment during the implementation phase. In sum, the charge that integrated rural development projects are incompatible with the learning process model is misleading. Clearly, the CADU-ARDU experience shows that integrated rural development projects need not be fixed and unopen to adaptation, and offers a tested approach for promoting learning and adjustment.

Fourth, CADU-ARDU provides an example of an integrated rural development project capable of carrying out a complex mix of administratively integrated tasks in a bureaucratic environment marked by low administrative capacity. As such it challenges the conclusion of Goran Hyden that:

> Rural development programmes will have to be made simpler...the trend must be away from the fashionable notion of 'integrated' programmes that imply the administrative integration of various institutional components involved in rural development.[20]

Perhaps the major fault critics find with integrated rural development is that it is administratively difficult to implement. The general argument is summed up by the Overseas Development Institute:

> In practice, IRD has looked far less convincing than the ideas which underpin it, particularly where all the administrative implications of integrating all aspects of government services related to the rural sector have not been fully considered.[21]

There is much truth to this point. The knowledge about administration of rural development projects was not extensive when the approach began to be applied in the mid-1960s, and, as noted earlier, it began as an operational effort not well grounded in theory or applied literature. But those who reject integrated rural development because of administrative implications appear unaware that a growing number of experts have been analyzing this constraint and formulating strategies for addressing it.

Drawing on existing case studies or their own on-site research of carefully selected integrated rural development projects, they are producing useful guidelines for designing projects that fit the policy space and administrative patterns characterizing their proposed task environments.[22] They are offering design and implementation principles expressly focused on administrative and management constraints and opportunities. In short, "administrative implications" are increasingly understood, even if the critics remain ignorant of the progress being made.

As for staffing, the critique usually runs that integrated rural development projects have low probabilities of success because of the lack of technical and administrative manpower in late developing countries. For example, Hyden concludes that in Africa:

> ... the creation of administratively integrated, multifunctional programmes in an administratively weak environment has proven a great mistake.[23]

This theme is picked up by the Overseas Development Institute which concludes:

> The manpower requirement of many IRD projects also tends to stretch government resources beyond their capacity. A common consequence is lack of contact with farmers and farmers groups, a poor staff quality and morale.[24]

The weak administrative context in which CADU-ARDU was implemented, as well as the project's strategy for responding to that constraint, was outlined in Chapters 4-6. Basically, the project recruited its staff without charges that it raided other ministries. In 1982, ARDU employed only 8 percent of the Ministry of Agriculture's high and middle level staffs; however, it employed 20 percent of the Ministry's field agents. It built their capacity through informal counterpart training at the upper levels and formal courses for technical staff at its training center. Despite the failure of the government to improve the provincial administrative system, the project carried out its integrated, multifunctional services and activities reasonably well. To be sure, a more competent, committed local government system would have helped the project better reach its objectives. But it would be hard to find the CADU project a "great mistake" on the basis of a review of its administrative performance.

To a great extent CADU's managerial capacity was due to the project's relative independence from the administrative environment in its early years and the presence of Swedish advisers. But by the mid-1970s the project had few expatriates and was being incorporated into the Ministry of Agriculture. Still, the project continued to provide its mandated services and activities, albeit in a more mechanistic and inefficient way. A major reason for this was SIDA's improvement of management of the ministry through the building of EPID and support for the MPP Phases. Maintenance of integration and performance was also due to the fact that effective systems of work planning, implementation reporting, evaluation, staffing, budgeting, and maintenance, for example, were designed in the early years of the project. So well did they fit and so well embedded were they in the project's administrative system, that they were carried on despite a revolution and subsequent decline in administrative capacity.

Still, the CADU-ARDU experience suggests that some long-term expatriate advisers with the skills to guide technical departments of an integrated rural development project are essential in weak administrative systems. It is simply hard to recruit and retain scarce nationals with both administrative and technical skills. But with attractive facilities, such as the project compound on the outskirts of Asella and its supporting Common Services Department, solid leadership and a sense of mission, good national managers can be found and attracted to move to the countryside, even in a country with Ethiopia's limited resources of trained manpower. This belief is supported by project figures showing the decline of high and middle level foreign employees from 36 in 1967 to 0 in 1980 and the increase in senior Ethiopian staff from 15 to 40 over the same period. These figures are remarkable given the fact that project employees are now subject to the salaries and terms of service of the Central Personnel Agency and that civil service salaries have been frozen since 1974.

The case study documented problems of excessive turnover in this staff after 1974, as well as immaturity in administrative judgment and declining skill levels. This was particularly the case in 1977 when ideological debates and turnover so hampered project management that SIDA considered early termination of its aid. But the fact remains that the government and SIDA kept the project's administrative posts largely filled and its administrative systems running under very difficult political and economic circumstances.

Importantly, the CADU-ARDU experience illustrates how a large integrated rural development project can help fill a national administrative void. This point is illustrated by the 1981 evaluation's finding that the project trained many of its staff for top level positions in Addis Ababa ministries, thereby making a contribution to the administration of agricultural development.

Fifth, the CADU-ARDU case demonstrates that an integrated rural development project can be successfully implemented in a centralized government that discourages innovation and, in the process, generate reforms in that government.

The problem administrative centralization is said to pose for integrated rural development projects is stated by Ruttan:

> Highly centralized administration of national programs make it difficult to carry out the experiments with program content and delivery methods that are essential if rural development programs are to meet the diverse needs of rural areas.[25]

Yet the CADU-ARDU project was conceived and implemented in a centralized political system, one no less dominated by post-1974 military officers and Marxist planners than the pre-revolutionary period was by aristocrats and senior officials loyal to Haile Selassie.

What allowed CADU-ARDU to "experiment" and "meet diverse needs of rural areas" was its initial separation from Ethiopia's unsympathetic national bureaucracy of development ministries. Yet this strategy of SIDA designers is strongly faulted in the literature on integrated rural development. Such criticisms are reviewed shortly.

CADU-ARDU experience suggests that the objectives, strategy, and activities of integrated rural development tend to make them progressive organizations. The staff they recruit are more likely to be highly motivated and creative in their approach to problem solving and provision of services. Hence, whatever the position of the highly centralized administration, such projects, activated by their staff, probably have more potential for carrying out experiments with program content and delivery methods than other kinds of projects.

This was the case in Ethiopia. Despite the autocracy of Haile Selassie's conservative provincial government system, and ideological posture of Colonel Mengistu's planners, project staff steadily experimented. Good examples are the model lease program, the shift to multipurpose extension agents in 1976, and current experiments with the Training and Visit System of extension delivery. Clearly, the evidence presented throughout the case study suggests that a highly centralized government need not preclude creative field level efforts to meet the diverse needs of rural areas.

Sixth, the history of CADU-ARDU illustrates that an integrated rural development project can be gradually incorporated into a line ministry as well as affect bureaucratic values and patterns in that ministry.

Designers of large-scale integrated rural development projects have tended to assume that effective coordination of services and activities requires the establishment of a semi-autonomous administrative unit. Certainly this was the case with CADU, given its obligation to perform functions cutting across divisions within the Ministry of Agriculture and between ministries and parastatals. But over the past few years serious questions have been raised about the wisdom of such a design strategy. For example, after reviewing the problems created by separate project implementation units, Uma J. Lele notes that achieving integration with the regular government administration without jeopardizing the performance of the project is a difficult, perhaps unlikely task:

> As the time approaches for transferring responsibility for some of the autonomous integrated rural development programs from the project authorities to the indigenous administrators, the gap between the capacity of the two administrative systems has become of particular concern to persons involved in designing rural development programs.[26]

After reviewing such concerns and relating them to the tendency of integrated rural development projects to seek to accomplish too much too fast, to advance services and activities without building institutional and manpower resources, Lele concludes:

> ...if there is not to be a considerable sag in the programs after expatriate managers have departed and project authorities have dissolved, programs may have to undertake only those activities on such a scale which, in the foreseeable future, can realistically be taken over and managed by indigenous manpower and institutions, even with ambitious assumptions about manpower training and institutional development.[27]

CADU-ARDU began as a semi-autonomous administrative unit with a ten year time frame and an ambitious set of objectives. These included the provision of a complex set of services and activities and the building of institutional capacity and trained manpower to run them. The full incorporation of the project into line ministries began with reforms placing the project within the jurisdiction of EPID in 1973, and was completed with the establishment of SEAD and promulgation of Ministry of Agriculture reforms in 1985. While there was a sag in programs with the departure of Swedish advisers, this must in part be attributed to the fratricide of the revolution that drove talented managers and technicians out of the country, underground, or to their deaths. It must also in part be attributed to the ideological debates that unsettled all Ethiopian government units and led to different policy objectives, such as the shift in ARDU from an emphasis on production to one on social mobilization.

Despite the gradualness of the process and the recent SIDA call for bringing back Swedish technicians to support SEAD, the fact remains that the project's case history demonstrates that a semi-autonomous unit can be integrated into the line ministries, that project management systems can be merged into a bureaucracy (as CADU did to EPID and it to the ministry at large), and that training and counterpart work can generate the administrative and technical manpower needed to maintain the project once donor support is withdrawn. Perhaps the key to this process in Ethiopia was the long-term view of the project taken by SIDA, a view most donors' aid control systems and changing strategy postures cannot tolerate easily.

Related to the critique of incorporation is the issue of disengagement. It is a common problem for integrated rural development projects because they are for the most part funded by international aid agencies.

SIDA always envisioned CADU as a long-term, although time-bounded investment. However, after the first two phases, internal SIDA discussion increasingly focused on the difficulty of disengaging from the project. To a large extent the problem arose from its success and status as the government's principal development agent in Arssi Region. Unsuccessful or inappropriate integrated rural development projects can simply be terminated by aid agencies. But projects that come close to reaching their objectives build powerful local and national constituencies that are hard to ignore. When the host government needs to satisfy such constituencies yet lacks the financial resources to cover the project under its own capital and recurrent budget allocations, donors are likely to be under significant pressure to continue providing the foreign aid needed to maintain the project.

This is the case with CADU-ARDU. Indeed, the disengagement problem has been compounded by the government request that ARDU be expanded to cover both Arssi and Bale Regions under the new SEAD initiative. In this sense, SIDA has become a hostage to the project's potential. Fortunately, the Swedish Parliament and SIDA have shown uncommon wisdom for donors, and are not yet embarrassed by nearly two decades of substantial funding. There is much debate today over whether donors should fund recurrent costs, under what conditions, and for how long. Perhaps the key to disengagement is a cycle of recurrent cost funding to gradually facilitate the project's absorption into the national budget. Certainly CADU-ARDU offers SIDA an interesting case to apply and study such a disengagement strategy.

A final aspect of the integration critique is that semi-autonomous implementation strategies hamper efforts to reorient the established bureaucracies that will ultimately have to absorb the activities and services needing to be sustained after the end of the project. This argument is stated by Coralie Bryant and Louise G. White:

> Acutely aware of the problems in getting organizations to make the necessary changes, development planners for many years assumed that the best procedure was to establish special project units to administer projects. The new emphasis in development administration on 'institutional development,' however, has changed this emphasis. Now developers are more concerned with finding ways to work with and strengthen the capacity of existing organizations to carry out development.[28]

Underlying this criticism is the new notion of "bureaucratic reorientation".[29] A still emerging concept of public administration, it argues that top down bureaucracies cannot serve the rural majority or be responsive to them until they institutionalize new values which recognize that development must be "by" rather than "for" people and establish new procedures and incentives to facilitate more responsive performance by the staff of development ministries.

There is much utility in this position, but it does not necessarily follow that bureaucratic reorientation must begin in a single ministry. Again, the history of CADU-ARDU as a separate unit that gradually came under the jurisdiction of the Ministry of Agriculture is instructive. As a separate unit, and with the external pressure and leadership of the Swedish staff, CADU provided a focus for the emergence of new orientations toward small-holders and tenant producers. While these views might have developed had the unit been located inside a line ministry, it is not likely, for imperial ministries under Haile Selassie were just that.

Chapters 4-6 document the new ideas of service and mobilization generated by CADU-ARDU and trace the spread of these ideas and staff supportive of them into the Ministry of Agriculture and the rest of the country. An example of major innovations based on a reorientation of the bureaucracy and field agents to small-holders and tenant farmers was the formation of EPID and the Minimum Package Program. Recent experimentation with the training and visit extension system by ARDU shows that these processes continue. Further, Chapter 6 describes the ideological debate that CADU's hothouse environment generated in the early 1970s, debate that was to make the project a center of political ideas for reforming the land tenure system, organizing the countryside, and linking development ministries with rural communities. Indeed, some assert that CADU staff provided an important core for the Ethiopian People's Revolutionary Party (EPRP) and used EPID's MPP extension system to push progressive socialist ideals throughout the country.[30] This assertion while probable, cannot be established. If true, it reflects bureaucratic reorientation far beyond that envisioned by its academic supporters. Hence, while the project was far from the people-centered strategy proponents of bureaucratic reorientation favor, the CADU-ARDU experience suggests that the complexities of integrating activities of several government units should not be rejected because of the emphasis on gradual bureaucratic reorientation within specific established organizations.

Seventh, the CADU-ARDU case challenges major propositions in the critical literature which assert that integrated rural development projects not backed by strong national support or directed by charismatic leaders have a low probability of being successful.

The first of these propositions is clearly stated by Dennis A. Rondenelli who argues that integrated rural development projects:

> ... simply will not succeed without strong and sustained commitment by national political leaders to goals of equitable economic growth...[31]

Strong national support makes project implementation easier, but the CADU-ARDU case suggests that it is not essential. Chapters 4 and 5 document the failure of Haile Selassie's government to undertake the reforms needed for the project to reach its objectives. The origins of this failure in the project design and negotiation period were reviewed. Yet, despite the fact that the government failed to provide the land tenure, local government, and agricultural policy reforms needed to raise the productivity, standards of living, and development participation of the target population, project staff found ways to overcome them or limit the negative effects.

To be sure, lack of national commitment to reform hampered project success in the early 1970s. So it must be asked: what if Haile Selassie had not fallen, what if a land based military or modernizing elite had succeeded him? Was the project in effect saved by the revolution and its removal of land, power, and status constraints described in Chapters 3-5? Counterfactual questions are important but difficult to answer. But if one can step back from the passion over tenant evictions and the anger over conservative local government officials and exploitive provincial elites, the project's success in increasing yields and income, broadening access to public infrastructure, generating design ideas and lessons for other projects, building improved management systems, and training of promising Ethiopians seems to argue that CADU-ARDU would be considered successful in the absence of a revolution. Clearly, whatever political direction Ethiopia might have taken in 1974, the project had already had, and would have continued to have, a long term impact as an agent of change on the larger agrarian sector and the central bureaucracies that served it. In essence, good project leadership, committed staff, and a supportive donor can overcome the absence of strong, sustained commitment by a nation's leadership.

A related criticism of integrated rural development is that it succeeds only where an unusual individual arises to direct it and that such individuals are extremely rare. This view is well expressed by Robert Wade:

> The experience of Comilla, Vicos and... other multipurpose projects, suggests that cases of successful multi-purpose rural development projects tend to be associated with highly skilled, highly dedicated and relatively autonomous organizers. What these projects do not give much guidance for is the question what components can be included if the programme is to remain within the limits of available organizing skills, and what components must be excluded.[32]

CADU had excellent direction and leadership in its early years from both Bengt Nekby and Paulos Abraham, a fact documented in the case study. But neither man was an Akhter Hameed Khan (Comilla) or Allen R. Holmberg (Vicos). After the beginning of the revolution, the quality of project leadership project declined, frequent turnover of top officers occurred, and the Swedish operating executives departed. This problem was noted clearly in the 1981 evaluation. Yet, CADU-ARDU continued to function through a period of great instability and expansion. Stronger project leaders might have made the project more successful, but the case study does not support the "great man thesis" of critics who use it to explain away apparent success.

Eighth, the CADU-ARDU case demonstrates that an integrated rural development project does not have to operate in isolation from indigenous administrative systems or separate from grassroots institutions in order to achieve its objectives.

Jon R. Moris illustrates an important critique of integrated rural development when he argues that:

> ...in order to meet ambitious production goals new projects exclude themselves from the very organizational frameworks they are claiming to influence.[33]

Clearly, the case study presented here does not suggest that project designers and managers attempted to isolate the project from the organizational frameworks they sought to influence in order to meet ambitious production goals.

Rather, the task environment made difficult most project initiatives to build linkages with the local government system and field ministries prior to the revolution. Patterns of power, wealth, and status in rural Chilalo also frustrated those efforts made by the project to promote grassroots institutions. To be sure the designers and managers of CADU failed to appreciate the need for participation and had little knowledge of strategies for building indigenous capacity under Ethiopian bureaucratic and political conditions. But in fairness it must be remembered this is a hindsight judgment, for these problems occurred prior to the emergence in the development literature of arguments and approaches for promoting participation, local organization, and bureaucratic reorientation. Most importantly, when faced with the full realization of government constraints, the project did not simply turn its back on them and promote food production. Instead it fought for reform of the land tenure system, promoted social awareness through its extension and information units, attempted to build a cooperative network, tried to organize model farmer groups, and promoted women's clubs.

CADU was not particularly successful at some of these efforts. But success is not important here. What is important is the fact that the project's leadership and staff spent energy and resources on efforts to understand and influence the organizational frameworks critical to the project's success and the maintenance of its achievements once SIDA funding ended. It would have been easy to use the milk and grain packages they developed and simply increase production. That this route was not taken is reflected in the internal conflict that hampered the project after 1973 and the influence the project had on the reorganization of the Ministry of Agriculture and the agrarian reforms that dramatically altered rural Ethiopia.

Ninth, CADU-ARDU demonstrates that an integrated rural development project can achieve acceptable internal rates of return and justify its high cost. As such it addresses Ruttan's concern that the benefits of such projects are unlikely to exceed their costs:

> Resources devoted to integrating the development and management of physical and institutional infrastructures are likely to have a relatively low return (because of)...absence of any well-defined or community development technologies around which professional capacity or resources can be organized or institutionalized.[34]

There is no question that some integrated rural development projects have been poorly conceived and designed without any clearly defined methodology for implementation. It is not hard to find projects that had relatively low returns. But as Chapters 4-6 establish, this need not be the case.

CADU-ARDU demonstrates at least one example of a well-defined strategy around which professional capacity and resources were organized and institutionalized. More importantly, it is a strategy that led to high returns, both in the Arssi Region and in Ethiopia's policy making arena. This position is supported by data in Chapters 4-6, which among other things document that: (1) the region has become one of the few surplus grain producing areas in the country; (2) Arssi's small-holders have potentially higher incomes than farmers elsewhere in the highlands; (3) the benefits of the project have exceeded the costs since 1972; and (4) the project has positively and significantly influenced Ethiopia's development policy, from the pre-revolutionary MPP innovation, to the conceptualization of the land reform and the formulation of PADEP.

Some project-generated benefits challenge the view that integrated rural development is too expensive to be justified. This criticism is restated in an Overseas Development Institute paper that argues integrated rural development represents:

> ...costly misallocation of resources...(because it attempts to) direct a process which cannot, and should not, be closely managed...(promotes) unnecessary duplication of functions...(and suffers from) lack of clear purpose.[35]

It is submitted that the cost-benefit data published by the project, the sections on economic impact in Chapters 5 and 6, and the general thrust of the project's 1974 and 1981 evaluations support an argument that the more than US$ 41.5 million (E$ 85 million) spent by SIDA and the Ethiopian government between 1967 and 1983 can hardly be considered a "costly misallocation of resources," either directly in Arssi or indirectly relative to rural Ethiopia. In fact, had the revolutionary government pursued supportive agricultural policies, as argued in Chapter 6, the benefits would have been even higher. Moreover, the case study illustrates the complexity of the cost issue. ARDU officials argue the project does not appear overly expensive if comparison is made to the total appropriations to other regions by the Ministry of Agriculture, particularly because ARDU carries infrastructure functions left to other ministries in such regions. Finally, the costs of important integrated rural development projects must be evaluated in terms of their wider impact. Such qualifications and claims set in high relief the fact that no data or cases of any kind underpinned ODI's charge that integrated rural development has "often proved a cost drain on scarce financial and human resources."[36]

As for the benefits of integrated rural development projects, critics tend to see them as distant, implying more direct and immediate projects are better. For example, Merilee S. Grindle notes that because such projects:

> ...are typically technically difficult, expensive, administratively complex...(they) promise tangible and intangible payoffs primarily in the distant future.[37]

To the contrary, CADU-ARDU provides a case where despite the conditions mentioned by Grindle and the long term view of SIDA's 1967 design, the payoffs were immediate. Tables in Chapter 4-6 testify to this. But most telling on this point was the constant pressure on the project by areas beyond its jurisdiction to expand and incorporate them. Clearly, the charge of lack of immediacy of benefits deserves to be questioned.

Tenth, the CADU-ARDU case demonstrates that an integrated rural development project can substantially raise food production. As such it challenges potentially devastating criticism that the intervention cannot promote reliable increases in food surplus. For example, based on a handful of cases, one of which is CADU, Carl K. Eicher and Doyle C. Baker claim:

> The decline of IRD does not reflect a retreat on equity goals as much as growing recognition that...IRD... was not solving the most fundamental rural problem – achieving a reliable food surplus.[38]

Yet, the CADU-ARDU case obviously challenges this conclusion. Increased yields are demonstrated in Chapters 4 and 6. Data on yields show that the project has turned its region of focus into one of the few grain surplus producing areas of the country. Table 12 summarizes the substantial yield increases achieved for food grains by the project, and other data show both increased household consumption and the fact that by the early 1980s only 31 of the country's 104 *awrajas* produced marketed surpluses, three of which were Arssi's. Given this significant exception to Eicher and Baker's charge, it is necessary to ask what might be the result of a systematic review of production data in areas where other integrated rural development projects have been implemented?

In a paper for the Council on Foreign Relations and Overseas Development Council, Leonard extends the Eicher and Baker critique with a more sweeping criticism of the potential of integrated rural development projects to increase crop production. After referring to only three successful projects, one of which is CADU, he argues that integrated rural development:

> ...is now counter-productive for agricultural development in most of Africa. First...the integrating organization provides services for only one crop or region and leaves others totally unserved. When a crop or livestock development opportunity falls between these specialized entities it will slip out of sight in the crack...[39]

Clearly, CADU-ARDU provides an exception to this criticism. For example, Chapters 4-6 document how the project sought to study and advance most of the diverse crops grown by farmers before 1967 while concentrating on food crops that were both consumed locally and marketed in Addis Ababa.

Eleventh, the CADU-ARDU case demonstrates that an integrated rural development project can create off-farm income opportunities and expand the technical skills of poor peasants, increasing in the process a community's capacity to engage in self-help activities. Some doubt that this can happen.[40]

Today Chilalo *Awraja* is one of the better developed rural areas in the country, and has a farm population with incomes potentially higher than those found in most other parts of Ethiopia. If the present government would end artificially low grain prices and allow private grain traders to operate, the higher income resulting could be used to increase the community's capacity to mobilize for self-help, thereby illustrating the benefits that can be generated by linking the two different development objectives in a single project. The new self-help program described in Chapter 6 is not entirely successful at mobilizing economic resources from the region's communities, in part because the percentage of local contribution required is higher than that set by the government for other areas of the country. CADU-ARDU steadily succeeded at promoting a wide range of new sources of income growth, largely because it was an integrated rural development project with a broad mandate. Among the sources reviewed in the case study are the milk production and bee-keeping programs, the industrial promotion of oil presses, flour mills and raw material fabrication sites, the training of craftsmen through the skill center program, and the promotion of women's crafts for market sale. The project was able to promote such a wide range of new income sources because it sought to find income generating activities beyond crop production, even those off-farm. In addition, the size of the project allowed for experimentation with such activities at the margin, without substantial cost in terms of economic resources or manpower. Coupled with these new technologies has been institutional growth, the new dairy cooperatives and skills centers described in Chapter 6 being examples of such change.

Twelfth, CADU's strategy, if not ARDU's, shows how an integrated rural development project can provide inputs and marketing facilities without taking advantage of producers or hampering private sector activities. This is important because critics argue that when a system of mutually interdependent activities, such as seed, fertilizer, and credit provision, are thoroughly integrated, dangers emerge. The major risks are said to be that if any part of the system fails the entire enterprise is hurt and that when one organization has a monopoly on services and activities, rural people lose options.[41]

This loss of options is stated at its most extreme by Grace Goddell who, on the basis of the Philippines' Masagana 99 project, argues that when an integrated project controls credit, fertilizer, and seed:

> ...it tightens central control over the 'masses' of farmers and over the untidy capitalist sector serving them...(it) enables the state's machinery to replace the supposedly avaricious middlemen on all three of their major areas of former 'oppression': credit, input supply...and harvest procurement. But from the small farmer's point of view, by exploiting his poverty, it robs him of all managerial or entrepreneurial options whatsoever. If he enjoyed little freedom under the old landlord, however, he may hardly know the difference.[42]

Surely the history of CADU's attempt to provide a fair market illustrates that integrated rural development need not be the conspiracy to eradicate the private sector that Goodell argues.

CADU's strategy was never one of displacing traders and merchants. Rather, as Chapters 4 and 5 demonstrate, the project excluded large-scale landowners and tenants, leaving them to use the private sector. Nor did it seek to unfairly undermine input suppliers and grain traders, even though their practices often disadvantaged CADU's target population. Instead, it sought to offer the price incentives and fair markets needed to induce traditional subsistence producers to adopt the project's production increasing package. It attempted to improve the marketing knowledge and bargaining powers of its target population through introduction of community weigh scales and adult numeracy programs. But prior to 1973 the project found the private sector difficult to reform, as illustrated by patterns reviewed in Chapter 5.

However, with the revolution the emphasis turned from creating a fair market to forging a government controlled market. The process of promoting service cooperatives, the government emphasis on the AMC, the bias toward cooperatives in the provision of inputs, and the state's attempt to limit private grain traders was described in detail in Chapter 6. Yet, despite these efforts, the private sector held its own, so that in late 1984 when the government was under domestic and international pressure to free up grain marketing, traders and merchants were in place to perform. Indeed, up to 1986 the private sector remained active in Arssi despite the Regional Administrator's efforts to eliminate it. The BARDU proposal recognized such strength and proposed to work with private traders. Hence, the CADU-ARDU case suggests that it is hard for even a large integrated and rural development project to destroy the market so favored by today's resurgent neo-classical economists and free market conservatives.

Thirteenth, CADU-ARDU demonstrates that an integrated rural development project can be designed to move beyond production and infrastructure objectives and address constraints in social structures.

Critics argue that integrated rural development projects are so large and complex that of necessity designers concentrate their limited resources on technical, managerial, and financial aspects, neglecting in the process critical cultural, social, and political variables. For example, H. Dupriez finds that such projects "typically ignore social structures and potential hierarchies, treating rural people and communities as undifferentiated target populations."[43] Yet, while CADU's designers misread such variables in 1967, the project's staff increasingly addressed them over the 1968-84 period.

There is no question that the design team had not done all the background work needed to understand the Chilalo area. This failure lends support to the call for more rapid rural appraisal techniques prior to the design of large complex projects, in part because it took so long for CADU's anthropological research to be completed.[44] But the project's basic and applied research on the area's communities and the impact of CADU's interventions on them was outstanding, particularly the work cited in Chapters 4 and 5 by Arne Lexander and, subsequently, Henock Kifle and Johan Holmberg. Contrary to Dupriez's observation, CADU-ARDU demonstrates how quickly an integrated rural development project with an appropriate research and evaluation component can move to inform project officers about cultural, social, and political factors affecting success. It also illustrates how large integrated rural development projects can mobilize resources to create unique sets of data. Surely Chapters 3-6 establish that CADU-ARDU has generated one of the richest collections of information presently available on rural development in one area. To a large extent this is to the credit of the Planning and Evaluation Section, whose products provided the foundation for other studies.

The impact of the project's success at shedding light on social structures and differentiation goes further than guiding the project. It enlightened a generation of students; for example, Henock Kifle's draft study of mechanization and tenant eviction passed from hand to hand at Haile Selassie I University in the early 1970s. It also provided insights needed to promote reform proposals before and after the revolution.

As for the constraints themselves, the CADU-ARDU case documents how integrated rural development projects can address them. This is illustrated by the land tenure constraint. The leading text arguing for the small-farm model admits that inequitable land tenure makes small-holder-directed projects difficult to implement successfully.[45] Hence, it is not surprising that integrated rural development projects are found to be vulnerable to the "talents effects" associated with the domination of a rural area by land based provincial elites. So Ruttan is generally correct when he concludes that:

> ...the structural characteristics of most rural communities, and of the societies of which they are a part, will continue to prevent them from obtaining access to many of the available development opportunities.[46]

CADU does provide a qualification on the generalization, however. Despite being implemented in an inequitable and exploitive task environment, it still managed to provide access to development opportunities for thousands of the community's poorest farmers. More importantly, the CADU-ARDU case raises interesting questions about Ruttan's observations that:

> ...great disparity in distribution of economic and political resources in many areas - e.g. land ownership – makes it difficult to design rural development program activities which can command a broad basis of community support.[47]

and that:

> ...rural development programs will rarely be able to mobilize the political and economic resources necessary for massive structural reform.[48]

As the analysis in Chapters 4 and 5 demonstrates, rural inequality based on the land tenure system made it difficult for the project to reach its full potential during the 1967-73 period and led to the eviction of large numbers of its target population.

However, notwithstanding a generally hostile local government system and distrustful landowners, CADU's field agents were able to make progress toward gaining the support of the area's small-holders. When the revolution began, it was CADU's presence in the community and the leadership it could provide peasants that greatly facilitated the land reform and mobilization that followed.

Ruttan is correct in noting that integrated rural development projects can't directly mobilize the political and economic resources necessary to remove major structural constraints such as inequitable land tenure rules. But the project does show that a committed project leadership backed by substantial support of its funding agency can go a long way toward facilitating such a process.

As Chapter 4 points out, SIDA designers were naive about the extent of the land tenure constraint and the government's promise to enact tenant protection legislation. However, once the patterns outlined in Chapter 5 emerged, the project's staff openly acknowledged them, producing reports on mechanization, eviction, rents, government land allocations, and market exploitation of peasants. These circulated widely and led to open discussion of land tenure reform in the national university and among progressives in the government, military, and private sector. Moreover, SIDA put open pressure on the government to pass reform, giving additional leverage to moderates promoting legislation through the Ministry of Land Reform and Administration. SIDA's stand on the need for reform emboldened other donors funding rural development projects to put their own pressure on the government and attracted the interest of the international press, interest an image-conscious Emperor wished to avoid. There is no doubt that CADU experience contributed to awareness of the need for reform.

Beyond this, it is clear that as the sweeping *coup d'état* and consolidation of military power took place, senior members of the project staff were deeply involved in formulating suggested agrarian reforms. They were particularly active in guiding the conceptualization of land reform legislation during the 1974-75 drafting exercise, Chapter 6 documenting the remarkable similarities between the laws, terms, and objectives and CADU's experience.

This summary suggests that integrated rural development projects on the scale of CADU, funded by agencies with the principles and commitment of SIDA, can both win broad community support from those oppressed by land based inequality and generate influential pressures for reform. Indeed, if the key premise in the small-farm strategy is correct – that land reform is essential to achieving the full benefits of small-holder strategies – then the promotion of integrated rural development projects with the size, visibility, and courage of CADU may be a far more attractive intervention for promoting progressive rural change than is currently realized.

One reason why critics believe integrated rural development projects cannot be effective in inequitable rural communities is they conclude that under such conditions people cannot organize to demand services from bureaucracies.[49] This generalization probably holds for integrated rural development projects implemented by host governments independent of donor funding. But most such projects are funded by donors pursuant to detailed project designs aimed at inducing rural development from above.[50] Whatever the rhetoric about decentralization and participation, the project design typically establishes an administrative strategy for reaching the target population, one that provides incentives for bureaucratic performance through the objectives and conditions set forth in the aid agreement between the funding agency and the host government. If the project is well prepared and based on studies of local needs and obstacles to reaching them, then the CADU-ARDU case suggests that integrated rural development projects can have a reasonable chance of serving the target population in a responsive and effective way. The sense of responsibility CADU staff felt to the Chilalo community certainly demonstrates this possibility.

Through careful monitoring of program performance and strong commitment to reach small-holders, CADU officers were able to adjust the project's operations to promote delivery of services. Credit provides a good example of this, for as Chapter 4 shows, the ceilings on land size that controlled access to project credit were steadily revised downward to ensure that project credit reached the target population. In effect, CADU staff received their incentives to serve the community from the project and its leadership.

Fourteenth, CADU-ARDU demonstrates that well led integrated rural development projects, staffed by motivated personnel, can effectively deliver resources to communities under conditions where participatory strategies and community organization are not feasible or too controlled to be useful, either because of conservative elite domination or excessive ideological penetration of the countryside. The CADU-ARDU experience raises questions about Hyden's sweeping conclusion that:

> The 'integrated' programme tends to be a hopeless venture...because by being designed in a blueprint fashion it tends to reduce popular involvement and certainly popular commitment to it. It is an effort that has to be imposed on the people.[51]

To be sure, CADU-ARDU was a project "for" rather than "by" rural people. But it was a project that sought to promote participation, though as Chapter 5 illustrates it was not particularly effective at doing so. Despite this failure, its monitoring and evaluation studies stayed in close touch with the community, providing a channel for identifying their needs and keeping senior staff aware of the field agent activities in support of them. As such, the case study challenges Hyden's conclusion by providing an important exception, suggesting that well-conceived, large, integrated rural development projects do not necessarily lead to a reduction in participation and can promote it.[52] In this regard, it is important to note that CADU's efforts to create a hierarchy of local organizations stretching from Model Farmer Area Development Committees to an *Awraja* Development Committee, as described in Chapter 5, had a powerful influence on the concept of "peasant association" as it emerged in the 1975 legislation of the revolutionary government and outlined in Chapter 6. Indeed, CADU's efforts provided the only example or model draftsmen could turn to, all because of the stubborn efforts of project officers to promote participation in a difficult task environment. Further, the social mobilization and awareness generated beneath the imperial provincial system during the CADU years quickly emerged as the revolution unfolded, leading to rapid implementation of the land reform and formation of peasant associations. Surely this fact illustrates how much more subtle and complex is the relationship between integrated rural development and participation.

From 1974 onwards, ARDU continued as an integrated rural development project, but as Chapters 6 shows, it functioned in a mobilized rural community. One of the major activities of the project became the formation of peasant associations, service cooperatives and producer cooperatives. Other important activities included the training of local people to lead these new organizations and to manage their administrative and financial affairs. So much effort went into social mobilization that recent evaluations found agricultural production objectives were jeopardized. Therefore, it is submitted that strong criticism of integrated rural development by the new school of "people-centered development" must be tempered by the realization that such projects are large enough to promote local participation in environments where "improvement strategies" are not possible and can have unexpected direct or indirect influence on the emergence of participatory environments at a future time, in part because of their struggles to "induce participation" in a resistant task environment.[53]

Fifteenth, CADU-ARDU provides an example of an integrated rural development project that successfully expanded its operations beyond a pilot area and reached an ever larger number of rural people during its implementation period.

Most integrated rural development projects begin with the assertion that they are "pilot projects" to be expanded into regional or national programs once they develop an appropriate methodology through experimentation. Based on a review of that standard objective and the experience of several projects that sought to expand beyond a pilot phase, Ruttan concluded:

> The success of many of the development pilot projects has been due to the relative intensity of the human resources devoted to organization, management, and technical assistance. When an attempt was made to generalize a pilot project on a national or regional scale, the intensity of human resource input could not be maintained.[54]

On the basis of this observation, he concluded:

> ...gains from even pilot 'integrated' rural development projects will remain low, until greater technical and institutional innovations that permit much greater efficiency in the use of human resources become available.[55]

Certainly the CADU-ARDU experience establishes that this conclusion on expansion need not always be true. The technical and institutional innovations described in Chapters 4-6 suggest that at least one project has made some progress in maximizing the scarce human resources needed successfully to implement expanding integrated rural development projects.

Not only did CADU expand within Chilalo *Awraja* between 1967 and 1973, it doubled the territory it covered in 1976 when it was given responsibility for all three *awrajas* of Arssi Region. More importantly, its central principles were used to design the nationwide MPP that was implemented after 1972. And, the PADEP initiative proposed in 1984 uses the CADU-ARDU experience as a basis for a proposal for several regional integrated rural development projects, one of which would be formed by expanding ARDU to cover both Arssi and Bale.

To be sure, the effectiveness of CADU declined after the revolution and the departure of most Swedish expatriates, as was documented in Chapter 6. But the project continued to perform over a much larger territory while losing staff to the administration of the separate MPP program it gave birth to. Importantly, it continued to function notwithstanding the political instability of the first revolutionary decade, an instability that led to the exile of many of Ethiopia's trained agricultural technicians and administrators. Hence, pilot projects can be expanded in government settings marked by limited technical and administrative capacity if the strategy is well thought through, the systems of administration well embedded in government operations, and the staff being asked to do more are committed to the project's objectives. Meeting these conditions is extremely difficult, but the CADU-ARDU experience testifies that sufficient progress can be made to allow expansion even in periods of great instability and loss of human resources.

Sixteenth, the CADU-ARDU case raises questions about the charge by critics that integrated rural development leads to undesirable regional inequality. This criticism is summed up by Lele who asserts:

> ... the objective of mass participation of low-income groups may be better served by a more equitable allocation of resources at the outset to ensure a minimum level of services and institutional development for removal of the most critical constraints before a few regions benefit from substantially greater allocation.[56]

A recent review of Swedish development policy in Ethiopia incorrectly concluded that by 1970 SIDA's focus had shifted from regional integrated agricultural development to stressing the importance of national agricultural development.[57] Specifically it argues that the Swedes learned from CADU's experience that integrated rural development projects tend to create regional disparity and disrupt government efforts to implement consistent national plans.[58] Of course the Swedes recognized these problems; however, in practice they continued to fund CADU-ARDU and draw upon its experience to guide the nationwide MPP program that they also helped fund. The Swedes did this because they reached a conclusion similar to that of Lele, who qualified her position by noting: "There are ... exceptions when unusually profitable opportunities may justify intensive development."[59] Indeed, in 1982 the Swedes decided to end all funding for MPP after mid-1983 and concentrate their resources on long term funding of ARDU's integrated rural development activities. Clearly, the wavering of the 1970's had given way to a strong preference for a focused project rather than dispersed nationwide funding. Here the Swedes were satisfied that area specific results and effective national influence outweighed concerns for possible contributions to regional inequality.

The CADU-ARDU project also illustrates the counter-intuitive aspects of regional inequality. Arssi is now one of Ethiopia's most productive areas. Ministry of Agriculture surveys suggest Arssi leads all regions in crop production per capita and yields per hectare.[60] CADU-ARDU's 17 year investment led to this productivity and the regional inequality it implies. But rather than simply decry the success of the project in turning a subsistence, food-deficit area into the country's second largest cereal growing region, critics should focus on whether the methodology developed in Arssi can be used to promote similar production gains in other smallholder regions. Here it is submitted that the project had much potential and influence. Its methodology led to the MPP and the benefits it generated nationwide, its officers and staff moved beyond the project and region to improve the Ministry of Agriculture and influence the direction of agrarian reform, and its relative success led to the currently debated regional development model of PADEP, the only viable alternative to the country's current policy of promoting agrarian socialism through producer cooperatives and state farms. Surely, CADU-ARDU demonstrates that intensive effort in one region through an integrated rural development project can yield substantial national benefits that offset the relative economic advance of the region selected.

WILL THE CASE STUDY HAVE INFLUENCE?

There are four grounds on which critics of integrated rural development could dismiss the contribution of the CADU-ARDU case to the debate.

First, they could conclude that the project was a failure. Such a conclusion is facilitated by the fact that CADU-ARDU's reputation is based on critical case studies more than ten years old. These emphasize land tenure constraints rather than design and implementation issues. Typical of statements dismissing the project on the basis of dated and narrowly focused studies is that of Johnston and Clark, who in their influential book note: "failures of programs like the much-touted CADU project in Ethiopia..."[61] So strong is this reputation that even a case study of this length will have difficulty overcoming it. This is particularly true because the project has had a troubled past and, like nearly all rural development projects, does not represent an unqualified success story.

Second, it can be argued that after 17 years the project's program of work cannot be sustained without SIDA's financial and technical assistance, implying thereby that the project did not succeed.

Third, even if the data presented in the prior chapters demonstrate that the project has been largely successful in reaching its objectives and that disengagement can occur, CADU-ARDU could be dismissed by critics as atypical. Efforts to distinguish cases generally occur in rural development when a positive experience is reviewed, for the literature in this field is, as every field professional realizes, critical and negative.[62] Probably the most visible evidence of this is the literature seeking to demonstrate that the Taiwan and South Korea cases are outliers that do not really establish the potential for effective small-holder-led growth strategies in other countries.

Fourth, it could be argued the case study is not relevant because the days of large-scale integrated rural development projects are over. This view rests on two positions. The first holds that integrated rural development projects are not workable, a position reviewed earlier in this chapter. The second holds that CADU-ARDU projects are unlikely to be attempted because of changed conditions in task environments, governments, and donor agencies. Specifically, it may be that CADU-ARDU type interventions require rural settings marked by weak, poorly articulated field ministry operations, national governments willing to tolerate large expatriate teams, and donor agencies willing to expend considerable resources over a sustained period of time. Such conditions, critics could argue, rarely occur in the Third World today.

In regard to the first two grounds, the case study must speak for itself. Sufficient detail is provided to allow others to prepare a brief critical of the one presented here. Such is the nature of debate in the social sciences. Still, it is asserted that in comparison to most rural development projects, not just those of the integrated rural development type, CADU-ARDU had remarkable success in bringing benefits to its target area and influencing national policy formulation and administrative reform while working in two different and difficult historical periods. As such it provides useful insights to those designing or implementing similar projects.

The effects of revolution, economic stagnation, inappropriate agricultural policies, and adequate budget allocations to the Ministry of Agriculture make it unlikely that SEAD's full program of work could be effectively performed if Swedish aid was withdrawn. But this does not mean that CADU-ARDU failed. Survival of the project's impact on the region's farmers and the country's agricultural strategy is the more important test of project performance. Here it is submitted that the research-extension-input-marketing model pioneered by CADU-ARDU will have a lasting impact on both Arssi's small-holders and small-scale farmers throughout the country, whether through CADU-ARDU influenced MPP initiatives or PADEP type approaches. Clearly, the project's long term benefits to the regional and national economy far exceed the 17 year Swedish-Ethiopian investment. To be sure, the government's ideological emphasis on villagization and producer cooperatives can undermine the longer term impact of CADU-ARDU's small-holder methodology. But whether small-holders and the CADU-ARDU model continue or not, the seed packages introduced by the project, as well as the physical infrastructure and conservation works created by it, will, if maintained, survive and continue to help Arssi remain a major agricultural surplus producing region.

The third criticism is less problematic. If the conceptual definition outlined in Chapter 2 is accepted, then the CADU-ARDU project is representative of a major type of integrated rural development project. CADU-ARDU is a Type 2 project. That is, it is an integrated rural development project combining both agricultural and non-agricultural services and activities. More broadly it meets the definitional requirement imposed by that conceptual framework and reviewed in the closing section of Chapter 2. If the project is atypical relative to the framework, it is that the "time bound" period to carry out its objectives was substantially longer than that found in the majority of projects. However, it is submitted that this is an important new qualification, perhaps requiring the phrase in Chapter 2 to be expanded to state "time bound but sufficiently long range in support to meet established objectives."

No major comparative study of a large number of integrated rural development projects has been carried out. Therefore it can only be hypothesized that Type 2 projects have been the most numerous and visible. Here it is assumed that the majority of donors and professionals do not accept the view that the principal purpose of such projects is to bring quality of life improving basic services to the rural poor. Rather, the centrality of agricultural production has been at the heart of most strategies and designs, with projects adding basic human service components as resources and capacity allow. It is also assumed that the pressures from the Basic Human Needs movement have been too pervasive and strong to allow aid agencies and host governments to fund integrated rural development projects that are designed only to promote agricultural production.[63] If this hypothesis and these assumptions are valid, then CADU-ARDU is more than typical; it is representative of the most numerous form of integrated rural development intervention.

The fourth reason for dismissing the CADU-ARDU experience, that changed conditions make it unlikely that integrated rural development projects will be tried in the future, presents the most difficult challenge. It is a challenge that requires another book, for to address it one must review the current policy statements and practices of nearly a dozen major donors, undertake a careful comparative study of integrated rural development projects to determine if the hypothesis underlying this book has any validity, and analyze the rural development strategies and internal administrative patterns of a number of agricultural based Third World governments.

There is evidence to suggest that while major donors such as the World Bank and USAID have turned their backs on integrated rural development, others have not. For example, in 1982, after briefly visiting and reviewing a failing integrated rural developmental project in the hill country of Jamaica, the Director of the United States Agency for International Development reportedly declared the Agency would no longer fund such interventions. Further, a senior agricultural officer in the Agency's Kenyan mission stated that if he had his way "agricultural and rural development projects would never involve more than a single ministry or two activities" because "it is now clear that bureaucracies in Third World countries simply cannot implement or sustain anything more complex." According to that officer, the Director's order was never made explicit but every professional in the Agency knew "no project labelled integrated rural development could gain approval, however defined or packaged."[64] Similar informal but powerful signals have passed through other aid agencies as well.[65] So clear is the trend that two perceptive reviewers, Carl K. Eicher and John M. Staatz, have identified the dates of the intervention's birth and demise: 1973-1980.[66]

The question is whether USAID's position holds for other donors and, if so, whether it will be translated into official policy guidelines. Only further research can determine this. But if Kenya is illustrative of current donor patterns, it suggests that they are still interested in funding large integrated projects aimed at increasing food production and protecting the natural resource base. There, as of 1986, 9 donors, including USAID, were funding 11 large arid and semi-arid lands projects that have many characteristics of the CADU-ARDU model.[67]

The Kenyan case also suggests that CADU-ARDU type projects need not be confined to countries marked by the rural poverty and administrative incapacity that characterized Chilalo in 1968. If integrated rural development projects can be mounted in Kenya, conditions are even more ripe in her less developed neighbors, such as Uganda, the southern Sudan or Somalia. Indeed, the strategy of integrated rural development has much to offer efforts to address the most serious problem facing the development community: assisting Africa to become self-sufficient in food production while protecting her resource base and improving the quality of life of her people.[68]

Whether donors and governments will turn to integrated rural development projects in the still rural and poor countries of the Third World depends on the flow of evaluative research and case studies over the next few years. The central argument made in this book is that integrated rural development projects should be evaluated more carefully than is the case in the critical academic literature or the brief site visits of senior international aid agency officers. What is needed are careful comparative studies based on original, detailed case studies. In this regard, it is hypothesized that such studies will conclude that with revision and careful application, integrated rural development interventions can play an important role in promoting rural development.

This hypothesis is supported by the conclusions of two recent comparative studies. The first, by George Honadle and Jerry Van Sant, reviews original field reports on 24 integrated rural development projects funded by USAID.[69] The second, by Cynthia Clapp-Wincek of USAID, synthesizes 12 detailed evaluations of major integrated rural development projects with a careful review of the literature and several lengthy commissioned studies of major integrated rural development experiences.[70] The Honadle and Van Sant study is particularly instructive because it is empirical, comparative and problem solving in its thrust, illustrating the strength of using numerous cases. Importantly, their systematic comparative review did not yield a rejection of integrated rural development. Rather, it generated positive design and implementation guidelines for increasing the potential of such projects to deliver goods and services, enhance local action, sustain benefits, and achieve integrated objectives.[71]

There appears to be a correlation between detailed research on integrated rural development and a recognition of the utility of the approach. In fact, the more analysts study these interventions and review promising projects in detail, the more inclined they are to concentrate on identifying constraints that hamper project success and offer guidelines for overcoming them. It is for such analysts that the case study presented here should be most useful.

But more than study is needed. Actual efforts to apply supportive guidelines in new projects must be carried out and carefully evaluated. Too much of the debate on integrated rural development is being waged in conference rooms and policy offices of aid agency headquarters by persons remote from the field. The next step in the debate must involve returning to project sites where learning and action can be combined to test and improve integrated rural development strategies. Here Siffin is correct when he argues:

> In the final analysis none of these problems can be solved on paper or through reflection. We can – and should – address the administrative problems of integrated

> rural development by laying out the issues and tendering possible answers. But the palpable problems can only be truly confronted and sometimes resolved in concrete and particular actions.[72]

Clearly, the evidence on integrated rural development is not all in. The question is whether donors and governments have the patience to look more closely at the strategy, the capacity to evaluate the lessons of the past, and the will to design and implement second generation projects based on such reviews.

CONCLUSION

The CADU-ARDU experience supports the central argument made in this book: well designed and flexibly implemented integrated rural development projects can make a substantial contribution to an agricultural area. As such it should be useful to those, like Derick W. Brinkerhoff, who are concerned that:

> ...IRD will be judged deficient prematurely and dispensed with before the cycle of learning can be completed.[73]

and to those, such as Eicher, who conclude:

> Particularly important is the reassessment of integrated rural development projects. The weakness of most IRD projects... can be corrected by restructuring some of the projects rather than phasing them out.[74]

If this book contributes to conceptually grounded and detailed comparative studies aimed at the reassessment and restructuring of integrated rural development projects, it will have achieved its principal objective. In this regard, it must be noted that Honadle and Van Sant are correct in their conclusion that:

> ... there are no algorithms for success. There are necessary ingredients, but no sure recipes, ideologies of the moment notwithstanding. There are basic contradictions within the process of induced development, and no single organizational form is effective at all stages in the process.

Guidelines and generalizations are possible, universal principles are not. Towards such ends, the successes and failures of the CADU-ARDU experience suggest that efforts of reassessment and restructuring should be focused on lessons related to organization for integration, management of delivery systems for goods and services, personnel training and incentives, knowledge building and macropolicy linkages, decentralization and local capacity building, and length of project support needed to sustain benefits while allowing donor disengagement.

It is a time for more empirical research on effective integrated rural development projects that have operated over an extended period and less criticism based on a limited number of inadequate observations coupled to deductive use of analytical principles drawn from the public policy and administration literature. Integrated rural development is too promising an approach toward ending agrarian stagnation to be dismissed as easily as has recently been the case.

This single study of CADU-ARDU can not alone begin to turn around this literature, but if the detailed case study of the project and the argument made in this closing chapter can keep the debate lively, it will be worth the pain caused by alternative positions likely to be constructed on the basis of the book's own case materials. The history of rural development is too marked by faddish promotions and dismissals to allow the strategy of integrated rural development to be buried without a sustained debate based on empirical evidence. Moreover, the approach is too promising to be abandoned before the constructive lessons that can be drawn from such studies and debate are tested in new, better designed and implemented integrated rural development projects.

Notes

1. Typical is a lengthy review of integrated rural development by Rainer Wulf. It cites 36 articles, few of which summarize a major project study, much less rest on detailed case evidence. A few of his references refer to case studies but only in an anecdotal fashion. The only exception is his reference to Uma J. Lele's book on Africa, but he does not draw on her case studies. "On the Concept of 'Integrated' Rural Development," *Economics*, XVII (1978), pp. 63-80.
2. For example, this is the case with John D. Montgomery's study of 8 integrated rural development studies: "Decentralizing Integrated Rural Development Activities," in *Decentralization and Development: Policy Implementation in Developing Countries*, edited by G. Shabbir Cheema and Dennis A. Rondinelli (Beverly Hills: Sage Publications, 1983), pp. 231-69. Uma J. Lele is one of the rare synthesizers who did manage to visit her project sites. But most of the analysis of documents was done by research assistants who after brief site visits synthesized information on the projects for her: *Design of Rural Development: Lessons From Africa* (Baltimore: Johns Hopkins University Press, 1975), pp. 6-12.
3. On "negative social science" see: Robert Chambers, *Rural Development: Putting the Last First* (London: Longmans, 1983), pp. 28-46. The need for and scarcity of successful projects is revealed by: Samuel Paul, *Managing Development Programs: The Lessons of Success* (Boulder: Westview Press, 1982).
4. Vernon W. Ruttan, "Integrated Rural Development Programmes: A Skeptical Perspective," *International Development Review*, XVII, 4 (1975), p. 14.

5. Vernon W. Ruttan, "Integrated Rural Development Programmes: A Historical Perspective," *World Development*, XII, 4 (1984), pp. 393-401.
6. Ruttan, "Integrated Rural Development," p. 14.
7. William J. Siffin, *Administrative Problems and Integrated Rural Development* (Bloomington: Indiana University, International Development Institute, a PASITAM Design Study, 1979), p. 1.
8. See Dennis A. Rondinelli's treatment of these constraints on management: "Administration of Integrated Rural Development Policy: The Politics of Agrarian Reform in Developing Countries," *World Politics*, XXXI, 3 (1979), pp. 402-15.
9. Robert Wade, "Leadership and Integrated Rural Development: Reflections on an Indian Success Story," *Journal of Administration Overseas*, XVIII (1978), p. 253.
10. For example: John C. Ickis, "Structural Responses to New Rural Development Strategies," in David C. Korten and Felipe B. Alfonso, eds., *Bureaucracy and the Poor: Closing the Gap* (Singapore: McGraw-Hill International, 1981), pp. 4-32.
11. Towards this end he reviews 8 integrated rural development projects and develops a number of propositions for better administrating their complexity: "Decentralizing Integrated," pp. 231-69. See also the analysis in: Robert E. Klitgaard, *On the Economics of Integrated Rural Development* (Cambridge: Lincoln Institute of Land Policy and John F. Kennedy School of Government, Harvard University, 1981); and his "Integrating Public Services for Rural Development: A Policy Framework," *Philippine Journal of Public Administration*, XXVI, 2 (1982): 93-127.
12. Wade, "Leadership and Integrated," p. 253.
13. David K. Leonard, "Choosing Among Forms of Decentralization and Linkage," in David K. Leonard and Dale R. Marshall, eds. *Institutions of Rural Development* (Berkeley: University of California, Institute of International Studies, 1982), p. 213. The Kenya case is described in: David K. Leonard, "Disintegrating Agricultural Development," *Food Research Institute Studies*, XIX, 2 (1984), pp. 177-86.
14. Leonard, "Choosing Among Forms," p. 213.
15. Robert Chambers, "Project Selection for Poverty Focused Rural Development: Simple is Optimal," *World Development*, VI, 2 (1978), pp. 209-19.
16. Johnston and Clark, *Redesigning Rural Development*, pp. 250-1.
17. David C. Korten, "Community Organization and Rural Development: A Learning Process Approach," *Public Administration Review*, XL (1980), pp. 480-511.
18. David C. Korten and Rudi Klauss, eds., *People-Centered Development: Contributions Toward Theory and Planning Frameworks* (West Hartford: Kumarian Press, 1984); Korten, "Strategic Organization," pp. 341-52.
19. Johnston and Clark, *Redesigning Rural Development*, p. 250.
20. Goran Hyden, *No Shortcuts to Progress: African Development in Perspective* (Berkeley: University of California Press, 1983), p. 94.
21. Overseas Development Institute, "Briefing Paper: Integrated Rural Development" (London: ODI, Briefing Paper No. 4, 1979), p. 4.
22. See the studies cited in footnotes 69 and 70; and such specialized studies as John D. Montgomery, "Managing Integrated Rural Development: View from the Field," *Rural Development Participation Review*, III, 3 (1982), pp. 6-9, which summarizes 630 incidents from 72 managers in 12 countries.
23. Hyden, *No Shortcuts to Progress*, p. 94. One of the few cases cited by Hyden in support of his view is CADU, suggesting that he did not look at it closely.
24. Overseas Development Institute, "Integrated Rural Development," p. 4.
25. Ruttan, "Integrated Rural Development," p. 15.
26. Lele, *Design of Rural Development*, p. 49.
27. *Ibid.*, p. 189.

28. Coralie Bryant and Louise G. White, *Managing Rural Development with Small Farmer Participation* (West Hartford: Kumarian Press, 1984), p. 50.
29. David C. Korten and Norman T. Uphoff, *Bureaucratic Reorientation and Participatory Rural Development* (Washington, D.C.: National Association of Schools of Public Affairs and Administration, Working Paper No. 1, 1981).
30. See: Marina and David Ottaway, *Ethiopia: Empire in Revolution* (New York: Africana Publishing Co., 1978), pp. 113-27. They identify CADU director Henock Kifle as an EPRP leader.
31. Rondinelli, "Administration of Integrated," pp. 395-6, 400 and 406.
32. Wade, "Leadership and Integrated," p. 52.
33. Jon R. Moris, *Managing Induced Rural Development* (Bloomington: Indiana University, International Development Institute, 1981), p. 49.
34. Ruttan, "Integrated Rural Development", p. 16.
35. Overseas Development Institute, "Integrated Rural Development", p. 4.
36. *Ibid.*
37. Merilee S. Grindle, "Anticipating Failure: The Implementation of Rural Development Programs," *Public Policy,* XXIX, 1 (1981), p. 55.
38. Carl K. Eicher and Doyle C. Baker, *Research on Agricultural Development in Sub-Saharan Africa: A Critical Survey* (East Lansing: Michigan State University, Department of Economics, 1982), p. 62.
39. David K. Leonard, "Developing Africa's Agricultural Institutions: Putting the Farmer in Control," (Paper prepared for Committee on African Development Strategies, Council on Foreign Relations and the Overseas Development Council, Washington, D.C., January 1985),p. 5.
40. Ruttan, "Integrated Rural Development," p. 16.
41. Leonard, "Disintegrating Agricultural Development," pp. 179-81.
42. Grace Goodell, "After Land Reform," *Policy Review*, 24 (1983), p. 4.
43. H. Dupriez, *Integrated Rural Development Projects Carried Out in Black Africa with EDF Aid: Evaluation and Outlook for the Future* (Luxembourg: Office for Official Publications of the European Communities, 1979).
44. See, for example: Robert Chambers, "Rapid Rural Appraisal: Rationale and Repertoire," *Public Administration and Development*, I, 2 (1981), pp. 95-106; George Honadle, "Rapid Reconnaissance for Development Administration: Mapping and Moulding for Organizational Landscapes," *World Development*, X, 8 (1982), pp. 633-49.
45. Johnston and Clark, *Redesigning Rural Development*, pp. 70-115.
46. Ruttan, "Integrated Rural Development," p. 16.
47. *Ibid.*
48. *Ibid.*
49. *Ibid.*, p.15.
50. Moris, *Managing Induced Rural Development.*
51. Hyden, *No Shortcuts to Progress*, pp. 94-5.
52. For a detailed analysis of CADU's efforts to promote participation, its missed opportunities and successes between 1967 and 1973, see: John M. Cohen and Norman T. Uphoff, *Rural Development Participation: Concepts and Measures for Project Design, Implementation and Evaluation* (Ithaca: Cornell University, Rural Development Committee, Monograph Series No. 2, 1977), pp. 176-302.
53. Induced participation is well illustrated by Bryant and White, *Managing Rural Development.*
54. Ruttan, "Integrated Rural Development," p. 15.
55. *Ibid.*, p. 16.

56. *Ibid.*, p. 186.
57. Seleshi Sisaye, "Swedish Development Aid Policy: A Discussion with Reference to Ethiopia," *Public Administration and Development*, II (1982), pp. 146-167.
58. *Ibid.*, pp. 152-4.
59. Lele, *Design of Rural Development*, p. 186.
60. Ministry of Agricultural data is most readily available in the tables in: Keith Griffin and Roger Hay, "Problems of Agricultural Development in Socialist Ethiopia: An Overview and a Suggested Strategy," *Journal of Peasant Studies*, XIII, 1 (1985), pp. 37-66; Ajit Kumar Ghose, "Transforming Feudal Agriculture: Agrarian Change in Ethiopia Since 1974," *Journal of Development Studies*, XXII, 1 (1985), pp. 127-49.
61. Johnston and Clark, *Redesigning Rural Development*, p. 198.
62. On "negative social science" relative to rural development projects, see: Chambers, *Rural Development*, pp. 28-46.
63. The overlap in conception between the green revolution, integrated rural development, and basic human needs is well illustrated in Ruttan's historical analysis: "A Historical Perspective," pp. 393-401.
64. Personal interview Nairobi, Kenya. Apparently efforts were made to issue formal directives. However, officers aware of the potential of integrated rural development projects blocked them through bureaucratic techniques, forcing the director and his supporters to rely on a "clear informal position widely signaled through the agency."
65. For example, David K. Leonard notes that after the failure of the Integrated Agricultural Development Project in Kenya, The World Bank "...has begun to design separate projects for the several aspects of the original IADP – in other words, to take a disintegrated approach to Kenyan agriculture." "Disintegrating Agricultural Development," *Food Research Institute Studies* , XIX, 2 (1984), p. 178.The effects of this abandonment are reflected on for Kenya in: Frank E. Bernard, "Planning and Environmental risks in Kenya Drylands," *Geographical Review*, LXXV, 1 (1985), pp. 58-70.
66. John M. Staatz and Carl K. Eicher, "Agriculture Development Ideas in Historical Perspective," in *Agricultural Development in the Third World*, edited by Carl K. Eicher and John M. Staatz (Baltimore: Johns Hopkins University Press, 1984), p. 21.
67. Steve Wiggins, "The Planning and Management of Integrated Rural Development in Dry Lands: Early Lessons from Kenya's Arid and Semi-Arid Lands Programmes," *Public Administration and Development*, V, 2 (1985), pp. 91-108.
68. Typical of numerous studies on this problem are: Stephen K. Cummins and Michael F. Lofchie, eds., *Africa's Agrarian Crisis: The Roots of Famine* (Boulder: Lynne Rienner Publishers, 1986); Carl K. Eicher, "Facing Up to Africa's Food Crisis," *Foreign Affairs*, LXI, 1 (1982), pp. 154-74.
69. George Honadle and Jerry Van Sant, *Implementation for Sustainability: Lessons from Integrated Rural Development* (West Hartford: Kumarian Press, 1985).
70. Cynthia Clapp-Winchek, "Draft Summary of the Impact of Evaluations on Integrated Rural Development" (Paper Prepared for the Center for Development Information and Evaluation, USAID, Washington, D.C., 1986). Case studies include: Cynthia Clapp-Wincek and Emily Baldwin, *The Helmand Valley in Afghanistan* (Washington, D.C.:USAID, Evaluation Study No. 18, 1983); Barbara D. Lynch, *The Vicos Experiment* (Washington, D.C.: USAID, Rural Development Paper No. 2, 1978).
71. Dennis Rondenelli summarized this comparative study well. In his words, the study found no universally applicable lessons. But it revealed the importance of proper organizational structure. This depended on choosing the most effective organizational level at which to locate the project to ensure integration of decisions and resources, the appropriate institutions to manage the project, and the best configuration of internal organizational divisions. The cases reviewed led to the conclusion that integrated rural

development projects could be more effectively managed if they were designed through a learning process aimed at building local and sustainable administrative and institutional capacity, in which the design is done in discrete phases rather than in great detail prior to project approval; a large amount of short-term technical assistance is provided to help the staff deal with particular technical problems as they arise; emphasis is placed on action-oriented, problem-related, field training of both staff to carry out project activities effectively; applied research is made a part of the project so that staff can test and learn from new ideas; simple, field-level information systems are used to collect new information after an inventory has been made of existing data; and provisions are made for redesign of the project as managers learn more about its operation and effectiveness during implementation. They found building local participation was important to project success. Finally, they concluded that integrated rural development projects should be kept small-scale, they should focus on overcoming critical constraints to rural development in the areas in which they are located, and that the projects should be designed to build up gradually the organization capacity of beneficiary groups so that they could participate in or eventually control project activities. "Development Administration and American Foreign Assistance Policy: An Assessment of Theory and Practice in Aid," *Canadian Journal of Development Studies*, VI, 2 (1985), pp. 227-8.

72. Siffin, *Administrative Problems*, p. 16.
73. Derick W. Brinkerhoff, "The Effectiveness of Integrated Rural Development: A Synthesis of Research and Experience" (Paper Prepared for USAID, Office of Rural Development, Washington, D.C., August 1981), p. 6.
74. Eicher, "Facing Up to Africa's Food Crisis," p. 165.
75. Honadle and Van Sant, *Implementation and Sustainability*, Chapter 5.

Selected Bibliography

A large number of published and unpublished materials underpin this case study. Each chapter is supported by detailed footnotes setting forth this literature. It would be unproductive to repeat those materials here. Hence, this select bibliography will include only general overview or consolidating studies likely to be found in most research libraries. It organizes these materials by the book's four major topics: (1) Integrated Rural Development; (2) Rural Development Under Haile Selassie; (3) Revolutionary Ethiopa and Rural Development; and (4) the CADU-ARDU Project.

Some of the most significant publications supporting the book are Ethiopian government reports and studies. The most important of these are the more than 100 documents published by CADU-ARDU since 1967 in its distinctive project series. These are not covered in this select bibliography even though some are of greater significance to it than publications listed. This is because such documents are not widely available. Most of these materials can be located, however, in such libraries as Addis Ababa University's Institute for Ethiopian Studies, Cornell University's Mann Library, and Israel's Rehovot Rural Development Center. Other libraries may have them as well. But effort must be made to locate many of the CADU-ARDU documents or other materials relied upon by the author. It is for this reason that full citations have been presented in the footnotes to each chapter.

I. Integrated Rural Development

Ahmad, J.J. "Administration of Integrated Rural Development Programmes: A Note on Methodology." *International Labour Review*, CXI, 2 (1975):119-42.

Armor, Thomas G., et al. "Organizing and Supporting Integrated Rural Development Projects: A Twofold Approach to Administering Development." *Journal of Administration Overseas*, XVIII, 4 (1979):276-86.

Belshaw, D.G.R. "Rural Development Planning: Concepts and Techniques." *Journal of Agricultural Economics*, XXVIII, 3 (1977):279-91.

Cohen, John M. *Administration of Integrated Rural Development Projects*. Cambridge: Harvard Institute for International Development, Development Discussion Paper No. 79, 1980.

-----. "Integrated Rural Development: Clearing Out the Underbrush." *Sociologia Ruralis*, XX, 4 (1980):195-212.

Crawford, Paul R. *Implementation Issues in Integrated Rural Development: A Review of 21 USAID Projects*. Washington D.C.: Development Alternatives, Inc., IRD Research Note 2, 1981.

Friedmann, John. "A Spacial Framework for Rural Development: Problems of Organization and Implementation." *Economie Appliquée*, XXVIII, 2/3 (1975):519-20.

Grindle, Merilee S. "Anticipating Failure: The Implementation of Rural Development Programs." *Public Policy*, XXIX, 1 (1981):51-74.

Holmberg, Johan. *Integrated Rural Development: A Discussion of this Concept and Its Implications for Swedish Aid.* Uppsala: The Swedish University of Agricultural Sciences, Report No. 120, 1977.

Honadle, George, et al. *Integrated Rural Development: Making It Work?* Washington, D.C.: Development Alternatives, Inc., 1980.

----- and Jerry Van Sant, *Implementation and Sustainability: Lessons from Integrated Rural Development.* West Hartford: Kumarian Press, 1985.

Kotter, H.R. "Some Observations on the Basic Principles and General Strategy Underlying Integrated Rural Development." *Monthly Bulletin of Agricultural Economists and Statistics*, XXIII, 4 (1974):1-12.

Lele, Uma J. *The Design of Rural Development: Lessons from Africa.* Baltimore: The Johns Hopkins University Press, 1975.

Leonard, David K. "Disintegrating Agricultural Development." *Food Research Institute Studies*, XIX, 2 (1984):177-86.

Leupolt, Manfred. "Integrated Rural Development: Key Elements of an Integrated Rural Development Strategy." *Sociologia Ruralis*, XVIII, 1/2 (1977):7-28.

Livingstone, Ian. "On the Concept of 'Integrated Rural Development' in Less Developed Countries." *Journal of Agricultural Economics,* XXXX, 1 (1979):49-53.

Montgomery, John D. "Decentralizing Integrated Rural Development Activities." In *Decentralization and Development: Policy Implementation in Developing Countries*, edited by Shabbir Cheema and Dennis A. Rondinelli. Beverly Hills: Sage Publications, 1983: 231-69.

-----. "Managing Integrated Rural Development: Views from the Field." *Rural Development Participation Review*, III, 3 (1983):6-9.

Morss, Elliott R. and David D. Gow. *Integrated Rural Development: Nine Critical Implementation Problems.* Washington, D.C.: Development Alternatives, Inc., Research Note No. 1, 1981.

----- and David D. Gow, eds. *Implementing Rural Development Projects: Lessons from AID and World Bank Experience.* Boulder: Westview Press, 1985.

Mosher, Arthur T. "Custom-Made Systems." *Ceres*, V, 4 (1972):33-7.

-----. "Prospects of Integrated Rural Development." Paper Prepared for Agricultural Development Council, New York, 1972.

Overseas Development Institute. "Briefing Paper: Integrated Rural Development." Paper Prepared by ODI, Briefing Paper No. 4, London, 1979.

Rondinelli, Dennis A. "Administration of Integrated Rural Development Policy: The Politics of Agrarian Reform in Developing Countries." *World Politics*, XXXI, 3 (1979):402-15.

----- and Kenneth Ruddle. "Local Organization for Integrated Rural Development: Implementing Equity Policy in Developing Countries." *International Review of Administrative Sciences*, XLII (1977):20-30.

Ruttan, Vernon W. "Integrated Rural Development Programmes: A Historical Perspective." *World Development*, XII, 4 (1984):393-401.

-----. "Integrated Rural Development Programs: A Skeptical Perspective." *International Development Review*, XVII, 4 (1974/75):9-16.

Siffen, William J. *Administrative Problems and Integrated Rural Development.* Bloomington: Indiana University, International Development Institute, PASITAM Design Study, 1979.

Wade, Robert. "Leadership and Integrated Rural Development: Reflections on an Indian Success Story." *Journal of Administration Overseas*, XVIII (1978):245-55.

Weitz, Raanan. *Integrated Rural Development: The Rehovot Approach.* Rehovot, Israel: Settlement Study Center, 1981.

Yudelman, Montague. "Integrated Rural Development Projects: the Bank's Experience." *Finance and Development*, XIV, 1 (1977):15-18.
Zaman, M.A. "Integrated Rural Development: FAO/SIDA Expert Consultation on Policies and Institutions." *Agricultural Administration*, V (1978):239-73.

II. RURAL DEVELOPMENT UNDER HAILE SELASSIE

Assefa Bequele and Eshetu Chole. *Profile of the Ethiopian Economy*. Addis Ababa: Oxford University Press, 1969.
Clapham, Christopher. *Haile Selassie's Government*. New York: Frederick A. Praeger, 1969.
Cohen, John M. and Peter H. Koehn. *Ethiopian Provincial and Municipal Government: Imperial Patterns and Post Revolutionary Changes*. East Lansing: Michigan State University, African Studies Center, 1980.
----- and Dov Weintraub. *Land and Peasants in Imperial Ethiopia: The Social Background to a Revolution*. Assen: Van Gorcum & Co., 1975.
Greenfield, Richard. *Ethiopia: A New Political History*. London: Pall Mall Press, 1965.
Hess, Robert L. *Ethiopia: The Modernization of Autocracy*. Ithaca: Cornell University Press, 1970.
Huffnagel, H. *Agriculture in Ethiopia*. Rome: Food and Agriculture Organization of the United Nations, 1961.
Levine, Donald N. *Greater Ethiopia: The Evolution of a Multiethnic Society*. Chicago: University of Chicago Press, 1974.
Mesfin Wolde Mariam. *An Atlas of Ethiopia*. Asmara: Il Polografico Priv. Ltd. Co., 1970.
Markakis, John. *Ethiopia: Anatomy of a Traditional Polity*. Oxford: Clarendon Press, 1974.
Nelson, Harold D. and Irving Kaplan. *Ethiopia: A Country Study*. Washington, D.C.: U.S. Government Printing Office, 1981.
Pankhurst, Richard. *State and Land in Ethiopian History*. Addis Ababa: Oxford University Press, 1966.
Perham, Margery. *The Government of Ethiopia*. 2nd ed. Evanston: Northwestern University Press, 1969.
Ståhl, Michael. *Ethiopia: Political Contradictions in Agricultural Development*. Stockholm: Liber Tryck, 1974).
-----. Contradictions in Agricultural Development: A Study of Three Minimum Package Projects in Southern Ethiopia. (Uppsala: Scandinavian Institute of African Studies, Research Report No. 14, 1973).
Stommes, Eileen and Seleshi Sisaye. "The Administration of Agricultural Development Programmes: A Look at the Ethiopian Approach." *Agricultural Administration*, VI, 3 (1979):219-39; VI, 4 (1979):253-67; and VII, 1 (1980):1-23.

III. REVOLUTIONARY ETHIOPIA AND RURAL DEVELOPMENT

Alulu Abate and Fassil G. Kiros. "Agrarian Reform, Structural Changes and Rural Development in Ethiopia." In *Agrarian Reform in Contemporary Developing Countries*, edited by Ajit Kumar Ghose. New York: St. Martin's Press, 1983.
----- and Tesfaye Teklu. "Land Reform and Peasant Associations in Ethiopia: Case Studies of Two Widely Differing Regions." *Northeast African Studies*, II, 2 (1980):1-51.

Brietzke, Paul H. *Law, Development, and the Ethiopian Revolution*. Lewisburg: Bucknell University Press, 1982.
Cohen, John M. "Revolution and Publication: Ethiopia Since 1974." *African Studies Association Review of Books*, V (1980):154-63.
----- and Nils-Ivar Isaksson. *Villagization in the Arsi Region of Ethiopia*. Uppsala: Swedish University of Agricultural Sciences, International Rural Development Centre, Rural Development Study No. 19, 1987.
----- and Peter H. Koehn. "Rural and Urban Land Reform in Ethiopia." *African Law Studies*, XIV (1977):3-61.
-----, John W. Mellor and Arthur A. Goldsmith. "Rural Development Issues Following Ethiopian Land Reform." *Africa Today*, XXIII, 2 (1976):7-28.
Eshetu Chole and Teshome Mulat. "Land Settlement in Ethiopia: A Review of Developments." Paper Presented at International Ethiopia Studies Conference, Addis Ababa, December 1984.
Food and Agriculture Organization. *Ethiopia Highlands Reclamation Study: Macro-Economic Review*. Rome: FAO, Report No. UTF/ETH/037/ETH, Working Paper No. 9, 1984.
Genberg, Björn, Michael Ståhl and Edvard Taube. "Report on Peasant Associations and Agricultural Co-operatives in Ethiopia." Report Prepared for SIDA, Addis Ababa, November 1982.
Halliday, Fred and Maxine Molyneux. *The Ethiopian Revolution*. London: Verso, 1981.
Henze, Paul B. "Communism and Ethiopia." *Problems of Communism*, XXX (1981):55-74.
----. "Beyond the Ethiopian Revolution: Anatomy of a Revolution," *Encounter* (June 1986), pp. 5-17; (July 1986), pp. 15-25; (September 1986), pp. 20-29.
Hoben, A. "Perspectives on Land Reform in Ethiopia: The Political Role of the Peasantry." *Rural Africana*, 28 (1975):55-69.
International Bank for Reconstruction and Development. *Agricultural Development in Ethiopia (with Particular Reference to the Highlands)*. 2 vols. Washington, D.C.: Eastern African Projects Department, Northern Agricultural Division, Report No. 3956-ET, May 28, 1982.
-----. *Ethiopia: The Agricultural Sector - An Interim Report. Washington,* D.C.: East Africa Region, Report No. ET 3956-ET, January 26, 1983.
Keller, Edmond J. "The Ethiopian Revolution: How Socialist Is It?" *Journal of African Studies*, XI, 2 (1984):52-65.
Markakis, John and Nega Ayele. *Class and Revolution in Ethiopia*. London: Spokesman, 1978.
Ottaway, Marina and David Ottaway. *Ethiopia: Empire in Revolution*. New York: Africana Publishing Co. 1978.
Wood, Adrian P. "Rural Development and National Integration in Ethiopia." *African Affairs*, LXXXII, 329 (1983):509-39.

IV. CADU-ARDU PROJECT

Alemneh Dejene. *Smallholder Perceptions of Rural Development and Emerging Institutions in Arssi Region Since the Ethiopian Revolution*. Cambridge: Harvard Institute for International Development, Development Discussion Paper No. 192, 1985.
Bengtsson, Bo M.I. *Rural Development Research and Agricultural Innovations* . Uppsala: Swedish University of Agricultural Sciences, Department of Plant Husbandry, Report No. 115, 1983.

Betru Gebregziabher. *Integrated Rural Development in Rural Ethiopia: An Evaluative Study of the Chilalo Agricultural Development Unit*. Bloomington: University of Indiana, International Development Research Center, 1975.

Cohen, John M. "Effects of Green Revolution Strategies on the Tenants and Small-Scale Landowners of the Chilalo Region of Ethiopia." *Journal of Developing Areas*, IX, 3 (1975):335-58.

-----. "Rural Change in Ethiopia: The Chilalo Agricultural Development Unit." *Economic Development and Cultural Change*, XXII, 4 (1974): 508-614.

-----. "Rural Change in Ethiopia: A Study of Land, Elites, Power and Values in Chilalo *Awraja*." Unpublished PhD. Dissertation, University of Colorado, 1973.

Central Statistical Office. *Report on a Survey of Arussi*. Addis Ababa: Central Statistical Office, 1966.

Fassil G. Kiros. "Learning from ARDU: Toward a Regional System of Rural Development in Ethiopia." Paper Presented to Seminar on Regional Planning and Development in Ethiopia, Ambo, April 1983.

Hunter, Guy, et al. *Final Report of the Appraisal of CADU and EPID*. Report by the Evaluation Team Appointed by the Imperial Ethiopian Government and the Swedish International Development Authority, Asella, May 1974.

Jonsson, Ingvar. *Diffusion of Agricultural Innovations in Chilalo Awraja, Ethiopia*. Addis Ababa: Haile Selassie I University, Institute of Development Research, Research Report No. 17, 1975.

Ministry of Land Reform and Administration. *Report on Land Tenure Survey in Arussi Province*. Addis Ababa: Department of Land Tenure, 1967.

Nekby, Bengt. *CADU: An Ethiopian Experiment in Developing Peasant Farming*. Stockholm: Prisma Publishers, 1971.

Seleshi Sisaye, "Development Aid to Rural Ethiopia, 1954-1977: The Political Economy of Swedish Rural Development Assistance Programs." Unpublished PhD. Dissertation, Cornell University, 1979.

Solomon Bekure, et al. *Evaluation of the Arssi Regional Development Unit (ARDU)*, June-July 1981. Uppsala: International Rural Development Center, Swedish University of Agricultural Sciences, 1981.

Swedish International Development Authority. *Proposal for Swedish Support to Rural Development in Arsi and Bale 1986/87-1988/89*. Addis Ababa: SIDA, December 1985.

-----. *Report No. 1 on the Establishment of Regional Development Project in Ethiopia* . Addis Ababa: SIDA, 1966.

Tesfai, Tecle. "An Economic Evaluation of Agricultural Package Programmes in Ethiopia." Unpublished PhD. Dissertation, Cornell University, 1973.

-----. *The Evolution of Alternative Rural Development Strategies in Ethiopia: Implications for Employment and Income Distribution*. East Lansing: Michigan State University, African Rural Employment Paper No. 12, 1975.

Wetterhall, Hans. *A Case Study in Contemporary Changes in Agrarian Structure, Ethiopia: Chilalo Sub-Province*. Stockholm: Food and Agriculture Organization, Human Resources and Institution Division, 1974.

Yelma, Kabada. "Chilalo Awraja." *Ethiopian Geographical Journal*, V, 1 (1967):25-36.